W9-BCG-675

DIOCESE OF BELLEVILLE

1887 1988

A TIME OF FAVOR

TimmermannPhilippsGraweScmittKruseVandeLooTheising WellinghoffGeoffrayHuene
KlinekorteGausepohlWesselmannWinkelerKolpFaukeDeterm
SchillerRibbingBergmannBrueggemannHuelsmannOverbeck
scherRobbeStueverKorandoTougawBrushShieldGaleKaercher
gayMeirinkFoppeScheibelDonneNieburTaphornReinekeGuttersohnGoewert
HusteddeRascheHitpasHorstmannLoddekeKluthoNiemannJansenDennoAngulisSpainKubrick
KolesinskisDrasdofskiNowickiZajokowskiVenegoniGaravagliaMossmanEovaldiGrezlakNagy
SwinjonskiVincentiZeboskiKonkielMazaiarzSimonDeMatteiLaurensEschmanVoellingerArnold
SchmidtBaquetHechenbergerFellnerSchobertHoffO'ConnellHladyshewskyBaggioStauderFrerker
ThousvenotVosmikBlaesDiekemarFleskrenLeonardMoerchenRensingZacharskiZimmermannHogg
IslerLeChienBretschVillemainReutermannVanCanhLeVoellingerKaefholdBeckWekemanIrose
KuhlsPeikeBeuchmannFreantPeppenhorstGerversmannFoecheHeitmannOstermannFidelerRoberg
EchelmannHilmesLandwehrRohrNordmannSimsMurphyHolthausSchoenKharkoffKampwerHusted-
deKahrhoffKampwerthHusteddeSchneiderPetersLanghauserVanDornBodenburgMahataFriederich
EllCunninghamDriscollDunnKastnerRo rgasonSchererLinnemannHutschMcEvilly
StetzenKlappBussonGuerrettazGa PoulterWaggandLevyBourqueTobin
TobinRombaughKovacHennebe inrichSartorySaugetVivianoSoucy
SmithRoustioRigneySchalten tztrauberSzewczykSzezepaniak
ThomasVosseWainwrightP WhiteheadPetersonNeffHayes
WigginsWilliamsZittelWh sBedelBresnahanDeMonge
BurnsDuffClimacoCourt edakCaraviaCannadyCipf
DreviciBarroncoAmesA arbieriAuthBerensGaskill
GoydaGrandcolasHass eyerMillerMaagPiekKoch
PratleReisO'BryanRuj aVogtWambergueYettke
WesterheideBergerBach ParkerFournieObernhefe-
manDuttonHahnmannL sRuenseterDemickMaty-
chowickFietsamMonken nainMcCormickEschenfel
derMeisenbeckPetrovich psonO'HaraDiverBurgess
TragesserKriegerCollignon lmannKunkelKeleherKolmer
MarquetteGravierAllouezSt leurinBergierLevadoixFlaget
BadenRivetOlivierLawlerDu uffyHanaganLambertZerrKlo-
ckeBauerHilgenbergMuenster neyHenkenDeGasperiSchauerte
ReuschEnzlbergerWiemarCluseSp erRoehrigOstlangenbergBrandmeyer
SeifertBrumleveAntonSchellerGajewski gerBerndtPanickLimasWegmanO'Halloran
BrennanHartungReinekeLohmannDemingCollinsDowneySauerGoeltzKorandoVossSpeckmanMohr
GieryMadajKowalskiPieszchalskiPriesRynakiGrajekZgoninaLabudaDudzikWollowskiTenepka
CzerniejewskiTerepkaRoesbergTecklenburgCimarolliTaggartBooshertKreinWittenbrink
WibretKillianMarhonicBurakMiddekePenjakPfisterMulliganLacroixChandlerDaussard
CoffeeMorrisonSullivanSwithLebkucherChewMcCarthyGoughBaumannSiekmannDutton
CoyneCraigCyganD'ArcyCywinskiClarkFoleyGajewskiGenettiFaheyFahrnerRaslawksiHalvachs
GroganGryzmalaKeserauskisHlavekHennessyMenestrinaMenendexMaldanadoKroupaMcDonnell
HowelMeehanManninoKlemmeDonzeSpannagelBottaniBueskingGregorichMojzisKeatingSchaefer
EckertSchottDelaneyWolfBussGreerWebbFlachMetzerGreimanTakmajianDonleyWilkinsonPruett
JonesJohnsonHarrisEdwardsCowgillBielickeCahnovskyBurkeBrelloBogachiBournDonahueDiaz
MerscherFruecheSchumacherHoltgaveMolitorStockmannStrubhartOttensmeierKolmer
SchultePeekPoettkerLampeGoestenkorsStrohmannLagerHempenLaurentDillmanLitteken
KuhlZurlioneKeimGoelzBartelsHoffmanMuellerKueterBeckerHeidemannGrimmerBretzBudde
TimmermannPhilippsGraweScmittKruseVandeLooTheisingGebkeWellinghoffGeoffrayHuene
KlinekorteGausepohlWesselmannWinkelerKolpFaukeDetermannDulleKoopmannDustFerguson
SchillerRibbingBergmannBrueggemannHuelsmannOverbeckMarkusFeldmannWempeStrootMer-
scherRobbeStueverKorandoTougawBrushShieldGaleKaercherHeiligensteinHaselhostPerjakBun-
gayMeirinkFoppeScheibelDonneNieburTaphornReinekeGuttersohnGoewertHentschelRuterman
HusteddeRascheHitpasHorstmannLoddekeKluthoNiemannJansenDennoAngulisSpainKubrick
KolesinskisDrasdofskiNowickiZajokowskiVenegoniGaravagliaMossmanEovaldiGrezlakNagy
SwinjonskiVincentiZeboskiKonkielMazaiarzSimonDeMatteiLaurensEschmanVoellingerArnold
SchmidtBaquetHechenbergerFellnerSchobertHoffO'ConnellHladyshewskyBaggioStauderFrerker
ThousvenotVosmikBlaesDiekemarFleskrenLeonardMoerchenRensingZacharskiZimmermannHogg
IslerLeChienBretschVillemainReutermannVanCanhLeVoellingerKaefholdBeckWekemanIrose
KuhlsPeikeBeuchmannFreantPeppenhorstGerversmannFoecheHeitmannOstermannFidelerRoberg
EchelmannHilmesLandwehrRohrNordmannSimsMurphyHolthausSchoenKharkoffKampwerHusted-
deKahrhoffKampwerthHusteddeSchneiderPetersLanghauserVanDornBodenburgMahataFriederich
EllCunninghamDriscollDunnKastnerRoweEichenseerMargasonSchererLinnemannHutschMcEvilly
StetzenKlappBussonGuerrettazGaffinettPanaraceBollheimerPoulterWaggandLevyBourqueTobin
TobinRombaughKovacHenneberryPabstPabarcusOssickSandheinrichSartorySaugetVivianoSoucy
SmithRoustioRigneySchaltenbrandSchlechtSchlueterSvobodaSwartztrauberSzewczykSzezepaniak

Profiles From Our Heritage

For me the measuring lines have fallen on pleasant sites;
fair to me indeed is my heritage.

Psalms 16:6

Profiles From Our Heritage

Stories of Catholics Who Helped Shape The Church Of Southern Illinois

Reprinted From *The Messenger*

Edited By
Raphael H. Middeke
& Stanley J. Konieczny

The Patrice Press
St. Louis, Missouri

Copyright © 1987
Diocese of Belleville, Illinois

There are no restrictions on the reproduction of any part of this book, for any purpose.

*Library of Congress
Cataloging in Publication Data*

"Reprinted from The messenger."
Includes index.
1. Catholics—Illinois—Belleville Region—Biography.
2. Catholic Church. Diocese of Belleville (Ill.)—
History. 3. Belleville Region (Ill.)—Church history.
4. Belleville Region (Ill.)—Biography. I. Middeke,
Raphael H., 1933- . II. Konieczny, Stanley J.,
1955-
BX4670.P76 1987 282'.092' 2 [B] 87-13386
ISBN 0-935284-49-4

The Patrice Press
1701 South Eighth Street
St. Louis MO 63104

Printed in the United States of America

To our forebears —
the men and women
whose faith is symbolized
in these Profiles.

Contents

Preface ix
Philippe Renault 1
Father Pierre Gibault 4
Nicholas Jarrot 8
The Pensoneau Family 12
Father Gabriel Richard 15
Pierre Menard 19
Father Elisha Durbin 22
Father J. F. R. Loisel 26
The Aydt Family 31
Mother Caroline Friess 35
Father Patrick McCabe 40
William Bissell 44
Michael Kelly Lawler 48
Father Louis A. Lambert 52
Bishop Peter Baltes 56
Father Theodore Gieryk 59
Mother Clementine Zerr 63
Father Charles Klocke 67
Bishop John Janssen 71
Monsignor William Cluse 75
Father Christopher Koenig 80
Father Patrick J. O'Halloran 83
First Men Ordained for Fledgling Diocese 87
Franciscan Presence in Southern Ilinois 92
Father Bernard Hilgenberg 96
Father Bartholomew Bartels 100
Father Frederic Beuckman 104
Father Kaspar Schauerte 108
Bishop Henry Althoff 112
Monsignor Christopher Goelz 116

Monsignor Francis Tecklenburg 121
Sister Theresa Repking 125
Marianist Presence in the Diocese 130
Monsignor Andrew Janiszewski 135
Sister Alma Juengling 140
Brother Eugene Frank 144
Dr. John T. Murphy 149
Father Charles Seifert 154
Mother Veronica Baumgart 159
Archbishop Joseph Schlarman 164
Joseph Buechler 169
Monsignor Charles Gilmartin 172
Father Joseph Pico 176
Monsignor Robert DeGasperi 181
Father Paul Drone 185
Kate Boismenue 190
Mother Veronica Schmitt 194
Father Peter Harrington 199
Monsignor Fred Witte 205
Monsignor John J. Fallon 210
Father Peter Minwegen 214
Felician Presence in Southern Illinois 219
Monsignor M. J. Gruenewald 224
Edwin Irwin 228
Brother Henry Heidemann 232
Monsignor Cyril Haffner 236
Sister Pacifica 241
Father Joseph Fontana 245
John Taylor 249
Archbishop Adolph Noser 253
Professor Bernard L. Miller 257
Father John Henken 260
Father Alphonse Simon 264
Father Elmer Schuhmacher 268
Monsignor John Fournie 273
Bishop Anthony Deksnys 278
Sister Rita Kampwerth 283
Imogene Wilson 288
Roslyn Waite 293
Bishop Albert R. Zuroweste 298
Father Edwin Guild 303
Anne and Bolen Carter 308
Robert Welzbacher 312
Father Francis X. Heiligenstein 317

Joe Hubbard 321
Bishop William Cosgrove 327
Sister Mary Catherine 332
Sister Madeline Dosmann 337
Bishop John Wurm 341
Nick Leone and Cy Vernier 344
Rose Zwilling and Elizabeth Meehan 348
Sister Suzanne Schrautemyer 353
Bishop James PatrickKeleher 358
Biographies of Contributors 362
Index 366

Preface

PROFILES FROM OUR HERITAGE started as a follow-up to a two-year syndicated series on the universal church and Catholicism in the United States in *The Messenger,* the Catholic newspaper of the Diocese of Belleville. The *Profiles* were originally planned as a one-year forty-part series in 1985. They developed into a second-year centennial series at the suggestion and urging of many of our readers.

We have attempted in these *Profiles* to represent clergy, religious and laity, the various immigrant and ethnic groups which have helped form our history, as well as areas of the diocese.

We're indebted to the authors who helped research and write the *Profiles.* We need to acknowledge, too, the suggestions of readers and the cooperation of many Catholics in southern Illinois who willingly shared their memories. We often called upon individuals for information, especially Sister Celine Laurent, ASC, the Belleville diocesan archivist.

All of us who have worked on the *Profiles* have gained an insight and an appreciation of the history of the Church of southern Illinois through these remarkable and unique people. The efforts, determination and faith of these pioneers and present witnesses have demanded reflection on a faith which is both old and new, a source of pride and humility.

If growth and inspiration have accompanied our efforts, the *Profiles* have also been a homecoming, where we shared a common humanity which welcomes the power of faith. It is our hope you will touch some of the same bases as you read these pages.

Raphael H. Middeke
Stanley J. Konieczny
April 30, 1987

Profiles From Our Heritage

CHAPTER 1

Philippe Renault: French Pioneer

By Rev. Theodore Siekmann

PHILIPPE FRANCOIS RENAULT, mining engineer and director of mines in the Illinois country, was born in France, where his father operated an iron foundry. Filled with adventure, Renault set sail in 1720 with a group of 200 miners, technicians, and laborers, plus a huge amount of mining and smelting equipment.

Like others in that era, his imagination was fired by rumors of vast amounts of precious metals in the new world. He was determined to develop a lucrative mining and smelting industry there, particularly in gold and silver. There were already extensive mining operations under way in the Illinois country, mostly coal mines. Stopping at Santo Domingo, Renault picked up 500 Negro slaves to work in the mines.

He arrived in the Fort de Chartres area in what is now southern Illinois convinced that there were treasures of precious ores in the bluffs along the Mississippi River, and particularly in the area north of Fort de Chartres. He formed his own mining company, the Company of St. Philippe, under the Company of the Indies chartered by the king of France.

He managed to obtain three tracts of land, two on the west side of the river and one on the east side, some miles north of Fort de Chartres. On the low land on the east bank of the river, on his treasured tract of land, Renault founded a town which he named St. Philippe after his patron saint. This town housed his mining personnel. It was surrounded by a palisade to protect against Indian attack. Within the palisade was a chapel of Our Lady of the Visitation, dependent upon and cared for by St. Anne Church at Fort de Chartres.

Renault had been appointed director of mines in the Illinois country, and he zealously examined the existing coal and other mines for evidence of precious ores, while he pursued his regular work. He also examined the banks of every stream in the broad area, always in the hope of coming upon some valuable find.

He did find traces of silver in what is now St. Clair County along the banks of Silver Creek, so named because of the small amount of precious metals he found on its shores. He also found traces of silver, copper, and perhaps gold in the coal mines, and a large amount of lead on the west side of the Mississippi. This lead continues to be mined and processed to this day.

But Renault found no silver and gold in any amount that would be commercially profitable.

There was a financial crisis at that time in France that affected the parent company. Supplies and additional personnel and financial backing were not forthcoming.

Pioneer Heritage — The altar and tabernacle have been restored in the chapel of Fort de Chartres, a state historical site located outside of Prairie du Rocher.

Disillusioned and disappointed, Renault sold the slaves to the French settlers, salvaged what he could of a failing project, and returned to France in 1742.

Renault and other French Catholics of his day did try to treat their slaves humanely. They provided for the basic needs of the slaves. They respected their dignity as children of God, endowed with immortal souls, and deserving of spiritual care and attention.

Although marriage was forbidden between blacks and whites, the black slaves were to receive instruction in the Catholic religion and to be given ample opportunity to practice the Catholic faith.

Notable was the concern not to break up slave families. There was also an honest endeavor to foster wholesome family life among the slaves, in sharp contrast to practices in parts of the world.

For many years, until quite recently, a sizeable group of black people lived in Prairie du Rocher, which lies between Fort de Chartres and the old St. Philippe. Some of these were descendants of the former slaves of Renault.

In the 1950s and 1960s, the school building once attended by the black children was still standing, although no black children were left, and only one aged and lovable black man remained.

The black Catholics in Prairie du Rocher had always attended Mass and received the sacraments along with the white people on an amicable basis. Indeed, two of the black girls became religious sisters.

The present village of Renault, founded in the early 1800s, long after Philippe Renault had returned to France, bears his family name.

The town, situated on the southeast edge and ridge of the Renault tract overlooks the old St. Philippe that was on the lower western edge near the river. The river swallowed it up. The new Renault, with its Church of Our Lady of Good Counsel, replaces the old St. Philippe with its chapel of Our Lady of the Visitation. The present village of Renault recalls the name and ambitions of the colorful Philippe Renault. It is his monument.

From the heights of Renault you can see the sprawling land of Philippe Renault's shattered dreams. In these hills and on these bluffs the starry-eyed Philippe Renault searched long to find his silver and gold.

It would be a mistake, though, to think that he was a failure. He did excellent work as a mining engineer and director of mines. His achievement was great, and his contribution to the solid mining industry of the Illinois country is acknowledged and respected.

But there was no "Eldorado," no fabulous lodes of silver and gold — only traces. And much coal and lead.

CHAPTER 2

Father Pierre Gibault: "Patriot Priest"

By Harold D. Olree

FATHER PIERRE GIBAULT, who became known as the "Patriot Priest of the West," was born April 7, 1737, in Montreal, Canada.

As a youth he studied at the Jesuit College of Quebec, then traveled with a fur trapping brigade in the Illinois country. Upon his return he studied at the Foreign Mission Seminary in Quebec and was ordained a priest on March 19, 1768, by Bishop Jean Olivier Briand.

In a letter from the bishop dated March 30, 1768, Father Gibault was assigned to the missions in the Illinois country to minister to "a folk unlearned and heavy laden . . . with grievous sins and deprived a long time of pastors."

Most Jesuit missionaries in the territory had been banished after the 1763 Treaty of Paris, which ceded all territory possessed by the French on the east side of the Mississippi River to England. Thus Father Gibault had to get permission from the British to enter the territory.

Catholics of Kaskaskia and Cahokia had been petitioning the Quebec bishop for a priest. The only priest in the area was Father Sebastian Meurin at Kaskaskia, the only Jesuit allowed to remain.

Father Gibault arrived at Kaskaskia in September 1768. Upon Father Gibault's arrival, Father Meurin moved to Prairie du Rocher.

From Kaskaskia, Father Gibault traveled to minister to Catholics at Cahokia, Ste. Genevieve and St. Louis, Missouri. He added Vincennes, Indiana, after Father Meurin's death in 1777 at Prairie du Rocher. He also served as chaplain of the British garrison at Fort de Chartres.

During his travels he not only had to endure the wilderness and unpredictable weather, but at times hostile Indians. For this reason he wrote to the Quebec bishop that he always carried two pistols and another gun. But he later abandoned the weapons because he felt safer traveling among the Indians unarmed. He was never attacked.

The incidents which were to give him the title "Patriot Priest of the West" began July 4, 1778. This was the date of arrival of Gen. George Rogers Clark at Kaskaskia, as he moved westward to secure territory for the new United States.

Father Gibault carried three guns at first as he ministered to the Illinois wilderness, but later discarded them, saying he felt safer among the Indians without them.

When the American Revolution began, Bishop Briand, whose see city was now under control of the British, forbade any of the clergy or laity of his diocese to help the American revolutionaries. The king of France, meanwhile, had made an alliance with the United States.

Upon the arrival of General Clark, Father Gibault, who seemed to favor the Americans over the British, cooperated with the military leader. In exchange for Father Gibault's role in persuading the mostly French inhabitants to capitulate to the Americans, Clark promised protection and religious freedom for settlers. With Father Gibault's similar influence, Clark's soliders were also able to take control of Prairie du Rocher, St. Philippe, and Cahokia without violence. Shortly thereafter, Father Gibault traveled with Clark's representatives to Vincennes where under the priest's influence, the inhabitants and the garrison at the British fort also yeilded to the Americans.

In the ensuing years floods ravaged Kaskaskia and the departure of the original French settlers, which had begun under the British, continued. The influx of new settlers from the East began and lawlessness reigned. Clark's soldiers could not back up his guarantees to Father Gibault of freedom and protection of the people.

The ordeals of ministering in the wilderness and being considered a traitor by both the British and Bishop Briand began to take their toll on Father Gibault. Beginning in 1782, for the next few years, he went first to Ste. Genevieve, then to Vincennes.

Father Gibault was appalled at the moral conditions he found among the people at Vincennes. He wrote Bishop Briand in 1786: ". . . I have enough confidence in God to hope to banish in a little while bar-

barianism from the Post Vincennes, whose inhabitants, especially the young people, had had no religious instruction during twenty-two years except during my short missionary visits."

Because of his health and ordeals, Father Gibault petitioned Bishop Briand for his return to Quebec in various letters from 1786-1788. His appeals were ignored, apparently because he had lost his good standing as a result of his support of the American Revolution.

Father Gibault was also unsure of his ecclesiastical authority since he was being shunned by the Quebec bishop and the Illinois Territory was coming under the jurisdiction of the first U.S. bishop, John Carroll of Baltimore.

The Catholics of Cahokia, who had previously sought Father Gibault's services, sent a courier to him at Vincennes requesting the embattled priest to come to the southern Illinois village. According to a letter from Father Gibault to Bishop Briand, the Cahokia offer was enough to spur Vincennes Catholics into action to help him build a church named "St. Francis Xavier on the Ouabache (Wabash)." The church was later to become a cathedral when the Diocese of Vincennes was formed in 1834.

However, some of the influential citizens at Vincennes, who did not like his attempts at reform there, were said to have sent accusations against him to the Quebec bishop.

Father Gibault did move to Cahokia in 1789 for a year. He then apparently ministered in various places in Missouri, Illinois, and Indiana until 1792. At the request of the Spanish, who had been ceded the west side of the Mississippi River by the French, Father Gibault went to the newly-founded settlement of New Madrid, Mo. He died there in 1802.

His burial place is thought to have been near the Church of St. Isadore, but it would have since been washed away by the Mississippi River.

The "patriot" designation came from Father Gibault's support of the American Revolution. Father Gibault wrote Bishop Briand that he was only doing what he felt was best for his people, and a number of prominent Americans, including Clark and Governor Patrick Henry of Virginia, credited Father Gibault with playing a major role in the accession of the Northwest Territory to the new American nation.

In a later request to the U.S. Congress for a grant of land, Father Gibault cited his services in the taking of Vincennes, "which are not unknown to you."

One of Father Gibault's parishioners came to his defense against the various charges by saying, "He was a true pastor wholly devoted to his people and to his duty as a priest." On various parish records, Father

Gibault always signed his name, "Priest, Missionary."

Father Gibault was the first secular priest to serve in the Illinois Country territory, since all of the earlier priests were of missionary orders.

Near the former Cathedral of St. Francis Xavier in Vincennes there is a memorial to Father Gibault which was constructed as part of a George Rogers Clark Memorial.

In the Diocese of Belleville, the early southern Illinois missionary priest is memorialized by Gibault Catholic High School at Waterloo, which was named for him on September 17, 1967.

CHAPTER 3

Nicholas Jarrot: Cahokia Pioneer

By Rose Josephine Boylan

CAHOKIA'S ORIGINS ARE FRENCH, but its historical importance was primarily Federalist. It was the government seat of St. Clair County of the Northwest Territory, which held the distinction of being the westernmost county in the original limits of the United States.

Its three surviving historic structures illustrate three foundations of American life: God, country, and home. The three are: Holy Family Church, which dates from 1799 (although the parish was founded in 1699); the old Cahokia courthouse, 1737, and the Jarrot mansion, 1798. The last was built by Major Nicholas Jarrot, the local tycoon who served as "marquillier" or trustee, of Holy Family Church and magistrate at the courthouse.

Born at Vesoul, Franche-Comte, France, in 1764, Jarrot was an adolescent during the American Revolution. After a solid upper middle-class schooling, young Nicholas went to Paris as a lay purchasing agent for the Seminary of the Foreign Missions (Vincentians). His clerical employers emigrated when "revolutionary atheism" became the French state "religion." They sought sanctuary from Bishop John Carroll of Baltimore and Jarrot sailed along with the Vincentians.

Since Bishop Carroll's diocese was nationwide, he welcomed the Vincentians as missionaries who could establish parishes in the Northwest Territory. He assigned a French priest to Cahokia. The young bookkeeper followed the French Vincentian on his new assignment to southern Illinois. They sailed along the eastern seaboard to New Orleans where they traveled the Mississippi River north.

Jarrot mansion in Cahokia.

The Federalist era featured an influx of French Revolution refugees who were Royalists and Catholics. They immediately fit into the St. Clair County scene. The early Cahokia settlers should not be confused with the French Huguenot Calvinists, who were the French equivalent to the English Puritans.

Nicholas Jarrot established himself in Cahokia and began to amass his fortune through fur trading and land speculation. He also married money twice. The first Mme. Jarrot was Marie Barbeau, daughter of the captain of the militia at Prairie du Rocher. In these colonial times, this was the most prestigious position in the community. Marie died shortly after the birth of their only child, Marie Louise, whose nickname was Elsie.

The second Mme. Jarrot was Julie St. Gemme Beauvais of Ste. Genevieve, Mo., which at the time was under the Spanish flag. The Beauvais family had migrated to Ste. Genevieve after the British occupation of Kaskaskia in 1765. The family was the mainstay of the Kaskaskia mission. When the Society of Jesus was temporarily banned by the pope, Vital Beauvais purchased the Kaskaskia church property so that the Jesuit missionaries would be provided with return passage to France.

Julie Jarrot, mother of six, lived to be ninety-five years old. A shrewd businesswoman, the matriarch of the Jarrot family skillfully administered all of Nicholas' properties for more than fifty years.

Nicholas Jarrot opened a school in his home for his children and their playmates under the direction of Samuel Davidson, an impoverished young lawyer. One of the youngsters studying in that "sitting room" school earned his own niche in American history. Col. Vital Jarrot became a lifelong friend of Abraham Lincoln during the Black Hawk War and was later appointed by Lincoln to negotiate treaties with the Sioux, opening the railroad route across the plains. He later joined the various gold rushes and died of exposure in the Black Hills of South Dakota.

In 1798 Nicholas Jarrot was a qualified voter in the territorial elections. Like many French refugees, he supported the more conservative candidates, transferring his loyalty from the late king of France to the new federal government. Jarrot proved the strength of his allegiance as a major in the St. Clair County militia regiment.

Major Jarrot aided Indiana Governor William Henry Harrison in establishing civil government under American procedure in the lands between the Mississippi River and the Rocky Mountains after the finalization of the Louisiana Purchase. Earlier, Major Jarrot had furnished the Lewis and Clark expedition with a winter campsite on his land near present-day Wood River, Illinois. Prior to the War of 1812, he served as an unofficial observer-courier for U.S. Army Intelligence. He forwarded detailed reports of observations made during his journeys into Indian country, seeking evidence that British traders from Canada were attempting to infiltrate the Upper Mississippi.

Nicholas Jarrot also generously proved his loyalty to the Church. Jarrot had acquired considerable wealth through land speculation. Part of this can be traced to his parish. The Holy Family mission was endowed by a royal grant of a tract of land "four leagues square." Incoming settlers held building lots and farms as "feudal tenants." The U.S. Congress considered the current tenants as the rightful owners of the tracts that they occupied since the mission's interest was previously alienated.

Major Jarrot bought up untitled tracts of land as well as acreage of neighbors who had exhausted their other assets. He purchased odd tracts of land not covered by any existing government land grants. One such tract was in an area north of the Madison County line which was long known for its concentration of prehistoric mounds. At this time, a group of Trappist monks arrived from France and were seeking a site for a monastery in the St. Louis vicinity. Jarrot turned over to them the property once used by the mound-builders, where they remained for several years. Finding the climate unhealthy, they turned the land back to Jarrot. The large mound is known officially as Cahokia Mound, but among local residents it is still called "Monks' Mound."

As "marquillier," Jarrot pressured Bishop Carroll to see the 1799 Holy Family Church through to dedication. Each year thereafter he paid top dollar at the New Year's auction of pew locations in the church. The pew holders took pride in their seating and the Jarrots always occupied the front pew on the right hand side. It was a weekly spectacle: Major and Madame, children and servants behind, walking the block from the mansion to the church for Mass.

The servants were black. The Illinois Territory residents considered the Northwest Ordinance prohibition of slavery as "post facto." Slavery had existed under France, Britain, and Virginia and continued through a transition period until it ended by attrition. The Illinois Supreme Court finally declared the transition complete in a law suit titled Jarrot vs. Jarrot in 1845. The parties to the suit were Madame Julie and Pete, her servant.

In his later years Nicholas Jarrot went on a binge of building mills both for lumber and grain. It is notable that provisions were made to safeguard the environment especially protecting "the fish of passage."

In early December 1820 Nicholas Jarrot was inspecting a new mill site north of Illinois Town, now known as East St. Louis. He caught a cold and died. He lay in state in the center hall of his mansion and was later taken to Holy Family Church for a stately Requiem Mass. He now rests in the peaceful churchyard along with veterans of the wars of his youth. To quote Governor St. Clair's favorite poet, Nicholas Jarrot "builded monuments more enduring than bronze."

CHAPTER 4

The Pensoneau Family: Laity in Action

By Stanley J. Konieczny

THE CHURCH IN SOUTHERN ILLINOIS was established through the the combined efforts and faith of devoted missionaries and settlers. Unfortunately, the names and sacrifices of so many of these lay Catholic pioneers were never recorded and they are seldom given proper recognition. In some ways, though, their religious and civic contributions are typified in pioneer chronicles like that of the Pensoneau family.

In his book, *The Romantic Story of Cahokia, Illinois,* Adolph B. Suess noted that two brothers, Louison and Etienne Pensoneau, and their cousin, Louis, arrived in Cahokia from France in 1798. Suess described the young settlers as "courageous, enterprising and comparatively wealthy Frenchmen."

Louis opened a ferry across the Mississippi River, connecting the village of Cahokia with Carondelet on the west bank. In later years, he built the first farmhouse in the Cahokia commonfields. Etienne constructed a two-story brick house in which he opened a tavern or inn for travelers who roamed the Mississippi River Valley.

By 1799 Etienne and Louis seemed to be active, influential members of Holy Family parish, because they were among the six laymen who joined their pastor, Father J. Olivier, in signing the parish regulations for church wardens at Cahokia. This document lends interesting insights into parish life in the eighteenth century.

The church warden of that time might be compared to today's parish trustee or the president of the parish council. The office required that the warden be a resident Catholic of the parish, live a good life and have "on this shore [the east bank of the Mississippi] sufficient funds to

Pensoneau house built in French Village (East St. Louis) in 1818.

answer for the moneys of the church." The church warden was authorized to hire a clerk to assist in keeping detailed records on pew rent and church inventories as well as recording all voluntary service rendered the parish. The church warden was also held accountable for "the maintenance and fencing of the cemetery." Fencing at the old cemetery seemed to be a very important matter since a considerable portion of the document was devoted to insuring that parishioners would contribute to maintaining the cemetery fence. Louis Pensoneau is cited as the third church warden of Holy Family parish.

Etienne Pensoneau's talents as a builder took him beyond the American Bottoms. In 1814 he was awarded the contract to build the first courthouse in Belleville. The two-story, unpainted frame building stood in front of the site of the present courthouse. The courtroom occupied the entire lower floor with the clerk's offices and jury rooms on the upper level. According to the stories told in the Pensoneau family, when St. Clair County outgrew this courthouse, Etienne was called upon to build a second municipal building. This time, he was deeded part of the public square as payment. Family "legends" hold that he swapped the land for a pair of leather boots.

At the time the elder Pensoneau was building Belleville's first county courthouse, his son Lawrence built a frame farmhouse out of water oak, lined with brick, for Pensoneau's grandson and namesake, Steven. This home still stands at 8107 Church Lane, East St. Louis, near St. Philip School. Vincent and Albert (''Abby'') Pensoneau still live in the old family ''homestead.'' The two brothers recount stories that have been passed down through the generations. Their tales of pioneer life in the Bottoms capture some of the hospitality and color that typifies our local Catholic heritage.

The early Catholic settlers in the vicinity of French Village would gather for the celebration of Mass at Madame Germaine's home or in the parlor of the Pensoneau house, which is designated as a state historical site, although it remains a private residence. From 1836 until 1842, when St. Philip church was completed, the fledgling parish met in these two private homes. In some ways, the roots of East St. Louis Catholicism took hold in these sturdy little houses.

Located on the old National Road which linked St. Louis with the East Coast, the Pensoneaus saw many pioneer families headed out West to seek their fortune. Abby and Vince recall their parents' stories of entire wagon trains camping on the grounds of St. Philip church, which often became a rest stop for these trailblazers.

During times of ''high water'' which inundated East St. Louis, boats brought people to dry ground around the Pensoneau house and St. Philip church where they would wait until the floods receded. ''The old people in those days seemed to be more hospitable,'' Abby noted, ''They just went out, helped and thought nothing of it.''

One story about family hospitality stands out in the brothers' recollections. During the Civil War, six Union soldiers rode onto the Pensoneau farm and wanted to shoot Stephen for being a Southern sympathizer. Pensoneau showed them his son, Jules' enlistment papers in the Illinois infantry and a note which he held proving that he loaned a Union Army doctor $65 to purchase surgical instruments; medical personnel brought their own supplies to the army.

The troops stayed the night, ate in the same house where Mass was once celebrated, and drank Grandpa Pensoneau's homemade wine. The next morning the detachment headed towards present-day Washington Park where they shot to death an eighteen-year-old man who had never registered for the draft. The Pensoneaus later heard that the soldiers were ambushed and killed somewhere in Missouri.

During this same time, in another branch of the Pensoneau family, Paschal Pensoneau's daughter Flavia joined the Sisters of Mercy, taking the name of Sister Mary Angela. Abby and Vince can be side-tracked for a few minutes talking about the problems and crises of the world today. Abby concluded, ''That's our whole problem; we've lost our connection with our past and what it stands for. That's an important thing to remember — where we've been.''

CHAPTER 5

Father Gabriel Richard: Multi-Faceted Missioner

By Stanley J. Konieczny

DURING THE LATTER PART of the eighteenth century, one of the most prominent figures in American Catholic history ministered in southern Illinois. Father Gabriel Richard, who from 1793 to 1798 served the Catholic communities at Kaskaskia, Prairie du Rocher and Cahokia, distinguished himself as a missionary, pastor, educator-scholar, editor-publisher, and U.S. congressman.

Father Richard is best remembered for the varied accomplishments which marked his thirty-four-year assignment to Detroit, where he earned the title "Apostle of Michigan." Prior to this mission, he spent six difficult years working among the French settlers in what is now the Belleville diocese.

Born October 15, 1767, at Saintes, France, Gabriel Richard was the son of a government employee. He entered the Society of Saint Sulpice (Sulpicians) and was ordained in 1791 at Issy, which is located near Paris. The Sulpicians seemed to be well-suited to the intellectual makeup of Gabriel Richard. Founded in 1642, the Sulpicians dedicated their ministry to seminary education. Young Father Richard began his career as a seminary instructor but when the French Revolution stepped up its anticlerical campaign, the priest was forced out of his native France.

Exiled along with Sulpician Fathers Marechal, Ciquard, and Matignon, Father Richard and his companions came to Baltimore, Maryland, where they were employed at the new St. Mary Seminary in 1792. The following year, Bishop John Carroll assigned the Sulpician priest to do missionary work in the French settlements of southern Illinois.

From February 1793 until February 1798 Father Richard is identified as the "Curé of Prairie du Rocher." Burial records indicate that during these years, he also ministered to the people of Immaculate Conception Parish, Kaskaskia. He moved north temporarily and served at Holy Family Parish, Cahokia, from June 1796 until May 1797. In his absence Father Pierre Janin was stationed at Kaskaskia.

Father Gabriel Richard.

Biographers of Father Richard describe his southern Illinois mission years as ones of "hardship and privation." Despite these relatively sketchy accounts of Father Richard, at least one historian, Father John Rothensteiner, was able to offer a glimpse into life in the early Belleville diocese.

In his article "The Sulpicians in the Illinois Country," which was published in 1962 in the *Illinois Catholic Historical Review*, Father Rothensteiner wrote, "In Kaskaskia he [Father Richard] lived among the ruins of former grandeur. Many of the houses were without roofs and doors. The better part of the Creoles had migrated to St. Louis. Fort Chartres lay deserted, and its mighty ramparts were falling piece by piece into the Mississippi. St. Anne's Church of New Chartres was no more. The Illinois Indians, that had formed the two flourishing missions of Kaskaskia were reduced to a pitiful remnant. All was desolation and despair. Yet Father Richard labored and prayed knowing that the result was in the hands of God. The parishes of Kaskaskia and Prairie du Rocher remained in his care from 1793 to 1798. On August 1, 1797, he inscribed his name in the baptismal record of Ste. Genevieve, Missouri, as "Curé de Prairie du Rocher."

In 1798 Father Richard was named the vicar general and pastor of St. Anne parish, Detroit. It is significant to note that Kaskaskia records indicate that Father Richard visited Immaculate Conception parish in November 1821. This was before the days of easy access to transportation. Kaskaskia and its people must have held a special place in Father Richard's heart for him to have made the effort to return for a visit.

Father Richard found himself in another challenging assignment when he arrived in Detroit, a rough frontier town which had once been an Indian trading center. He sent out to improve this community by introducing education to the town. In 1804 he opened an academy for young women and a preparatory seminary.

The territorial governor invited Father Richard to give a series of lectures on religion and morality for the legislature and government leaders of the Michigan territory in 1807. Within two years this pioneer Sulpician traveled to Baltimore where he bought type and a press which he took to Michigan. Father Richard became editor and publisher of the first newspaper in Michigan, entitled *Michigan Essay or Impartial Observer*. Father Richard's press over the next three years would produce seven educational and religious books, including *The Epistles and Gospels for all the Sundays and Feast-days of the Year*, the first publication of a part of the Scriptures west of the Allegheny Mountains. As an educator and a publisher, Father Richard was considered a dangerous element by the British force during the War of 1812. When Detroit was captured by English troops, the priest was arrested and imprisoned in Canada. At the end of hostilities Father Richard returned to Michigan where, collaborating with a Protestant minister, John Monteith, he co-founded the University of Michigan, which evolved into the present-day University of Michigan. Father Richard served as vice-president of the school and taught six of the thirteen courses offered at the university. In 1821 he was named trustee of the University of Michigan.

Bishop Plessis of Quebec visited the French community at Detroit in 1816 and left this picture of Father Richard in his journal: "He has the talent for doing, almost simultaneously, ten entirely different things. Provided with newspapers (*gazettes*), well informed on all political questions, ever ready to argue on religion, when the occasion presents itself, and thoroughly learned in theology, he reaps his hay, gathers the fruit of his garden, manages a fishery fronting his lot, teaches mathematics to one young man, reading to another, devotes time to mental prayer . . ."

This is the man of energy and reflection whom the people of the Michigan Territory elected as their representative in Washington in 1823. Father Richard experienced some problems in getting to the nation's capital though. As pastor of St. Anne parish, he had excommunicated one of his parishioners who had divorced his wife. The disgruntled man charged Father Richard with defamation of character and sued him for $1,000. Unable to pay the judgment, the priest was thrown into jail. Friends in the French community raised bail so that he could be freed in time to go to Washington. The suit was later overturned.

He was the first Catholic priest to win a seat in the United States

Congress. As a congressman, Father Richard proved to be a very persuasive orator, although his faulty English had to translated by a friend and fellow legislator, Henry Clay. He was defeated in a bid for reelection and returned to his pastoral work in Detroit.

When the Diocese of Detroit was created in 1827, Gabriel Richard was proposed as the first bishop of the new see, although he never received the mitre. One source speculated that he turned down the appointment while another hinted that it might have been ''suppressed.'' While ministering to Detroit's cholera victims, Father Richard contracted the disease and died on September 13, 1832.

In addition to these accomplishments it is interesting to note that the missionary who once served in our diocese spoke five European languages fluently as well as the dialects of various Michigan Indian tribes; he introduced wool-carding as an industry on the Michigan frontier; he proved himself to be a great humanitarian. After the War of 1812 when settlers were going hungry because the soldiers had taken their crops, Father Richard bought wheat at his own expense and distributed it to those in need.

CHAPTER 6

Pierre Menard: First Lieutenant Governor

By Patricia A. Hamilton

ON THE STATEHOUSE GROUNDS at Springfield east of the capitol stands a bronze statue of an Indian trader. He is standing erect beside an Indian seated upon a bale of furs, each displaying a sample of his merchandise to the other. On the eastern face of the ten-foot pedestal which serves as the base for the statue is the single word "Menard."

Known to us mainly as the first lieutenant governor of Illinois and owner of the beautifully-restored home at Kaskaskia in Randolph County, Pierre Menard was widely recognized by his contemporaries for his fair dealings with the Indians.

He was born October 6, 1766, at Saint-Antoine, Quebec. His father was an officer in the French Canadian army. Menard left Canada at about age fifteen, signing on with a trading expedition to the "Illinois country." By 1788 he had come to Vincennes, in Indiana Territory, and in 1789 he accompanied Francis Vigo to Carlisle, Pennsylvania, to interview George Washington concerning the Western frontier.

It is perhaps not surprising that he might be attracted to Kaskaskia. As an early French settlement on the frontier, it offered him the opportunity to surround himself with both his fellow Frenchmen and the Indians in whom he had such a great interest.

Kaskaskia had begun as a settlement of traders, priests, and Indians. Parish and village were identical communities — the members of the one were the citizens of the other. Most of the business of this early local government was conducted in "assemblies" held after Sunday Mass, either in front of the church or in the house of one of the leading citizens.

Menard settled in this community in the early 1790s. His Kaskaskia trading company ledgers began in the spring of 1791 and he was granted a St. Clair County commercial license in 1793.

On June 13, 1792, he married Therese Godin in Kaskaskia. Four children were born of this marriage. She died in 1804, and on September 22, 1806, also in Kaskaskia, he married Angelique Saucier. Six children were born of this union.

Pierre Menard, first lieutenant governor of Illinois.

Between 1795 and 1818 Menard received such appointments as major in the militia, judge of the Court of Common Pleas of Randolph County, member of a commission of enquiry concerning crimes in the territory, delegate to the territorial legislature of Indiana Territory, and sub-agent of Indian Affairs. From the formation of the separate territory of Illinois until Illinois became a state, he was a member of and the presiding officer of the legislature (four terms), then called "the Council." During all these early years, he was the only Frenchman in this part of the state who was honored with an important office.

There was but one political party in Illinois at this early period; all citizens were members of the Democratic party, with Andrew Jackson as their idol. But there were two strong factions in the party, and both were striving for control of the new state government. A truce was agreed upon between the Bond and Edwards factions: Shadrach Bond and Pierre Menard became unopposed candidates for governor and lieutenant governor, and Ninian Edwards was elected a U.S. senator.

Menard had helped frame the first Illinois constitution, and he was being strongly promoted for the position of lieutenant governor. The provision that the governor must have been born in the United States was retained in the constitution's final form, but a paragraph was added stating that this should not be a requirement for lieutenant governor. This has been cited as an unusual instance of a paragraph having been added to a basic law intended to apply to but one person. Menard, strongly favored, could not otherwise have assumed the position.

The first general assembly of Illinois, composed of fourteen senators and twenty-eight representatives, convened at Kaskaskia on October 5, 1818. Kaskaskia, which had been the territorial capital, was also the first state capital. Governor Bond, a prosperous farmer residing near Kaskaskia, and Lieutenant Governor Menard, a wealthy merchant in Kaskaskia, had but a few steps to walk to their offices where they administered their duties and guided the new state. Menard's name was perpetuated by the state government in 1839, when the newly-formed Menard County was named in his honor.

Pierre Menard died at his residence near Kaskaskia on June 13, 1844, just a few months short of his seventy-eighth birthday. Mention was made in his obituary in the Belleville *Weekly Advocate* of his dealings with the Indians and of his truthfulness and fairness in his relationships with all persons. He was characterized as a great and good man who loved his country and his fellowman and was possessed of strict honesty and integrity of character. Having become wealthy through his dealings as a merchant and having been blessed with a long life, he was thus given the opportunity of exercising to his heart's content the virtues of charity and benevolence. He helped many poor young men with families to secure their homes and farms, and his obituary claimed that "no poor man was ever turned away from the door of Colonel Menard without having his wants relieved so far as possible."

Although he left what was a large estate for the time, his family was also left with many worthless promissory notes from those he had aided who were unable to repay him.

John Reynolds, in his *Pioneer History of Illinois*, described Menard as a "liberal and enlightened member of the Catholic church" who "died happy, confiding in the doctrines of that church."

Pierre Menard was among the most distinguished of the French emigrants who came to Illinois during and after the Revolution. He maintained an enviable popularity for more than fifty years in Illinois, and he lived and died "the favorite of the people."

CHAPTER 7
Father Elisha Durbin: Circuit-rider

By Lucille Lawler

TODAY, SOUTHEASTERN ILLINOIS is a stronghold of Catholic faith, but before the early 1800s there was no Catholic living in this area. In 1819 John and Elizabeth Lawler arrived at Shawneetown with their son, Michael Kelly. They were followed by former neighbors and friends from Ireland and established the nucleus of the Catholic Church in the five county area.

These faithful Catholics were concerned because the nearest priests lived in Kaskaskia, Illinois, and Vincennes, Indiana. After a few years of praying and looking for a pastor, a young priest on horseback arrived at the clearing in front of the Lawler cabin in May 1824. He told them that he had come to serve them. This young priest was Father Elisha John Durbin from St. Vincent, Kentucky.

This pioneer priest of Kentucky came from a long line of hardy ancestry. A relative of the pioneer priest, Ross Durbin, who lives in St. Louis, has traced the family genealogy back to Samuel Durbin, who was born in 1698, and to Ann Logsdon, who was born around 1703. Elisha John Durbin was born February 1, 1800, in Madison County, Kentucky, to John D. Durbin and Patience Logsdon Durbin. His parents were natives of Baltimore, Maryland.

While the Logsdons of Kentucky were reported to be of large stature, Father Durbin was only five feet ten inches tall and weighed about 160 pounds. He attributed his surprising energy and good health, despite exposure to the elements, to simple foods and exercise from horseback riding.

After completion of his studies at St. Thomas Seminary, Bardstown,

Father Elisha "Daddy" Durbin.

Kentucky, Elisha Durbin was ordained on September 21, 1822. Two years later, Father Durbin was entrusted with the care of the entire population of southeastern Illinois, western and southwestern Kentucky and southern Indiana. His pastoral jurisdiction covered thousands of miles of territory where isolated Catholic families lived. His "parish" was extended in 1832 to include an annual visit to Nashville, Tennessee.

These many miles were traveled in good and bad weather on horseback. A priest friend calculated that Father Durbin's combined journeys during his sixty-two years in the priesthood would be underestimated at 500,000 miles!

The newly-appointed circuit-rider priest made his headquarters at St. Vincent, Kentucky, home of the Sisters of Charity of Nazareth. When Father Durbin first arrived at St. Vincent, there was a small log church. Within two years of his arrival, Father Durbin was able to point with pride to two churches that he was instrumental in erecting: a new one at St. Vincent near the site of the log church and a second one at St. Ambrose in Union County, Kentucky.

Eventually, the Sisters at St. Vincent expanded their institution, which grew into an outstanding girls' school. Many families from southern Illinois as well as from Indiana and Kentucky sent their daughters to this school. It was a place of higher education where Catholics and nonCatholics alike could learn music, art, stitchery, and religion.

Records show that Father Durbin began his pastoral ministry in the present Belleville diocese in May 1824 with the baptism of Margaret Lawler, the four-year-old daughter of John and Elizabeth Lawler. In September of the same year, three children of area families were baptized by Father Durbin, according to early church records kept at St. Vincent's. Separate records were opened for the Illinois parishes in 1842. These children, John Milney, Edward Mattingly and Peter Sanders, were from two to five years old, leading to the belief that no priest had been in the area for baptism for at least three or four years.

In his memoirs, written after his service in the Civil War, Gen. Michael Kelly Lawler left the following comments about the young Father Durbin: "To the Catholics eager to learn of the next visit of Father Durbin, the message of his coming brought cheer and great preparations . . . Oxen were put to the yoke and family readied for a three-day visit, the one the day before Father Durbin's arrival and the day after the services."

The children must have loved going to Mass as it was a holiday, although there were no schools to close. Parents provided both academic and religious instruction in their homes in the early 1820s and 1830s. The people's love for the missionary is evident in their nickname for him: "Daddy" Durbin.

While riding this circuit, it was Father Durbin's custom to carry the sacred vessels and vestments for Mass in his saddle bags. In *The Centenary of Catholicity in Kentucky*, written by Hon. Ben J. Webb and published in 1884, a story related how Father Durbin's bulging saddle bags and florid complexion was once the occasion of a humorous incident.

Riding along the road one day, Father Durbin raised his eyes from the pages of his breviary to greet a stranger who had stopped his horse to visit for a moment.

"Halloo, stranger! You are just the man I'm looking for. Give me a swig from your jug," the traveler said to the priest. "My friend," Father Durbin replied, "I have no jug nor do I have use for one. I do not drink."

"No jug! Then what sort of bulge is that in your saddle bags?" the stranger challenged the missionary. "I told you the truth the first time, I have no spirits at any time," Father Durbin said.

The man looked intently at the priest's red face and the bulges in the saddle bags for a full half minute and rode away saying, "If I were in your place, then, I'd take in my sign."

Father Durbin may have endured many hours in the saddle, but he lived to see the fruits of his labors toward establishing the Church in southern Illinois. The first church built in Gallatin County was at Waltonboro, or Pond Settlement. Built in honor of St. Patrick in 1853 it grew from the early visits of "Daddy" Durbin.

This was a small log structure with most primitive furnishings; split logs with sticks for support served as pews. The poverty of the church reflected the poverty of the parishioners. For example, shoes were so rare that they were carried under the worshippers' arms until they reached the church door at which time they were slipped on.

Thirty miles north of St. Patrick's was another Irish town, known as Dolan Settlement, or Enfield. Patrick Dolan was possibly the first

Catholic in White County and was there to welcome Father Durbin. By 1847 the town of Carmi had its first Mass offered by Father Durbin in the home of John and Catherine Rebstock, natives of Baden, Germany. Their home became a shrine for worship when Father Durbin came to that corner of White County.

In 1841 Father Durbin started visiting the Catholics at Auxier Prairie in the neighborhood of Piopolis. A number of families from Ersinger and Bilsenger, Baden, Germany, had sailed for forty-one days to New York City, from which they traveled to Pittsburgh where they took flatboats down the Ohio to Shawneetown. Led by John Leonard and Cajetan Aydt, who had come earlier to scout for good land, they decided to build their homes on land which today comprises the parish of St. John the Baptist, Piopolis. Father Durbin was the first priest to visit and celebrated Mass in the log cabin of Nicholas Engel.

Other parishes in southeastern Illinois, including Equality, Metropolis, McLeansboro, and Olney, as well as parishes in western Kentucky, were fortunate to have Father Durbin minister there during their early years. Catholics in many local parishes no doubt have signatures of this venerable priest in their early records. St. Mary Church, Shawneetown, has relics of this pioneer priest including his monstrance, chalice, paten, and altar stone, which was used when he said Mass in the home of Mary Handmore.

It is untrue that Father Durbin received only praise while ministering to his scattered flock in three states. Father Durbin was not perfect and his people admitted that he could not preach. During his first year at Bardstown, he would memorize his sermon, then proceed to forget his lines, stammer, stop, and at times just walk away from the pulpit.

Although St. Mary Parish, Shawneetown, received its first resident pastor in 1847, Father Durbin's signature can be found in parish records until 1859. At age seventy-three, Father Durbin was released from his pastoral duties in Union County, Kentucky, but the aged missionary continued to minister to Catholics living along a route from Elizabethtown to Paducah, Kentucky. He finally retired to the College of St. Joseph, Bardstown, where he was surrounded with much care and love until he died in his eighty-seventh year.

CHAPTER 8

Father J. F. R. Loisel: A Friend From the West

By Rose Mansfield

IN THE TROUBLED and chaotic times following the American Revolution, many of the "paisible" French Creoles of the Illinois villages crossed the Mississippi to begin anew at Laclede's settlement, which was named St. Louis for the French Crusader King Saint Louis IX. In 1778 the French of Cahokia had sworn allegiance to a new country. And the Catholics of the oldest of French villages no longer looked to France, Quebec, or New Orleans for their French priests. They now looked west to the bishop of St. Louis because, although separated by the Mississippi, the people of St. Louis and Cahokia had a common French heritage and central to both was the Catholic Church.

During the long periods of disorder following the American possession of Illinois, Holy Family Parish, Cahokia, often had no priest at all; this situation existed for a period of eight years after Father Olivier left in 1803. In 1808 America's first bishop, the Most Rev. John Carroll, created four dioceses out of his see, which had encompassed the entire United States. Illinois was placed in the newly-established Diocese of Bardstown, Kentucky. At this date, in all of Illinois, Bishop Carroll counted three old French parishes, one at Cahokia, another at Kaskaskia, and the third at Prairie du Rocher. There was one lone priest, Father Pierre Gibault, the Patriot Priest of the Revolution.

Since Bardstown was so far away, it was only natural that the Catholic history of western Illinois became part of that of St. Louis in the early nineteenth century. On June 26, 1826, Father Joseph Rosati succeeded Louis William Du Bourg as bishop of Saint Louis, and, upon his request, the western half of Illinois became part of the St. Louis diocese.

Holy Family Church in Cahokia where Father Loisel served as pastor.

In this transition period of the Catholic Church in Illinois, there came as a missionary to Illinois in 1828 Father Jean Francois Regis Loisel from St. Louis. Father Loisel was the son of Regis Loisel, who came from lower Canada. The Loisel ancestors were of Norman stock from the Diocese of Bayeux, France. One of the earliest Loisels was a soldier of France at the Citadel at Quebec. Rose Josephine Boylan, author and historian, tells us that the name Loisel is a form of the French "Loiseau" which is related to the French "Mademoiselle."

Regis Loisel died in October 1804 at the young age of thirty- one. He was survived by Helen Chauvin, whom he had married on May 27, 1800; two baby daughters; and a son, Jean Francois Regis, who was born after his father's death. Jean Francois Regis went on to become the first St. Louisan to be ordained a priest.

When Father Loisel was born in St. Louis on March 24, 1805, the village had fewer than 1,000 residents. As a boy of thirteen, he was enrolled as one of the first students of today's Saint Louis University, which opened its doors in 1818, the year Illinois became a state. The school was chartered as a university in 1832.

At age fifteen, Jean Francois Regis Loisel entered St. Mary's Seminary at the Barrens to begin his studies for the priesthood. This seminary was established near Perryville, Missouri, by Father Joseph Rosati under Bishop Du Bourg.

In spite of his ill health, Father Loisel was ordained by Bishop Rosati on June 29, 1828, the feast of Sts. Peter and Paul, at Bishop Du Bourg's brick cathedral on the St. Louis riverfront. He served the next nine years as assistant there. His chronic illness forced him to go often to his mother's home to recuperate.

Father Loisel was assigned to Cahokia, first as an assistant to Pastor Joseph Antoine Lurz von Odenheim, for the months of August and September 1828. The parish at Cahokia had existed for more than a century and a quarter, when, in August 1836, Father Loisel returned as pastor to succeed the much-loved Father P. J. Deutreluingue, C.M. The old log church to which Father Loisel came had been built by the Voidrie brothers during the tenure of Father Olivier.

Peterson, in his *History of Cakokia* tells us that Father Loisel evidently brought money to the parish, because the church was freshly painted in 1840 and a wide lean-to against the rear was added. In 1838 Father Loisel, at his own expense, built the fifth rectory. It stood just west of the church and was quite the grandest ever seen at Cahokia. French architecture was not discernible; rather the home was in the Greek style, made of brick with a colonnade in front supporting the roof. This private residence of the priest was built well and survived many and varied tenants for a century. While Father Loisel was pastor, a new cemetery, located a mile southeast of the village, was opened. It is recorded that Julia Touchette, wife of Pierre Voidrie, was the first to be buried at that place.

The year Father Loisel became pastor at Cahokia, Sisters of the Order of St. Joseph came from France and opened a school that became known as the Abbey. Their chapel was blessed by Bishop Rosati on August 17, 1838. A bell for the occasion was sent from Lyons, France, by Mother St. John Fontbonne. This school was lost at the time of the great flood. The sisters took their services and their school to St. Louis and today it is well known as Fontbonne College.

Although Cahokia became part of the Diocese of Chicago during the pastorate of Father Loisel, the priests of the old French villages continued to look to St. Louis and Bishop Rosati for their leadership.

Father Loisel's duties were not confined to his church and congregation at Cahokia. Father Deutreluingue before him had established little mission stations at French Village, St. Thomas near Millstadt, and Belleville. So, like his predecessor, Father Loisel evangelized the whole neighboring territory east of the Mississippi River. The *Illinois Catholic Historical Review* lists Father Loisel as a missionary whose field of labor included Prairie Du Rocher, Cahokia, French Village near Cahokia,

La Cantine near Cahokia, and Belleville.

St. Thomas the Apostle near Millstadt should have been included in the priest's field of labor. The first mention of a little Catholic chapel near Millstadt can be found in the register of Cahokia where Father Loisel recorded that on "November 17, 1836, I said Mass . . . for the first time at the house of James Powers for the new congregation of St. Thomas . . . about twenty-five persons were present . . . we spoke to them about building a little chapel . . . next Wednesday the 23rd . . . the parishioners should assemble to cut down trees for the construction of the chapel." On November 26, 1837, a log church built on the farm of Thomas Laughlin was dedicated by Bishop Rosati of St. Louis in honor of St. Thomas, Apostle. The location of the little church was also called the "Johnson Settlement." Father Loisel continued his visits until 1839. The little chapel served these early German Catholics until 1851 when a new brick church was ready for services at the village of Millstadt.

In 1814 Belleville was founded in a cornfield on land originally given a soldier for his military service in the American Revolution. Typical Americans from the eastern and southern states chose this site for a new county seat because they thought the French of the Bottoms inferior, and they liked neither the customs nor the religion of the Catholics who lived there. Cahokia was one of the first seats of government in the Northwest Territory and the first county seat of St. Clair (1790).

Priests came to offer Mass in the private homes of the Catholics and sometimes in the county courthouse built by one of the early Catholics from Cahokia, Etienne Pensoneau. Father Loisel made the journey to Belleville on horseback through the American Bottoms' swamps and marshes. At the time, many of the French-speaking immigrants at Belleville were from Alsace and Lorraine.

In 1800 French speaking Catholics from Cahokia established "Village Francais." Now known as French Village, it became the site of one of the small mission parishes created by Cahokia pastor Father Deutreluingue. In 1836 when Father Loisel made the twelve-mile journey from his home to French Village on his old slow-footed, hesitant horse, he was described as an old man, while in truth he was only in his thirties.

Father Loisel recorded that he celebrated Mass for the first time on October 27, 1836, at the home of Madame Germain. Mass was celebrated regularly by Father Loisel at the homes of Mrs. Germain and Steven Pensoneau. He was never a resident pastor of St. Phillip, but he did make a record of the formal establishment of the parish when he wrote in the Cahokia records that on April 18, 1841, St.

Philip parish was separated from the parish of the Holy Family at Cahokia. At the same time, Father Loisel formally opened the parish records when he celebrated Mass at the home of Madame Germain and then baptized Jules Cyril Pensoneau and Nicholas Boul.

With the "June rise" of the Mississippi of 1844 came the worst flood the American bottoms had ever witnessed. L. U. Reavis in his *History of East St. Louis, 1776-1876,* wrote, ". . . ordinary steamboats plied between the bluffs and second and third street in St. Louis, over the roofs of some and along the roofs of other remaining houses in the area."

Father Loisel ignored his own ill health and ministered tirelessly to his flock who lived in the flooded alluvial bottom lands of Cahokia. After the flood he became ill, most probably a victim of the epidemic that swept the village, due in part to its poor sanitary conditions. He returned to his sister's home in St. Louis. There he lingered until May 10, 1845, when he died at age forty. He was buried in St. Louis.

In the 1940s John L. Keeley, along with other contractors, developed the area in the vicinity of the old Boul homestead on the bluff and the original Boul farm opposite in the bottom land. Mr. Keeley and his associates remembered the faithful priest who came to Village Francais. They named the area Loisel Village and Loisel Hills. In 1961, the year of the East St. Louis centennial, St. Philip parish float depicted Father Loisel celebrating the Eucharist.

CHAPTER 9

The Aydt Family: Influence of German Settlers

By Stanley J. Konieczny

WITHOUT A DOUBT the Germans have played a vital role in the establishment of the Church in southern Illinois. Immigrants from Germany laid the foundations for many communities in today's Belleville diocese while their descendants made significant contributions to the continuing growth of the local Catholic Church. A case study of the German influence in the Belleville diocese is seen in the story of the Aydt family of Hamilton County.

The Aydts trace their roots to the village of Ersingen, Germany, a relatively poor farming village in the Baden region. John Aydt, a peddler popularly known as "Cheap John," came to the United States and plied his wares as far south as Mexico. When he eventually made his headquarters in Shawneetown, "Cheap John" became the "forerunner" of the first Catholic settlement of Germans in this (southeastern) portion of the state," according to Father Joseph Lawler in his book, *Cradle of Christianity*.

By 1840, Cajetan Aydt, who had at one time been a hotel manager near Ersingen, journeyed to America. After staying awhile in Baltimore, he roamed the West, traveling through Ohio and Indiana. Cajetan returned to his native land where he recruited other pioneers to settle the midwestern prairies. His eloquence persuaded Mathias Kaufmann, Albert Eswein, Anthony Kaufmann, Urban Anselment, William Aydt, and Marcellus Zachmann to leave Ersingen and start new lives in America.

Father John Nepomuk Enzelberger, former pastor of St. John the Baptist parish, Piopolis, had the foresight to preserve the story of these courageous settlers in a pamphlet which he wrote, entitled *History of a*

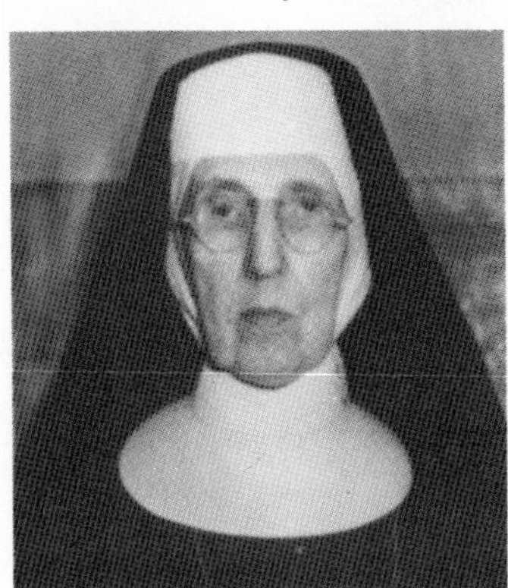

Sister Salome Aydt

Father Henry Aydt.

Country Parish. The late Father August Reyling, OFM, a native of Piopolis, translated the work into English in 1956.

Headed by Cajetan Aydt, the twenty-five settlers began their trek to the United States on April 19, 1841, after attending Mass at their home parish church in Ersingen. The pioneers embarked from Rotterdam and after forty-two days on the Atlantic, they landed in New York City.

By way of Philadelphia and Pittsburgh, the band of German immigrants reached Troy, Indiana, where they made their home in a cooper's workshop, where barrels were made, while Cajetan scouted the territory for a suitable location for their settlement. Ferdinand, Indiana, was ruled out even though the German parish there offered a warm welcome to the newcomers. The land there was considered too expensive at $15 to $20 per acre.

When it was learned that John Aydt, a fellow countryman, was living in Shawneetown, Cajetan sought out his advice. The two Aydts, who probably were cousins, followed the recommendation of an innkeeper that land was good in Auxier Prairie and the two inspected a parcel of land in Hamilton County. After purchasing a plot of land, the Aydts led their charges to Shawneetown and then to Auxier Prairie, arriving at their new home on August 21, 1841.

The next two years passed quickly as the German pioneers struggled to survive and build their homes on the Illinois prairie. Throughout these years, one of their principal complaints was that they had no one to meet their spiritual needs. "Cheap John" came to the rescue. In his travels, the peddler had met the famed circuit-rider priest Father Elisha Durbin. John Aydt went to "Daddy" Durbin's home in Kentucky and made arrangements for the famed missionary to visit the German settlement.

On February 12, 1843, Father Durbin baptized the first child, Joseph Haller, in what is now St. John the Baptist Church, Piopolis. Mass was celebrated in the home of Nicholas Engel. After so many years, the devout Germans were anxious to reconcile themselves and to seek forgiveness of their sins through the sacrament of penance.

There was a snag in their joyful welcome for Father Durbin. The priest did not speak German. John Aydt had to serve as a confidential interpreter for priest and penitent. "Cheap John" would be seated in the "reconciliation room" facing away from Father Durbin and the person going to confession. Aydt would announce a commandment in German. If the penitent had sinned against this commandment, she would nod her head toward him and indicate the number of incidents with her fingers. Such a silent "confession" facilitated the celebration of the sacrament while insuring the individual's privacy.

Cajetan Aydt purchased a tract of land for a parish church and construction of a log chapel was begun in 1845. Father Durbin celebrated Mass in the new building on Ash Wednesday of the following year. A German parish in southern Illinois was founded.

This parish is now known as Piopolis and seemed to be the springboard of several other adventures. Cajetan Aydt left the community in 1854 and resettled at Aydtstown, Minnesota. Then in the latter part of the nineteenth century, another resident of Piopolis, Charles Aydt, left the village and opened a store in Cottonwood. He was later joined by his brothers, Thomas, Joseph, Solomon and Alphonse. Their settlement was soon named Dahlgren and as the community grew, a Catholic church was built there and dedicated to St. John Nepomucene.

Two parishes in the Belleville diocese, Piopolis and Dahlgren, were built on the adventurous spirit of members of the Aydt family. In turn, these parishes were home to at least two Aydts, who made significant contributions to the church in southern Illinois.

The longtime pastor of St. Dominic parish, Breese, the late Father Henry Aydt, was born in Dahlgren on April 20, 1895, one of Solomon Aydt's seven children. Ordained in 1920, Father Aydt served in East St. Louis, Murphysboro, St. Sebastian, Fairfield, Todd's Mill, and Hecker before he began his twenty-eight year pastorate at St. Dominic, Breese, in 1942.

Father Aydt had a lasting impact on the Clinton County community that he served. He was instrumental in organizing Breese Council 2869 of the Knights of Columbus and Precious Blood Circle 718 of the Daughters of Isabella.

When Bishop Albert Zuroweste introduced the plan for Mater Dei High School to Clinton County, Father Aydt was a major organizer of the program. He was instrumental in the final selection of the institution's present site and served as Mater Dei's first president for ten years. The ordination of several young men to the priesthood from St. Dominic's and the many women religious who are natives of the Breese parish also testify to Father Aydt's influence.

An updated history of St. John the Baptist parish, Piopolis, which was compiled by Mrs. Leo J. Aydt, noted that thirty-five women of that community entered religious life. Four of these women were Aydts. The chronicles of the Adorers of the Blood of Christ, Ruma Province, record the pioneer educational efforts of the late Sister Salome Aydt at the former St. Teresa Academy, East St. Louis. Sister Salome organized the first high school classes at the East St. Louis school for girls.

In 1896 Sister Salome initiated the STA high school program. In her latest book, *Ruma: Home and Heritage,* Sister Pauline Grady, ASC, noted, "She [Sister Salome] was to become the soul of the academy, directing the elementary and secondary divisions of the school from 1903 to 1928 and serving as bookkeeper from 1936 to 1951 . . . It fell to Sister Salome's capable hands to lead the school into a period which placed added emphasis on scholarship and business competence. She also began the production of operettas and other dramatic performances, started an active alumnae association and gained state accreditation within a year when in 1919 the state of Illinois set up specific standards for high schools."

CHAPTER 10

Mother Caroline Friess: An Academy for Girls

By Sister Barbara Brumleve, SSND

ONE HUNDRED TWENTY-FIVE years ago, in September 1859, the *Weekly Belleville Advocate* advertised the first Catholic girls' school to open in Belleville, the Immaculate Conception Academy. Here a girl, whether Catholic or not, could receive a "thorough English, German, or French education." Board and tuition for languages, plain or fancy needlework, and vocal music would be $25.00 per quarter. At a time when the entire area that is today the Diocese of Belleville had only a few more than eight priests, and when the only higher education for girls was available at Kaskaskia, the opening of Immaculate Conception Academy was an important event.

More than two years earlier, the pastor of St. Peter Church, now the cathedral, had begun a fund drive. He collected $5,000 from his parishioners and another $800 from non-Catholics of the city, but he was still short of the $8,400 price of the building. For a time it looked as though the courts would take over the building; but then the pastor, Father Peter J. Baltes, and the bishop turned to Mother Caroline Friess, superior of the School Sisters of Notre Dame. They offered her the building free if she would assume the debt.

Mother Caroline was thirty-five years old, twelve years a missionary in the United States and three years a citizen of the country. In 1859 she was responsible for two other academies in Baltimore and Milwaukee, plus six orphanages and some twenty-eight elementary schools spread across the United States from New York, Maryland, and Virginia to Wisconsin and south to Louisiana. Only nine years earlier, she had moved the motherhouse, or main house, of her sisters to Milwaukee, a comparatively new city, but one which had a German bishop and many German immigrants. Already she had to expand that house and she had debts on it.

To assume another debt in Belleville would be a hardship for the community. She described her dilemma: "I was not able to decide quickly. Finally, love and confidence triumphed over reason." In the fall of 1859 Mother Caroline traveled to Belleville with nine sisters and two candidates (young members of the community) to open the academy. On the first day, seventy-five children enrolled and there were twenty boarders. This was the beginning of St. Peter Cathedral Parish School and also the introduction of the School Sisters of Notre Dame (SSND) into the Diocese of Belleville.

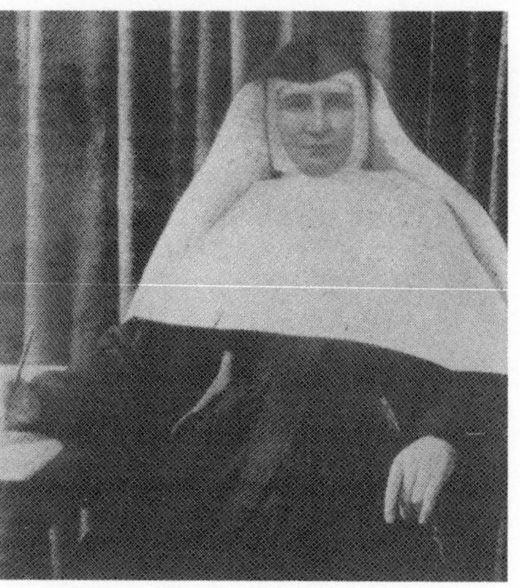

Mother Caroline Friess.

Immaculate Conception Academy grew and already that first year paid for its own maintenance and managed to pay the interest on the debt. Mother Caroline hoped that soon she would also be able to pay the principal. She knew that "the Sisters are saving in every possible way and depriving themselves of many things. May God bless their sacrifices."

Although Mother Caroline was concerned about Immaculate Conception Academy and her community's other academies in Baltimore and Milwaukee her main concern was the parish school, especially in rural areas and small towns. One time she explained to the young members of the community how she saw the sisters' work in the United States. The country was, as it were, a wilderness overgrown with brush, trees, and weeds, that needed to be cleared. She saw her sisters helping the bishops and priests by moving as quickly as possible, in small groups of two or three, to as many places as possible in order to light fires that would clear this land. Their many little fires would be more effective than several very large fires.

St. Dominic, Breese, and St. Liborius, St. Libory (then called Mud Creek), were two of the places where Mother Caroline sent her sisters in 1865 and 1869. In both places the pastor and people had sacrificed to build a school and a convent. They asked the sisters to instruct their children in the faith. Father Reineke, pastor at St. Dominic, Breese, had requested sisters for three years, but Mother Caroline was unable to accept his invitation. Despite the number of women entering the community, she never had enough to fill all the requests. So in Breese, as in many other places, a lay woman, Mary Mueller, taught for three years until Mother Caroline could send sisters.

The ever larger number of schools and orphanages meant more places for Mother Caroline to visit. Much of her year was spent on the road; by train, steamboat, wagon, or carriage. Sometimes her travels meant fording a creek in high boots lent by a kind farmer. Often she was one of the very few women on board a riverboat or train. Only sixteen months before she came to Belleville, she had survived a riverboat explosion on the Mississippi. The motherhouse chaplain traveling with her from New Orleans to Milwaukee was killed. Mother Caroline escaped only to face several years of harrowing nightmares.

Mother Caroline's childhood had not prepared her for the physical hardships of life on the frontiers of North America. As a young member of the community in Germany, she had often been ill, mostly from overwork. By her own admission she was not good at pushing wheelbarrows, gardening, splitting kindling wood, or carrying water. Josepha Friess had been born on the outskirts of Paris, the oldest daughter of a Bavarian farmer and a French mother. Her father had served as translator for the army of Napoleon and had moved to Paris where he married the only daughter of one of Napoleon's officers. At the age of four, Josepha and her family moved to southern Bavaria, so that her father could take over the family business in moroccan leather. On their way from Paris they stopped to see Josepha's priest-uncle and her grandmother who persuaded the family to let the four-year old girl remain with them. For the next twelve years Josepha spent summers with her family and the rest of the year with her uncle, a strict disciplinarian, and her grandmother, who spoiled her.

She received an excellent education for a girl of her day. In addition to the school subjects she learned to play the violin, make fancy embroidery and to keep a tidy house. She liked the styles of her day and once threw a temper tantrum when her uncle would not allow her a wide satin ribbon for her hat. She also loved to share her allowance with the poor. When she decided to enter the convent, she chose the School Sisters of Notre Dame, then only seven years old as a congregation. She found their poverty difficult, but when a bishop from the United States requested sisters for the children of immigrants, she volunteered, even though it meant leaving for a lifetime, and despite the fact that her mother refused her blessing. Mother Theresa of Jesus Gerhardinger, foundress of the congregation, recognized the gifts of the young Sister Caroline and at the age of twenty-six made her the superior in North America, a position she held for forty-two years.

Mother Caroline's heart went out not only to the children of German immigrants but to any children who needed her sisters: English-speaking, Polish, Bohemian, Italian, black, Indian, Dutch, French. In

1880 she sent Sister Tita Hutsch and another sister to Radom, Illinois, where Sister Tita, herself Polish, could teach the twenty-five children of Polish families attracted to the southern Illinois site by the promise of inexpensive fertile land. Many of the families had come directly from Poland or from the Polish parish of St. Stanislaus in Chicago, where SSNDs already taught. Mother Caroline understood the plight of immigrants lured by advertisements which told only part of the truth. In 1847 she arrived in the United States with Mother Theresa, the foundress, and four other sisters. Their destination was St Mary's Catholic colony in the forests of Pennsylvania. In Europe they had read the advertisements describing the colony as a metropolis connected with many other cities. She remembered their disillusionment as they forged through the Pennsylvania woods, jolting along on a buckboard wagon. In the months that followed sometimes they had only cucumbers to eat.

At times Mother Caroline worried about the rapid growth of the SSNDs in North America. Her "compassion . . . for the youth of America" and her "desire to promote God's glory" were always the compelling reasons for opening new missions. Sometimes, she wrote, this rapid growth "inspires me with fear when I consider that, ordinarily, all that is good and noble thrives slowly." As the years passed, she accepted orphanages and schools in still more distant places: Kentucky, Minnesota, and Canada.

In 1884 Mother Caroline was in New Orleans for one of her many visits. She had agreed to stay a few days longer to rest, a decision unusual for her. On the feast of the Epiphany, January 6, she and the other sisters had eaten an early lunch and were enjoying their time together when a telegram was handed to her. As she read it, her face became deathly pale and she leaned back against her chair, her eyes closed. Only gradually could she announce: "Our Academy in Belleville burned last night. Four sisters and twenty-two pupils lost their lives."

The night before Sister Jerome, the superior, and several other sisters had stayed up late in order to fill the stockings of the children for Little Christmas. It was a very cold night, and the sisters in charge of the furnace had stoked it with coal. Fire broke out and, fed by a strong wind, filled the building with smoke and flames. Today crosses in Green Mount Cemetery mark the graves of Sister Jerome and the other three sisters killed in the fire. A monument topped by an angel records the names of the girls who lost their lives in the Immaculate Conception Academy fire.

Mother Caroline heard the criticism leveled against the sisters after the fire. She knew that all the bedrooms had been on the third floor. She ordered that all her sisters' schools and orphanages have fire escapes and she sent inspectors to assure herself that such a tragedy would not happen again.

When the academy was rebuilt, the pastor of St. Luke parish in Belleville donated a bell in memory of the fire victims. That bell rang in the rebuilt academy and later at Notre Dame Academy on West Main Street. Today it calls parishioners to church in Ghana, West Africa.

Until the fire, the English-speaking children of St. Luke parish were instructed in the basement of the Immaculate Conception convent. After the fire, the pastor at St. Luke's fitted up a former stable on the church property to serve as a school. Here, for more than four years until a school building could be erected, two sisters taught the children of the English-speaking St. Luke parish in Belleville.

After the Belleville diocese was formed in 1887, Mother Caroline accepted two other schools in the diocese: St. Charles Borromeo in DuBois and Sacred Heart in Du Quoin, both in 1891. Mother Caroline marked forty-one years since she had first shared with the sisters in Milwaukee the news that Mother Theresa had appointed her superior in North America. There were now over 1,900 SSNDs in the United States and Canada caring for more than 66,000 children in schools and orphanages. Mother Caroline was tired. She returned from a visitation trip in New Orleans, knowing that her days of missionary work in North America were nearing a close.

For seven months, first from her wheelchair and later from her bed, she continued to respond to her sisters and to the needs of the Church in North America. Only weeks before her death on July 22, 1892, she agreed to send sisters to work in an institute for the deaf in Louisiana. She had no one trained for the work, but the need was there. She would accept. For years Mother Caroline had dreamed of a chapel of perpetual adoration where sisters could pray day and night for the Church. Now, in that chapel only nine days before perpetual adoration began (and continues today), she was waked. The bell that announced her death was inscribed: "The mother I mourn; the daughters I call."

CHAPTER 11

Father Patrick McCabe: Irish Apostle

By Raphael H. Middeke

HE WAS A pioneer priest in a pioneer church in southern Illinois during the decades preceding the nation's Civil War. He was one of the circuit-rider priests, who plied the same trails followed by peddlers and settlers to minister to the scattered Catholic immigrants.

Though the history of Father Patrick McCabe is sketchy, it has been noted that "the galaxy of heroic missionary priests of early days who labored so disinterestedly in planting the seeds of religion on the virgin prairie soil of Illinois would remain incomplete were the name of Father McCabe omitted."

In that pioneer church of the land between the rivers of the Mississippi, Ohio, and Wabash, this down-to-earth Irishman grew into the hearts of all who knew him as a "big-hearted and whole-souled" priest whose long, and by every account, faithful ministry, ended in sad disappointment. "Tears come to my eyes when I think back at this man of God's labors and sufferings," a priest who knew him wrote in his memoirs.

Father McCabe was born in Ireland and was probably ordained there. It is not known exactly when he came to America, but he probably came to southern Illinois through Chicago, though at least one account says he came from Perryville, Missouri. It is known that he opened the baptismal records of Ss. Peter and Paul parish, Waterloo, presumably as a traveling priest. Waterloo is probably one of several dozen churches — though no churches were there — where Father McCabe began the recorded history of a parish.

The Diocese of Chicago was formed in 1843 and Father McCabe was one of thirty-two priests who participated in the first synod of the new diocese in 1847.

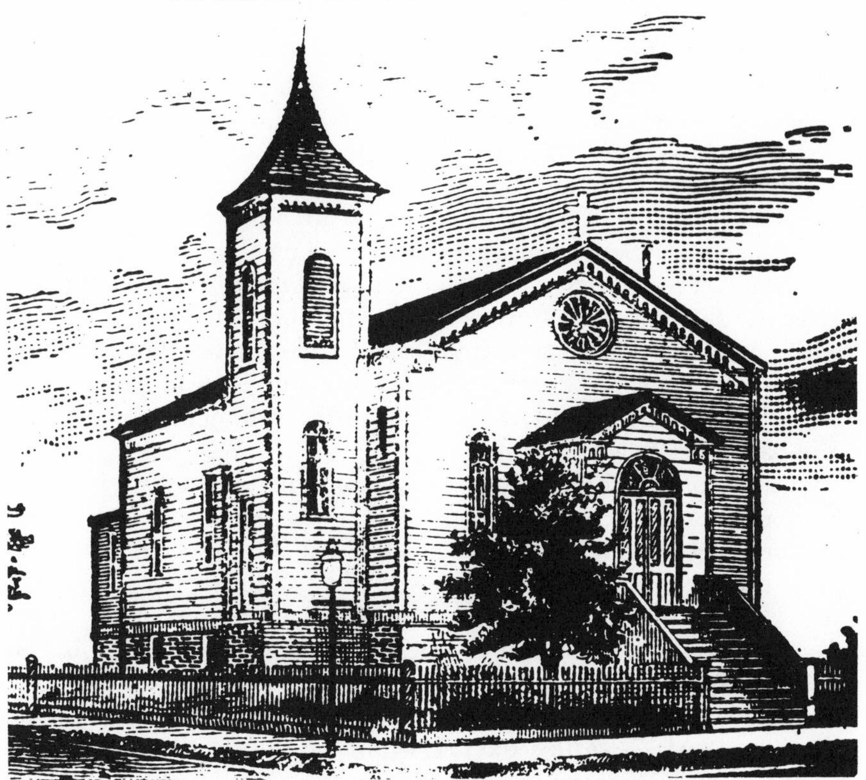

Father McCabe's St. Patrick Church in Cairo was built to withstand Cairo floods.

Father John Larmer, himself a pioneer priest and the pastor of Shawneetown in 1863, says in his memoirs: "I don't know how many years Father McCabe was a missionary in Illinois but it must have been a long time, as I rarely ever went to a cabin or out of the way settlement in the forest or swamps but the first question from the old settlers was: 'When did you see or hear from Father McCabe?' God prosper him."

The itinerant priest in those early days worked on the railroads during the week as a common laborer for 75 cents a day, paid in food or supplies, and offered Mass on Sundays for the few Catholics. "Jeans were his clothing," Father Larmer said "Corn bread baked in the ashes and badly cured hog meat his food; such was the living those days in southern Illinois."

A priest acquaintance in St. Louis recalled Father McCabe coming to St. Louis once or twice a year. "So poor was he," Father Patrick O'Brien said, "that he would take the out-of-the-way streets to get to [my] house to borrow a coat so he could appear decently on the streets."

General Michael Lawler, whose parents came to Illinois from Ireland in 1799 wrote of him: "Often he gave his last dollar to the unfortunate persons without food or clothes, whom he came across when traveling in boats between Cario and Shawneetown on the Ohio."

In 1850 Father McCabe was assigned as the pastor of Shawneetown and surrounding areas. He built the first church in Gallatin County in what is now Pond Settlement, then probably known as Doherty, in the early 1850s. The church, which he called St. Patrick, was a thirty-five by twenty-five-foot structure. Father McCabe and a man named Welch personally cut the trees used to build the church. The primitive benches were log splits and the altar rail and altar were of native wood construction. The project was the work of the two men, by this time, white-haired Irishmen.

Dates become a bit confusing and accounts differ as to Father McCabe's next move. One account has him moving to Mt. Sterling and the surrounding settlements of Pittsfield, Jacksonville, and Beardstown.

But by 1854 the itinerant priest certainly went to Cairo. Cairo at the time was without a church. The original St. Patrick Church, built in 1838, was swept down the Ohio River during the flood in 1843.

Father McCabe carefully selected the site for a new church — the site of St. Patrick's to this day. The building of the church became something of a nineteenth century Noah's Ark. Father McCabe studied carefully the highest point of the 1843 flood and raised the basement, built of stone brought down the Ohio River on flat boats, higher than any point observed in the freshets of the river. Father McCabe was chided for this stone basement above the ground. The building was viewed by some "with sarcasm and derision," according to Father Larmer.

But when in the following year another flood devastated Cairo, the church became a refuge from the raging waters, serving as a temporary infirmary for people who couldn't leave the flooded city.

The bell from the original church which had been hung in the fork of a tree survived the 1843 flood. It was hung in the new church and later in the present St. Patrick's, built in 1894. The bell was removed and replaced by the bells of St. Joseph when that parish was closed in 1961. The whereabouts of the historical bell, which had hung in three St. Patrick churches for over a century, is presently unknown.

Father McCabe's status as a resident pastor didn't end his travels. In 1856 he made an arduous trip to Chicago on horseback to make a spiritual retreat.

The seasoned and veteran priest who had survived the harsh pioneer days with generosity, "whose name was one to conjure by in every

Irish cabin,'' as one historian puts it, was hardly prepared for his final battle.

When a new diocese was formed in southern Illinois in 1857, the first bishop of Alton, Henry Juncker, wanted Father McCabe to leave Cairo. The old priest, who considered the decision unfair and unjust, pleaded to stay, to no avail.

A test of wills developed and when the bishop came to Cairo to remove him he found the church doors locked. The bishop broke them down personally and was arrested but not indicted.

As a result Father McCabe was suspended and forbidden to offer Mass or administer the sacraments. He evidently remained in Cairo, living for some time at his niece's boarding house. His niece, ''a bounding, vigorous Irish girl, kept him in comfort he never knew in the active life of a priest,'' according to Father Larmer's memoirs.

Father McCabe died on January 31, 1863. He was buried in Perryville, Missouri. Father Larmer closed the memoirs of his beloved friend with this account:

''Curious things happen in every station. I think the following Sunday after Father McCabe's death, I, being ordained some time, was requested by the same bishop to meet him in Cairo. I sang High Mass. A military band of one of the regiment's company there, awaiting orders to go to battlefield in Tennessee, played and sang in the choir. The bishop preached an eulogistic sermon on Father McCabe's life, missionary career and the humility with which he accepted the censures imposed on himself. I myself was not edified, but I suppose it went down with my people.''

Father Larmer added: ''I can only say that Illinois can be proud of such an apostle. In zeal, sufferings, labors, and charity unseen, Father McCabe has not been excelled by any apostle,'' — feelings of respect and love shared by many both before and after his retirement.

CHAPTER 12

William Bissell: First Catholic Governor

By Harold D. Olree

WILLIAM HARRISON BISSELL was the first Catholic to be elected governor in Illinois. He was also the first Republican to hold the highest office in the state. Many people in the mid-nineteenth century and many historians since have speculated that had Bissell lived, the Belleville resident would have been the first Catholic president of the United States. Had it occurred, there would have been a Catholic president exactly one hundred years before the election of the late President John Fitzgerald Kennedy in 1960.

But that was not to happen. Bissell died in 1860, shortly after the end of his third year in office at age forty-nine.

Who was Bissell and what led him to the brink of reaching the highest office in the land before his death?

Bissell was born in April 25, 1811, near Cooperstown, New York. He studied medicine in Philadelphia and practiced in New York before coming to Illinois in 1837. He settled in Monroe County and opened a physician's office southwest of Waterloo, according to an article by Rose Josephine Boylan in the *Combined Journal of St. Clair County Historical Society, 1975-76.*

Dr. Bissell and Emiline James, daughter of the owner of the mills at the Monroe County site, were married in 1840. They had two daughters, Rhoda and Josephine, before Emiline died in 1844.

Bissell wasted little time in becoming active in politics in his new home state. He was elected a representative from Monroe County in the Illinois General Assembly in 1840, serving one term.

He then studied law, practiced in area counties, and opened an office in Belleville. He served as St. Clair County prosecuting attorney in 1844-48.

His service in politics was interrupted by the Mexican War (1846-47), for which he volunteered. He was captain of one of two companies from Belleville, then became colonel in command of one of the regiments formed at Alton. He was praised for his service in the war when he returned to Belleville in 1847 and resumed his law practice.

William Bissell

But Bissell soon was back in politics. The next year, 1848, he was elected to the first of three consecutive terms (1849-55) in the U.S. House of Representatives. It was during these years that he and Elizabeth Kane of Kaskaskia were married in 1851.

Miss Boylan wrote that Bissell and Miss Kane were married in the home of a friend in Belleville by Father Kasper H. Ostlangenberg, pastor of St. Peter Catholic Church.

This historian explained that Bissell was a native of a New York area "settled chiefly by Lutherans and Scotch-Irish Presbyterians" but that he had not previously been active in any church. But, Miss Boylan continues, "he agreed to respect his fiancee's faith and practice."

In 1854, while serving his last term in Congress, Bissell suffered a paralytic stroke, which required him to use crutches the rest of his life.

It was during his convalescence that Bissell became a Catholic in 1854.

As a result of the paralysis, he decided not to seek a fourth term in Congress and he returned to Belleville in 1855.

Prior to his illness, Bissell had gained a national reputation in Congress as a "skillful debater" and leader. In one action in 1850 he strongly defended the contributions of troops from the northern United States, including Illinois, in the Mexican War, against an attack by a southern representative. The dispute led to a challenge to a duel from Jefferson Davis, the future president of the Confederation of American States. Bissell accepted, naming "muskets at twenty paces," but friends of Davis, including President Zachary Taylor, intervened to settle the dispute.

Bissell's stand against Davis and strong opposition to slavery gained respect for the Belleville congressman. Other positions which strengthened his popularity were support of the Homestead Act, of facilities for the mentally ill, and for assistance to military veterans.

Bissell also had an ability to gain the respect of persons and groups of widely different interests. There were many of these divergent views in the years just preceding the Civil War (1861-65). The country was not only becoming divided on the slavery issue but along other lines, such as native-born Americans vs. foreign-born. Bissell defended the latter, who were growing in number with the increased immigration.

The Know-Nothing Party, composed of members of secret societies, protested against immigration and was strongly anti-Catholic.

A staunch Democrat, Bissell joined many other members of his party in opposition to the Kansas–Nebraska Act, which was passed in 1854. The act decreed that any new state coming into the Union could declare itself "slave" or "free" on the slavery issue.

When the act was passed, many of the opposing Democrats began organizing a National Republican Party. In Illinois Bissell joined a number of others to establish the Republican Party in the state.

Thus it was that the state Republican convention in July 1856 at Bloomington nominated Bissell, who was absent, as the new party's candidate for governor. Though crippled, he did some campaigning and was elected, despite the election of a Democrat president, James Buchanan. Bissell's support came from the various groups he had supported and even included some members of Know-Nothings, who were split over slavery.

During Bissell's election campaign, Abraham Lincoln, who became the nation's sixteenth president in 1860, visited Belleville for the second time and supported the gubernatorial candidate.

It was during Bissell's time in office that the 1858 Lincoln-Douglas debates were held on the slavery issue. The debates helped publicize Lincoln before his 1860 election.

After Bissell's election as governor, many prominent persons thought he would be the "favorite son" candidate for president for the Republicans in Illinois in 1860. One of them wrote, ". . . if he had not become an almost helpless invalid, he would have become president . .."

Also attesting to Bissell's popularity in the governor's contest, another historian said, ". . . Bissell's election gave Lincoln the necessary home base for his national campaign four years later."

Speaking of Bissell's election as the first Catholic governor, Miss Boylan wrote: "To the credit of the voters of Illinois, there seems to have been little, if any, religious antagonism." She noted that McKendree College, a Methodist institution at Lebanon, gave Bissell an honorary Doctor of Laws degree in 1857.

In *Illinois, a History of the Prairie State,* Robert P. Howard, noted

Bissell's popularity with the various diverse factions of people in the country at the time "in spite of the fact that he was of the Roman Catholic faith."

Miss Boylan reported that Bissell was the first Illinois governor to die while in office. He died on March 18, 1860, of pneumonia. She also noted that "Reverend John J. Janssen, a recently-arrived German priest, who later became the first bishop of the Catholic Diocese of Belleville" was among those assisting at the funeral service for Illinois' first Catholie governor.

The governor's widow returned in 1862 to Belleville, where she died three years later. Both are buried in Oak Ridge Cemetery in Springfield, where President Lincoln is also interred. A monument at the Bissells' grave site honors the first Catholic governor in Illinois as "Patriot, Statesman, Hero."

CHAPTER 13

Michael Kelly Lawler: Fighting Irishman

By Lucille Lawler

WHEN JOHN AND ELIZABETH Lawler, immigrants from County Kildare, stepped off a flatboat in Shawneetown on a wintry day in 1819 with their two-year-old daughter, Mary, and a five-year-old son, Michael, few would have predicted that little Mike would grow up to have such influence. Michael Kelly Lawler went on to become a licensed lawyer, surveyor, farmer, merchant, father of ten children, and a distinguished hero in our country's military history.

Young Lawler's life paralleled the early growth of the new state of Illinois. Although schools in the newly formed "Prairie State" were scarce, Michael became a well-educated man, a man of great faith. This was due largely to the efforts of his parents, who were regarded with some curiosity when they arrived as the first Catholics in southeastern Illinois. John Lawler bought land in what is now known as Pond Settlement. Through his influence, former neighbors in Ireland came to the area and the first Catholic church was built on Lawler land.

The first Mass was celebrated in Pond Settlement in May 1824 with Father Elisha Durbin, the circuit-riding priest, coming from nearby Waverly, Kentucky, to worship with the pioneers in their log cabin chapel. The Lawler family also grew in Pond Settlement, where two other members of the family, Margaret and Thomas, were born.

John Lawler died in 1835, leaving his farmland to Michael and Thomas. In 1837 Michael courted and married Elizabeth Crenshaw, daughter of John Crenshaw, the wealthy landowner who operated the saltworks. The newlyweds moved into a log cabin across the road from the Crenshaws on eighty acres of land given to them by the bride's father. Within three years land had been acquired and the 1840 census

General Michael Lawler

noted four "hired hands" in the household. Also listed in this census were the young Lawler's two children, Margaret and John.

Records indicate that Michael Lawler was a prosperous farmer, owning 930 acres. He also owned a store in Shawneetown and showed an early interest in public affairs. He was a leader of a group known as the "Vigilantes," which was formed to oppose the "Regulators." The latter had been organized to "regulate" blacks, both free and bound to slavery. The blacks and their friends appreciated Lawler's help in preventing their being beaten and threatened. Illinois Governor Thomas Carlin recognized Lawler's ability to organize men and appointed him captain of the Fourth Regiment of the Illinois militia.

Governor Thomas Ford issued a call for 3,000 volunteers when President James Knox Polk declared war on Mexico in 1846 in a dispute over the Texas border. Captain Lawler left his farm and his position as bookkeeper with the Crenshaw Salt Works and recruited Company G of the Third Regiment, Illinois Volunteers.

Patriotic songs were sung and the colors were flown as the troops boarded boats, which would take them down the Ohio and the Mississippi rivers. At New Orleans the recruits from southern Illinois began their march overland to join General Zachary Taylor at the Rio Grande. The 350-wagon military contingency encountered plenty of trouble in Texas.

Horses and mules dropped dead in the heat of the warm winter in the Southwest. Soldiers suffered from disease, lack of water, and blistered feet. When the regiment reached Cerro Gordo, General Santa Anna, victor in the famed Battle for the Alamo, and 5,000 Mexican troops were well-entrenched.

One of Lawler's men, Zacariah Sisk of Equality, recalled how the southern Illinois troops later caught up with Santa Anna on the Jalapa road to Encerro. The Mexican general was taken by surprise and escaped to the nearby woods, leaving behind his dinner, his cork leg, his carriage, all his papers, and $20,000. Lawler is said to have yelled to his men, "Here's Santa Anna's cork leg! Catch him boys, and we'll put it back on him!" They obviously never did since the "trophy" is now in the custody of the adjutant general's office in Springfield.

After a triumphant march into Mexico City, a lieutenant proctor of the Third Regiment praised Lawler in a letter to General John A. McClernand. "In infantry tactics, he [Lawler] cannot be beat and in cavalry, he is superior to any officer from Illinois."

The discharge of the units came on October 26, 1848, in Shawneetown. As an attorney, Captain Lawler spent many months after the war presenting and adjusting claims of his fellow soldiers for bounty lands and their losses incurred during service. The Lawler brothers' business in Shawneetown continued to thrive. An 1849 newspaper advertisement showed the witty approach they used to get customers. The ad read, "The children of Adam, who had the misfortune to be born bare-foot, can obtain boots and shoes, all sizes from M.K. and T.R. Lawler's, on Main Street next door above the bank."

Elizabeth kept busy with the couple's five children and with running the farm while her soldier-husband was away.

The routine of life was shattered on April 12, 1861, when the Confederate States launched an attack on Fort Sumter in the harbor of Charleston, South Carolina , ushering in the Civil War. On the day that President Abraham Lincoln called 75,000 volunteers to preserve the Union, Michael Lawler was out plowing. Although he was fifty years old, he, along with 1,360 men of Gallatin County, made the momentous decision to leave their families and join the fight. With Confederate troops training for war just ten miles away across the Ohio River in Kentucky, these volunteers feared an invasion.

Father Louis A. Lambert of Shawneetown decided that he should accompany his parishoners as chaplain of Colonel Lawler's Eightenth Regiment, which was engaged in some of the fiercest fighting of the war in Tennessee, Alabama, and Mississippi. General Ulysses S. Grant observed, "When it comes to just plain hard fighting, I would rather trust old Mike Lawler than any of them." Lawler was severely wounded at Fort Donelson. His meritorious service earned him a commission as brigadier general.

General Lawler led 1,100 men in storming the rebel stronghold at Vicksburg, which had blocked the Union's southern advance. In a letter to Elizabeth, Lawler wrote, "Hold up your head and thank God with all your heart that I passed through two days of battle unscathed; and remember that your prayers and spirit hovered near me. Keep the children for me. God preserve you all. Fourteen men died in the charge and 185 were wounded."

General Lawler was recognized as a prayerful man, although he was criticized by his men for going behind enemy lines to attend Sunday Mass. Towards the end of the war, he assumed command of 18,000 men and was promoted to the rank of major general in March 1865. Two months later he learned that his family home was burned, but his family was safe. At the end of the war, General Lawler returned home to rebuild his farm.

At the suggestion of his pastor, General Lawler spent some time writing, *Memoirs of Michael Kelly Lawler,* in which he described in detail various battles and other events of his life. The chronicle is stored at Southern Illinois University, Carbondale, where historians still refer to it.

In these later years as writer and gentleman farmer, General Lawler was described by a friend, Bluford Logsdon, as "a strict Catholic man, strictly temporate, who reprimanded anyone using profanity." Seventeen years after returning home from the battlefields, General Lawler died quietly at his home near Equality at age sixty-nine.

At his request, family and neighbors prepared his body for burial. The general was wrapped in a winding sheet, the traditional burial shroud of his Irish ancestors. The local pastor celebrated the funeral liturgy and his remains were transported to Lawler Cemetery in a simple farm wagon. General Lawler also requested that there be no "military rites."

He wanted no eloquent testimonies or monuments erected in his honor because he felt the silent battlefields with fallen heroes offered enough eloquence. However, in 1913 the general's friends and the State of Illinois erected a fitting monument in Gallatin County to honor Michael Kelly Lawler, the fighting Irishman.

CHAPTER 14

Father Louis A. Lambert: "The American Newman"

By Rev. Paul W. Stauder

FATHER LOUIS A. LAMBERT was born February 11, 1835, in Allenport, Pennsylvania. This priest did outstanding pioneering missionary work, in what is now the Diocese of Belleville, ministering especially in Cairo and Shawneetown. His service took him further north, all the way up to Enfield, Carmi, McLeansboro, Piopolis, and many other sections of the diocese.

His father came to America in 1811 from Inniscorthy, Wexford County, Ireland. His mother was of English descent. Her ancestors came to this country with the colony of William Penn. Besides Father Louis, another of the Lamberts' sons became a priest, and one daughter became a nun. At the age of nineteen, Lambert decided he wanted to become a priest and began his classical studies at St. Vincent's College in Westmoreland County, Pennsylvania, in 1854.

After completing his classical studies he went to the St. Louis Archdiocesan Seminary in Carondelet, Missouri, and completed his ecclesiastical studies in 1859. He was ordained to the priesthood that year in St. Louis for the diocese of Alton.

Father Lambert's first assignment was as assistant to Father Walsh in the parish at Cairo in 1859. Riding a horse long distances from Cairo brought Father Lambert to the Catholics who were meeting together in selected log homes, where Mass was offered, and confessions heard.

He spent less than a year in this assignment when Bishop Henry Juncker appointed him the rector of the cathedral in Alton. Again, in less than a year he was appointed pastor of the parish at Shawneetown, 1860-1862.

The new parish assignment extended his missionary work to White, Hamilton, Saline, Gallatin, Pope, and Johnson counties. The present-day parishes that he served by horseback include Enfield, Piopolis, Pond Settlement, Equality, Carmi, McLeansboro, and Shawneetown.

Father Louis A. Lambert

There was at this time a bitter agnostic living in Shawneetown named Robert Green Ingersoll. Ingersoll tried to tear down the Catholic Church with eloquent speech, blasphemy, and lies. Father Lambert was a kind priest, but in time lashed out against Ingersoll. The priest very effectively defended the Catholic Church.

In 1862 Father Lambert's pastorate at Shawneetown came to an end with the outbreak of the Civil War. The governor of the State of Illinois, Richard Yates, commissioned him to be a chaplain for the Eighteenth Cavalry Regiment of Illinois. The southern Illinois priest held the rank of captain.

The war took Father Lambert a long way from his former Shawneetown parish. He was in twenty battles of the Civil War including, the Battle of Shiloh at Pittsburg Landing. He also served in companies in Missouri, Kentucky, Tennessee, and Mississippi, where he ministered to the spiritual and material needs of the young men at war with their own brothers. Some of these men were from his former parishes.

On March 15, 1862, the bishop of Alton recalled Captain Lambert from his military assignment and appointed him pastor of St. Patrick parish, Cario, where he served until 1868.

With his enthusiasm Father Lambert searched through the baptismal records and found Catholics living fifty to sixty miles from Cairo. Thomas McCabe, who lived fifty-four miles north of Cairo, was one of his parishioners. From his reminiscences we learn the following: Father Lambert, on a Monday morning, mounted his horse at six o'clock riding the fifty-four miles to a cabin near Reynoldsburg. It was there he found Thomas McCabe's residence. The priest had been instructed to look for a double log cabin with two glass windows facing the road.

When he arrived he found Mrs. McCabe milking the cows. It was evening. As he guided his horse in the clearing to their log cabin, he dismounted and asked Mr. McCabe to give his horse some water and some shelter for the night. With great joy and happiness, the McCabes welcomed Father Lambert. They had supper together. After supper Thomas McCabe walked five miles to the nearest Catholic family and informed the Murphys that there would be Mass on Wednesday. The Murphys in turn notified the Murrays, the Hughes, the O'Keefes, and the Zimmers.

On Tuesday morning all these families and even some of their Protestant neighbors, along with seven Protestant ministers, came to the McCabes. They all hitched up their oxen teams and took along bedding and provisions for their families. That night Father Lambert heard confessions up to eleven o'clock. In all, two-hundred families showed up for the Mass. They came from Pope County, Stonefort, Vienna, New Burnside, and other places no longer in existence.

On Wednesday the congregation was devout and in deep contemplation, but a voice in the group could be heard before the Mass started, saying "I don't see any long horns on that priest's head like Ingersoll said. Why this priest looks like he is a pretty smart man."

Once a year for the next five years, Father Lambert would ride his horse up to the double log cabin of the McCabes and schedule the Mass by word of mouth, just as the first time. More families showed up each year.

In the first year of Father Lambert's pastorate, he was responsible for bringing the Sisters of the Holy Cross to Cairo, to set up a hospital for Civil War casualties. When the sisters arrived General Ulysses S. Grant was staying in Cairo, too. He convinced the sisters to also staff a hospital in Paducah, Kentucky. Later, he also requested the sisters to staff the new military hospital in Mound City.

When Mound City was devastated by the 1864 flood, Grant gave orders to move all the patients by boat up the Mississippi to the new Jefferson Barracks near St. Louis.

Father Lambert purchased, with his own money, the cemetery for the Cairo parish. It was named Calvary Cemetery and was located thirteen miles north of Cairo. The road to the cemetery was most difficult, and at first the caskets were carried by wagons. Later the Illinois Central Rail Road was used, until motor vehicles were introduced.

In 1868, Father Lambert was offered a professorship of moral theology at the Paulist Institute in New York City. He recieved permission from the bishop of Alton and accepted the assignment. After a year of teaching, he asked for a parish. Father Lambert was then appointed pastor of St. Mary Church, Waterloo, New York.

He founded the *Catholic Times of Philadelphia* (1892-1894) and edited *The Freeman's Journal of New York* (1895-1910). An able linguist, Father Lambert translated several works into English, including Paul Merz's *Handbook of Scriptural Reference.* This was the first Catholic scriptural concordance published in the United States. Another translation he undertook was *Kerkhoff's Grammar of Volapuk.*

His *Notes on Ingersoll* refuted the current rationalistic statements of Ingersoll which were heard by curious listeners on a national scale. These internationally popular books and his *Christian Science Before the Bar of Reason* inspired contemporary Catholics to call Father Lambert "The American Newman."

When Father Lambert transfered his *Catholic Times* to the publishing company of Rochester, New York, he became read on a national and international scale. Protestants, especially, wanted to read his book *Notes on Ingersoll,* since Ingersoll had traveled throughout America and Europe preaching his stinging lies about the Catholic Church.

In 1892 the University of Notre Dame in South Bend, Indiana, conferred upon Father Lambert an honorary Doctor of Law degree. This great defender of the faith was transfered to serve as pastor of Assumption Church in Scottsville, New York, where he remained until his death on September 25, 1910, while he was visiting Newfoundland, New Jersey.

The Catholic University of America in 1955 announced that it had acquired Father Lambert's papers. A Catholic University spokesman described him as one of the most noted American priests of the late nineteenth century. In southern Illinois, where his ministry began, Father Lambert is memorialized in the Knights of Columbus Council in Ridgway that bears his name.

CHAPTER 15

Bishop Peter Baltes: A Man Often "Alone"

By Rev. John Myler

WHEN PETER JOSEPH BALTES was consecrated in early 1870 he found himself to be the only bishop for the 27,000 square miles of terrain and fifty-six separate counties in all of central and southern Illinois. And he found himself to be just about the only bishop in all the United States.

Vatican Council I, called by Pope Pius IX, had summoned to Rome the bishops of the world and so — during that cold January of 1870 — it was difficult to find in America a prelate to officiate at the consecration of Bishop Baltes. By January 20 — the day of the ceremony — Bishop John H. Luers of Fort Wayne, Indiana, one of the few who had remained at home, was contacted and agreed to be consecrator.

But the next day, Peter Joseph Baltes was again the only bishop for hundreds of miles around.

In many ways, he remained for the next sixteen years a "lone bishop." Bishop Baltes lived alone in his residence in Alton; he single-handedly and aggressively reorganized the Church in every corner of the diocese; he issued voluminous, stern, and demanding *Pastoral Instructions* to clergy and laity, and he rigidly maintained a distanced, dignified, commanding mien, always demanding obedience and respect for episcopal authority.

And as Bishop Baltes ruled and reigned, his diocese prospered.

Born in 1824 in Bavaria, Peter Baltes had emigrated with his parents to America when he was six years old. They settled in Oswego, New York, where at age of sixteen young Peter took private lessons. He continued his classical studies at Holy Cross College in Worchester,

Massachusetts. Desiring to become a priest, he completed his philosophy and theology in Montreal. While a student, he himself was instructor of German and acted as perfect of studies.

Bishop Peter Baltes

He finished his own schooling at the grand Seminary of Montreal, where he was ordained to the priesthood on May 21, 1853, at the age of twenty-nine.

His first mission was St. Peter and Paul parish, Waterloo, in Monroe County, where he remained for two years.

Father Baltes' varied experiences, quality education, and familiarity with languages were not wasted when, in 1855, he was ordered to St. Peter parish, Belleville. His first concern was to give the parochial school there a solid basis. For this purpose, he called for the assistance of the School Sisters of Notre Dame. The membership of the parish increased steadily, and Father Baltes directed his attention to the building of a new church. On June 29, 1863, the cornerstone was laid by Bishop H. D. Juncker of Alton; and in spite of many difficulties with the construction (including its collapse when it was once nearing completion) St. Peter's in Belleville was dedicated on November 6, 1866. Bishop Junker officiated at the ceremony, assisted by Father Baltes who in three years would be named as Bishop Juncker's successor.

It was in St. Peter's, his own church, and later the cathedral church of the Belleville diocese, that Peter Joseph Baltes was consecrated the second bishop of Alton in 1870.

He had been singularly ambitious as a pastor and became uniquely active as a bishop. He often found himself alone in his strident endeavors "to bring about as complete a uniformity as possible" in Church governance, administration, and rites. Bishop Baltes submitted the whole diocese in all its varied activities to a complete reorganization; even "The Use of Church Bells" and a chapter on "Bees-Wax Candles" were included in his three-volume *Pastoral Instructions*. In regard to deviation or exception, many found him "unapproachable."

He wanted his priests to be the finest body of clergymen in the country, and his authority in matters of discipline was often publicly assailed, not by the priests themselves, but by many of the foremost Catholic newspapers in the land. They attacked Bishop Baltes' various regulations and laws, some of which were more demanding than those which were promulgated for the Church in the United States at the Plenary Councils of Baltimore.

But "a time came," one of his eulogies read, "when it was deemed an honor throughout the country to be one of Bishop Baltes' priests."

Bishop Baltes died in 1886 at the age of sixty-one. At the time of his death, there were in the Alton diocese 190 churches, 169 priests, 100 parochial schools, and 11,000 pupils taught by Brothers of the Holy Cross and sisters of many religious communities.

In addition to the numbers, history shows Bishop Baltes was a man of faith and a man of work, work that effectively organized the Church in his diocese into an efficient, uniform institution.

He prepared the Church in central and southern Illinois during the 1870 and 1880s for the challenges America was to face with the coming of the twentieth century.

For it was the well-organized Catholic Church that accommodated immigrants from Ireland, Poland, Italy, and so many other European countries. It was the strong Catholic school system, governed by the bishop, that helped produce Catholic civic and cultural leaders during an era of anti-Catholic prejudice. It was efficient, disciplined Catholic organization that provided war relief during the first and second World Wars. The strong, demanding American bishop of the nineteenth century insured many successes for the people of the Church in the United States during this century.

CHAPTER 16

Father Theodore Gieryk: Immigrants' Friend

Stanley J. Konieczny

WHAT CAN AN individual accomplish in six years? Father Theodore Gieryk, the first resident pastor at St. Michael parish, Radom, ministered in the United States for only six years. Yet his deep faith, compassion and concern enabled him to help establish a national organization which continues to assist his fellow countrymen in sharing their common faith and cultural heritage with future generations.

Theodore Gieryk was born in 1837 in the Prussian section of partitioned Poland near Marienwerder. He served as a chaplain in the Prussian army before he migrated to the United States in 1872. Father Gieryk first ministered to Polish immigrants in America as Pastor of St. Adalbert Church, Detroit.

Many of his parishioners in Detroit were refugees of Otto Von Bismarck's Kulturkampf. Years of repression and religious persecution instilled in these immigrants a strong sense of nationalism and they were determined to maintain their ethnic identity. These strong ties to their native language and customs targeted the Poles for a certain amount of discrimination. The newcomers from eastern Europe were also seen as unwelcome competition in a very tight job market. This overall situation was compounded by the economic depression of 1873, which put many of these immigrants in an even more precarious financial situation.

Ethnic parishes helped their members to a certain degree by serving as buffers between the Old World immigrants and the new society in which they had to function. Such parishes and local Polish organizations across the United States tried to address these universal problems, but it soon became apparent that a national, "umbrella" organization was needed to protect the Polish immigrants as well as to preserve their cultural heritage and identity. Father Gieryk was among the earliest advocates of such a national organization.

Father Theodore Gieryk

Using the few Polish-language weekly newspapers that were published in the United States at the time, Father Gieryk wrote open letters in June 1873 encouraging Poles in America to unite in a national effort. This idea was warmly received by John Barzynski, editor of the *Pilgrim* in Washington, Missouri. This Polish newspaperman promoted Father Gieryk's idea and on October 3, 1873, he, along with Father Gieryk, Peter Kiolbassa, Joseph Giosewski, and Father Vincent Barzynski, CR, met in Detroit to implement this dream. At that meeting, Father Gieryk was named chairman of the fledgling group known as the Polish Roman Catholic Union of America.

The following year, October 14-16, 1874, St. Adalbert parish, Chicago, hosted the first national convention of the PRCUA and Father Gieryk was elected national president. At the convention, the group issued a statement of its purposes which included preserving the Catholic faith and national spirit of Polish Americans and passing on these values to future generations. Convention participants also voted on establishing a bank, hospital, local libraries, teachers' seminary and other institutions of higher education for Polish Americans.

While the groundwork was laid for this national organization, Father Gieryk stressed the need to maintain the group's Catholic identity and this special apostolate to Polish immigrants was placed under the patronage of the Sacred Heart of Jesus. The religious tone of the organization lent special support to Polish clergy who often had to struggle to maintain their ethnic parishes, which were opposed by some of the hierarchy. This was viewed as a threat of total assimilation by Polish priests such as Father Gieryk.

Such was the formidable task that faced Father Gieryk. Within six months, the priest's health deteriorated and he had to seek a more peaceful, rural pastorate. Father Gieryk read a newspaper ad about the boomtown that the Illinois Central Railroad was building at Radom, Illinois. At that time, General John Turczyn, a Civil War hero, was recruiting Polish immigrants for the railroad to settle in southern Illinois. The priest was determined to go to Radom where he hoped he could continue his ministry and regain his health.

In April 1875 Radom fell short of the paradise which had been promised in Illinois Central advertisements. St. Michael parish had just marked its first anniversary and there was no rectory. So Father Gieryk, the first resident pastor of St. Michael parish, moved into the nearby barracks where the railroad workers slept. Although he was in poor health and was new to the Radom scene, Father Gieryk could not help but be concerned for the spiritual and material welfare of his people. This concern, which became the hallmark of Father Gieryk's life, proved to be his downfall in southern Illinois.

Father John Terepka, currently the pastor of St. Mary Magdalen parish, Todds Mill, recalled the stories of Father Gieryk's downfall that he had heard as a priest from the old-timers in Radom. "The people remembered Father Gieryk for the good that he tried to do for them and for the sacrifices he made. Look at the conditions he lived under." Father Terepka said.

"Father Gieryk was a priest and a priest is supposed to look after the good of his people. He learned that people were buying land and farming it, but they didn't hold the deeds. Father Gieryk started asking people where their deeds were and told them they should have the titles for their land," Father Terepka recounted, adding, "Well, the land agent heard about all this. He called the people together, probably bought a few beers at the tavern and assured them of his honesty. The agent then told the people that their pastor was a troublemaker and that they had better get rid of him." In April 1876 Father Gieryk was asked to leave Radom.

The priest then served in Berlin, Wisconsin, for a while, but he soon returned to southern Illinois. "One of the older gentleman that I talked to in Radom said that Father Gieryk was offered a parcel of land by the Louisville and Nashville Railroad to establish a church about fourteen miles northeast of Radom," Father Terepka noted. Father Gieryk moved to this farm in Jefferson County and served German Catholics living in the vicinity. He never built a church, though. In late September he became critically ill.

Father Dezyderjusz Liss, OSF, brought him the sacraments and on his deathbed Father Gieryk forgave the people of Radom for any hurt that they caused him, according to the Radom parish history published in 1924 on the occasion of the dedication of the present church. Father Theodore Gieryk died on November 3, 1878, at the age of forty-one.

His grave was marked by a small tombstone placed by his housekeeper, Matilda Stryzyzewska.

On May 31, 1937, hundreds of PRCUA members from throughout the Midwest gathered at Radom to honor their co-founder at the unveiling of a fourteen-foot, granite cross which the organization erected at Father Gieryk's gravesite at a cost $1,175. The June 3, 1937, edition of the *Nashville Journal* noted that forty-six scouts from Chicago joined youths from Nashville and St. Louis in the colorful procession from St. Michael church to the parish cemetery. The American Legion color guard from Nashville and the Nashville band lent a special solemnity to the occasion.

Bishop Henry Althoff addressed the assembly in both English and Polish. "This festivity then carries us back in thought over a period of almost sixty years to the pioneer days of this town and parish. It recalls the origins and progress of this community and tells of its sturdy Polish people who by their industry, sacrifices, and strength of faith converted this barren wilderness into a paradise of happy homes and fertile fields. Moreover, it especially concentrates our minds upon the life and ministry of a noble, self-sacrificing priest whose interest in the Polish immigrants prompted him to found an organization that would preserve their national ideals and customs, lend material assistance, give proper guidance and protect the priceless treasure of the Catholic faith," the bishop stated.

At the gravesite, vice-chaplain of the PRCUA, Father Paul Janeczko cited Father Gieryk's zeal and understanding of the temporal concerns of his people. "With all of his heart, Father Gieryk sought the good fortune and progress of the Polish people. He looked to the future. Therefore his works have such a profound meaning for all Polish people in America," Father Janeczko said.

The impact of Father Gieryk's ministry was further recognized in 1970 when the pioneer priest's remains were exhumed and transferred to the honor section of the cemetery at the National Shrine of Our Lady of Czestochowa, Doylestown, Pennsylvania, where Father Gieryk now rests with thirty-six other outstanding Polish Americans. Perhaps the most enduring tribute to Father Gieryk is the present membership of the Polish Roman Catholic Union of America, approximately 200,000 people who still benefit from the faith and vision of an immigrant priest: Father Theodore Gieryk.

CHAPTER 17

Mother Clementine Zerr: Pioneer Educator

By Sister M. Pauline Grady, ASC

MOTHER CLEMENTINE ZERR, who founded the Ruma Convent, is an important link in the historical chain of Catholic education and health care in the Belleville diocese.

Two pictures come to mind as we recall the life-story of this pioneer educator, who is given credit for assuring the international character of the Adorers of the Blood of Christ at a time in history when God's will for the struggling American Church had to be sorted out amid very confusing circumstances.

The first picture is of the tall, energetic woman in the habit, frill, and red sash of a Precious Blood Sister, standing before a crowded, typically ungraded country classroom in the late nineteenth century. The youngsters are singing lustily, acting out their words — a favorite teaching method when books were few and the Catholic schools were poor. One of Clementine's songs that survived begins:

I am a little Catholic, and Christian is my name,
And I believe in the holy Church, in every age the same.
I love the altars where I kneel my Jesus to adore;
I love my Mother Mary; O may I love her more!
I love the saints of olden time, the places where they dwelt;
I love to pray where saints have prayed and kneel where they have knelt.

But there is another equally characteristic picture of the sister who founded sixty schools, traveled back and forth between Rome, Baden, Bosnia, and throughout the midwestern and western United States, and spoke and wrote in four languages. Mother Clementine not only taught her sisters to teach but she gave them an example of the adoration inherent in their charism of sharing the riches of Christ's redeeming blood. A favorite memory is of Mother Clementine at her spinning wheel, especially in the early, needy years, lost in contemplation and apostolic dreams which surged up to the calming rhythm of the turning wheel.

Mother Clementine Zerr

The life which was to end in honor and grace in Wichita in 1906 began very simply on a farm in the Black Forest area of Baden, Germany, in 1832. Barbara (the future Clementine) Zerr inherited from her parents, members of the rising middle class, both physical and moral strength. In 1848 when she was a teenager, Europe exploded into revolution. Religious orders were proscribed in her native Sasbachreid, but she matured in deep piety and took on her young shoulders responsibility for the sins of the world, practicing self-denial in food and drink and sleeping on a bare wooden board. Like her compatriots, she loved the blood of Christ and decided to join other Baden women in Ottmarsheim, in the new Precious Blood sisterhood founded in Steinerberg, Switzerland, and relocated from there after persecution.

Her enthusiasm had been intensified immeasurably by her contact with Mother Maria De Mattias in Acuto, Italy, from 1864 to 1865. (Mother Maria was beatified in 1950.) Between Sister Clementine's entry into religious life in 1851 and her meeting with Mother Maria in 1864, profound changes again and again redirected her path. From her early contemplative years in Ottmarsheim to the position of leadership which brought her to Rome in 1864, Sister Clementine and her fellow sisters had gone through various phases of negotiation with Mother Maria De Mattias and the Italian Adorers of the Blood of Christ from an initial 1847 document granting them affiliation through study of the still-developing rules to formal adoption of the Roman rule and habit in 1860. The contemplative life had broadened to embrace an apostolate of teaching and care of children. In Gurtweil, Baden, where she was sent in 1858, Clementine Zerr's call to spiritual motherhood had begun to grow.

As novice mistress from 1860 and "praesidentin" from 1865, she had formed the new members of the Gurtweil convent, taken care of the sick, guarded the observance of the rules, counseled novices and sisters alike. In America, where Sister Clementine arrived in 1873 with the last fifty of the exiled German Adorers fleeing Bismarck's Falk Laws, she became increasingly distressed to see that the hard-won bonds with the Italian Adorers were being weakened and even discarded. This was perhaps inevitable, given the strong hand of the American bishops and the difficulties of communicating with the Old World. Not only was physical communication by letter or visit difficult, but circumstances were further complicated by understanding and applying European ways and the old canon law to the situation of the American immigrant Catholic.

It had been extremely hard to keep the line of Church authority clear. Most of the sisters, led by Mother Augusta Volk, left the Alton diocese because of the demands of Bishop Peter Baltes of Alton. The sisters established themselves in Missouri. After months of prayer, the offering of Masses by Rev. John Neuhaus, pastor in Piopolis, and agonizing consultation, Mother Clementine separated herself from her fellow sisters, many of whom she had trained as novices. When the St. Louis-based community dedicated their motherhouse at O'Fallon, Missouri, in 1875, Mother Clementine with four other sisters, a few novices and postulants announced that they would stay in Piopolis and submit to Bishop Baltes' demands. Mother Clementine felt that under the Most Rev. Henry Muehlsiepen, archdiocesan vicar for German-speaking immigrants, the sisters were giving up their relationship with the congregation of Mother Maria De Mattias, something she had vowed never to do.

John Merlini, De Mattias' spiritual director, had once said of Mother Clementine: "If you told her that it was the will of God that she throw herself out the window, she would jump out immediately." Convinced as she was that to remain bound to her fellow sisters in Italy was the will of God, she took that symbolic leap.

Returning from Europe the following spring after the first of several trips to collect money and new members and to discuss her anomalous situation personally with the superiors in Rome, Mother Clementine found that Bishop Baltes had changed her plans for building a motherhouse and told her to buy the newly-closed Sacred Heart Seminary in Ruma. The sisters moved there in July of 1876 and spread through the Alton diocese. After Bishop Baltes' death, they quickly branched out to Missouri, Iowa, Kansas, and other states to the west and south, including New Mexico.

Mother Clementine wrote enthusiastic letters to Europe about fields ripe for the harvest in the German immigrant parishes of southern Illinois, where immigration peaked in 1882. Her little flock grew rapidly amid hardships that make fascinating reading but must have greatly taxed the young women who endured them. Characteristically, she did not wince at the cost. Bishop Baltes had begun with impossible demands, writing to Father Neuhaus on June 28, 1876:

"Please accompany Mother Superior and another sister to the Ruma College without delay. Do it tomorrow, Thursday a.m. I offer them the College and all the land belonging to it for $12,000 of which they shall pay $6,000 on time at the rate of 6%. . . Before you return to Edwardsville come here so that the matter may be settled . . . The sisters better buy the two horses, the cow, calf. . ." It was a steep price for a woman with few resources, but for Clementine "nothing was impossible with God." She taught her sisters that obedience worked miracles.

Even though befriended from the beginning by the gracious parishioners of St. Patrick parish, her sisters suffered hunger, want, and a great deal of skeptical nonacceptance, even from the clergy, during the first winter. Grandma Larkin of Prairie du Rocher, whom the author met in the 1930s, used to say, "I would never have joined that order. As I walked across the fields I saw the sisters working like men in the hot sun, wearing those awful black bonnets."

By 1879 Sisters M. Catherine and M. Thomas of the Dominican Sisters of Jacksonville (now of Springfield) were helping the immigrant sisters learn English, music, and American ways. Proudly these sisters claim Ruma as "our first Illinois mission." During the ensuing decades Mother Clementine's sisters opened schools in many places in the twenty-eight counties that became the Belleville diocese. They also built the congregation's first hospital, St. Clement's, in Red Bud, Illinois. Its original building is now called Clementine Hall.

Even though Mother Clementine eventually moved on with the German settlers to develop the apostolate and a new center in Wichita, Kansas (now the Wichita Province), her sisters had become so much a part of the growth and development of the Belleville diocese that the two can hardly be separated. St. Teresa Academy, which she built in 1894, was destined to develop secondary education for women during its eighty years of leadership in East St. Louis.

At Mother Clementine's death on January 24, 1906, the Ruma Vicariate (now Ruma Province) had 168 living sisters with twenty-six preceding her in death. There were fifty-two local communities of sisters. Ruma's founder and leader had left the convent many traditions, customs, and memories crowned by her favorite expression, the motive of her driving energy and almost reckless courage: "*Der himmel ist es wert!*" (Heaven is worth all!")

CHAPTER 18

Father Charles Klocke: He Loved His Only Parish

By Raphael H. Middeke

THREE MONTHS AFTER his ordination on June 21, 1868, Father Charles Klocke was named the first permanent pastor of the growing Sacred Heart mission in Du Quoin. The priest, born in Germany and ordained in Montreal, remained in Du Quoin all his priesthood years. He died in February 1911 and was buried in Scared Heart Cemetery, where five years later a monument in his memory was erected with the inscription: *Delexit suam parochiam unicam* (He loved his only parish).

The year of his death was exactly 100 years after the death of Chief Jean Baptiste Du Quoin, the son of a Frenchman and a woman of the Tamaroa tribe. Chief Du Quoin, buried at Fort Kaskaskia, was the first Catholic to set foot on Perry County soil.

The Indian chief, who had fought under the French General Lafayette in Virginia and who had received a citation from George Washington, gave his name to a town closed to his decendants, after the remnants of his tribe of which his son, Louis Jefferson Du Quoin was then the chief, were moved west in the early 1830s.

Before Father Klocke's appointment to Du Quoin and the surrounding missions, priests from Vandalia, Illinois, and some itinerant priests celebrated Mass and baptized in the homes of settlers at irregular intervals. By the time Father Klocke was named the pastor a church had been built. It was completed by Christmas 1867. About twenty Catholic families were present for the first Mass and about thirty resided in Perry County.

When the German priest arrived in Du Quoin the Illinois Central Railroad and a new coal industry were changing the rural German farming community, not only in numbers but also in nationalities.

He was the only priest stationed on the Illinois Central from

Father Charles Klocke

Effingham to Cairo, and after his appointment in 1868 he attended the missions of Pinckneyville, DeSoto, DuBois, Radom, Centralia, Odin, and Sandoval.

If Du Quoin became the only home and parish of the missionary priest, the parish and home during his almost forty-three years of priestly service in the area literally went on a binge of change and growth.

In a period of twenty-five years the thirty Catholic families of Perry County multiplied to over 300. By 1871 two new congregations were founded in Pinckneyville and Todd's Mill. Father Klocke, who supervised the building of the first St. Bruno and St. Mary Magdalen churches, served them for several more years as missions. By the early 1880s, however, there were eight established parishes with resident pastors in the territory of which he had been named the pastor just a few years after the Civil War.

It was the day of the immigrant, the railroad, and the mines. Those were the three influences which in the last decades of the nineteenth century formed Du Quoin and the surrounding communities — influences to which Father Klocke could respond but which he couldn't control.

The new railroad sometimes replaced the horse as a way to get to the outlying missions. Anton Berg, a seventy-eight-year-old present-day parishioner of Sacred Heart recalls his parents talking about Father Klocke going to Tamaroa on a railroad handcar. The handcar was used by section hands and in this instance was supplied by a Mr. Sanford, who was a section foreman and at whose home Father Klocke stayed before his return to Du Quoin the following day.

Berg, born in 1907, was baptized by Father August Hunnewinkel, who was helping out at the parish during Father Klocke's illness. Anthony was the young priest's first baptism and his mother insisted the priest's surname be included in his baptismal name; seventy-eight years later Anton tells the story of how he happened to be baptized Anthony Sylvester Hunnewinkel Berg, during the final years of Father Klocke's pastorate, with a wry smile.

Berg's grandfather, Nicholas Mueller, sawed the big timbers for the new church, which was dedicated in 1890 after a storm damaged the old church extensively. The melting-pot nature of the immigrant farming-railroad-mining community was perhaps never better demonstrated than the day the new church was dedicated. In the last Mass in the old church sermons were preached in Polish and Italian. In the first Mass in the new church sermons were preached in German and English.

Father Klocke was a large, jovial man, Mr. Berg says, with a round, full face. He proudly showed me his parents' 1899, ornate marriage certificate filled in and signed in German script by Father Klocke.

Father John Bergmann, born in Du Quoin in 1893 and presently retired in his hometown, who was ordained as a Jesuit and served for many years as a diocesan priest in the Diocese of Winona, Wisconsin, recalls the good and loud voice of his pastor as he was growing up in the southern Illinois town around the turn of the century. "To this day I remember how his *"per omnia saecula saeculorums"* rang through the church. I didn't know what it meant, but I remember it," he says. "He was a hardworking, zealous and holy priest," Father Bergmann says. "He did an awful lot," says the retired priest.

He talks about the days when pot-bellied stoves heated the church, horses pulled the hearse out to the cemetery several miles out of town, and he and his brothers raced home from school together on their donkeys to the family farm four miles south of Du Quoin.

Father Klocke preached every Sunday in German and English and Father Bergmann remembers him bringing his grandfather holy communion in his "chauffeured' buggy, in a day when receiving communion more than once or twice a year was rare. Today Father Bergmann remembers the regular communion calls as one example of Father Klocke's zeal and pastoral solicitude. (He also remembers the pastor bringing along a big pitcher to be filled with buttermilk — "The only thing he ever asked for.")

The more than forty-two years of his pastorate were necessarily years of building. New churches in missions, new schools in the parish — keeping up with the booming immigrant population. In 1892 twenty-three years after Father Klocke opened a one-room school in his rectory for eight pupils, a new school was built to replace a two-story structure erected in 1872. The School Sisters of Notre Dame came to staff the school that year. The annual report of his last year as pastor of Sacred Heart parish indicates that more money was received from pew rent than from the Sunday collection. Parish organizations were active and contributed heavily to the parish, donating more than twenty-five percent of total receipts of the nearly $9,000 budget. An $11,950 debt was outstanding, which resulted in interest payments of over $500, or over five percent of total expenditures.

Buried next to Father Klocke in Sacred Heart Cemetery is Msgr. Cyril N. Haffner, who came to Du Quoin in 1922. When he died in 1966 he had been, as the parish's third pastor, the pastor for forty-four years. In 1966 it had been ninety-eight years since Father Klocke had begun a resident pastorate in Du Quoin — almost eighty-eight of them shared by these two priests.

Father Klocke came to a small villiage — the only pastor in an area of new missions and new settlers. Even then only the name, Du Quoin, remained of the first Catholic to set foot in Perry County. When Sacred Heart's first pastor died in 1911 he left an area of established parishes — a legacy of faith which both formed him and which he formed.

His memorial monument says it best: "He loved his only parish."

CHAPTER 19

John Janssen: Belleville's First Bishop

By Harold D. Olree

THE FIRST BISHOP of the Belleville diocese, Johannes Janssen, was born March 3, 1835, in Kepplen, near Cleaves, in the Rhine area of Germany. He was one of eight children of Henry and Mechtilda Peters Janssen. Janssen was completing his studies at the Borromaeum when Bishop Henry Juncker of Alton, Illinois, visited there in 1857. The Alton bishop was seeking priests to "come to America where there are so many souls to save." Janssen was among those who responded to Bishop Juncker's invitation. He arrived in the United States in 1858.

After making his "classical studies" in nearby Calcar, the young Janssen enrolled in the Collegium Augustinium at Gaesdonck. He later began to study for the priesthood at Collegium Borromaeum in Muenster.

After his ordination at Alton November 19, 1858, Father Janssen was assigned by Bishop Juncker first as assistant pastor, then as pastor of the "German congregation" at St. John Church, Springfield. Bishop Juncker called him back to Alton in 1863 and named him chancellor. After Bishop Juncker's death in 1868, Father Peter J. Baltes, rector at St. Peter Church, Belleville, became bishop of the Alton diocese in 1870. Bishop Baltes appointed Father Janssen as vicar general. From 1877 to 1880, Father Janssen served as pastor at Quincy and upon Bishop Baltes' death in 1886, he became administrator of the Alton diocese.

Pope Leo XIII divided the Alton diocese January 7, 1887, forming the Springfield and Belleville dioceses. Father Janssen continued to administer affairs at Alton, even after he was named February 28, 1888, to head the new diocese of Belleville.

Father Janssen arrived in Belleville two days before the consecration, which was scheduled for April 25, 1888. A Belleville newspaper said, "His arrival on the twenty-third was the occasion of one of the greatest civic demonstrations that Belleville had ever witnessed . . . practically all inhabitants of the city were in waiting and cheered the Bishop . . . That evening, an elaborate civic welcome was given at the Court House . . ."

Bishop John Janssen

The firing of cannon in the city and the tolling of bells of the two Catholic parishes in Belleville, St. Peter and St. Luke, at 5 A.M. on April 25, 1888, heralded the day of consecration of Bishop Janssen.

At the end of 1888 Bishop Janssen reported on the state of the new diocese. He said he found 50,000 Catholics in the 11,678-square mile, twenty-eight county diocese. There were sixty priests, eighty-two parishes (fifty-four without resident pastors) and forty-four parish schools.

The bishop had vowed to visit every parish and mission by the end of 1889. He apparently had a good start during the nine months of 1888 as he reported confirming 4,643 persons. He also held two retreats for the priests, with half attending a program in English and the other half in German.

In the 1888 report Bishop Janssen said, "This was the beginning of the new Diocese of Belleville. Although the times were hard, the crops have been a failure for several years and work being scarce, yet all were full of hope for the future."

Some of the "hope" began to be fulfilled with the influx into the new diocese of immigrants and the start of coal mining and other industries. After twenty years, Bishop Janssen was able to report 71,500 Catholics, 119 priests, 113 parishes and missions, and eighty schools with nearly 9,000 students.

The diocese began to grow through various new facilities: St. Mary Hospital, East St. Louis, was established in 1890; St. Teresa Academy was begun in that city in 1894; St. John Orphanage was opened in

1901 as a successor to St. Agnes': St. Vincent Hospital was opened in 1909; Cathedral High School was begun in 1905; the first issue of *The Messenger* was published in 1907; a diocesan school board was appointed by Bishop Janssen at the third diocesan synod in 1909; the first diocesan teachers' institute was held in 1910 at St. Elizabeth parish hall, East St. Louis.

Expansion of St. John Orphanage was continued by Bishop Janssen, who took a special interest in homeless children. He was often referred to as "A Father to the Orphans." A painting which hung in the cathedral was entitled "Bishop Janssen at Glen Addie," which was the former name of the orphange site.

A major event in the life of Bishop Janssen occured on the night of January 4, 1912, when the cathedral was gutted by fire. When informed of the fire by the rector, Father Joseph Schlarmann, Bishop Janssen was said to have responded, "The Lord giveth. The Lord taketh away. That again will be built up. God's will be done." Reconstruction began immediately with Masses celebrated first in St. Vincent Hospital chapel and later at Cathedral Hall.

Bishop Janssen's fifieth anniversary as a priest on November 19, 1908, was marked by a two-day celebration. It included a torchlight parade through downtown Belleville the night before.

The silver anniversary of Bishop Janssen's episcopal ordination and the establishment of the diocese occurred on April 25, 1913. However, the bishop discouraged any celebration, saying, "one is enough for any man." The parish and the diocese had decided to dedicate the rebuilt cathedral to the bishop's silver anniversary. In the *Souvenir of the Cathedral Fire* publication, to raise funds for the reconstruction, Father Schlarmann said, "Let our offerings for the reconstruction be a jubilee donation to Bishop Janssen, and let the new Cathedral, which will rise from the ruins of the old, be an offering of loyal submission and filial devotion to our Venerable Bishop in his declining years."

Following a heart attack April 25, Bishop Janssen's health steadily declined. On occasion, he had his staff members take him to the cathedral so that he could check on the rebuilding process.

However, he was not to see the completion of his cathedral nor the delayed celebration of his silver jubilee, which had been scheduled for the fall of 1913. He died July 2, 1913.

The fire-gutted cathedral church was crisscrossed with workmen's scaffolding as arrangements were made for Bishop Janssen's funeral. Some scaffolding was removed; the rest draped in black and white cloth. Carpeting was put over the unfinished floor of the sanctuary. Some 1,500 chairs were brought in to replace the burned-out pews.

The Messenger reported that "By Sunday, the entire church had gone through a transformation, greatly to the astonishment of all who came to see. It really looked beautiful.'' Chronicling those days of mourning through the July 8, 1913, funeral and burial of Bishop Janssen in the crypt below the cathedral, the diocesan newspaper said, ''We confess that we never saw anything like it.''

In his last message to the diocese January 25, 1913, Bishop Janssen said: ''My parting words to you, beloved priests and faithful of the Diocese of Belleville, are the words of Tobias to his son: ''Hearken therefore my children to your Fathers; serve the Lord in truth, and seek to do the things that please him; and command your children that they do justice and almsdeeds, and that they be mindful of God, and bless him at all times in truth, and with all their power.'''

Bishop Janssen's final message concluded, ''When they shall have laid my body to rest remember me at the altar of the Lord.''

CHAPTER 20

Monsignor William Cluse: The Diocese's First Vicar General

By Raphael H. Middeke

FATHER WILLIAM CLUSE was the pastor of St. Boniface parish, Germantown, when the Diocese of Belleville was formed in 1887. The crucifixion setting in the parish's cemetery and the unusual stations of the cross along the cemetery's roadway are a heritage of his pastorate in the Clinton County parish, which ended in 1899. Without the tensions of Catholic immigrants from various countries growing, sometimes clumsily, into one American church, he might very well have ended his active ministry there.

A pastor, educator, scholar, writer, poet, lecturer, and administrator, Monsignor Cluse was the first vicar general of the new diocese, a post he held for thirty-one years. The talented and respected monsignor played an important role in the formation and development of the southern Illinois diocese.

He is perhaps best remembered as the man most influential in the appointment of the young pastor of Okawville, Father Henry Althoff, as the second bishop of Belleville. Bishop Albert R. Zuroweste said in an interview many years later: "Yes, they [Bishop Althoff and Monsignor Cluse] were close friends. He was the vicar general. He was also known to be responsible for Althoff becoming bishop. He was his candidate. After [Bishop John] Janssen died, there were two factions in the diocese. One group wanted [Father Joseph] Schlarmann and the other wanted a monsignor in Alton."

The vicar general had retired as the pastor of St. Henry parish, East St. Louis, in 1911, and lived in his retirement home, the Cluseton hermitage, across the street from St. Barbara Church in Okawville where Father Althoff was the pastor.

The new bishop had been Monsignor Cluse's assistant at St. Henry's and had inherited from him an interest in languages. (Bishop Althoff could speak six languages fluently and could read and write several others.)

Monsignor William Cluse

The exact role and influence of the vicar general in the naming of Belleville's second bishop isn't known, but oral history has left this version. When asked to be a bishop, the appointee could talk to one person confidentially. Father Althoff walked across the street to Cluseton to talk to Monsignor Cluse. Monsignor Cluse suggested they go to the chapel and pray for guidance from the Holy Spirit. One version of that prayer session retold by a priest of the diocese was that the Holy Spirit appeared that night to Father Althoff in the form of an old retired priest with a long grey beard.

Ordained in 1868, Father Cluse had already been a priest for almost twenty years when the Belleville diocese was formed. He was the pastor of the Catholic parish at Petersburg with missions at Virginia and Greenview from 1868 to 1872.

For the following four years he was the president of the ill-conceived Sacred Heart College at Ruma, Illinois, before the campus was purchased at the insistence of Bishop Baltes of Alton, by a group of immigrant German sisters looking for a motherhouse. The former campus is still the motherhouse of the Adorers of the Blood of Christ, Ruma province. The college president also attended the mission at Evansville during those years. After the closing of the college, he was named pastor of Assumption Church in Litchfield until his appointment as the pastor "irremovable" of St. Boniface in Germantown in 1881.

William Cluse was born at Heiden, Westphalia, Germany, on March 8, 1845. His studies for the priesthood, begun in Germany, were completed at the Salesianum of St. Francis in Wisconsin. He was ordained by Bishop Henry Juncker in the cathedral of Alton on April 3, 1868.

As a German Catholic immigrant, Father Cluse shared with many Catholics in southern Illinois an uneasiness over the political and religious climate in their native country under Bismarck — which led to the imprisonment of tens of thousands of clergy in the 1870s — and was a major reason for the influx of German immigrants in the mid-1800s.

In 1889 Monsignor Cluse resigned his irremovable pastorate at St. Boniface in Germantown at the request of Bishop Janssen in order to be assigned as pastor of St. Patrick parish, East St. Louis — an assignment which brought to the respected vicar general the bitterest months of his sixty-five years of ministry in the immigrant American church.

The new St. Patrick pastor became the catalyst of the fear — and perhaps in a few instances, the hope — of German nationalism in the American church. A few radical organizations supported the imposition of the manners and customs of the German church on the entire American church, fostering the fears of non-German American Catholics — especially the Irish.

In the Diocese of Belleville, while almost half of the Catholics in the late 1880s were non-German,the vast majority of the clergy was German.

The large, 800-family St. Patrick's had requested that their assistant, Father James Downey, be named pastor, after their pastor, Father Patrick O'Halloran died in 1898, but said they would accept any non-German pastor.

The appointment of Father Cluse mobilized the Irish Catholics of East of St. Louis into one of the most famous rebellions in the American immigrant church.

Father Cluse was met at the front door by an armed honor guard and denied entry into the church. The popular rebellion, which sometimes gathered several thousand Irish Catholics into St. Patrick church for combination prayer and rally meetings, retained its obstinacy for months of often bitter confrontation — ignoring an official proclamation of excommunication. Boycotts of German merchants and slogans such as "armed with an Irish blackthorn in one hand and a rosary in the other, we are ready," became instruments of the confrontation.

In a letter to Bishop Janssen, Father Cluse officially offered his resignation as the pastor of St. Patrick on August 30, 1899. Waiving the resignation "for the present," Bishop Janssen appointed the Rev. J. Harkins as parish administrator so the school could be reopened, and shortly afterward named the Rev. Charles Sweeny pastor, ending the rebellion.

Accounts of the incident indicate that the decision to name an Irish pastor came from the Vatican Congregation of the Propaganda.

The documentation of the "scandal," as the whole incident was often referred to by all sides, was carried out mostly in the secular press — especially the St. Louis daily newspapers. The Catholic press biographies of Monsignor Cluse later extended his pastorate at St.

Boniface to 1902, when he was named the pastor of St. Henry Parish in East St. Louis — leading one historian of the account to recall the supposed words of Pope Leo XIII to his Vatican librarian: "You may be sure if the Gospel had been written today the treachery of Judas and the denial of St. Peter would have been suppressed for fear of scandalizing weak consciences." During the confrontation, Father Cluse lived at St. Mary Hospital — the place of his death thirty-four years later.

Several years later two new parishes were formed in East St. Louis. Non-German pastors were named to found both of them.

In 1911 Monsignor Cluse resigned his pastorate of St. Henry and retired from the active ministry, but remained the vicar general for another ten years. He built a house across the street from the young priest he hoped would be the next bishop of Belleville.

The hermitage of Cluseton — a name created from his father's and mother's names — became a place of study, writing, counseling and prayer — sometimes to the chagrin of neighboring pastors. A poet at heart, although not necessarily in literature, the retired monsignor decided to translate an epic German poem. When the publisher contacted Bishop Althoff for an "Imprimatur" and the naming of a censor, and the censor made the judgment that the translation was "peculiar" and hardly worthy of the original, the bishop first asked the publisher not to continue publication. When Monsignor Cluse persisted, he allowed publication on the condition that it be published without his imprimatur, without the intended dedication to him, and with no reference to him.

When the translation was finally published, the aging monsignor wrote his friend, the bishop: "If the saying proves true: 'Was lange waehrt, wird gut (What is long in completing is in the end good), I may live in good hopes."

"Living in good hopes" was perhaps the hallmark of this pioneer of the Belleville church — a man as influential as any in first century of our history.

He died at the age of eighty-eight in 1933 and was buried from St. Henry Church in Holy Cross Cemetery. He was the last of the priests who were active in the Belleville diocese when it was formed in 1887. During those forty-six years he had been involved in every way in the growth and struggles of that church.

Even those who forcibly kept him from entering St. Patrick's were careful to say that their objection was not to the person or the character of one of the most respected and esteemed priests of the diocese.

His funeral homily was preached by Msgr. Charles Gilmartin, later to succeed him as vicar general, who was also the first assistant at St.

Patrick's after the great and bitter controversy and was the founding pastor of Sacred Heart Parish — one of the two new parishes formed in East St. Louis in 1902.

By the time of Monsignor Cluse's death the melting pot of America had touched the American church in a way it could not in 1889.

CHAPTER 21

Father Christopher Koenig: Endearing German Immigrant Pastor

By Harold D. Olree

FATHER CHRISTOPHER KOENIG was pastor of the historic Old St. Henry Church, East St. Louis, for thirty-three years. He led his parishioners in building the former parish complex and also in founding St. Mary Hospital.

However, when Father Koenig was named pastor of St. Henry in 1869 by Alton Bishop Peter J. Baltes, he was shunned by his new parishioners.

St. Henry had been established in 1866. In the three years before Father Koenig was named pastor, the parish had seen several priests come and go. Their most recent pastor, Father G. Leve, had led them in building their first frame church and school building at Collinsville and St. Louis avenues.

This building had resulted in a debt of $5,000 and the parishioners did not want another change. "There were only forty families at the time and the frequent change of pastors had not proved a benefit," wrote Father Frederick Beuckman, a diocesan historian and native son of St. Henry parish.

St. Henry had been established for German immigrants of East St. Louis. The immigrants were unhappy going to St. Patrick, the first Catholic church of the city and predominantly an Irish parish.

So, St. Henry became the first "national" parish of the city.

The new pastor, Father Koenig, "endeared himself to the people in a few years," wrote Father Beuckman. The priest-historian continued, "The main problem was to keep the few people together and to cancel the debt of the parish . . ." Over the next four years, the number of families doubled to eighty and the debt not only was paid off, but the parish reportedly had a $750 surplus.

Father Christopher Koenig

The next year, 1874, they erected a church on a new site, at Sixth Street and what was then the end of Broadway. St. Henry parishioners, in general, disagreed with the new location of the church. They claimed that it would take too many years for the town to grow out to it.

Father Koenig was pastor of St. Henry when the Diocese of Belleville was formed January 7, 1887. At the diocese's first synod, October 24, 1890, Bishop John Janssen named Father Koenig to the first board of consultors.

It was also in 1890 that St. Mary Hospital opened. The hospital was built by St. Henry parish in a campaign led by Father Koenig.

At that time there was no hospital in East St. Louis and the sick and injured had to be taken to hospitals in St. Louis.

To raise funds for the hospital, a fair was held in the city. Father Beuckman reported that, "Catholics vied with Protestants to make this affair a financial success and the result was that approximately $4,000 was raised."

Father Koenig was said to have used his own funds in helping to construct the hospital. Msgr. Christopher Goelz, a nephew of Father Koenig who was also a native son of St. Henry parish wrote: "To this institution [St. Mary Hospital], he gave his talent for organization as well as the greater part of his earthly possessions." (Monsignor Goelz was ordained while his uncle was pastor of St. Henry.)

St. Mary Hospital was first administered by Hospital Sisters of the Third Order of St. Francis from Springfield, Illinois. The Poor Handmaids of Jesus Christ took over the administration in 1903 and acquired the institution from St. Henry parish in 1922.

Father Koenig's success in guiding the German immigrant church was phenomenal, considering that he had little parish administrative experience. He had only served as an assistant to Father Paul Limacher of Ss. Peter and Paul parish at Waterloo for a month prior to taking over the St. Henry pastorate.

But he was a German immigrant himself. He had come to the United States with his family in 1863 from Germany, where he had been born on October 6, 1842, in Huelschotten, Parish of Attendorn,

Westphalia. The family lived in Columbia. The young Koenig entered the Salesianum in St. Francis, Wisconsin, in 1864, a year after his arrival. He was ordained at the seminary December 19, 1868, then was assigned to Waterloo.

In addition to being one of the first consultors of the Diocese of Belleville, Father Koenig was also one of the incorporators for both the St. Francis Student Aid Society, which assisted priesthood education, and St. John Orphanage. He was also a charter member and president for twenty years of St. Henry branch of Western Catholic Union which was founded in 1880.

It was while he was pastor in East St. Louis that St. Henry parish cemetery was established in 1870. The cemetery was the only one for Catholics in the city parishes until Mt. Carmel was opened by St. Patrick and St. Mary parishes in 1890.

Father Beuckman, the native son of St. Henry parish who was ordained during Father Koenig's pastorate, said, " . . . his home was noted for its hospitality, where priests, old and young coming to the city, loved to visit."

One priest of the time cited the "line of cleavage between Irish and Germans in East St. Louis.

"However," he continued, "Fathers [Patrick] O'Halloran [pastor of St. Patrick] and Koenig, both big men physically and spiritually, were able to settle the differences in an amicable manner and remained good friends."

On the objection of the original St. Henry parishioners to the site of the church, it was noted that at the time of Father Koenig's death in 1901, the location was at the center of town.

CHAPTER 22

Father Patrick J. O'Halloran: Close to His People's Hearts

By Stanley J. Konieczny

THE POPULAR POSTER ADVISES, "If life hands you a lemon, make lemonade." This bit of contemporary wisdom is reflected in the life and ministry of Father Patrick J. O'Halloran, who served as pastor of St. Patrick Church, East St. Louis, during the latter part of the nineteenth century. Father O'Halloran's years as a priest were marked by considerable challenges, but he always seemed to be able to turn the most trying situation into a profitable experience.

Patrick J. O'Halloran was born August 15, 1830, in New Kildima, County Limerick, Ireland, one of the seven children of Patrick and Margaret Kelly O'Halloran. When Patrick was ten years old the O'Halloran family emigrated to the United States, settling in Cincinnati, Ohio. Following studies at Bardstown seminary in Kentucky and Mount St. Mary in Cincinnati, he was ordained on September 14, 1862, in Alton at age thirty-two. Father O'Halloran's biographies offer no insight into why he became a priest relatively late in life or why he chose to relocate in Illinois. It could be attributed to typical O'Halloran adaptability.

After ordination, Father O'Halloran was assigned first to Jacksonville and then to Bunker Hill. Bishop Peter Baltes directed the young pastor of Bunker Hill to establish St. Michael parish in nearby Staunton. According to the St. Michael's centennial history, the Catholic pioneers of Staunton had few opportunities to attend Mass and receive the sacraments until Father O'Halloran arrived on the scene and began organizing the parish. It must have been somewhat difficult for Father O'Halloran to be transferred just as he was laying the groundwork for the new parish in Staunton. He turned over his pastorate to Father John Clifford and moved on further south to St. Patrick parish, Cairo.

During these early years in the priesthood, Father O'Halloran distinguished himself as a capable parish administrator and Bishop Baltes appointed him as vicar general of the Alton diocese, an office which he held during his five years in Cairo. Father O'Halloran was then named pastor of St. Patrick parish, East St. Louis, on December 1, 1873.

Father Patrick J. O'Halloran

This assignment posed special new challenges. The entire nation was expreiencing the effects of the Bank Panic of 1873. The fledgling town of East St. Louis was not spared the consequences of this economic hardship. Many St. Patrick parishioners found themselves unemployed and in a dire need when the rolling mill in East St. Louis shut down in 1873 as a result of the economic panic. The parish was in debt because a new rectory had just been built and the church had been enlarged at St. Patrick's original location on Illinois Avenue between Sixth and Seventh streets.

"Father O'Halloran assumed the $45,000 debt and not only made other extensive improvements but was able to retire the original debt," recorded a 1957 history of the East St. Louis parish. Within a year, he commissioned an artist in Munich, Germany, to execute two hand-carved, wooden statues of the Blessed Virgin, Queen of Heaven, and St. Patrick, the parish patron. What do those two works of art symbolize — an act of confidence that the debt would be reduced or a sign of gratitude for divine intervention in a difficult situation? Or was it his way of challenging his parishioners to greater things? Whatever Father O'Halloran's intention was in ordering those statues, they seem to have marked an upswing in this community which had faced such dire financial straits.

In 1887 Father O'Halloran shifted his concern from the needs of the parish plant to the church community at large. He helped organize the St. Patrick Mutual Loan and Building Association which helped parish families obtain funds for housing at a fair mortgage rate. It is reported that seventy-two homes were financed and built with loans from this parish project.

Father O'Halloran directed the formation of East St. Louis' first parochial grade school at St. Patrick's, just one year after the Belleville diocese was established. A new rectory was built and the pastor's former residence became the home of the Loretto Sisters, who staffed St. Patrick School. The sisters' house had been somewhat of an albatross to the parish. The two-story brick structure had been constructed by Father O'Halloran's predecessor, Father F. H. Zabel, D.D., who conducted the short-lived St. Aloysius College there. The debt from this building had contributed to the unsound financial situation that had greeted Father O'Halloran upon his arrival sixteen years earlier. Now he managed to salvage Father Zabel's dream of a Catholic educational institution in East St. Louis.

The pastor of St. Patrick's was instrumental in persuading the diocese to purchase seventy-one acres of land on the bluffs to be used as a parish cemetery. On May 19, 1891, Mt. Carmel Cemetery was consecrated. The first burial recorded was that of the infant son of J. W. McGlynn.

A devastating tornado struck East St. Louis at 5:22 P.M. on May 27, 1896. In the wake of the storm, 102 were dead, hundreds were injured and the property damage was estimated in the hundreds of thousands of dollars. The tornado gave birth to the Queen's Daughters, a charitable organization of women founded by Father P. J. O'Halloran. After the storm subsided, a group of Catholic women joined the relief effort to feed, clothe, and provide shelter for the area residents who had lost their homes in the tornado and the fire which followed. The women's generosity and dedication so impressed their pastor that Father O'Halloran insisted that they form a permanent outreach ministry.

Mrs. Harry F. Parry was elected the first president of the women's group in 1897, and Father O'Halloran served as spiritual director of the organization for three years. In 1903 the women affiliated with the Queen's Daughters General Council in St. Louis. In keeping with their purpose of giving glory to God and the Blessed Mother by performing the corporal works of mercy, the Queen's Daughters reached out to those in need. The group is best remembered for the many holiday food baskets which the members prepared and distributed. The Queen's Daughters disbanded in 1976.

This gives an overview of the dynamic Irish pastor who made outstanding contributions to the formative years of the Church in East St. Louis. Owen Roe described the man behind the pastorate in the following personality sketch, "The Very Rev. Father O'Halloran was an ideal man and priest. Underneath the plainness of manner and diction which characterized him, there was a tenderness of feeling and a purity of mind which were most admirable. . . . He was eminently practical and a hater of all nonsense and humbuggery, exceedingly hospitable and appreciative of genial humor. Dear Father O'Halloran was a typical Irish priest who was close to the hearts of his people."

Father O'Halloran suffered at great length from Bright's disease. When Bishop John Janssen visited the old Irish pastor, who was on his deathbed, it was reported that Father O'Halloran told him, "If I must die, God's will be done; but I have this supreme consolation: I have done my duty."

Father Patrick O'Halloran died on December 30, 1897. The funeral procession was headed by Holten's band and included three suburban line streetcars, each holding 200 passengers. Archbishop Patrick Ryan of Philadelphia led the delegation of 100 priests who escorted Father O'Halloran to his final resting place at Mt. Carmel Cemetery.

CHAPTER 23

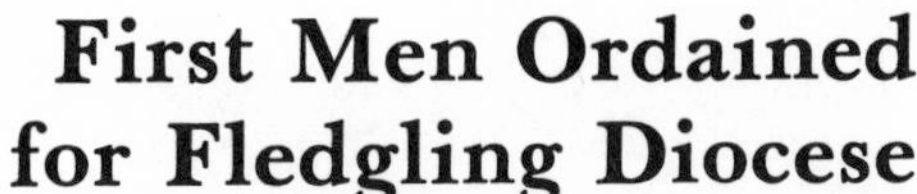

First Men Ordained for Fledgling Diocese

By Stanley J. Konieczny

THIRTY-TWO DAYS AFTER his installation as the head of the newly established Diocese of Belleville, Bishop John Janssen ordained the first two priests for this new diocese. Father Henry Goosens and Aloysius Wegmann became the first priests ordained for the Belleville diocese on May 27, 1888. Being first, in most cases, is a singular distinction, whether it is earned by hard work and endurance or it is a mere accident of history.

Father Henry Goosens and Father Aloysius Wegmann, though, merit a place in the diocesan chronicles beyond mere coincidental completion of seminary training just when a new diocese was being created. These men distinguished themselves by their ministries in southern Illinois. Their years of work were characterized by a special dedication and creativity. They stand at the front of the ranks of Belleville diocesan priests, both in seniority and in exemplary service to the Church of southern Illinois.

Born on February 5, 1856, at Oeding, Westphalia, Germany, Henry Goosens was not a "cradle Catholic." Rather, he chose the faith after a conversion experience which he had while serving in the German army. Henry Goosens was received into the Catholic Church on December 17, 1874. Within ten years of his reception into the church, this German soldier would be a seminary student halfway around the world.

After completing his military service, Henry Goosens emigrated to the United States in 1880. He embarked on a new venture by enrolling in St. Joseph College, Teutopolis, Illinois, where he took his classical studies. In 1884 he continued his training for the priesthood at St.

Father Henry Goosens

Father Aloysius Wegmann

Meinrad Seminary. Four years later, during that first ordination ceremony in the Belleville diocese, Father Henry Goosens reached a milestone on what must have been a remarkable journey of faith and spiritual growth.

In his first assignment, Father Goosens was named pastor of Holy Cross parish, Wendelin. The newly-ordained priest built and opened the parish's first one-room schoolhouse, which was used until 1899. He also brought in the Adorers of the Blood of Christ to serve the community. The sisters remained for the next seven years in this East Deanery parish.

Father Goosens was then appointed pastor of the historic Immaculate Conception parish at Kaskaskia in 1893. Bishop Henry Althoff would later remember this portion of Father Goosens' ministry as a "period of hard labor, sacrifices and discouragement." The new pastor arrived to find his church shuttered and abandoned. The Mississippi River had cut a new channel and Kaskaskia Island was a shambles. The town and its church would have to be relocated three miles further north on the island.

The following year, Father Goosens supervised the drive to move Immaculate Conception Church, which was built in 1843, to its present location on higher ground. The landmark was moved brick by brick and reconstructed at the new site. The treasured relic of the past was embellished by a bell tower which was constructed alongside the entrance.

"Father Goosens was deeply interested in the welfare of Kaskaskia," Bishop Althoff observed. The second bishop of Belleville recalled that Father Goosens once sent him a history of the island with the note, "What will become of Kaskaskia in the future is hard to tell on account of the ever-changing Mississippi. May the Immaculate Mother Mary, its patron, continue to protect this old and venerable parish.

The 1903 pastoral assignments found Father Goosens beginning his thirteen-year ministry at Immaculate Conception parish, Columbia. The pastor encountered new challenges for his talents to build, design, and create. Father Goosens constructed a new rectory, which one Columbia parish chronicle noted was "very spacious and substantial and was considered the best of its time." He also completely remodeled the church, installing pillars in the nave.

Carl Reis, a lifelong member of Immaculate Conception parish, remembers that Father Goosens also installed electricity in the church when that convenience was considered an experiment for laboratories and industry. The pastor of Columbia installed an electric generator in the church vestibule to power the tower clock and to provide limited lighting on the main altar. Because of his small stature, the young Reis was elected to drag two electric wires from the generator through the crawlspace beneath the church to the lamps on the altar.

"Father Goosens was an individual who couldn't just sit down and rest. He was always tinkering," recalled Reis, who is the retired president of the Missouri Pacific Employees' Hospital Association. "Father would sit in his room, say his prayers and then start tinkering with his clocks or the lawnmower or the buggy." This "tinkering" led Father Goosens to invent a device for horse-drawn buggies which would insure greater comfort for passengers and less effort for the horses. The invention was patented by the U.S. Patent Office but the product never went into production.

Deteriorating health forced Father Goosens to a seek a less demanding pastorate. He served briefly at St. Michael parish, Paderborn, before he entered "retirement," which took him to Belleville, Columbia, and even a brief stint as temporary pastor of Immaculate Conception parish, Madonnaville. He finally settled in Red Bud, where he died on October 20, 1928, after serving his church for forty years. Father Goosens was buried at Immaculate Conception parish cemetery, Columbia.

The other priest ordained on May 27, 1888, Father Aloysius Wegmann, distinguished himself especially through his special devotion to Catholic education in the Belleville diocese. Aloysius Wegmann's vocation can be traced back to Altendorf, Germany, where he was born on April 9, 1865. He had originally intended to be ordained for his home diocese and began his studies for the priesthood in Germany, but soon he discerned the missionary aspect of his vocation.

The young Wegmann came to the United States in 1881 and studied at both St. Joseph College, Teutopolis, and St. Meinrad Seminary. After ordaining his first two priests for the new Belleville diocese, Bishop Janssen commissioned Father Wegmann to St. Stephen parish, Flora. That year Father Wegmann led the construction of Flora's first parochial school. Lay teachers taught in the parish institution which attracted between thirty and sixty children a year.

Then sixty-one families of St. Stephen parish experienced a crushing setback when a fire destroyed their church on Christmas Day 1892. The community met temporarily in the parish school until a new brick church was built under the direction of Father Wegmann. The structure on the corner of Eighth and Main streets could accommodate 200 people and served the community for sixty-one years.

For the next sixteen years, Father Wegmann served at St. Philip parish, East St. Louis. In this community, he was again closely identified with Catholic education. In a St. Philip parish history by Sister Barbara Brumleve, SSND, it was noted, "The parish school had been Father Wegmann's great love. He established it as a free school so that no child would be barred for non-payment of tuition. He was even the diocesan superintendent of schools for a time, but conditions were not ripe for that position in the diocese."

In later years, *The Messenger* editors would eulogize Father Wegmann, recalling, "The school [St. Philip's] was one of the favorite haunts of the diligent priest, and it must be admitted by all, that in the course of a few years he made out of the old time country school of the [French] Village, a school that is on a level with the most modern and up-to-date schools in any of our larger cities." It was noted that Father Wegmann maintained a reputation as a popular confessor in both Belleville and East St. Louis. He was in demand as a speaker, especially with youths such as the St. John's Club.

St. Philip Church was remodeled and new art glass windows were installed in 1907 under the direction of Father Wegmann. The Catholic community in French Village earned a special place in the heart of Aloysius Wegmann. At his death, he willed his chalice, a gift from his father, to St. Philip Church. He was also commemorated by a marble plaque honoring St. Philip's former "pastor and benefactor."

Father Wegmann succeeded Father John Enzelberger as pastor of Germantown on December 11, 1907. Within a year and a half, the new pastor of St. Boniface Church was dead. He was in the midst of making plans to return to Europe to study sociology when he suddenly became ill with what seemed a relatively minor ailment. On April 24, 1909, Father Aloysius Wegmann died of apparent heart failure at the age of forty-four.

St. Boniface Church was filled to capacity for the solemn funeral liturgy. Pallbearers from Germantown and French Village took turns in carrying their pastor to his grave in St. Boniface parish cemetery.

Fathers Henry Goosens and Aloysius Wegmann, as the first priests ordained for the Belleville diocese, set a standard of creative service and undying devotion for the men who would succeed them in the years leading up to the diocesan centennial and beyond that festive occasion.

CHAPTER 24

Franciscan Presence in Southern Illinois

By Stanley J. Konieczny

THE FOLLOWERS OF ST. FRANCIS OF ASSISI have been part of the Illinois scene for over 300 years. The famed explorer of the Mississippi River, Robert Cavelier Sieur de La Salle, was accompanied by three Franciscan friars as he meandered down the great river, which creates a natural western border for Illinois. One of La Salle's Franciscan companions, Father Gabriel de la Ribourde, was murdered in 1680 by Kickapoo Indians in northern Illinois.

Franciscans ministered to the many immigrants who settled in southern Illinois beginning in the mid-nineteenth century. At the time of the organization of the Belleville diocese, a Catholic census indicated two communities of religious men working in the area: the Benedictines with headquarters at Wetaug and the Franciscans with their ministry based at Radom. One of these pioneer Franciscans in Washington County was Father Luke Mierzowski.

A native of Peiskretscham, which is located in the Diocese of Wroclaw, Poland, Victor Mierzowski was born December 22, 1857, the son of Francis and Mary Kroll Mierzowski. Upon entering religious life, the young Mierzowski was given the name Luke.

"He came to the United States in 1875 as a candidate for the Order of Friars Minor. Presumably, he accompanied thirty Franciscan clerics and nine novices who came that year from the Saxonian Province of the Order of Friars Minor, as refugees of the Kulturkampf," explained Father Ladislas Siekaniec, OFM, Ph.D., a historian and past archivist for the Sacred Heart Province of Franciscans.

On July 19, 1879, Luke Mierzowski, OFM, entered the St. Francis novitiate friary at Teutopolis, Illinois. He took simple vows as a Franciscan the following year and began his seminary studies. "He made his solemn profession in the order on August 15, 1883, at St. Anthony

Father Luke Mierzowski, OFM

friary, St. Louis,'' Father Siekaniec noted. ''At that time, St. Anthony's was also a house of theological studies. Here he received the tonsure and minor orders in 1882. Bishop Patrick John Ryan ordained him a deacon on May 21, 1884, and a priest on the following day,'' Father Siekaniec added.

Records indicate that Father Mierzowski's original apostolate was to the Indian missions. After three years, though, he was assigned to work with Polish-speaking immigrants in the vicinity of St. Michael the Archangel Parish, Radom. For twenty years Father Luke Mierzowski labored in Washington County.

The village of Radom was founded in 1873, when the Illinois Central Railroad recruited Polish immigrants to settle in Washington County. The struggling young community was visited occasionally by Franciscans from Teutopolis. In 1877 the town sent a delegation to Alton to petition Bishop Peter Baltes that a parish be established in Radom under the administration of the Franciscans. Bishop Baltes consented and Father Desiderius Liss, OFM, arrived that year. A small, five-room house served as both school and friary for this first Franciscan community. From this mission headquarters in Radom, Franciscans went out to minister to the Catholics living in DuBois, Scheller, and Tamaroa. The Radom parish encompassed parts of three counties in its early years and the Franciscans at Radom spent many days on the road visiting the various farms and settlements.

In 1887 Father Luke joined St. Michael friary and was put in charge of the St. Charles Borromeo Church, DuBois. The 1924 history of St. Michael parish, written in Polish and issued to commemorate the dedication of the new church in Radom, recalled Father Luke as a very mild and meek man who was characterized by a thriftiness which bordered on austerity. Such virtues must have proved invaluable as he embarked on various ambitious undertakings in the newly-established diocese.

An account of the November 5, 1890, dedication of the new Sacred Heart Church, Du Quoin, conveys the multi-national nature of the early Belleville diocese and the need for priests who could serve their congregations in their native languages. "A farewell Mass was said in the old church at 8 o'clock at which Vicar General Cluse preached a sermon in the Italian language. He was followed by the Rev. P. Lucas Mierzowski, OFM, who spoke in the Polish language . . . At the dedication of the Sacred Heart Church of Du Quoin, sermons were preached in the Italian, Polish, German, and English languages. . . . Like on Pentecost day, everyone was able to hear God's message in his own tongue."

At the time the Belleville diocese was formed, Father Mierzowski and his DuBois parishioners were purchasing five acres of land and planning St. Charles Borromeo cemetery. That same year, Bishop John Janssen visited the mission parish and confirmed 151 people. In 1891 Father Luke led the construction of the DuBois parish school and arranged for School Sisters of Notre Dame to staff the two-classroom school, which opened October 5, 1891. Three years later he became the superior of the Radom friary and assumed the duties of pastor of St. Michael parish. In 1895 Father Luke constructed a two-story, brick friary at the cost of $12,000. The spacious building was a necessity for the friars who spent much of their week visiting the neighboring communities. St. Michael's gave them a welcome retreat where they could rest, pray, and restore themselves before they hit the mission trail again.

A new convent was constructed for the sisters at Radom in 1901 and their former residence was converted into a boarding school for children who lived too far from Radom to return home everyday.

Although he had remodeled St. Michael Church once and installed an organ and some ecclesiastical art, Father Luke had a dream of building a new church. In addition to his regular pastoral duties, he began to travel around his extensive parish, soliciting pledges for the great "house of the Lord," which he envisioned. Although the concept was well received and plans were made, neither Father Luke nor the Franciscan fathers ever realized this dream.

The pastor of Radom overtaxed his strength and caught a cold, which gradually developed into "consumption." On November 16, 1907, Father Luke collapsed in the arms of a religious brother and was dead before he could be laid upon a nearby couch. Father Luke Mierzowski was fifty years old.

The 1924 Radom parish history observed that as a tribute to Father Luke's twenty years of ardent service in the Belleville diocese, a throng of mourners attended the Mass of Christian burial for the Polish Franciscan, making it the largest funeral ever remembered in Radom up to that time. Father Luke was laid to rest in St. Michael cemetery among the parishioners he had so faithfully and humbly served. Gradually the

Franciscans relinquished the administration of DuBois and Scheller and in 1914 they left Radom, which was then staffed by a diocesan priest.

The Franciscan presence in southern Illinois does not end with the burial of Father Luke Mierzowski, nor is it merely some remembered landmark like the old St. Michael's friary. Living the rule of St. Francis, the Poverello's followers still serve the Belleville diocese through parish, health care and educational ministries and social outreach. Franciscan friars of various provinces continue the pastoral ministry of their predecessors, like Father Luke. Among the women religious of the diocese, there are Franciscan Sisters of Our Lady of Perpetual Help, Franciscan Sisters of Perpetual Adoration, Hospital Sisters of the Third Order of St. Francis, School Sisters of St. Francis, Sisters of St. Francis of the Providence of God, and Poor Clares. The secular Franciscan order, St. Peter fraternity, operates a thrift shop in Belleville as part of its outreach.

CHAPTER 25

Father Bernard Hilgenberg: The Pastor of the Coal Fields

By Raphael H. Middeke

WHEN HE CELEBRATED his golden jubilee as a priest in Carlyle in December of 1944, Father Bernard Hilgenberg had been gone from the mission coal fields, the place of his ministry in the early 1900s, for over thirty years. But at the jubilee he was still toasted as "the pastor of the coal fields."

When he died in 1952, Father Hilgenberg had spent thirty-eight years as the pastor of St. Anthony parish, Beckemeyer, and St. Mary parish, Carlyle. But the far-flung and nationally diverse group of Catholic immigrants from Italy and Eastern Europe who settled in the often turbulent and confusing new coal mine camps of southern Illinois always remembered him as the coal belt missionary — a title born out of an accident of time and place.

Born in Coesfeld, Germany, in the diocese of Muenster June 19, 1872, Bernard Hilgenberg began his studies in Germany and completed his philosophy and theology courses at Floreffe and Louvain in Belgium. He was ordained by Bishop John Janssen on December 26, 1894, at the age of twenty-two in St. Peter Cathedral in Belleville, only seven years after the Belleville diocese was formed.

His first assignment was as an assistant to Father Kaspar Schauerte in Murphysboro. The Murphysboro parish also attended missions in Ava, Raddle, Grand Tower, and Carterville. Within a year, Father Hilgenberg built the first church in Carterville, the beginning of a career as a builder even he couldn't have envisioned. Within a few years, he built a rectory at Ava.

When the Illinois Central Railroad moved its division office from Centralia to Carbondale, Catholic employees moving to Carbondale were anxious to begin a parish and Father Hilgenberg was asked in

1900 to establish the parish and continue the mission in Carterville. In the same year, he organized a parish in the new coal town of Herrin and said the first Mass in Herrin in the town hall, the only building in town big enough for the growing number of Catholics in the area.

Monsignor Bernard Hilgenberg

Coal was changing the face of Little Egypt, as well as the social environment. The discovery of rich coal deposits brought an influx of immigrants, most of them Catholic, to a strange and often hostile environment. Unlike the Irish and Germans, who left because of social conditions in their own countries and not only because of the promise of work, native priests did not accompany the coal camp immigrants — adding to the cultural shock of a religious environment which not only did not welcome them but often hated them simply because they were Catholic.

It was in this environment that Father Hilgenberg, who in 1907 was named the first pastor of Herrin, became a familiar figure along the muddy roads leading from mining camp to mining camp.

Even before he became Herrin's first pastor, the coal belt missionary had established a parish in Johnston City in 1904. A year later, he was the founding pastor of St. Andrew parish in Christopher and St. Mary parish in Sesser. He also started collecting funds for a church in Royalton, but didn't begin the building of it before Father Charles Seiffert was named as the first pastor of the parishes in Royalton and Ziegler.

At one time the pioneer priest visited four churches each Sunday, traveling by buggy over the rutted roads. An obituary in 1952 in the *Benton Standard* ran under the headline: "Last Rites Held for Founder of Most of Franklin County's Catholic Churches." The writer ties the beginning of the parishes in Marion, West Frankfurt, and Benton and missions in Cambria and Bush to Father Hilgenberg's missionary efforts.

The coal camp priest brought with him to the missions of southern Illinois a special gift — without which his ministry would have been difficult if not impossible. He was a gifted linguist who learned the languages of the Catholic immigrants, as needed. At one time, eight nationalities were under his care. He preached in four languages and spoke Italian, Polish, Lithuanian, Slovak, and French, besides his native German and the English of his new country.

Alluding to the new Catholic presence in the suspicious and often unfriendly environment of the American Protestant frontier culture the *Benton Standard* writer said, "He [Father Hilgenberg] changed the religious complexion of Franklin County. [He] became the Catholics' counterpart of Egypt's Protestant circuit-riding preachers."

The German priest's multilingual religious family, scattered in the sprawling coal camps, was hardly greeted with cheers to Little Egypt by its neighbors. The Ku Klux Klan was a growing organization and the Catholic immigrants were one of their objects of prejudice and fear, fostering in the minds of earlier Americans "rumors about the dreaded Catholic." Not many years later, it wasn't unusual for the white-robed Klan members to circle a Catholic church or burn a cross on church property.

In 1913 after a two-day sick visit forty miles from his home, driving a two-wheeled cart in inclement weather, the forty-year-old priest was admitted to a hospital for a rheumatic condition. He went to Hot Springs, Arkansas, to recuperate, but returning with not enough strength to continue his pastoral work, he took an extended sick leave.

The illness was a mixed blessing. Father Hilgenberg, not prevented from traveling, visited every country in Europe and traveled in North Africa. He went on to India for six months, where he visited a distant relative who was the Bishop of Poona. He stayed for a while in Russia and studied Lithuanian at Kaunas and spent a month at the university in Krakow, Poland, where he studied Polish. After an eighteen-month tour he returned to the United States and was named the second pastor of St. Anthony parish, Beckemeyer, where he stayed for twenty years.

It is easy to think of Bernard Hilgenberg, the priest and coal camp missionary, without thinking of the builder of churches, schools, rectories, and convents. The coal belt missionary returned from his study tour to Clinton County with less energy and stamina, perhaps, but he did not come with less vision. In Beckemeyer he enlarged the school, the hall, and the convent, and repaired the old church. Before he left, he laid the foundation of the new church, but postponed the program because of the depression.

When he went to St. Mary parish, Carlyle, in 1934, his final pastorate, he renovated every building . The parish was in the midst of extensive renovations on the old church in May 1940 when a disastrous fire gutted the building. On the old foundation and the remaining walls, the present St. Mary's was raised, "a monument to his zeal and administrative ability," as one obituary account put it. In Carlyle, the now-aging pastor dedicated much time and effort to enlarging the facilities of St. Mary's Central Catholic High School. On the occasion of his fifty-fifth anniversary celebration, he announced his plans to build a new Catholic Central High School and gymnasium/auditorium by the time he celebrated his diamond jubilee. Those plans never materialized, because it was decided to build a new central Catholic high school for the entire county, the present Mater Dei.

For many years, Monsignor Hilgenberg (he was named a monsignor a year after his golden jubilee) was associated with the National Catholic Rural Life Conference and was diocesan moderator of the conference at the time of his death.

Perhaps symbolic of his wide interests, his undeniable accomplishments and his talents and zeal are a few recorded relatives: the cousin who was the Bishop of Poona, India; the uncle who was the rector of the seminary in Muenster, Germany, when Hilgenberg was a boy; the sister, Sister Mary Columbe, who was a religious superior in St. Louis.

From coal camp Masses to the St. Mary Church in Carlyle, which cost $120,000 to construct in the early 1940s, Father Hilgenberg was always the doer and the dreamer, the builder and the man of arts and languages. But more than anything, he was the coal belt missionary — the priest who converted the coal camps into parishes.

CHAPTER 26

Father Bartholomew Bartels: Bartelso's "Great Benefactor"

By Harold D. Olree

IN HIS HISTORY OF ST. CECILIA PARISH, Bartelso, Father John Keim referred to Father Bartholomew Bartels as the "greatest benefactor" of that Clinton County community. Not only did Father Bartels, who came as the second pastor of St. Cecilia in 1888, donate the property for the parish and personally provide many of the items for the church, but he gave the town its name.

Father Keim wrote from experience, having served as assistant, then as St. Cecilia administrator during the last two years of the pastor's life, 1892-94. He succeeded Father Bartels as St. Cecilia pastor shortly after his death in 1894.

Father Bartels was named pastor of St. Cecilia parish succeeding the founding pastor, Father John Spaeth, who had resigned in 1887, two years after the parish was formed. Father Spaeth left because of continuing financial problems of the new parish. At the time of his appointment, Father Bartels was sixty-five years old and had been in retirement for six years at Quincy. For sixteen years he had served as pastor of St. Boniface parish, Germantown. After the Diocese of Belleville was formed in 1887, he moved to Carlyle.

It was Father Spaeth, his predecessor, who had proposed that the location of Cecilia parish be named Bartelso for Father Bartels when the parish was opened in 1885. Area residents desired a post office and the name "Bartelso" was accepted by officials in Washington after they had rejected several others, including "Bartelsville" because there were already too many towns with "ville" in their names.

St. Cecilia parish and the town of Bartelso were founded for "convenience" sake. Some seventy-five families, mostly German immigrants who farmed the area east of Germantown, had serious difficulties in getting to Mass. They were in either St. Boniface parish, Germantown, or St. Mary parish, Carlyle. But frequent flooding of Shoal Creek, poor roads, and few bridges made Mass attendance impossible at times.

Father Bartholomew Bartels

Oddly enough, it was Father Bartels, while he was pastor at Germantown about 1870, who first proposed a parish near Shoal Creek, but the plan was vetoed by Germantown businessmen.

Parish historical accounts say that Father Bartels, while still in retirement at Quincy, ordered and paid for a new altar, two side altars, a communion rail, pulpit, confessional and baptismal font, and vestment case for St. Cecilia Church. He also donated a statue of St. Bartholomew and a crucifixion group for the parish cemetery.

Most of the church furniture donated by Father Bartels was used by Jetty (Justin) Vandeloo in building the present St. Cecilia Church altar. Vandeloo's grandfather, Gerhard Van De Loo, a Dutch horticulturist, had served as Father Bartels' caretaker in Quincy and came with him to Bartelso, according to a St. Cecilia parish centennial feature story in *The Messenger* in 1984.

Bartelso's "greatest benefactor" was born Bartholomeus (anglicized to Bartholomew) Bartels on March 10, 1823, in Cleve in Rhineland, Germany. He studied at Cologne, Bonn, and Muenster, Westphalia. He was ordained there and served his first eleven years as a priest in Germany.

He came to the United States in 1858 in response to one of the visits to Germany by Bishop Henry Damian Juncker, seeking priests for the Alton diocese, which then included the area of the Belleville diocese.

Father Bartels was accompanied by his mother, Bartholomaea Bartels, and two nieces, Dominica Ingendaa (later Wolting) and Anna Ingendaa. His nieces served as his housekeepers and donated the statues of St. Dominic and St. Anne, respectively, in the Bartelso church.

The priest who gave Bartelso its name first served as pastor at Teutopolis and also at Quincy and St. Marie. He was pastor at Teutopolis when the first group of Franciscans arrived there September

23, 1858. The nine friars resided in Father Bartels' home until a new rectory was built and space provided for the Franciscans, who were given control of the parish in late 1858.

When the Franciscans built a new parish complex, Father Bartels was invited back to dedicate the order's convent October 4, 1886.

Bishop Juncker asked Father Bartels to become founding pastor of St. Dominic parish, Breese. Father Bartels instead went to Highland, where, according to Father Keim, "he had an experience similar to St. Athanasius [a strong opponent of Arianism in early church history] with his persecutors. . . ." (St. Dominic's founding pastor in 1858, was Father Augustine Reineke, who remained there for forty-one years until his death in 1909.)

Father Bartels served at Millstadt and Freeburg before being named pastor of St. Boniface, Germantown, in 1865. He asked Bishop Juncker for a different location because of malaria which had caused the death of the previous Germantown pastor, Father Augustin Berger. He had also heard of much dissension among Germantown parishioners. He was appointed to St. Libory but was reassigned to Germantown a few months later. Some historical accounts also had Father Bartels serving at Fayetteville, Paderborn, Columbia, and Pocahontas.

Many improvements were made in the Germantown parish during Father Bartels' sixteen-year pastorate, 1865-1881. The bell tower was completed, the interior of the church was renovated, including a new high altar, two confessionals, stations of the cross, and a new tower clock was installed. In addition, a new rectory, high schools for boys and girls and residence for the sisters were built.

His retirement in 1881 lasted until he agreed to become pastor of St. Cecilia parish. In the 1935 parish history, Father Keim said, "Everyone knew him since he had from 1865-1881 the great majority of the Bartelso Catholics as members of his parish in Germantown," referred to as "the mother church of Clinton County."

The Bartelso parish's centennial history book in 1984 noted that Father Bartels, during his priestly life, "adopted" two young children, whose families were unable to care for them properly. Mary Gebke, who came to live with him when she was four years old, grew up to become his housekeeper and continued to live in his home after Father Bartels' death.

The other young girl raised by Father Bartels was Annie Rite, who joined the Poor Handmaids of Jesus Christ. She gave money inherited from her mother which went to purchase the present crucifixion group on the main altar of St. Cecilia Church, and she continued to visit Bartelso until her death in 1960.

Father Bartels was also a great benefactor of the German Catholic press. He was on the board of directors of the German Literary Society of St. Louis and a strong supporter of *Herold des Glaubens*, a German Catholic weekly, and of *Die Amerika*, a daily which also published a bi-weekly edition.

While pastor at Germantown in 1872, Father Bartels was credited with saving the *Amerika* publication, which was having financial problems, by influencing his fellow board members to install a new editor. Another board member, who had appealed to Father Bartels for help, described him as "*Gottes Segen vom Lande*" (God's messenger from the country).

Father Bartels wrote *Notes on the First Settlements of Catholic Low-Germans in Clinton County*, which was published in *Die Amerika* in 1881. He described the *Notes* as "based on statements during several meetings of a number of farmers of Germantown, Illinois."

As Father Frederic Beuckman, diocesan historian-writer observed, Father Bartels' *Notes* have proved a "most valuable document" on the "religious and civil beginnings and the advancement of the County."

Upon Father Bartels' death on May 4, 1894, in his seventieth year, he was buried in St. Cecilia parish cemetery.

CHAPTER 27

Father Frederic Beuckman: History Maker

By Stanley J. Konieczny

EACH OF US CHERISHES, to a certain degree, a very special legacy: our personal family histories. These treasures are passed on from generation to generation and such stories of sacrifice, hardship, endurance, achievement, and growth instill in us a sense of pride, belonging, and security. This is evident in the growing interest in genealogy.

As a family of faith, the Church in southern Illinois also possesses a rich heritage. The popularity of *The Messenger* features such as "Profiles From Our Diocesan Heritage" and "Parish Spotlights" indicate that members of the Belleville diocese want to know more about the selfless women and men who planted and nurtured the faith here for so many years.

Today, whenever we read one of these profiles, we benefit from the tireless wŏrk of a southern Illinois priest who recognized the tremendous wealth of local Catholic history and who dedicated much of his energy to preserving this great story of faith. This distinguished historian-pastor was Father Frederic Beuckman. Through his efforts both as a scholar and as a community leader, Father Beuckman can be truly recognized as a "maker of history."

Frederic Thomas Beuckman was born December 19, 1869, in East St. Louis, a son of Frederic and Theresa Schamoni Beuckman. After completing his studies at St. Joseph College, Teutopolis, and St. Francis Seminary, St. Francis Wisconsin, the twenty-two-year old seminarian received a papal dispensation and was ordained in his home parish, St. Henry Church, East St. Louis, on June 24, 1892.

Writing his autobiography in later years for St. Francis Seminary, Father Beuckman reflected, "My ambition was a university career

Father Frederic Beuckman

which was planned and I think would have been realized if my father's death previous to my ordination and then the great need of good and saintly Bishop Janssen of priests in his small diocese had not dictated my immediate assignment to pastoral work." Father Beuckman was not a man of understatement. He never served as an associate pastor. Immediately after ordination, he was named acting pastor of St. Mary Church, Shawneetown with the attached parishes of St. Joseph, Rosiclare, and St. Joseph, Equality.

This first assignment posed a considerable undertaking. Equality was twelve miles west of Shawneetown by rail. Father Beuckman started a drive there to build a two-story, frame rectory for a resident pastor at the mission. Upon completion of the residence, St. Joseph's parishioners petitioned that Father Beuckman be assigned to Equality. Instead, Father Thomas Day was named the first resident pastor of Equality, which became an independent parish in November 1893.

Father Beuckman used to travel by packet steamer or horse and buggy into Hardin County to minister to the isolated German Catholics living at Rosiclare. This mission was attached to the newly-established parish at Equality in 1893. Then the historic mission of St. Patrick, Doherty, now known as Pond Settlement, was given to the care of Father Beuckman.

At his home base, St. Mary parish, Shawneetown, Father Beuckman won the respect and esteem of the entire community for his relief work following the devastating flood of 1898. The community marveled at the way in which the young priest assumed responsibility for the organization of aid and reconstruction programs after the town was virtually destroyed when a levee broke and inundated Shawneetown.

In 1908 the pastor of Shawneetown began construction of a new St. Mary Church. Learning from past experience, Father Beuckman had the Gothic church built upon a high basement to place the church floor well above the swirling waters whenever the Ohio River might overflow its banks.

Shawneetown lost one of its leading citizens in 1910, when Bishop John Janssen transferred Father Beuckman to St. Mary parish, Belleville. Throughout the years of ministering in the southeastern corner of the diocese, Father Beuckman became imbued with the rich Catholic heritage of that area, which can trace its roots to the famed missionary Father Elisha "Daddy" Durbin. The scholarly inclination of St. Mary's new pastor led Father Beuckman to do in-depth historical research and from 1910 to 1912, the monthly diocesan *Messenger* published his series of articles entitled, "An Early Catholic Mission of Southeastern Illinois."

On July 1, 1912, Bishop Janssen commissioned Father Beuckman to write a history of the Belleville diocese. Seven years later, Bishop Henry Althoff directed the priest-historian to furnish the editorial material for *The Messenger's* St. John Orphanage edition, which benefited the diocesan children's home at Glen Addie and which today is an invaluable reference tool to anyone doing research on the early Church in southern Illinois. His expertise was soon recognized beyond the boundaries of the Belleville diocese and Father Beuckman was made associate editor of the scholarly journal, *Illinois Catholic Historical Review*, later known as *Mid-America*.

Justice demands that a complete picture be given of Father Frederic Beuckman. While he was a reputable scholar, this man was not locked into the musty past of his Church. First and foremost, Father Beuckman was a pastor who served his people to the best of his ability. When Belleville was stricken by the great influenza epidemic, Father Beuckman spent most of his time visiting the sick in makeshift hospital wards that had been set up in schools and churches.

He was an outspoken critic of socialism, which made him very unpopular in the city's west end parish where many coal miners and factory workers lived. Father Beuckman used his position to debate area socialists and to confront the problems which workers faced in the early twentieth century. Although the priest and his working-class flock often found themselves at odds over various issues, undoubtedly Father Beuckman became a champion in the cause of at least some of his workers.

Father Beuckman wrote, "About the year 1926, quite a number of my parishioners, stove foundry sandblasters, were dying the slow and agonizing death of silicosis strangulation. Daily, I saw these victims of industrial wrongs and neglect die an undying death, to which even strangulation of an unsuccessful hanging on the gallows is but momentary to the many months of strangulation of an incurable silicosis victim." Father Beuckman pressed the issue until it entered the legal arena; corpses were exhumed for autopsies to prove criminal neglect at the work place and laws were enacted to improve working conditions in area stove foundries.

During his twenty-four year pastorate at St. Mary's, Belleville, Father Beuckman saw the parish grow to 380 families. Parish property was acquired and the present school and auditorium were built. These pastoral responsibilities coupled with his social crusades and scholarly endeavors wore down the pastor and Father Beuckman suffered a complete breakdown; his health had been undermined by overwork and fatigue.

On June 26, 1934, Father Frederic Beuckman died. He was buried in his family's plot at Mt. Carmel Cemetery, Belleville, where a simple headstone marks the grave of a great history maker of the Belleville diocese.

CHAPTER 28

Father Kaspar Schauerte: Pastor, Educator

By Sister M. Pauline Grady, ASC

EVERYTHING ABOUT THIS GERMAN IMMIGRANT, Kaspar Schauerte, was big. He was large of stature; he had a big heart; he possessed a broad vision which helped shape the future of the Belleville diocese and its educational system. Father Kaspar Schauerte was a great priest of southern Illinois who built up the Church through the parish school.

The French missionaries laid the foundations for the Church in southern Illinois during the late seventeenth century. The providential growth of this faith was nurtured by the Irish and German immigrants who came to this area in the nineteenth century. Father Schauerte represents a cadre of outstanding priests who for many years were the moving force in the acculturation of these immigrant Catholics to southern Illinois. Dedicated clergymen like Father Schauerte helped settle newcomers to America in a wholesome way so that they were no longer strangers, without losing a great number of them to frontier materialism or Protestant evangelization.

Born March 7, 1862, in Marmecke, Westphalia, one of seven children of William and Regina Schauerte, Kaspar Schauerte's early ambitions were geared toward education. He enrolled in the "teachers' seminary" at Bueren, Westphalia, and after completing his studies, he taught for one year at Huelschotten, Westphalia. The young educator was destined for greater things. Young Schauerte soon discerned a vocation to the priesthood.

Father Christopher Koenig, pastor of St. Henry parish, East St. Louis, invited the young teacher to come to America, live at St. Henry's rectory and catch up on his studies. Traveling aboard an old, all-steerage steamer, Kaspar Schauerte arrived in the United States

Father Kaspar Schauerte

and in 1880 was admitted to the Salesianum at St. Francis, Wisconsin, where he completed his philosophy and theology studies. Father Kaspar Schauerte was ordained on June 24, 1887, three years after the Third Plenary Council of Baltimore, which placed so much emphasis on building the American Church on parish schools. There was to be a very strong link between that landmark council and this young man's priestly ministry, which began in the Belleville diocese with the celebration of his first Mass at old St. Henry Church on July 3, 1887.

The Very Rev. John Janssen, administrator of the Alton diocese, appointed the newly-ordained priest as the administrator of St. Andrew Parish, Murphysboro. The next January Father Schauerte was named pastor of the Murphysboro Catholic community where he would serve his entire thirty-seven years of priestly ministry.

The History of St. Andrew's Parish, written by Marie Palmer and Mary Slechticky, notes the problems that the young priest encountered upon arriving in Murphysboro. His predecessor, Father Frederick Bergmann, returned to his native Germany, unable to cope with the continual pressures of poverty and pioneer "disorder." Murphysboro at the time shared in the mixture of nationalities, uncertain conditions in the coal mines, poor health, and epidemics which were typical of life in many southern Illinois parishes of the time.

Like his conferees from Germany, Ireland, and Poland, Father Schauerte sought to address the problems facing rural pastors in the light of the Third Plenary Council of Baltimore, which encouraged a good Catholic school standing beside every Catholic church!

These parish schools, while making sure that religious freedom was not put into question by enforcing the presence of Catholic children in parish school, proved to be a real boon to rural pastors of the late nineteenth and early twentieth centuries. These men became the ombudsmen and leaders of their solidly Catholic compatriots who sought new lives in southern Illinois. These pastors, like Father Schauerte, depended on the schools to help their people preserve their faith and identity in a land that was often inimical to the Church.

A struggling parochial school was established at Murphysboro in 1872. In the summer of 1893 a new St. Andrew School was built under the direction of Father Schauerte. Students, who met in a three-story brick structure, were under the direction of five Sisters of the Precious Blood from Ruma who taught the regular curriculum of the day as well as science and music.

Father Schauerte used the school to encourage his youths to greater academic achievement. He would use little tricks like challenging the little ones on the playground to spell his name correctly for a nickel, and instituted academic medals which were awarded by the local Knights of Columbus to outstanding grade school graduates. This reflects his deep commitment to the notion that only a Church of knowledgeable, educated Catholics could survive.

During these years, Father Schauerte recognized the more comprehensive needs of the Church. In 1890 he extended his ministry to Ava, where he celebrated the first Mass in Wagner's Hall, thus establishing St. Elizabeth parish. Following a train accident in 1895, when St. Andrew School had to be used as a makeshift hospital, Father Schauerte led his people in building one of the early Catholic hospitals in the diocese.

Yet throughout his years of pastoral ministry, education seemed to be a driving force in the life of Kaspar Schauerte. He served on the various school committees and boards of the diocese and was chairman of the diocesan school board for many years. This strong and authoritative board, set up by the diocesan synod of 1909, included men such as Msgr. Charles Gilmartin, Fathers Christopher Goelz, John Bruns, Francis Pieper, Peter Engel, James Gillen and Fred Witte. These men dreamed of an educated Catholicity and they worked step by laborious step to have one. From diocesan and motherhouse archives, we learn of carefully planned "teachers institutes," which called upon sisters to improve their classroom methods and techniques. Papers were delivered at these meetings anonymously by women religious from various orders who were experts in their fields. The first of these meetings attracted almost 200 teachers from sixty-two of the diocese's seventy-four schools.

It is important that in spite of his drive to share the Good News with his people, Father Schauerte demonstrated exemplary appreciation to the religious and parishioners who helped him realize his goals. It is said that the convent at St. Andrew's was considered to be the best in the diocese. It should have been — after all, a saint was entertained there. Mother Francis Cabrini and a companion enjoyed Father Schauerte's hospitality at Murphysboro when they missed their train on the way to Chicago.

In 1924 Father Schauerte learned that he had incurable cancer and after lengthy treatments, died on December 7, 1924. Flags flew at half-mast; shops closed in tribute to this man who did so much for Murphysboro and the entire Catholic school system in the Belleville diocese. The *Murphysboro Daily Republican* eulogized the pastor-educator as "a man of activity but never too busy, nor too deep in thought to greet his friends and acquaintances cordially and whisper a word of cheer, commendation, inspiration, and congratulations to those who had achieved a small or great success, or extend the healing mantle of sympathetic words to those in sorrow or despondency. Truly he was in every sense a man of God."

CHAPTER 29

Henry Althoff: Our Second Bishop

By Raphael H. Middeke

FOR SEVERAL MONTHS beginning in late summer and extending through the fall, an old German pastor had led the altar boys after Sunday Mass to St. Joseph's altar, where they knelt and prayed for a good bishop to succeed Belleville's first ordinary, Bishop John Janssen, who had died on July 2. The year was 1913.

In late November — a months-long pilgrimage to St. Joseph's altar notwithstanding — a young teenager saw the old pastor ruefully shake his head as he said: *"Ai, ai, ai, das hat den Schlarmann sein solt."* (Loosely translated: My, o my, that should have been Schlarmann — then pastor of St. Peter Cathedral. (He was later ordained bishop of Peoria.)

The young pastor of St. Barbara parish, Okawville, Father Henry Althoff, had been named Belleville's second bishop. A quiet, soft-spoken, almost shy priest, Father Althoff had been ordained only eleven years, all of which, after a few years as an assistant at Holy Family, Cahokia, St. Damian, Damiansville and St. Henry, East St. Louis, had been spent as the pastor of the small rural parish, with the mission of St. Ann's in Nashville.

For thirty-three years Bishop Althoff was the diocese's chief shepherd. Mention his name to people who knew him and they speak of his simple life, his personal austerity, his uneasiness with crowds. They are quick to add that his demeanor and his personality overshadowed a brilliant and personally confident man who was hardly an unlikely candidate as Belleville's second bishop.

Henry John Althoff was born in Aviston, Illinois, August 28, 1873, the oldest of six children. Two of them — his brother, John, and sister, Catherine — would later live and work with him in his residence above

Bishop Henry Althoff

the chancery office at 222 South Third Street.

Before entering the seminary at the age of twenty-one, he worked on Clinton County area farms and in St. Louis. He went to Innsbruck, Austria, for his theology studies and was ordained on July 26, 1902, just a few weeks before his twenty-ninth birthday.

The new bishop shared with his successor, Bishop Albert R. Zuroweste, the rather unique fact that both their fathers were not Catholic in a day when mixed marriages were severely frowned on. They both joined the church in their later years.

By 1913 the great wave of immigration had ended. The thirty-three years of Bishop Althoff's ministry were a time of stabilization. The diocese grew by only slightly more than 10,000 Catholics. It had grown by more than 20,000 in the diocese's first twenty-five years — and from only a few thousand the twenty-five years before that. During those first twenty-five years of the diocese's history, the number of priests had grown from only fifty to 115. Bishop Althoff buried seventy-one priests and ordained more than 120. At the time of his death more than 800 women religious were ministering in the diocese. Diocesan institutions were strengthened and broadened. In 1914 there were two Catholic high schools; in 1946 there were thirteen; nineteen new parishes and missions were established. More than 100 church and school buildings were dedicated and parish and diocesan institutions and organizations multiplied.

The year 1913 was the eve of the first of the two great world wars during the bishop's thirty-three years of leadership. The immigrants who came to a new country with hope and the promise of better lives, found themselves losing their private lives and being drawn into the realities of a growing and powerful nation. By 1946 their sons and grandsons had fought in those two world wars, sometimes fighting against their own relatives, and many of them never returned. They had survived a crippling depression and the natural disasters of crop failures, floods, and tornadoes.

Immigrants continued to come to work in southern Illinois coal mines (mostly Italian and Lithuanian) and the Fairmont City zinc smelters (Spanish). The bishop's interest in languages made him aware of these immigrants' special needs. He established the Spanish-speaking parish in Fairmont City and made efforts to meet the language needs of southern Illinois coal miners, many of whom did not have priests who spoke their languages.

The bishop's interest in languages was more than just a hobby. As the pastor of the mission in Nashville he learned Polish so he could speak to his parishioners in their own language. As years went by he mastered German, Italian, French, Spanish, Polish, Lithuanian and several other Slav dialects, including a knowledge of some Russian and Croatian. Bishop Zuroweste recalls taking a Croatian priest into his office one day and saying: "Father speaks a language you don't know, Bishop." The bishop responded by speaking to him in Croatian.

The bishop, who was known as a strict disciplinarian, was not without a real sense of humor, and he befriended his priests, especially in times of difficulty. "He was most exact in demands for the fulfillment of the law, but he never failed to pardon the frailty of human nature," Monsignor Zuroweste wrote in *The Messenger's* funeral edition editorial. (Monsignor Zuroweste was the editor of *The Messenger* prior to his selection as bishop in 1947). "Priests in trouble found a real friend in him," one pastor said recently.

His sense of humor was experienced only privately. The bishop, who Bishop Zuroweste said was uncomfortable in crowds, presented a sober and almost austere image in public. But his close friends remember his humor even today. A stickler for rules, he once told a pastor whose cemetery rules irked a number of his parishioners: "Those silly rules of yours don't help anyone." And he told a meticulous young priest overly concerned about records and details: "*Salus animarum* (the salvation of souls), Father, is the one law."

The bishop whose concern for social justice is generally not remembered, wrote a thirty-five-page commentary on Pope Pius XI's encyclical on social justice promulgated in 1933. Commenting on a social justice newsletter published in Germantown, the bishop wryly said: "I don't think those people in Clinton County are going to follow him. Their motto is: *Es ist immer so gewesen.* (It has always been that way.)"

For thousands of Catholics in the Diocese of Belleville over the age of fifty, the only encounter with Bishop Althoff was at the time of their confirmation. They remember the months spent in memorizing every answer in the Baltimore Catechism to prepare for the bishop's briefing session before confirmation.

The bishop, who was seen only in the sanctuary, sat unsmiling on a straight-back chair during the questioning. The class was carefully arranged with the smartest kids in the front, since the bishop always started his questions with the first bench.

One former seventh-grader shares with many the trauma of knowing every single word in the catechism, but catching only a single word of the soft-spoken bishop's question -- in this instance the word "three." When his first effort at an answer — "Father, Son and Holy Spirit?" — received a "no" headshake, he went on to "faith, hope and charity?" — which was accepted with a "yes" headshake, as most second answers were.

A full one-third of the Belleville diocesan history has been under the leadership of this quiet, retiring, but knowing and reflective priest — whose leadership was surely marked by the times. But that history was formed by a truly simply, humble and intelligent man.

In the spring of 1947 Bishop Althoff was told he had cancer. He suffered for several months without complaint and died on July 3 of that year — one day after the thirty-third anniversary of the death of his predecessor.

CHAPTER 30

Monsignor Christopher Goelz: Pastor and Historian

by Raphael H. Middeke

When Elizabeth Koenig came to the United States from Germany with her parents and brother, Christopher, in 1863, she began a tradition of rectory life which would become a major influence for her own son, to be born Christopher Goelz eight years later.

The parents and two children of the immigrant Koenig family (the other brothers and sisters remained in Germany) moved into the rectory of their newly-ordained son and brother, Father William Koenig, who had been named the pastor of Immaculate Conception parish, Columbia. (Father William Koenig died of tuberculosis three years later.)

In 1864, following in the footsteps of his brother, Christopher Koenig entered a seminary and was ordained in 1868. He was named pastor of St. Henry parish, East St. Louis, in January 1869, and Elizabeth, then twenty-one, went with him as his housekeeper.

In the spring of 1870 she left her brother's rectory to marry Peter Goelz. But she returned in the fall of 1871 with her infant son, Christopher, named after her brother and father, following the unexpected death of her husband. For the next sixty-one years, until her death in 1931, she was the parish housekeeper for her brother (who died in 1901) or her son, first in Cobden and Anna and then at St. Philip parish, East St. Louis. Christopher Goelz grew up in his uncle's and mother's rectory. It wasn't surprising that he followed in his uncle's footsteps and went to St. Joseph College, Teutopolis, in 1886 before entering St. Francis Major Seminary in Milwaukee in 1889. He was ordained by Bishop John Janssen March 19, 1894, just a few years after the beginning of the Diocese of Belleville.

Within months after his ordination, Father Goelz was named the pastor of the Anna and Cobden parishes, where his mother joined him in 1901. The young priest gave to the mission parishes a stability which had been lacking for decades.

Monsignor Christopher Goelz

While the parishes had had resident pastors for short intervals in the 1870s, they had been cared for as mission outposts of Cairo or Mound City when necessary and for some years had been the responsibility of the Benedictine monks from Wetaug, the nearby ill-fated monastery. In some real sense Father Goelz was the mission parishes' first "pastor" and his memory lingered gratefully in southern Illinois. At his golden jubilee celebration in 1944, Bishop Henry Althoff said: "As the good people (of Anna and Cobden) still hold their former pastor in high esteem so he retains for them an enduring friendship." When his mother died in 1931, several busloads — a significant percentage of the parishioners — traveled the 150 miles to East St. Louis for her funeral.

In 1908 the thirty-six-year-old priest was named the pastor of St. Philip parish in East St. Louis and remained there until his retirement in 1951, several months before his death.

The St. Philip parish of 1908 was a thirty-square-mile challenge. In his writings the pastor spoke about his educational and pastoral efforts in Caseyville, Country Club, Signal Hill, and Oak Park.

Some of the spirit and the energy of Father Goelz is obvious in his involvements in the St. Stephen and Blessed Sacrament parishes in Caseyville and Belleville.

Caseyville was at the time a mission parish of St. Philip. But the walls in the church building, which had frozen while wet, aggravated by the vibrations of trains rattling over tracks adjacent to the building, had become a physical hazard to worshippers because of falling plaster.

Because the parish was financially unable to make the necessary repairs, Father Goelz, who had once too often seen and heard the chunks of loosened plaster hit the floor and benches, ended Sunday Masses in the building in 1911. For some years occasional weekday Masses were celebrated, but even those eventually became too dangerous and the doors were locked permanently in 1918.

Years later, when Father Goelz wrote a history of the Caseyville parish, he expressed his joy at the naming of a resident pastor in the parish in 1931 — his assistant at St. Philip, Father Joseph LeGrand. Reflecting, perhaps, on his real gift to the parishes of Anna and Cobden, he said that the parish had "suffered from too many priests." But the naming of a pastor also removed a gnawing and haunting memory. "It is not a pleasant task to close the doors of a church," he wrote.

During those same years that he wrestled with the closing of St. Stephen's and plotted its reopening, the pastor looked at the southeastern edges of his sprawling parish and recognized the need for the establishment of a new parish there. In 1923 he purchased land at 95th and West Main streets for the site of a new parish. He traded that plot for property at 8800-8900 West Main street. In 1926 Blessed Sacrament parish was established and Father Joseph Mueller, later bishop of Sioux City, Iowa, was named the first pastor. The enduring ties to his former "parish" is perhaps best recognized by the fact that Father Louis Ell, longtime pastor of Blessed Sacrament, preached Father Goelz's eulogy in 1951.

The efforts, energies, and interests of Father Goelz, who was named a monsignor forty years after his ordination in 1934, were never confined to his parish. His avocations and the demands of his vocation as a diocesan priest are obvious in a simple noting of areas of work in which he was involved:

Education: He was a charter member of the diocesan school board, established in 1909. He served in that capacity until his death. Education, both religious and secular, was a major concern of the longtime East St. Louis pastor. But in his retiring years, when St.Philip mushroomed after the war, the parish school became a burden for the aging pastor. He no longer had the energy to build the new school the parish desperately needed. Available space, eked out of every possible building, owned and rented, was no longer adequate. Efforts were made to hold enrollment down and for several years admission was refused to some. In 1950 Monsinor Goelz told one of his parishioners: "I am going to leave the school to my successor, but I've been putting money away for it." Six years later school enrollment had doubled to over 600 students.

Vocations: For almost fifty years, beginning in 1902, Monsignor Goelz devoted his time and energy to the St. Francis de Sales Student Aid Society, an organization which aided seminarians. At the milestone personal and parish celebrations in his later years at St. Philip's — the parish's centennial, the pastor's golden jubilee and his funeral liturgy — the presence of four priests was especially gratifying to Monsignor Goelz. They were sons of the parish, ordained while he was the pastor. He had baptized three of them. There is little doubt he considered Fathers Theodore Siekmann and Robert Hutsch, Oblate Father William Coovert and Franciscan Friar Joseph Hagen his sons, too. Bishop Albert Zuroweste established a seminarians' burse in his honor at the time of his death.

Diocesan Responsibilities: For many years, until 1950, for Bishops Althoff and Zuroweste, he was a diocesan consultor. He worked with the diocesan Marriage Tribunal in several capacities. And he was the assistant editor of *The Messenger* for several years beginning in 1912. For many years he contributed features and articles to the diocesan newspaper.

Historian: When the Diocese of Belleville celebrated its golden anniversary, Monsignor Goelz was assigned the task of writing the official record of those fifty years. His account, *Fifty Golden Years*, continued the work of Father Frederic Beuckman in documenting the history of the diocese. The two native sons of St. Henry parish, East St. Louis, shared an interest in the people and events that formed the church of the Diocese of Belleville. It has been said that Monsignor Goelz's library contained the most complete record of early Catholic history in southern Illinois. Every celebration in his honor took note of his historical interests and contributions.

If the parishes of St. Stephen in Caseyville and Blessed Sacrament in Belleville exemplify the pastoral concern, energy and hope of Monsignor Goelz, two other parishes formed out of portions of his once thirty-square-mile parish became a burden in his last years as St. Philip's pastor. They are also, perhaps, sad memorials to the former custom of non-retirement for priests.

Near the end of his pastorate, the almost eighty-year-old pastor wrote that Fairview Heights had been "ready for a pastor in 1941." In fact, he recommended and requested that a parish be formed at that time, but was told that no priests were available. For several years, before St. Albert the Great was established, St. Philip parishioners in Fairview Heights, encouraged by their pastor, sponsored a benefit picnic. The pastor also announced in 1950 that parishioners in Fairview Heights could mark their envelopes with an "F" and they would be credited to their new parish. St. Albert the Great was formally established in late 1951, eight months after Monsignor Goelz' death.

The second parish, St. Cyril, was not formed until 1958, and because residential trends did not develop as expected, was closed fifteen years later.

When he asked to resign in January 1951, heavy burdens — the burdens of a large and struggling parish — weighed heavily on him.

The forty-three-year pastorate at St. Philip's is a reminder of "hard toil and sacrifices. I never reached the comfortable country fields of Clinton County," he wrote. Alluding to the areas of his parish ripe for new parishes, he said: "In my days of an easy chair, I am carrying a burden of three parishes, with little sign of relief anywhere." And he complained that while he requested meetings to talk about his problems and concerns, diocesan officials were too involved in "so many affairs of importance, apparently, that I could not get a hearing."

He added: "I am not able to leave the house. I am sick and cannot go on anymore. I want to resign."

His resignation was accepted on February 1. He died on April 15, exactly one month after his successor, Father John Fournie, was installed as the pastor of St. Philip. His body was laid to rest in Holy Cross cemetery, the cemetery opened by his uncle as St. Henry parish cemetery. He was not buried in a "place of honor," but was laid to rest "with the ordinary people" between the graves of his mother and his father. When he buried his mother in 1931 he reserved that plot for his own resting place. He had come home.

The influence of the fifteen-year-old immigrant girl, who moved to the rectory in Columbia in 1863, had been completed.

CHAPTER 31

Monsignor Francis Tecklenburg: A "Maverick"

By Rev. Theodore C. Siekmann

MONSIGNOR FRANCIS TECKLENBURG, or "Father Teck," as he was invariably called, was a legend in his day, a genius, a man way ahead of his time. Francis Joseph Tecklenburg was born in Auenhausen, Germany, March 5, 1883, son of John Tecklenburg and Theresa nee Kroemke. He came to the United States as a boy of twelve, making his preparatory studies at St. Joseph College, Teutopolis, Illinois. His college and philosophy courses were taken at Quincy College, Quincy, Illinois, where he earned his B.A. and M.A. degrees. Following his theology studies at the University of Innsbruck, Austria, he was ordained to the priesthood at Brixen, Tyrol, June 29, 1906.

His first assignment was as assistant at St. Peter Cathedral in Belleville, 1906-1914. Just one year after his ordination, Father Teck founded the diocesan paper, *The Messenger* in 1907. Three years later he became a naturalized citizen.

Father Teck's first pastorate took him to Mounds City and Mounds, 1914-1919. Later he served at Mt. Vernon, 1919-1923, then at Harrisonville and Valmeyer, 1923-1926. In 1926 Father Teck was appointed pastor at St. Boniface, Evansville, where he remained until his death in 1965. He was appointed dean of the West Deanery on October 23, 1940, and named a monsignor on July 21, 1959.

From the start he was a dynamic young priest. Though by no means a climber or a man of vain ambitions, he saw in this great land, and specifically in southern Illinois an opportunity for his solid, priestly zeal, and a partial outlet for his many talents.

Unfortunately, he never reached his full potential. Not that Father Teck lacked ability; he had it in abundance. Rather, his routine work in the priesthood consumed most of his energies. He never had the luxury in his early years to be solely the scholar for which he was so richly endowed. But whenever there was a challenge open to him, he met it head-on. And all the while his innate abilities were being sharpened by a growing experience.

Father Teck was not a pious-appearing priest. He would have scoffed at the very idea. He was a good, solid, down-to-earth person, warm and gregarious, hospitable, a bit loud and raucous, humorous always, but with a sense of duty and a knack for responsibility. He liked a drink, and he could play cards until dawn. He enjoyed sports, and encouraged sports among the young. He reveled in the normal wholesome recreations and relaxations of life. When people said he was full of life, that is just what he was.

His rectory rang with the happy voices of hospitality. His faithful housekeeper, Hedwig Foerster, who was so very good to him to his dying breath, was the soul of friendliness and helpfulness to his many and frequent priest and lay friends.

Among the notable accomplishments of Father Teck was his founding of the diocesan paper, *The Messenger*, serving as the first publisher and editor of the paper. That was an example of his meeting a challenge. The time was ripe for the establishing of diocesan papers. He would not be the last, but among the first to foresee the future and value of such a publication.

Another challenge was his foray into the writing of a church history for children and young people. He and the sister in school were dissatisfied with the existing school texts in church history, especially as tools for teaching the history of the church to the children. He found the texts in use dry, uninteresting, hard to follow, and boring to the youngsters he was so eager to teach. The books in use were in striking contrast to his own, lively, enjoyable presentation.

What did he do? He met the challenge and wrote his own church history called *That Mustard Seed*. In it he traced the story of the church from its tiny beginning to its later spread all over the world —just like the mustard seed that grew into the great bush, harboring the birds of the air.

That Mustard Seed is a simple though highly informative book that is geared to young people. It is practical, and purposeful, not scholarly. Yet anyone can see that he simplified and coordinated much scholarly research and years of reading into a usable text for children and young people in school. He saw a need and he met it.

But no book could ever match his own manner of teaching history. Older people can testify now that as children they sat spellbound before him, as he made the characters of history come vividly to life, and they could never get enough of it. And so, too, was his explanation of the Bible. It was interesting. It was alive.

Monsignor Francis Tecklenburg

One did not have to be with Father Teck long to realize that he was up on everything. He was a truly educated man. Some failed to appreciate the depth of his learning because he always simplified a complex subject with his analytical mind and made even difficult concepts seem easy to grasp. He might not have sounded or seemed profound, but he really was both profound and understandable. All this was cheerfully blended with mirth and laughter and good humor.

In his declining days, he was nearly blind and could read only for short periods of time. Yet he did not stop reading and studying to the very end. Unless he had a visitor, he would be at his reading. He would read until his eyes could take it no more. Then he would lie down on the couch in the living room and rest his eyes. Then before long he was up again, poring over his book, perhaps the latest on the market, for he kept up on all the latest trends and theories.

Even after his eyesight failed completely he procured recordings and continued gathering knowledge by hearing it. He was one of the first to appreciate and use tapes.

What must be emphasized in the life of Father Teck was his avant-garde outlook on new thinking. He was deep in ecumenism and in his association with and cooperation with non-Catholic clergy, long before it was the accepted thing to do. He was way ahead of his time on matters of theology and scripture studies. While many Catholic priests, sisters, teachers, and lay people were still holding to a kind of fundamentalist, literal reading of the Bible, Father Teck was reading the latest scholarly periodicals, books, and treatises that were cautiously exploring a new and broader view of scripture interpretation and theological discovery.

I can still see the shocked expressions on the faces of the priests and hear their spontaneous outcries of disbelief. Never had they heard anything like this. Truly, Father Teck was simply ahead of his generation.

Today, the shocking new things that he described are accepted by almost everyone, supported by papal decree, and enshrined with universal approval in the decrees of Vatican Council II.

Back in Father Teck's day, it was customary for the bishop to have all the deans made monsignors. In his capacity as dean, Francis Tecklenburg was also made monsignor, though interestingly enough, after a delay of nineteen years.

After his investiture Father Teck remarked: "And to tell you the truth, I never thought I'd ever make it." He was something of a maverick and he knew it. He was an original thinker. He had definite views on everything and he never hesitated to say what he thought. If he felt something was wrong he criticized it loudly, but always with a twist of humor. He was indeed something of a maverick, but his sincerity or his loyalty could not be faulted. He thought deeply, and he spoke freely.

Father Teck died December 8, 1965, in his beloved rectory at Evansville. It was very early in the morning — 3:30 — on the Feast of the Immaculate Conception. Years before he had picked the title of Immaculate Conception for the church at Mt. Vernon.

Msgr. Francis Joseph Tecklenburg was a man of warm emotions and deep loves. He loved St. Boniface parish at Evansville. He loved every year of his pastorate — almost forty years. He loved its people. He saw the children grow up and have children, and those children have children. He was truly a patriarchal figure, a consolation for the elderly and an inspiration for the children and young people. He once told me: "You know, the parish at Evansville is tailor-made for me." This tells it beautifully. It fitted him so well. Life itself fitted him well. No one denies that he was a rare, a lovable, a remarkable priest.

CHAPTER 32

Sister Theresa Repking: Faithful Maintainer of the Ruma Tradition

By Sister Loretta Berra, ASC

GOD IS THE LORD OF HISTORY. He has plans for humanity as a whole as well as for individuals. In the pursuit of his plans, God uses people and events as his tools. These are loving plans motivated by an infinite love — plans that serve the interests of many. It was the plan of Divine Providence that led Mary Theresa Repking to heed the words of Isaiah (45:4-6);

I have called you by your name, giving you a title, though you knew me not . . .
It is I who arm you, though you know me not.

In central Illinois, near Effingham, lies the village of Bishop Creek, the birthplace of Mary Theresa Repking. She was born July 23, 1857, in this rural area where her father farmed.

Mother Mary Theresa's life was like a puzzle consisting of many pieces, plots, and plans, challenging and difficult to put together at times. She spent her years in religious life, developing and maintaining the apostolic works begun by Mother Clementine Zerr in convents in Illinois, Missouri, Kansas, and Nebraska. Her faithful service ensured a lasting foundation for the future of the community. Her spiritual life and experiences were also like the puzzle, consisting of highs and lows, starts and stops. She trusted in her faith experiences in order to have a meaningful relationship with God and all with whom she came in contact. Her love of God was evident to everyone, especially her sisters. Mary Theresa was the first young lady from her village to enter religious life. Because of government suppression during the Franco-Prussian War, a band of Precious Blood sisters and novices came from Gurtweil, Germany, in 1870. They resided in St. Agatha Convent in St. Louis. Sister Clementine Zerr and novices moved to Belle Prairie (Piopolis), Illinois in 1873.

These young sisters placed their total trust in Sister Clementine Zerr as their leader. Their ardent zeal for the welfare of their little community prepared them for any kind of labor, and their efforts in surmounting the numerous hardships they encountered were unfaltering.

Mother Mary Theresa Repking, ASC

Mary Theresa entered the postulancy of the Sisters of the Precious Blood on July 23, 1873, and received the religious habit at St. Agatha's. One year later, she and five German-American sisters and a young immigrant were professed.

The parishioners at Belle Prairie loved the sisters and generously offered them a home and some adjacent land for the construction of a motherhouse. But permanent residence in Belle Prairie presented problems. The isolation of the area made the establishment of a motherhouse there impractical.

In August 1876 Mary Theresa Repking was one of ten professed sisters who left Piopolis with Mother Clementine Zerr for an abandoned college and twenty-six acres of land in Ruma. They found acres of uncultivated ground with overgrown, tangled brush, weeds, and briars.

Through their efforts it was later to assume a simple loveliness and repose and became a haven of rustic beauty for the "Ruma sisters."

Mary Theresa's background from the rural environment of Bishop Creek was an asset to this community living in primitive conditions. She had learned some carpentry from her father and displayed skill in it. The sisters improvised ways to produce what they needed; they abounded in creative ideas. During these years, the sisters bravely faced and endured many hardships. To the sting of poverty was added intense anxiety caused by a fever which affected some of the sisters during their first summer. They were too poor to obtain medical care.

Their meals were frugal. Breakfast consisted of thin soup, a piece of black bread, and coffee made from acorns or roasted wheat. Lunch was a vegetable soup made from greens, black bread, and coffee. Thin soup made from cornmeal, a bit of cornbread, and coffee constituted the evening meal.

James O'Hara, a neighbor, often shared the fruits from his orchards, which helped to solve some of the sisters' economic problems.

Frequently the sisters were unable to sleep at night because of hunger, but they tenaciously clung to the duty they recognized as theirs — to lay a lasting foundation for their community.

Sister Mary Theresa, recognized as a capable young teacher and an excellent organizer, was sent to found one school after another during the fourteen years between her profession and her appointment as director of novices. The schools she founded are still in operation today at St. Mary, Chester; St. Rose, St. Rose; St. Clare, O'Fallon, and St. Cecilia, Bartelso.

As director of novices, she had an excellent rapport with the novices and sisters. She was regarded with great respect, sometimes feared, but deeply loved because of her motherly consideration.

During these years, St. Clement Hospital in Red Bud was under construction. Although St. Clement's originally was planned to serve the aged and infirm sisters, it soon attracted the attention of doctors and the public. Because of the pressing demand to admit patients, more provisions were made for medical care.

At St. Clement's completion, Sister Mary Theresa was assigned to the hospital staff as superior. She also gladly undertook the duties of nurse and gardener. Since the garden furnished much of the food for the hospital, she was seen in the garden early in the morning before the sisters rose for prayer. The financial accounts she kept in her characteristically neat handwriting are still extant.

Mother Mary Theresa Repking assumed the responsibility of vicaress for the Ruma Convent in 1906 and remained in office sixteen years to serve about 150 sisters. To the sisters she was "Mother Mary," an endearing title because of her calm, peaceful personality. The sisters revered her for her motherly qualities and she was their trusted counselor.

Mother Mary Theresa lacked the initiative and daring confidence of her predecessor to continue the expansion and progress of the vicariate. She was the type of person who clung to tradition and pioneer times. She spent most of her years adjusting the internal affairs of the vicariate to catch up with the pace of her predecessor's expansion. She was more like a mother to the sisters than an administrator. Mother Mary Theresa's caring qualities were demonstrated in the following excerpt from a letter to her sisters:

"As writing day is near [she was accustomed to write to them on the fourteenth of each month], I will now have a little chat with you. I must state I am well pleased with the information I received through your letters. Let it be good or bad, anything that befalls you arouses my sympathy. What interests you also interests me. I feel for every one of you. It hurts me to the bottom of my heart that some of you have to go to school or work so much whilst you feel so bad. I am glad for all of you that vacation is so near. Let us hope you will rest and gain new strength, bodily and spiritually."

In her first year as vicaress, she was sent to St. Teresa Academy, East St. Louis, as superior to resolve existing problems. The chaplain often stood in for her as the acting administrator.

During 1905 and 1906 the aging Mother Clementine Zerr, then in Wichita, Kansas, left Mother Mary Theresa in charge in Ruma. She struggled with the plans for a new hospital in Taylorville, Illinois, which the people were clamoring for. Her reluctance and apprehension were born of tightened finances and lack of personnel. Despite her resistance to the project, the citizens of Taylorville continued their efforts for the construction and the hospital to this day serves the Christian County area, a monument to their concern for the sick and aged. St. Vincent Memorial Hospital has been staffed by the Adorers of the Blood of Christ since its opening in 1906.

Mother Mary Theresa realized the importance of education. She herself was an experienced teacher and principal and had held a state teacher's certificate as early as 1885. Circumstances made it difficult for her to provide systematically organized summer school for the sisters. Pastors demanded the sisters' services during summer months, and accommodations at the motherhouse were inadequate.

She encouraged the young sisters to study hard and to pass the county examinations for certification. Those who could spent the summer months at Ruma or at St. Teresa Academy, East St. Louis, studying. But in her staunch traditionalism, Mother Mary Theresa failed to take the necessary steps to meet the demands of the rising standards for the education of the sisters. It would devolve on her successor, Mother Veronica Baumgart, to intensify the Ruma sisters' professional preparation.

Financial affairs of the vicariate, construction of a new motherhouse, education of the sisters, and other problems confronted this tired and aging vicaress. In 1922 after sixteen years of service, Mother Mary Theresa was released from her office. Like her beloved model, Mother Clementine Zerr, upon leaving Ruma, she became superior of St. John Academy, staffed by the Precious Blood sisters in Wichita, Kansas. When the division of the Ruma vicariate was made in 1929, Mother Mary Theresa expressed her desire to remain in the Wichita Province. She was assigned to St. Francis Xavier Hospital in Carlsbad, New Mexico, where she spent the rest of her long life as the superior and later as a member of the religious community. She died on February 6, 1935.

There is a quiet peace about her grave at the Adorers' Provincialate in Wichita, a peace characteristic of her whole religious life. Her final farewell to the sisters attending her bedside reveals her joyful faith. "Adieu," she whispered calmly, "until the happy reunion in heaven. What a joyful meeting it will be." So, the puzzle of Mother Mary Theresa's life was completed.

CHAPTER 33

Marianist Presence in the Diocese

By Brother Leo Willett, SM

THE MARIANIST EDUCATION APOSTOLATE in southern Illinois can be traced back eighty-one years to the arrival of the first Brothers of Mary in Belleville. The efforts of talented Marianists, like Brothers Charles Aul in Belleville and Albert Kaiser in East St. Louis, laid the foundation for outreach that has touched thousands of lives since the turn of the century.

The Marianists were founded in 1817 by Father William Joseph Chaminade at Bordeaux, France. Its members strive to form a single family in serving God's people under the motto, "Through the Mother, to the Son." The first Brothers of Mary arrived in the United States in 1849, and the brothers were indirectly associated with the Church in southern Illinois from the very start.

Originally, it had been decided that Marianist Father Leo Meyer and Brother Charles Schultz were to serve in Cincinnati, but they were unable to reach their mission because of a cholera epidemic which was especially severe in southern Ohio. Cincinnati's Bishop John B. Purcell asked Father Meyer to assist at the German-speaking Emmanuel Church in Dayton, Ohio. The pastor of Emmanuel Church was Father Henry Juncker, who became the first bishop of Alton in 1857.

Forty-eight years later, Father George Meyer, provincial of the Society of Mary with headquarters at Dayton, accepted a new school in Belleville, Illinois. Brothers Charles Aul, Philip Fink, and Thomas Seebald were welcomed on September 1, 1905, upon their arrival in Belleville cathedral parish by Bishop John Janssen and the rector of the Cathedral of St. Peter, Very Rev. Henry Hagen.

Brother Charles Aul

Brother Albert Kaiser

These first Brothers of Mary in Belleville taught cathedral boys from grade four through grade eight and they also began a two-year commercial high school. Classes began September 6, 1905, with 129 students in attendance.

The man in charge of this pioneer venture was Brother Charles Aul, who was born in Pittsburgh, Pennsylvania, in 1866. After professing first vows in 1883 Brother Charles taught in Ohio for two years. He was then sent to teach in Paris and later in Spain. It is no wonder that he would be described as an "accomplished linguist," who had mastered German, French, and Spanish.

Upon returning to the United States, he served as both teacher and administrator before joining the team of brothers who established the Marianist presence in southern Illinois. Brother Charles was principal at Belleville from 1905 to 1910. He headed schools at Dyersville, Iowa, and Winnipeg, Manitoba, before he requested a teaching position at St. Mary College, San Antonio, Texas. He died there on July 29, 1920, after enduring a long battle with cancer, at the age of fifty-five.

Brother Charles' biographer noted, "He was every inch a gentleman in costume, bearing, speech and attitude. He was an ideal religious. There was distinction in him in every way. As director, he was firm, just, patient, and gentle and he set the example of what he expected from his fellow Brothers."

Eventually, the School Sisters of Notre Dame took over the lower grades and in 1923 Msgr. Joseph Schlarman announced the organization of a regular four-year high school under the direction of the Marianists. Eleven young men made up the class of 1927, Cathedral

High School's first graduating class.

During the Great Depression, Cathedral High faced serious financial difficulties since the tuition-free school was supported solely by cathedral parish. However, in the early 1940s, Cathedral became more and more an area school. A tuition program began and the school grew.

In 1962 diocesan officials decided to build Althoff Catholic High School, which would absorb the students from Cathedral High School. The Marianists were offered the administration, but declined, due to the numbers of brothers available to teach in Belleville. School records show that 1,822 students graduated from Cathedral High School.

Reflecting on the withdrawal of the brothers from Belleville, Bishop Albert Zuroweste, commented, "During these years, the brothers have rendered invaluable service to Cathedral parish and the entire city of Belleville. They have educated thousands of Catholic boys during these years and have won the gratitude and affection of the bishop and the people of Belleville."

On the eve of the Great Depression, Bishop Henry Althoff extended his blessing and welcome to three Marianists, who were sent by their provincial, Father Joseph C. Ei, to establish Central Catholic High School in East St. Louis. This group of Brothers of Mary included Brothers John Kessler and Louis Meinhardt and was directed by Brother Albert Kaiser.

A native of Baltimore, Brother Albert professed first vows in 1878. He attended Stanislaus College in Paris and had his first teaching assignments in Switzerland. In 1892 he introduced the Marianists to St. Aloysius parish, Chicago, and remained there as principal until 1908, when he took an active part in the creation of the St. Louis Province of the Society of Mary. At the provincial level, he served as treasurer from 1908 to 1916, while directing various St. Louis area Marianist schools. Before coming to East St. Louis he was principal in Dyersville and Chicago. Brother Albert directed that first year of Central Catholic's existence when classes were held at Wabasha and St. Clair avenues in a remodeled storefront.

On September 4, 1929, after the opening day Mass at Sacred Heart Church, the seventy-four students, faculty, and staff walked to the school which was then blessed by Msgr. Charles Gilmartin. The following year the growing enrollment necessitated a move to the former St. Patrick school at Sixth Street and Illinois Avenue. Remodeling progressed slowly, but the brothers transferred to the new location on October 9, 1931, and conducted classes although the renovation work was not completed until February 1932.

Brother Louis Meinhardt was among the three pioneers of Central

Catholic, remaining there until 1937. From 1933 to 1937, Brother Louis served as the school's third principal. He returned to direct the school again from 1948 to 1952. He is remembered for his firmness as a teacher and athletic coach.

For a number of years Brother Louis has been a part of the Marianist community at Chaminade College Preparatory school, Creve Coeur, Missouri. Since 1981 this Central pioneer has served as a full-day volunteer, four days a week at St. John Mercy Hospital, St. Louis. He was eighty-four years old on September 1, 1986.

During the twenty-four years which followed that first school day in East St. Louis, when the school was conducted by Brothers Albert, Louis and John Kessler, Central Catholic was characterized by steady increases of student enrollment. By 1943 the Marianist community grew to twelve to help staff the school along with lay teachers and diocesan clergy. At that time, the annual salary of the religious also increased from the original $300 to $750.

The Belleville diocese purchased a tract of land at the intersection of routes 50 and 111 where it planned to construct a new Catholic high school. Groundbreaking ceremonies were held April 13, 1951, and within two years, Brother Leo Rothermich, principal, led the faculty and students in the move from the old Central Catholic High School to the new Assumption High School. Later expansion enabled this facility to accommodate up to 1,000 youths.

Assumption High School was consolidated in 1974 with St. Teresa Academy, an East St. Louis Catholic girls' school directed by the Ruma Province of the Adorers of the Blood of Christ. Brother Eugene Meyerpeter served as the first executive director of the coeducational school.

Throughout its fifty-six-year history, Central Catholic/Assumption has had the whole-hearted support of the Province of St. Louis Society of Mary. This was strongly expressed by the provincial chapter of 1984, which decided to make a five-year grant of $20,000 annually for tuition assistance to the school. The chapter expressed a desire to continue collaborating with the mission of the Church in East St. Louis, "the most important effort in our province directed to the black community."

As of September 1985, the Assumption Marianist community numbered twelve members who ministered at Assumption High School, Vincent Gray Alternative High School, and the Marianist House of Prayer.

The Marianists are involved in a special outreach through the Vincent Gray Alternative High School, which operates out of the former St. Adalbert rectory at 705 Summit Ave. In 1980 the provincial chapter approved the opening of this alternative school for high school dropouts. The school honors the memory of Brother Vincent Gray, a black Marianist who taught in the St. Louis area before he died at the age of thirty-eight in 1967.

The philosophy of Vincent Gray Alternative High School is to provide an opportunity to high school dropouts to acquire academic skills, vocational experience and spiritual and social traits necessary for self-esteem and the power to contribute to a better society.

The three members of the Marianist House of Prayer belong to the Assumption Marianist community and pledge themselves to pray two extra hours each day in addition to the prayers of the Marianist rule. They remember all the members and apostolic works of the St. Louis Province, the church's ministry in East St. Louis, and the intentions of the people throughout the Belleville diocese.

Those active in the House of Prayer are also involved in spiritual direction, retreat work and chaplaincy work.

Father Chaminade had envisioned a comprehensive "Family of Mary" when he founded the Marianist sisters and brothers. One extension of this vision is the Marianist affiliates, a community of clergy and laity who form a spiritual union with the Marianists according to their individual states of life. The Metro-East affiliates meet monthly at Assumption High School.

This far-reaching ministry, affecting thousands of lives, came about as unassuming men like Charles Aul and Albert Kaiser planted seeds of the Marianist presence in southern Illinois. The late Brother Gerald Schnepp's *Province of St. Louis 1908-1983* provides additional information on the Society of Mary.

CHAPTER 34

Monsignor Andrew Janiszewski: Polish Immigrants' "Good Shepherd"

By Stanley J. Konieczny

MSGR. ANDREW JANISZEWSKI'S MINISTRY among Polish immigrants in southern Illinois aptly reflected Christ's image of the Good Shepherd. His thirty years in the priesthood demonstrated a pastoral concern for the total person.

An immigrant himself, Monsignor Janiszewski indeed knew his people and their specific needs. He could empathize with them and acting on his firsthand knowledge of their circumstances, he set out to meet both their spiritual and physical needs. This immigrant pastor spent himself helping his flock fit into the mainstream of American life while preparing for their entry into eternal life.

Andrew Janiszewski, the son of Adalbert and Josephine Szulgitow Janiszewski, was born November 20, 1869, in the town of Lubstowek, which was located in Poland's western province of Poznan. His uncle, Bishop John Chrysostom Janiszewski, had been imprisoned for the faith during Bismarck's Kulturkampf.

In his youth, Andrew studied for two years at Poznan's St. Magdalen Gymnasium or high school. At age seventeen he emigrated to the United States. Entering Ss. Cyril and Methodius Seminary in Detroit, he completed his secondary schooling as well as his philosophy and theology studies. Father Andrew Janiszewski was ordained by Detroit's Bishop John Foley on July 1, 1900, and shortly after ordination day he celebrated his first Mass at Our Lady of Perpetual Help church in Chicago.

July 1900 brought Father Janiszewski his first challenge in ministering to the Church in southern Illinois. The newly ordained priest was assigned as the substitute pastor at St. Mary Magdalen parish, Todd's Mill, for five months. He then spent one year as associate pastor of Ss.

Peter and Paul parish, Waterloo.

At the turn of the century, Bishop John Janssen decided that another church was needed in south-central Washington County. The Polish farmers, who settled this area more than twenty years earlier, had to travel to DuBois or Radom in order to worship. With the enthusiasm of a pioneer pastor, Father Janiszewski accepted the bishop's assignment. The young priest not only founded Our Lady of Perpetual Help parish, but named the small village Posen, in honor of the fertile Polish province where he was raised.

Monsignor Andrew Janiszewski

His former classmate, the late Msgr. Joseph Ceranski, pastor of DuBois, would later recall, "At Posen, it was a life of self-sacrifice and he [Father Janiszewski] even performed hard manual labor."

Upon arriving at the farm settlement in October 1901 Father Janiszewski worked right beside his parishioners in laying foundations for Posen's first church, school, and rectory which would be located on a 140-acre tract of land donated by Martin Gryna. In these early days, he would use the home of Joseph Kitowski for his headquarters.

The first parish school was opened in 1901 and Father Janiszewski arranged for Franciscan sisters to teach in Posen. Our Lady of Perpetual Help school grew and in 1904 he headed the drive to build a new two-story frame structure which served as both a school and convent. Prior to his assignment in Posen, Bishop Janssen had asked Father Janiszewski to study the feasibility of creating a parish for Polish-speaking Catholics in East St. Louis. The twenty-fifth anniversary history of the former St. Adalbert parish, East St. Louis, noted that since he was unfamiliar with the area, Father Janiszewski relied on the opinion of certain people. These "advisors" assured the priest that there were only ten Polish families in East St. Louis and there was no need for such a national parish.

Father Janiszewski reported his "findings" to the bishop and the matter was dropped, until two years later, when a young priest at St. Casimir church in St. Louis, Father Simon Zielinski, was called to bring the sacraments of the sick to a young Polish girl in East St. Louis. Father Zielinski recognized the serious need for a Polish-speaking priest in the city.

With Bishop Janssen's approval, Father Julian Moczydlowski from St. Stanislaus Kostka church, St. Louis, began to minister to the fifty families and fifty single men who, at that time, made up East St. Louis' Polish community. These original members of St. Adalbert parish met in St. Henry's parish hall every Sunday morning at seven o'clock in order to worship and celebrate together in their vernacular. The Knights of Columbus eventually sold the diocese their former hall on Summit Avenue and these immigrants' dream for a home parish, St. Adalbert church, became a reality.

In an ironic twist which might point to a divine sense of humor, Father Andrew Janiszewski became the second resident pastor of St. Adalbert parish in 1907. The people of St. Adalbert's would come to see Father Janiszewski as a godsend. Under his administration, the parish prospered and the pastor became a special champion of his people.

The early weeks and months after his arrival in East St. Louis were marked by the enterprise and determination which characterized Father Janiszewski's twenty-year pastorate at St. Adalbert's. He immediately had the church repainted and repaired. By the fall of 1907 St. Adalbert school opened its doors to forty-eight children.

At first, Franciscan Sisters of St. Cunegunda conducted classes in Polish and English in makeshift basement classrooms. As the parish debt decreased St. Adalbert school grew. First a two-room school was built in 1915. Five years later, a nearby residence was purchased and renovated to accommodate the growing student body.

There was a certain vibrance in the parish since the influx of immigrants meant parish growth for St. Adalbert's. Yet these people faced special challenges in American society, and like immigrant Catholics across the country, they turned to their parish priest for help. Father Janiszewski served as a buffer between his parishioners and society. "He acted here for his people as an interpreter and defender in matters pertaining to their temporal welfare," Monsignor Ceranski remarked about Father Janiszewski. "To stamp out various abuses, he was constrained to use drastic methods but it was in a spirit of charity. Due to his efforts, today eighty-five percent of the parishioners own their own homes," Monsignor Ceranski commented in 1930.

Father Andrew Janiszewski wore many hats as pastor of St. Adalbert parish. In addition to serving as spiritual advisor, he acted as an interpreter whenever his Polish-speaking parishioners entered any contract that they could not read or when they were involved in any litigation.

He was the financial advisor of the parish. Single men would turn over most of their paychecks to their pastor, who banked the money and insured that dubious saloons or gamblers would not take advantage of his younger, vulnerable parishioners. When these young men would bring their fiancees to the rectory for marriage instructions, they would receive a nest egg for their new life together, which they had saved with Father Janiszewski.

The pastor of St. Adalbert's is often remembered for his constant encouragement of the Polish immigrants to improve their lives. He urged his congregation to buy their own homes, operating on the premise that home ownership would bring a certain stability and pride to the immigrant neighborhood which sprung up around St. Adalbert church.

Father Janiszewski offered his counsel, encouragement and support when some of his parishioners were exploring the opportunity of opening their own meat packing business, the former Circle Packing Company. "Father Janiszewski encouraged them that it was a good idea, and when they started he blessed their building, a duplex on Winstanley Avenue," recalls Edmund Kubicki, former president of Circle Packing and son of one of Circle's founders.

Father Raymond Malec, whose father was also involved in the organization of Circle Packing in 1919, commented, "Father Janiszewski was the impetus behind the packing company. He saw that his people had to do something to make money."

While the pastor of St. Adalbert's grew in confidence and respect with the Polish American community in East St. Louis, he also assumed various responsible positions of service to the Belleville diocese. Father Janiszewski had been named a diocesan consultor, a member of the council on vigilance and the board of examiners of the clergy.

This life of service was recognized in 1912 when Father Janiszewski was given the title of monsignor by Pope Benedict XV. The official announcement noted that Bishop Henry Althoff had recommended the East St. Louis pastor for this honor in recognition of his ministry to people of Polish extraction. At Monsignor Janiszewski's investiture, the homilist, Father Simon Zielinski noted, "A priest by consecration and an American citizen by adoption and a Pole by birth, these are the ideals for which Monsignor Janiszewski has lived and labored."

St. Adalbert parish continued to grow until it became one of the largest Catholic communities in East St. Louis. Diabetes, though, robbed the pastor of his health and vigor. In 1928 Monsignor Janiszewski was forced to resign his pastorate. He returned once to old St. Adalbert church and in a very poignant liturgy, the nearly blind pastor groped his way through the sanctuary to the pulpit where he delivered his farewell homily. The monsignor spent most of his last two years under the care of the Hospital Sisters of the Third Order of St. Francis at St. Elizabeth Hospital, Belleville.

His struggle ended May 5, 1930. Bishop Althoff celebrated the funeral liturgy and gravesite services were conducted by Monsignor Janiszewski's nephew, Father Anthony Zielinski. Msgr. Andrew Janiszewski was buried at the top of the hill at St. Adalbert cemetery, which he established for his people in Fairview Heights.

CHAPTER 35

Sister Alma Juengling: Motherly Care for Orphans

By Sister Catherine Lampe, PHJC

SISTER ALMA JUENGLING, PHJC, might never be accorded a place in the Hall of Fame but she does have a place in the hearts of hundreds of people in the Belleville diocese. She gave almost all of her religious life to the service of St. John's Orphanage. Her name is indelibly linked with the baby house of the children's home, for it was here that she ministered to the wee folk for over forty years.

St. John's Orphanage was an outgrowth of St. Agnes Children's Asylum which in the late 1880s housed approximately forty orphans when the Belleville diocese was part of the former Alton diocese. The asylum was located on the corner of South and Third streets where St. Elizabeth's Hospital now stands. The Franciscan sisters were in charge of the children's home.

When the Belleville diocese was established, even a casual observation on the part of the authorities gave them to understand that the orphan asylum was inadequate for the needs of so many children. Something had to be done, purchased, built. Speculations focused on what was then known as the beautiful Morrison mansion at "Glen Addie," whose history and description is a chapter in itself.

The original tract on which the August Morrison mansion had been built encompassed 640 acres. The mansion and forty surrounding acres became a single unit apart from the rest of the land area. This unit was purchased in 1900 by Bishop Janssen for the purpose of converting it to the orphans' needs. It did not take long to reconstruct the elegant building for this purpose. After an official opening, forty-three children were transferred from St. Agnes Asylum to St. John's Orphanage. The Poor Handmaids of Jesus Christ were placed in charge. Renovations and improvements were constantly in order. In 1902 it was decided to house the infants separately.

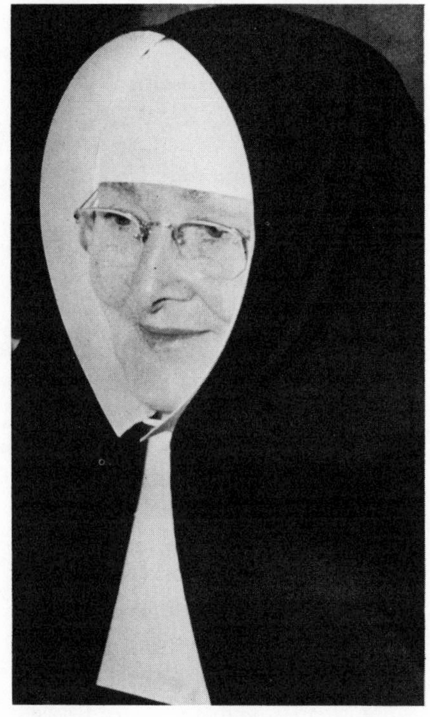

Sister Alma Juengling, PHJC

The onetime servants' quarters to the rear of the mansion seemed appropriate. When completed it would boast an addition of a dormitory, a playroom, and a bathroom for the babies — more correctly, the pre-school children.

This was the setting for Sister Alma's part in the history of St. John's. She did not come on the stage until 1909, but her intensely enduring part in the drama from then on left a mark on hundreds of her charges and their future children and grandchildren. Documents in the Ancilla Domini archives state it briefly:

"February 8, 1909, Sister Alma came to St. John's as the twelfth Sister."

Sister Alma was born on February 15, 1887, in Columbia, Illinois, the daughter of Carl and Catherine (nee Nuers) Juengling. Five days later she was taken to the Immaculate Conception Church for baptism and received the name Maria Louisa. Her mother died when Louisa was very young and the care of rearing the family fell to the father. Though not a Catholic, Carl Juengling took the responsibility of his children's Catholic education very seriously. Sister Alma would relate the story that every Sunday before she and her brothers set out for Mass, he kept a dress review: "All cleaned up? Clothes brushed? Shoes shined? Nothing showing that should not show?" It was not just a matter of: "Do you have a prayer book and a rosary?" The adoration of God and Carl Juengling's promises demanded that the ordinary things of life be geared in the right direction.

We do not know just what it was that impelled Louisa Juengling to choose the religious life as her vocation. The Poor Handmaids of Jesus Christ were in charge of the Catholic school and home nursing care in Columbia during the early part of the 1890s. There is mention in the sisters' chronicle of that period about a Sister Thais, who may have been the superior. The chronicle simply states: "April 18, 1906: (Sister

Thais accompanied Miss Louisa Juengling to the Motherhouse in Fort Wayne, Indiana.'') Louisa became a postulant. Another act in the drama of life had begun.

On February 4, 1909 she made her first profession of vows. Five days later she came to St. John's and assumed the responsibility of the ''baby house.'' The assignment was challenging for one so young.

From day to day, hour to hour, it meant having to meet the needs of twenty, thirty, sometimes forty little people. While the original setting of St. John's mirrored the name ''mansion,'' there was little mansion glory reflected in the four walls of Sister Alma's work-a-day world. From 1909 to 1951 she shared a small corner of the children's dormitory for her nightly rest. That rest was frequently interrupted by a whimper, a cry, a sob of a child's discomfort.

Many times the warmth and snugness of Sister Alma's arms provided the love and assurance that all was well. ''You are all angels,'' was an oft-repeated phrase of hers. She had the help of some of the older girls so that her own physical and spiritual needs could be provided for. There were times, too, when another sister would be called in to share the burden. The necessities of food, clothing and shelter were provided for, but the ''over and above'' were long in coming.

Running water was a luxury. Father Arthur Niemeyer in his *History of St. John's* writes ''. . .in those early days water was carried from wells and cisterns to do the washing. The sisters would rise early in the morning to do the washing over scrub boards, working by the light of kerosene lamps and lanterns. All of this was done before the children demanded their attention.''

Bishop Albert R. Zuroweste, who was superintendent at St. John's for some years, said in an editorial tribute at the time of Sister Alma's death, ''. . .alone, to do most of the work, Sister Alma never complained because she had to do the laundry over a hot stove. Nor did she become impatient when the cold winds froze the washing on the line outside.'' As late as 1926 a laundry improvement became a reality and made possible the washing of the babies' clothes by simpler means. Until then it had to be done by hand each day.

The water supply was only one of the many inconveniences that faced Sister Alma in caring for her brood of little ones. There was the year-round possibility of children's diseases; tonsil removal ''en masse'' was practically an annual occurrence. The surgical part would be taken care of in a nearby hospital, but the care of the post-surgical traumas fell to the mercy of Sister Alma. There were contagious diseases to contend with and then she or another sister would be isolated for weeks. Wrapped up with all of this were the tears caused by countless cuts, scratches, and bruises of childhood. Regardless of how bad the mishap or accident, sister always knew how to bind and heal.

Hers was the daily round of supplying the necessary apparel for everyone, from the buttons on the underwear to the ribbon in the hair. Her kindness and forethought had a way of seeping in to all around her. It is said that the orphanage pony got the notion that he was in on the deal; he learned how to nuzzle the doorknob of the baby house and expected his daily handout.

Her health was not always good and from very early days at the orphanage she suffered from severe foot trouble, so much so that there is frequent mention of hospitalization because of it. Other health deficiencies became apparent but nothing daunted Sister Alma from the care of her "first love," as she affectionately called her little charges.

In the early 1950s St. John's took on a more modern appearance. Old buildings were razed so that new ones could replace them. So it was that an up-to-date infants' cottage with all its ramifications came into being. Sister Alma experienced the thrill of the new surroundings for a brief time, then graciously yielded to others what had been denied to her.

In 1952 she gave up her responsibilty of the nursery and took on nursing care for both children and adults. It may be assumed that many a youngster feigned a mishap of some sort just to get her motherly attention, the smile, the pressure of her hand, the "love you" in her eyes.

On February 7, 1959, she celebrated her golden jubilee of her first profession. The high point of the celebration was the Pontifical High Mass by Bishop Zuroweste. Many relatives, friends and former proteges came for this occasion. There was a repeat of this kind when she observed her eightieth birthday and again when she took her final leave from St. John's in 1970.

It is said by many who knew her that she had a remarkable memory. At the above-mentioned occasions and at other times she recalled the names and faces of countless of her "former babies." Often, too, there was a pertinent story that emerged from her "I remember when . . . ." In 1970 she retired to the Catherine Kasper Home, the community's home for retired sisters. Her life of devotion and concern for others continued in the few years that were left to her

She died December 23, 1973. To the words of Bishop Zuroweste, we would all agree: "Sister Alma was a spiritual giant. We are all a little closer to God because she passed by and touched our lives."

CHAPTER 36

Brother Eugene Frank: Martyred Missioner

By Father John Vogelgesang, SVD

NEW GUINEA IN 1929 was not the familiar, almost household term that it became less than two decades later during World War II. Most people, if they knew anything at all about New Guinea, knew only that it was an island somewhere in the South Pacific; an island inhabited by sundry Stone Age tribes frequently at war with one another. Indeed, New Guinea was "the land that time forgot." To that remote forgotten land Brother Eugene Frank was missioned in September 1929.

Anton Frank, the future Brother Eugene, was born at Mount Carmel on December 21, 1900, the fifth of eight children of Anton and Louisa Frank. One of his brothers became a Passionist priest and missionary to China. Anton attended St. Mary's school in Mount Carmel, though, according to the sisters who taught there, he was "a difficult boy — hating his lessons — a tough kid only too willing to prove his toughness on the playground."

Nevertheless when he graduated, Anton felt attracted to the priesthood and studied for a while with the Precious Blood fathers. Later he spent three months with the Trappists in Gethsemani, Kentucky, but found the vigorous regimen of the monks too severe for his frail health. Back home again he worked as a carpenter and cabinet-maker. Still he was restless and unhappy; the call to the religious life did not go away.

One day he came across an appeal for missionary brothers and the thought came to him that perhaps if he started out as a brother he could later shift more easily to studies for the priesthood. So he answered the advertisement and on August 31, 1921, entered St. Mary's Mission House as a candidate for the missionary brotherhood in the Society of the Divine Word.

Brother Eugene Frank

St. Mary's Mission House, Techny, Illinois, was the American headquarters of the Society of the Divine Word, a religious missionary community of priests and brothers founded in 1875 by Father Arnold Janssen at Steyl, Holland, to recruit and train missionaries for the foreign missions. The society's first permanent foundation in the United States was made at Techny, Illinois, where in 1900 a technical school for boys was opened. In 1909 the technical school was phased out and a seminary for the training of missionary priests and brothers took its place. So when Anton Frank entered on August 31, 1921, he was a candidate for the missionary brotherhood. He began his novitiate on July 2, 1922, received the name Eugene, and made his first profession of vows on May 1, 1924.

When he entered Techny, Brother Eugene was assigned to work in the bakery. He became adept at baking bread — especially the whole wheat bread for which the seminary was famous — and at making pies, cakes, and other pastries. In November 1924 Eugene was transferred to Sacred Heart Mission Seminary in Girard, Pennsylvania, where he was put in charge of the bakery, a position he held for the next five years. Baking, however, was not Eugene's idea of apostolic missionary work. He requested an assignment to the foreign missions and was delighted when in 1929 his request was granted. He was assigned to the island of New Guinea, where the Society of the Divine Word had been working since 1896. Brother Eugene departed for his mission on September 29, 1929.

In New Guinea, Brother Eugene was stationed first in Alexishafen along the seacoast where he was put in charge of an extensive coconut plantation. This assignment involved not only the care and cultivation of the coconut trees, but also the harvesting of the nuts and the drying of the copra. In this latter task, his years of experience in the bakeries of Techny and Girard came into play. He did not dry the copra in the sun; he dried it in ovens. The end result was copra of an excellent quality.

The dehydrated coconut was much in demand by the bakers and confectioners of Australia, where seventy-five tons of the copra was shipped each month.

Nevertheless, Brother Eugene longed to become involved in more basic missionary work. He was overjoyed, therefore, when he was chosen in 1934 to accompany Father William Ross, SVD, on his expedition to the Whagi Valley for the purpose of establishing the first mission stations there. Many of the tribes in the area had never seen a white man. The Mount Hagen area was all virgin mission territory.

To his family in Mount Carmel, Brother Eugene wrote: "Hip, hip, hurray!. . . Our destination is Mount Hagen. It's about 13,000 feet high. That the good bishop has appointed me to work in the interior of our vicariate, among the wilds and cannibals, makes me feel very happy. Thousands of natives are there, some fifty to sixty thousand. We will take over a hundred young men as carriers, and enough food for a year. . . . Am happy and healthy as ever."

It is noteworthy that Brother Eugene, who found the strict routine of the Trappists, more than he could take, was blessed with such good health in the tropics. He never contracted malaria. He slept soundly, had a good appetite and was an indefatigable worker. Perhaps the very variety of his work contributed to his happiness and good health. One of the first things he and Father Ross did on their arrival in the new mission of Wilya was to plant gardens to insure an adequate food supply for themselves and their native helpers. Various kinds of beans, wild corn, and sweet potatoes thrived in their garden beds. In addition they planted brussels sprouts, a variety of other edible greens, bananas, sugar cane, Irish potatoes, peanuts, carrots, cabbages, and celery.

Besides, in these new stations, Eugene could put his building skills to excellent use. In quick succession he built a missionaries' residence, church, kitchen, workers' quarters, poultry house, and pigpen. From June to September 1934 he built not only the main station but also nine outstations. The natives supplied the necessary materials: kunai grass, treebark rope, and wild sugar cane for walls. Eugene was rightfully proud of his accomplishments and looked forward to the day when he could build the first Catholic school in the Hagen territory. As he was setting out on what was to be his final trek, his last words to Father Ross were: "Father, please do not build that school until I get back. I really want to have the privilege — the first Catholic school in the western highlands." But Brother Eugene never got back.

Father Ross and Brother Eugene celebrated Christmas of 1934 together at Hagen, unaware that on December sixteen natives in the Chimbu district had killed Father Karl Morschheuser. Brother Eugene planned to leave Hagen soon after Christmas to hike to Bundi to meet some fellow missionaries and to make his annual spiritual retreat. On January 2, 1935, he left Mount Hagen with fifteen carriers. Six days later he reached Mingende where he learned about Father Morschheuser's death.

Although friendly natives warned Brother Eugene not to pass through the Chimbus River district, he felt he would be in no danger and was determined to go ahead. However, he did take certain precautions. As required by law he armed his little party with five shotguns, one small .22 caliber rifle, one revolver, and a small supply of ammunition. And so, trusting in the Lord's protection, the little party set out again on January 7. The first indication of impending trouble came when Chimbu tribesmen volunteered to help carry the cargo, and promptly vanished with their parcels in the tall kunai grass, only to reappear moments later with more tribesmen all fully armed, some even carrying their war shields.

The Chimbus attacked twice. In the first skirmish no one was wounded, but in the second encounter several were, including Brother Eugene, who received a total of eight arrow wounds, mostly in the chest and back. Most serious was the wound caused when a native crept up behind him as he knelt in the kunai grass and thrust an arrow into his back so deep that the right lung was perforated. When the attack ended, sympathetic natives carried Brother Eugene and two of his boys into a nearby hut where they were cared for in the native manner. For Brother Eugene this was the beginning of a long week of agonizing pain.

The Chimbu tribesmen had robbed Eugene of all his possessions — his clothing, his watch, and his revolver. When brought in he was clad only in a pair of short khaki trousers. Banana leaf bandages were applied to his wounds and tied with vines to hold them in place. From time to time he was fed an occasional roasted sweet potato or roasted banana. He drank a lot of water or sometimes sugar cane juice. As a result his abdomen became bloated, causing him such pain that he moaned aloud the whole night through. As his wounds festered and his fever mounted, natives came and lanced his wounds with a stone knife. As the pus oozed out it was wiped away with leaves and then the banana-leaf bandages were re-applied. The treatment brought only momentary relief to the sufferer.

A government patrol finally reached Brother Eugene and his two companions on January 16. Mr. Melrose, the government agent, was appalled by the revolting stench, the swarms of flies and the emaciated appearance of Brother Eugene, who nevertheless greeted his rescuer in a weak but cheerful voice: "At last God has sent someone in answer to my prayers.'' Because his condition was critical, Eugene was flown the next day to the mission hospital in Salamaua. There, in spite of the excellent care he received, he died alone without a priest present on January 23, 1935, attended in his last hours only by a Protestant doctor and a Catholic nurse, fortified only by his constant praying of the rosary. He was buried in Salamaua, but later his remains were brought to Alexishafen.

In May 1984 Pope John Paul II paid a pastoral visit to Mount Hagen where he was welcomed by more than 200,000 natives; some twenty-two archbishops and bishops concelebrated a Mass in pidgin English. Was there a break in the clouds that day, and did Brother Eugene look down with special satisfaction on the mision he had helped establish some fifty years earlier?

CHAPTER 37

Dr. John T. Murphy: A "Vigilant Knight" of the Diocese

By Harold D. Olree

DR. JOHN T. MURPHY'S ELECTION as the first officer of the Illinois Knights of Columbus Council from downstate was symbolic for this representative of the "Church militant," who was born near the beginning of the twentieth century.

Dr. Murphy was an East St. Louis dentist, but he distinguished himself in the diocese and in the state by his example as a Catholic leader and pioneer, especially in K. of C. Council 592 and in the state council. Those who knew him agree that Dr. Murphy was a "no nonsense," sometimes hard-nosed Irishman when it came to faith and business. But they also readily agree that this strong defender of the faith was a person of great sensitivity and humility.

He was elected state deputy of the Illinois Knights of Columbus Council in 1951. He was the first member from downstate and only the second outside of the Chicago area to be elected to a top Illinois K. of C. office in the first fifty-four years of the organization.

"He convinced the downstate dioceses to get together and then he went to Chicago and told them," said Bill Hubbard, building manager of Council 592. Hubbard, who served on K. of C. degree teams with Dr. Murphy, said that the fellow Council 592 member's action resulted in the "all-state movement" policy of the Illinois K. of C. The policy promoted by Dr. Murphy provides that the top state K. of C. officers are alternated each term between the Chicago and downstate areas, explained Hubbard.

Dr. Murphy's action resulted in his appointment as state secretary to complete an unexpired term, then election as the first Illinois K. of C. state deputy from downstate.

The K. of C. pioneer and leader joined East St. Louis Council 592 in

Dr. John Murphy

1908, when he reached the eligible age of eighteen. He served in a number of council offices, including grand knight, and held the offices of Master of the Fourth Degree for the Southern Illinois District, Marquette Province, for ten years and of district deputy for eleven years.

John T. Murphy was born November 25, 1889, in East St. Louis. He was the third son of Thomas and Elizabeth (Walsh) Murphy, natives of County Wexford, Ireland. The family were members of St. Mary parish in the "South End" of East St. Louis. Young John attended the parish school, "was a regular server at Mass and played violin in the St. Mary school orchestra," recalled a niece, Kitty Keeley Gleeson, Belleville.

Like most youths in those days, John Murphy went to work after graduating from grade school, taking a job with the Louisville and Nashville Railroad. By attending classes at night he worked himself up to a secretarial/stenographic position.

The studies also enabled him to meet the requirements for entering dental school at Saint Louis University. His shorthand and typing abilities payed off when John started to make copies of his course notes and sell them to fellow students.

His pursuit of a dental degree was interrupted by his military service in World War I, but he returned to graduate in 1919. He maintained his dental practice in East St. Louis until he retired in 1947.

Another of Dr. Murphy's nieces, Eileen Murphy Orlet, also of Belleville, remembers her uncle as quite often "sober and business-like." But, she pointed out that "Uncle Doc," as his nieces and nephews referred to him, had difficulty maintaining his stern disposition because of his brother and her father, Thomas Murphy, also a member of Council 592, who served with the dentist on degree teams. Mrs. Gleeson also noted, "Nobody could be Tom Murphy's brother and not have a sense of fun."

Mrs. Gleeson received a firsthand view of her "Uncle Doc " since she lived with Dr. and Mrs. Murphy, (the former Loretto Sullivan), who had no children of their own, from age six. Mrs. Gleeson's mother was the former Catherine Sullivan, a sister of Mrs. Murphy.

Mrs. Gleeson's parents moved to Mt. Vernon, where there was no Catholic school, she said. She went to live with "Uncle Doc and Auntie" Murphy and attended Holy Angels school.

She said Dr. Murphy "sometimes seemed stern and formidable in public," but that he was a dutiful husband and father at home. She recalls that after each meal," he walked around the table to kiss Auntie and to thank her and tell her he loved her."

Mrs. Gleeson also pointed out that in the 1930s when her mother had diphtheria, all of the Keeley children went to live with "Uncle Doc and Auntie" Murphy.

Dr. Murphy "could seem stern . . . if a matter of principle happened to be involved," Mrs. Gleeson continued. "I'm sure his life during the times when Irish Catholics, indeed all Catholics, were subject to the terrorism of KKK [Ku Klux Klan], colored or formed his belief. He, like all good Knights of Columbus, was a member of the Church militant. He never compromised on matters of faith and morals," she added.

Charles W. Gruninger, also a past Master of the Fourth Degree who is a member of *The Messenger* staff, recalled doing typing and other work for Dr. Murphy, who was serving as state K. of C. Newman chairman at the time. "He was airtight financially," Gruninger noted. "And when Doc would get something in his mind, you couldn't change it.

Gruninger also explained that Dr. Murphy had the courage of his convictions. "When the Ku Klux Klan came to East St. Louis he was the only one willing to lay his life on the line. Doc disguised himself and went to KKK meetings so he could report back to the council — he was a vigilant knight — and the Klan later died out," Gruninger concluded.

Dr. Murphy became well known early in Council 592 in the post of lecturer, which is involved with fund-raising. In that post, he became chairman for the Council 592's legendary annual picnic when it began in 1919. The proceeds from the picnics funded numerous East St. Louis community and diocesan projects, including priesthood education and youth retreats.

The picnic attracted crowds from both Illinois and Missouri. Its location was moved frequently to provide more space. At one time, it was held at Fairmount Race Track.

Mrs. Gleeson related, "The old K. C. picnics were the social events of the summers for many years in wonderful East St. Louis."

The picnic was continued for nearly fifty years and was discontinued with the advent of bingo and shortly before Council 592 moved into its present quarters at 9600 Lebanon Road.

Mrs. Gleeson reported that Dr. Murphy "had much to do with the building of the fabulous Knights of Columbus building," five stories tall, at 1447 State Street in East St. Louis. He was grand knight of Council 592 when it was built, 1924-25. She described the building as "the hub of Catholic social life, with its roof garden for dances under the stars, its ballrooms for wedding breakfasts and receptions, its swimming pools, gymnasium, and bowling alley."

The building had living quarters for bachelors and housed *The Messenger* and some other diocesan offices for a few years. It was razed in 1976.

Mrs. Gleeson shared one story to show that Dr. Murphy knew his faults and limitations and was humble enough to admit them. An East St. Louis group asked him to run for political office. He declined, "because I am an uncompromising man." This showed that he correctly assessed his one shortcoming: he could not compromise," Mrs. Gleenson said.

Dr. Murphy retired from dentistry in 1947 and was named administrator of East St. Louis Public Library. Mrs. Murphy was ill with cancer and he wanted more time to spend with her.

Mrs. Gleeson reported, "During World War II, he worked six days a week with office hours two and sometimes three evenings a week. He was anxious to have a 9-5 job during the years of her illness."

Mrs. Murphy died in 1950 and the city librarian and retired dentist married Addie Mulconnery Chamblin, who had been a family friend.

Dr. Murphy reportedly made many improvements in the East St. Louis library and its facilities. Andrew F. Keeley, a nephew of Dr. Murphy who worked as a clerk at the library, said that his uncle indexed all of the early issues of the former *Journal* newspaper for the reference department.

When Dr. Murphy became state K. of C. secretary, then the deputy in 1951, he established an office in East St. Louis and continued as city librarian.

Both in Council 592 and in his state offices, Dr. Murphy emphasized increasing membership in the Knights of Columbus. In 1953 near the end of his second one-year term as state deputy, he reported that Illinois had become third in the United States with new memberships, with 5,000 added in the previous year. Council 592 was one of the largest in the state.

When he retired as state deputy in July 1953 Dr. Murphy said, "The year now ending can be recorded as the most successful in the past quarter century." He also noted that the Knights of Columbus program in Illinois "showed decided improvement and progress."

In addition to his Knights of Columbus leadership and accomplishments, Dr. Murphy was a pioneer in a number of other diocesan areas as well. He was a founding member of Holy Angels parish under Father William Trombley and served on the board of trustees for many years. He was also instrumental in organizing the Serra Club in East St. Louis and the Father and Friend club at the former Central Catholic high school in the city. He also served on the diocesan Catholic Charities advisory board and was active in the Council of Catholic Men and the Lay Retreat Program as well as having membership in a number of other organizations.

Bishop Albert R. Zuroweste, who served as state K. of C. chaplain for many years, recommended to Pope John XXIII in 1959 that Dr. John T. Murphy be named a Knight of the Order of St. Gregory. In November of that year Bishop Zuroweste instituted the ''vigilant'' Catholic and K. of C. leader with the honor for his ''self- sacrificing and notable achievements'' in behalf of the Church.

Dr. Murphy died February 13, 1965 at age seventy-five. His funeral service was held at Holy Angels church. He was buried in Mt. Carmel cemetery. At the time of his death, he was still a member of the Council 592 corporation's board of directors.

CHAPTER 38

Father Charles Seifert: Man of Charity

By Raphael H. Middeke

"THE TOWER OF LIGHT, strength, and hope in Royalton and Zeigler was Father Charles Seifert. When times were tough — and they were with monotonous regularity — there always was Father Seifert at the work of rescue. He'd hunt for the desperately needy who were too proud to ask. He didn't have to hunt far. With a few dollars at miserable moments when the whole community was under the economic gun, the frail padre gave pretty fair replays of the miracle of the loaves and fishes."

The *Chicago Sun Times* columnist who wrote the above in 1953 learned about Father Seifert from a group of Catholics in Chicago. In 1939 they had organized a dance and social on Chicago's west side for the pastor of two parishes in coal mining towns in southern Illinois — Sacred Heart, Zeigler, and St. Aloysius, Royalton. The group had grown up in the two parishes and had left for economic reasons when the mines, on which their hometowns were built, struggled with the effects of the depression and the turmoil of unionization.

Father Seifert's parishes needed financial assistance and the annual dance — which continued for over twenty-five years and often netted $3,000 a year — was a unique tribute to the man who always remained their "pastor" and for whom they retained a love, respect, and admiration few priests in the diocese of Belleville have engendered.

The Chicago dance became homecoming for former parishioners as far away as Detroit, as well for former residents from towns such as Christopher, West Frankfort, Herrin, and Marion.

"The dance was a big and merry affair held each year as a grand demonstration that it's more blessed to give than receive, and considerably more fun, too," the *Sun Times* columnist said.

The organizing committee "promised their beloved pastor he would never want for anything as long as they lived,'' said Father Vic Sulkowski, St. Mary, Carlyle, pastor and the first priest ordained from the Zeigler parish.

The dance was an effort to repay a personal debt of gratitude to the man who, as Father Sulkowski put it, ''was like a father to us.''

''The dance caught on like a wildfire,'' he said ''because they knew it was for a man of charity.''

Father Charles Seifert

A ''man of charity'' is as good a description as any for this genuine and generous priest. Those who knew him insist he was the best the diocese ever had. ''He did a lot of favors for people, which he kept to himself,'' said Eugene Prudent, longtime mayor and lifelong parishioner of Sacred Heart parish. Indeed, his charity — and the way he went about it — is almost legendary.

Charles Seifert was born in Quincy, Illinois, on June 23, 1889. After completing his high school and college studies at St. Francis there, he went to Rochester, New York, to finish his preparation for the priesthood. He was ordained in Rochester June 12, 1915, and for the next three years served as an assistant, twice in each parish, at St. Lawrence, Sandoval, and St. Andrew, Murphysboro. In 1918 he became a chaplain in the army until the war ended. ''He always was a veteran,'' Prudent said, serving as chaplain of the local American Legion post.

''Memorial Day was a big day in his life. He and his servers went to all the cemeteries in the area to pray,'' it was recalled. When he was hospitalized for lung cancer in 1953, he admitted himself to Jefferson Barracks Veterans Hospital in St. Louis. He died on Memorial Day.

After returning from the war in 1919 Father Seifert spent several months at St. Elizabeth, East St. Louis, before he was asked to organize a parish church or churches in the coal mining towns of Franklin County. He stayed there till the day he died, opting several times not to accept another appointment.

No account and no memory of Father Seifert continues long without noting Father Seifert's special rapport with the young people, not only of his parishes, but of the towns of Royalton and Zeigler. The incidentals become part of a mosaic which today would probably be called a model youth ministry. He didn't call it anything. The kids just learned to love and lost the need to fear.

"We knew God was good because he was good," said Father James Blazine, pastor of St. Stephen, Caseyville, and the last of the three diocesan priests he considered his "sons."

"I was always amazed at how he did his religion classes," said Father Don Lenzini, pastor of St. Damian, Damiansville. "He had all eight classes at once. Everyone looked forward to going. We also looked forward to going to his house and to church." Father Seifert baptized Father Lenzini and also took part in his first Mass in 1951.

In Zeigler the church basement became a youth center. In Royalton he built an old wooden "gymnasium." There were no boundaries. When the ball hit the wall, it was out of bounds.

His house was always open. The corkballs were in his bottom desk drawer, Father Blazine recalled, and the soda was in the refrigerator. The sacristy sported a Ping-Pong table. "We had to stop playing fifteen minutes before Mass started," someone said.

The debt of gratitude never stopped. "Thank God we had him. I don't know what we would have done without him," said Minnie Laurenti Kapustas, originally from Royalton.

Minnie started cooking for him at the age of sixteen. "I did some cooking in school and one day he said: "If you can cook for the school faculty, surely you can cook for me." After high school she went to Chicago to work, but returned several years later when her brother was killed in a mine disaster, and cooked for Father Seifert again. She later returned to Chicago, became involved in the Chicago dance and married Albert Kapustas, who grew up with Father Seifert in the Zeigler parish. Father Seifert went to Chicago, to officiate at the wedding, as he did for many of his "kids" Mr. Kapustas echoed the sentiments of many when he said: "He was like a Father to us. He raised us."

Minnie and Albert were active for many years in the planning of the Chicago dance and social.

The Kapustases recalled a few of the other incidentals of the mosaic.

"He taught us all how to drive in his Model T. (After the late 1920s he always drove a Roadmaster Buick, a gift from a New York friend who not only replaced the car occasionally, but also paid for expenses.)

"He taught us to drive and he taught us to swim. He took us out to one of the "duck ponds" in the area," Minnie said.

He introduced corkball to Zeigler, Prudent said, "and he always played with us."

"He was one of the first to have a radio and all the kids used to congregate in the quarters behind the church to listen to the ballgame," a former "kid" said.

"And every time he went to Belleville [to the chancery], someone had to shine his shoes."

All the incidentals add up to the fact that the kids felt very comfortable with him. He was their friend.

"I didn't know anyone could be afraid of a priest," Father Blazine said.

"I thought all priests were like that," Father Lenzini said. "He had no axe to grind with anyone. He had no ambition and he was good to his people. He was a thoroughly good person. I haven't found anyone better."

The coal boom towns never really came through on the promises they held out for the immigrants. Zeigler was planned by a Chicago industrialist whose mines were the finest and the best in the country. The town was designed by the country's best engineers. But union struggles kept the miners unemployed many times and the depression dealt a fatal blow for many others.

Father Sulkowski remembers that during the early years of the depression, Sunday collections ranged between $2 and $3. "But not once did I ever hear him complain or gripe that there wasn't enough money to operate the parish."

He received a lot of support, but he also had a way of getting things done. "He made a deal with the coal companies during those years to provide the parishes with fuel. When he had money, he paid. If not, they forgot about it," Father Sulkowski said.

During those depression years, when he seldom drew a salary, one of the coal companies appointed him their spiritual director and paid him a $35-a-month salary until the day he died.

Everyone talked about his charity.

"He would get money in one hand and give it away with the other."

"If he had it he shared it."

"He made sure the First Communion kids had new clothes and new shoes. He'd send them down to the store if they couldn't afford them. What kind of deal he had at the store, no one knew," Father Lenzini said.

Father Seifert today would be called a pastoral priest. He was not a legalist. He was "broadminded," one parishioner said. "I'd rather go to hell for being lenient than for being to strict," he once told Father Lenzini. His "broadmindedness" included advising a young couple to get married by a justice of the peace until the conditions and circumstances in their lives warranted a church wedding. "Knowing all the rules of the church doesn't make you a good Catholic," he once told Father Blazine.

One of the stories often repeated is that he got along with everyone — respected by Catholics and non-Catholics alike. He was a special advisor and counselor for many people from other Christian denominations. "Often he was called to the hospital by people of other faiths and he buried many of them," Father Sulkowski said.

In a special way he was a counselor for the politicians and would-be candidates and servicemen. When the young men went into the service during World War II, they all — Catholic and non-Catholic alike — came for a blessing, a medal, and parting words of advice.

For many years he lived in two rooms behind the church, until he or someone else purchased two "left-behind" houses for $50 each in 1932, out of which he built a rectory next to the church.

The stories of Father Seifert did not end when he died of lung cancer on Memorial Day 1953. He wanted to die in his own home and was cared for by parishioners the last several weeks.

The news of his lung cancer hit him hard. He had lived a lot and looked forward to many more years of living. The day of his death a group of grown men sat on his front porch and cried.

There wouldn't have been enough money to bury him (five priest friends had agreed to pay for the funeral expenses) but a small life insurance policy was found, still in the name of his mother, who had died twenty years earlier.

The funeral was a celebration of his life. The towns shut down. People came from all parts of the country. Loudspeakers were installed outside so everyone could hear. The chief of police, a non-Catholic, said: "There was the finest man who ever lived in this area." People had always talked about his saintliness; a few now talked about making him a saint.

The memories of the priest continue to live. The fiftieth anniversary of Sacred Heart parish in 1970 became a reunion of Father Seifert's former parishioners. A history of the two parishes, written by Prudent in 1983, is dedicated to Father Seifert "on the thirtieth anniversary of his death."

"He kept going with the divine fire under his boiler until cancer took him away," the *Sun Times* columnist said.

And so he did — and continues to do so. A few conversations prove his spirit lives on in the lives of many who know they would be different people with different values had they not been one of Father Seifert's "kids."

CHAPTER 39

Mother Veronica Baumgart: Progress at Ruma

By Sister Loretta Berra, ASC

"Your ways, O Lord, make known to me, teach me your paths; guide me in your truth and teach me, for you are my God, my Savior."
— Psalm 25

THROUGHOUT THE HISTORY of the Ruma sisters, there were leaders recognized for their courage, self-sacrifice, and accomplishments. Mother Veronica Baumgart has a true claim to admiration for responding to the challenge unique to her time. Her name translates "true image of Jesus" and she lived it by trusting in the Lord as a pilgrim on a journey.

Mother Veronica, a woman of genuine humility, craved no honors, no privileges, nor was the responsibility of major superior of the Ruma community an office that she sought. She would have preferred to continue as inconspicuous teacher and administrator at St. Andrew school, Murphysboro, where she had served for twenty-nine years. She accepted the office reluctantly, but fulfilled her duties efficiently as the third vicaress of the Ruma sisters.

Mother Veronica shared with the pioneer members in the hardships and difficulties of Ruma's primitive beginnings, entering religious life from Mt. Carmel in 1889, thirteen years after the sisters had arrived in Ruma. Her appointment in 1922 brought Ruma's pioneer period to an end.

She guided the destiny of the community in the days of transition, when a new era of religious life and education was dawning in America. Mother Veronica as vicaress and Father Fred Witte as chaplain led the Ruma sisters firmly into the American mainstream.

In the 1920s vocations at the Ruma convent were flourishing. The motherhouse was overcrowded. Lack of space made religious formation difficult and the professional education of the sisters impossible. A building project was inevitable.

Mother Veronica Baumgart

Soon after Mother Veronica assumed office, she called a chapter to consider the construction of a new motherhouse. In an informal meeting with Bishop Henry Althoff, the chapter unanimously gave full charge of the undertaking to Father Witte, a man of vision and great managerial ability.

The location of the new motherhouse at Ruma presented a weighty transportation problem. The sisters purchased a tract of land east of the property of the Oblate fathers near Belleville in September 1922 with the thought of moving the motherhouse there. By November 1922 the building of a paved road (Route 3) connecting Waterloo, Chester, Red Bud, and Ruma solved the dilemma. Gratefully, the sisters decided to build in Ruma.

Mother Veronica carried on her duties of placing the sisters in various communities, guiding their spiritual lives, visiting convents, and informing the sisters of the plans for the new construction. Despite many financial burdens, work on the building began under the protection of the Sacred Hearts of Jesus and Mary.

The motherhouse was dedicated on August 9, 1925. Numerous priests and friends as well as the Knights of Columbus from East St. Louis and Murphysboro were present. Bishop Althoff officiated. Work on the incomplete chapel progressed so well that the chapel wing was ready for dedication June 17, 1926.

The following year the grounds were landscaped to add beauty to the new building. With new roads between the convent and highway, transportation was no longer a problem by 1930.

The cemetery was enlarged, graves were leveled, new crosses of Tennessee cedar replaced the old, and a new crucifixion group was erected on a terraced plot.

Finances were not available for so many improvements. A loan, the sisters' small salaries, their daily sacrifices, and donations from generous relatives and friends made it possible to undertake these many projects.

During the summer of 1926 the majority of sisters spent their vacation at the motherhouse for the first time. Mother Veronica was solicitous that adequate furnishings and conveniences should be provided for the sisters after a year of hard work in school, hospital, and community. The sisters have continued to spend vacation time at Ruma for retreats or relaxation, continually adapting and remodeling for changing times, but always within the space Mother Veronica had provided.

With the completion of the motherhouse, Mother Veronica and Father Witte made the education of the sisters the top priority. Precious Blood Institute, begun in 1923, received state recognition as a four-year high school in record time. During the summer months sisters attended summer school at the new high school in Ruma or at St. Teresa Academy, East St. Louis, unless they were attending college elsewhere.

In 1925 another opportunity for the sisters' advancement occurred when Saint Louis University admitted women to the School of Education. The community enrolled several sisters as full-time students. It was the summer of 1927 when the Jesuits at Saint Louis University granted a college extension center at Ruma. Sister Etheldreda Heard was the first Precious Blood sister to receive a doctorate from Saint Louis University. She was an excellent educator and, as educational director, led the members of the province to a higher level of professionalism.

Sister Etheldreda, now retired at the provincial house, commented recently: "Mother Veronica transfered me from St. Teresa Academy to the motherhouse with the assignment to set up a science department. Texts and equipment were purchased and on April 23, 1923, I began teaching general science. Sister Evangeline Ludwig, now residing at Clementine Residence, was assigned as physics teacher. Mother Veronica gave full support in later implementing and determining the scope and direction of the educational program."

Mother Veronica's vision of education extended further than the teaching field. She began upgrading the nurses' education as she saw the need to meet state qualifications. Sister Marian Wansing, St. Louis, stated: "Mother Veronica urged every nurse to acquire a state nursing certificate, a necessity at that time. Her successor continued her interest and sent me to our hospital in Taylorville to teach chemistry to the sisters. Everyone studied assiduously and met the state demands."

Mother Veronica was a woman of prayer, a woman who relied not only on her own prayers, but also the prayers of her sisters. Her sisters experienced her spirituality powerfully, through her example and witness. In prayer, she found the strength and courage to fulfill the role to which she was called. New decisions concerning the vows and lifestyles of the sisters were coming from Rome. Her conscientious observance of all details caused her to take personal responsibility for her sisters' conformity to these new decisions.

During these years, the Sisters of the Most Precious Blood were still following the constitution written in 1897, by and for Italian Adorers not yet aware of their order's budding internationality. In her letter of appointment, Mother Veronica was given the assignment to bring the U. S. into closer conformity with the religious practices of the congregation in Italy.

One of the rules that perplexed Mother Veronica was the distinction between choir and lay sisters. Such a distinction had never been observed in Germany or the United States. It became imperative that a change in the rule be made to offset the differences in practice and lifestyle between American and Italian sisters. Mother Veronica, aided by Father Witte, who was the mastermind behind this undertaking, sought the revision of the constitution so the rules would be adaptable to the community in America and in accordance with canon law.

For a time a struggle occurred between the Old World and the New. It took several years of communication, sometimes marked by painful misunderstandings, before the Roman Generalate consented to a revision which recognized American needs. Bishop Althoff in his ''ad limina'' visit had the pleasure of bringing the long-awaited manuscript of the constitution.

On June 30, 1935, Mother Mary Stella, provincial superior, presented each sister with a copy of the English translation of the constitution blessed by Bishop Althoff. The annals of Ruma reflect the sisters' immense joy on that long-anticipated day.

When Mother Veronica's term as vicaress ended in 1929 she continued to serve in responsible positions as provincial economa (treasurer), local superior at Our Lady's House of Studies in St. Louis, and the first local superior at St. Ann's Home for the Aged in Chester, which opened in 1937. When her health was failing, the aging superior retired to the Provincial House until her death October 19, 1955.

Sister Serena Haas, now sacristan at the Provincial House, treasures her memories of Mother Veronica: ''I was in the first group of sisters to profess vows with Mother Veronica as vicaress. She was a very kind person, who loved us sisters, and who was very concerned about our future. If she saw us scrubbing the floors she took a brush and bucket and joined us. And when she left her post as vicaress she helped Sister Edwiga Degenhart care for the chickens. She was a remarkable woman.''

Mother Veronica Baumgart, "true image of Jesus," was a prayerful and loving religious who trusted in the Lord as she journeyed through life.

CHAPTER 40

Archbishop Joseph Schlarman: Tall Son of the Illinois Soil

By Harold D. Olree

ARCHBISHOP JOSEPH SCHLARMAN referred to himself as a ''tall son of the Illinois soil.'' He was tall, well over six feet, and came from a family which had farmed in southern Illinois since 1837. He also was a strong supporter of rural interests.

But rural problems was only one of the areas in which Archbishop Schlarman demonstrated strong leadership in his more than forty-seven years of service to the church. When he became bishop of the diocese of Peoria in 1930, he was already widely known as a linguist, traveler, historian, public speaker, educator, author, administrator and builder.

Joseph Henry Leo Schlarman was born February 23, 1879, near Germantown. He was one of ten children of Bernard Joseph and Philomena (Keyser) Schlarman. The family, members of St. Boniface church, and the future archbishop attended the parish grade school. He then went to St. Francis Solanus (now Quincy) College for six years.

He completed his priesthood education at the University of Innsbruck at Tyrol, Austria, and was ordained at Brixen cathedral there June 29, 1904.

After ordination, the new Father Schlarman was sent by Bishop Janssen to Gregorian University in Rome to study canon law, where he received a doctorate degree in 1907.

The future archbishop's first assignment in the diocese of Belleville, July 1, 1907, was as assistant at the Cathedral of St. Peter, Belleville. Soon afterwards, he became secretary to Bishop Janssen; subsequently, administrator of the cathedral, then rector, as well as chancellor of the diocese.

Archbishop Joseph Schlarman

Father Schlarman was given the title of monsignor in 1921 by Pope Benedict XV. On April 19, 1930, Monsignor Schlarman was appointed bishop of the diocese of Peoria, Illinois. Pope Pius XII gave him the personal title of archbishop on June 29, 1951, the forty-seventh anniversary of his ordination.

Cathedral parish grew rapidly during Archbishop Schlarman's twenty-one years as rector and chancellor. Major changes which he made in the cathedral building and interior were destroyed in the January 4, 1912, fire which completely burned out the interior and the roof.

The rector edited a book on the fire which was sold to help raise funds for restoration, but also, he said, "to give a first-hand and authentic account" of the catastrophe.

Bishop Janssen was in declining health at the time and left supervison of the cathedral's reconstruction to his rector and chancellor. For this reason, many persons said the restored cathedral was like a monument to the future archbishop.

After Bishop Janssen's death July 2, 1913, the rector and chancellor continued under his successor, Bishop Henry Althoff.

Archbishop Schlarman underwent some fifteen major surgical operations 1915-23, while continuing in his assignments. When he eventually regained his health, he credited "the grace of God and the intercession of the Virgin Mary and her mother, St. Anne," whose shrine at Beaupre in Quebec, Canada he visited.

During World War I, Archbishop Schlarman taught French to servicemen at Scott Air Force Base and other army posts. He reportedly could preach in seven languages.

In the 1918 flu epidemic in Belleville, the cathedral rector set up emergency treatment quarters for about sixty patients in the parish hall.

He was sponsor of the parish St. Vincent de Paul Society and directed that the poor be provided assistance without regard for race, creed, or color. He also served as the diocesan director of the Society for the Propagation of the Faith.

Archbishop Schlarman had a keen interest in history and its meaning for people of the times. He is credited with inspiring the restoration of Fort de Chartres, the historic French fort near Prairie du Rocher. He wrote a pageant, "Romance of Fort de Chartres," 1927-28, and had it staged at the site to raise funds. He dedicated the restored fort and gave the main address when the museum was officially turned over to the state of Illinois in 1930.

His first major book, published by Buechler Printing Co. of Belleville in 1929, was *From Quebec to New Orleans, The Story of the French in America.* He thought it was important for people to learn about the men who established the early French missions and settlements, such as Cahokia and Kaskaskia. In other words, he said, "we should like to get in touch with the souls of these men . . . whose spirits still seem to hover about the ruins of Fort de Chartres."

The then Monsignor Schlarman was consecrated bishop of Peoria June 17, 1930, in St. Peter cathedral, Belleville. He was installed in St. Mary cathedral, Peoria, a week later.

As if to emphasize his interest in the welfare of the priests of his diocese, on the day of his installation Archbishop Schlarman announced he was contributing $1,000 to establish a Clergymen's Aid Society.

He began the Aledo-Peoria plan of religious education centers for rural children not in Catholic schools — a pattern which was followed nationally. Schlarman High School in Danville was one of three opened under his leadership. He introduced a Peoria diocese edition of the *Register* newspaper in 1934.

Archbishop Schlarman took an active interest in the penal institutions in Illinois. In 1936 Governor Horner named him to head a commission to study the state prison system. In a summary of the commission's report, entitled *Why Prisons?,* published by Paulist Press, Archbishop Schlarman called for smaller prisons and for special schools to train prison staff members so they could "retrain and re-fit the lawbreaker to go back into the free world a better citizen."

The "tall son of the Illinois soil" wrote a letter to President Franklin D. Roosevelt in 1933 proposing the use of gasohol. He said the "alky-fuel" would provide a use for farmers' surplus grain, especially corn, which was selling for only ten cents a bushel during the depression.

Archbishop Schlarman was an active supporter and participant in the National Catholic Rural Life Conference. He was elected president of NCRLC for two terms and wrote the NCRLC constitution. He was a life member of the board of advisors and in 1950 the NCRLC presented him with a distinguished service citation.

When Albert R. Zuroweste became the third bishop of Belleville, on January 29, 1948, Bishop Schlarman presided as consecrator at St. Peter cathedral. At the dinner which followed the consecration, Archbishop Schlarman spoke on the theme, ''For the strong obey when a strong man shows them the way.''

But he didn't believe that a bishop should be overly visible. ''As pastor of the cathedral,'' he said at the consecration dinner, ''I never favored the idea of the bishop living right across the street from the front door of the cathedral.'' He recommended ''a house somewhere between Belleville and East St. Louis.'' He added, ''The present bishop's house would make a good chancery office. . . .''

When the U.S. bishops established Montezuma Seminary in Mexico to train priesthood aspirants during persecutions south of the Rio Grande, Archbishop Schlarman was one of the strongest supporters of the project. He visited Mexico frequently and also South America to study their rural problems.

From his research, he authored in 1949 his second book, *Mexico: A Land of Volcanoes,* ''an unbiased scholarly view of the violent social, economic, and political eruptions which have shaken Mexico during the last 400 years.'' The book was published in Spanish and German and received wide acclaim throughout the world.

Bishop Zuroweste later said the book was ''recognized as the most authoritative work on Mexican church history published in modern times.''

Archbishop Schlarman authored a number of other publications. In the Diocese of Peoria, these included *Catechetical Sermon Aids,* which outlined a three-year series of sermons on the catechism. In the Diocese of Belleville, he also authored *The Magnificat,* a Catholic prayer book, and sponsored a *Cooking for Christ* publication.

In 1950 Pope Pius XII named the Peoria bishop an ''Assistant to the Pontifical Throne.'' When he was given the rank and personal title of archbishop the next year, he became one of only five in the U.S. holding the honor.

Also in 1950 Archbishop Schlarman visited Father Jacques Marquette's birthplace, Laon, France, to help design a memorial statue of the Jesuit missionary for Illinois. Shortly before his death in 1951, he dedicated the memorial at Utica, Illinois, for the 275th anniversary of Father Marquette's first Mass celebrated in the Illinois area.

Archbishop Schlarman died November 10, 1951, of a heart attack, as his fellow bishops were meeting in Chicago. At the time of his death he was writing a history of the Montezuma (Mexico) Seminary at the bishops' request.

Bishop Zuroweste, delivered the sermon at the funeral service. Bishop Zuroweste said that Archbishop Schlarman's motto, *''Domine dirige nos''* Lord, direct us) ''briefly summarized his mode of action.'' He described Archbishop Schlarman as a strong, strict, fearsome, demanding leader and worker. But, he added, ''his courage was grounded in divine truth.''

The funeral sermon continued: ''His assistants found him demanding but always understanding; his people loved him because their interests were his prime concern. He urged his co-workers to use their talents in the spread of God's kingdom.

''Archbishop Schlarman realized the dignity of his epsicopal office,'' Bishop Zuroweste added. ''He insisted upon proper respect, not for personal glory but because of the office. He was always the bishop, the successor of the apostles and wanted to be ever worthy of that dignity. Strict and unbending at times, he was, nevertheless, genial and humane and loved his fellowmen.''

CHAPTER 41

Joseph Buechler: Catholic Press Pioneer

By Robert Welzbacher

JOSEPH NICHOLAS BUECHLER, Knight of St. Gregory, typified the hardworking second-generation German immigrants, carving out careers in a new world. He followed in his father's footsteps to become a successful, self-made printer-publisher who felt there was no substitute for hard work, diligence, and faith in God. Buechler specialized in Catholic publications, which earned him national recognition.

After young Joe completed his studies at St. Nicholas grade school, St. Louis, his father, a Bavarian immigrant, introduced him to printcraft in 1890 at the *National Livestock Reporter,* an East St. Louis daily newspaper. Soon he moved to Belleville, where he worked for a short while with the *News Democrat* before opening his own print shop at 220 West Main Street in 1902. As his business prospered he moved to larger headquarters in the 300 block of West Main. His final location was at 332 West Main, a site now enveloped by various downtown business expansions.

The year 1902 was a landmark year in the life of Joe Buechler. Not only did he embark on the business venture which would serve both church and community, but that same year on August 20 he married Caroline Koch of Trenton at the Cathedral of St. Peter. The couple raised four children: Rita Heck, now of Glendale, Arizona, the late William Buechler, Louise Buechler, and Frances Vernier.

Upon establishing his own print shop, Buechler was encouraged to enter the field of the Catholic press, which at that time was relatively new in the Midwest. Buechler was ready for such a move since he had kept improving his printing facilities. He was capable of providing flat-run printing, newspaper style format, bound magazines and books. When Buechler Printing began working in the area of religious publishing, producing hardcover prayerbooks, histories, and religious texts, the hardcover work was contracted to special binderies.

Joseph Buechler

Joseph Buechler took the plunge into the Catholic press in 1907 when the first issue of this quarterly magazine, entitled the *Diocesan Messenger,* rolled off of his presses. Actually, he was only a co-laborer in the cause for the diocesan newspaper which his company published. Initially, *The Messenger* was the editorial product of Father Francis Tecklenburg of the cathedral parish. Father Teck, the original editor, served the paper until his transfer to southern Illinois in 1914.

The following year, the Buechler Company purchased "the right, title and good will" to *The Messenger* and changed its format from a monthly magazine to a regular weekly newspaper. The late Professor B. L. Linderberger, who also taught at St. Henry Seminary, was the first in a line of clergy and lay editors of the new *Messenger.*

Official news of the Belleville diocese originated at the chancery office of Bishop Henry Althoff, where Monsignor M. J. Gruenewald served as press officer. Meanwhile, Buechler Printing assumed responsibility for subscription sales, advertising sales and the costs associated with publishing and distribution.

Originally, the diocesan paper had a circulation of 4,200, but through the encouragement of Bishop Althoff the eight-page weekly was soon sent to the homes of 16,000 Catholic families throughout southern Illinois. During these years, Beuchler drew his editors from such talented men as Father Frederick Beuckman, Father Ed Dahmus, Arthur Pruess, Professor Bernard L. Miller, KSG, George Thebus, and Sebastian Weygandt.

The scope of Joe Buechler's Catholic publishing expanded with the introduction of the *Schoolmate,* edited by Father John Henken. This pioneer newspaper for Catholic students reached a peak circulation of 90,000 and was published forty times during the school year. Father Henken also was instrumental in Buechler's publication of *The Catholic Girl,* a monthly magazine for young women that had a national circulation of 10,000. Among Buechler's co-workers in his Catholic publishing ventures were such authors as Bishop Joseph Schlarman, Msgr. Christopher Goelz and Father Albert Zuroweste. Buechler also enlisted writers from across the country.

Much of the early history of the Belleville diocese was disseminated by Joe Buechler, who printed various historical pamphlets, annual diocesan reviews and the 1919 St. John's Orphanage benefit edition. This interest in history and an eagerness to enter new fields led Joe Buechler to undertake the publication of his firm's first book, *From Quebec to New Orleans, the History of the French in America,* by Bishop Schlarman of Peoria. Bishop Schlarman also compiled *The Magnificat,* the popular children's prayerbook and hymnal which was a product of Joe Buechler's presses.

Bishop Althoff named Father Zuroweste, who was the superintendent of St. John's Orphanage, the editor of *The Messenger* in 1935, after the young priest completed his journalism studies at the Catholic University in Washington, D.C. The parish plan was introduced by the new editor and the weekly's circulation grew. In 1937 the Buechler Company notified the diocese that it chose to withdraw as the printer of *The Messenger.*

For his work in the field of Catholic publishing, Pope John XXIII named Joseph Buechler a Knight of St. Gregory in 1959. The honor was bestowed on the veteran publisher by one of his former editors, Bishop Albert Zuroweste, during ceremonies in the Cathedral of St. Peter, Buechler's home parish.

Throughout his life, Buechler was active in cathedral parish organizations. He served as first president of the Cathedral Holy Name Society and before that was a member of the parish men's society. He was closely identified with the Knights of Columbus, Catholic Knights and Ladies of Illinois, the Western Catholic Union, St. Vincent de Paul Society, and Te Deum International. It was only natural that he become active in numerous political and civic organizations including the Republican Club, Optimists, Kiwanis, and Turners. He served terms on the county board of supervisors and the board of health.

This life of service to community and church ended when Buechler was stricken with a cerebral hemorrhage March 12, 1961, at the age of eighty-five. This pioneer of the Catholic press was laid to rest at Green Mount Catholic Cemetery, Belleville.

CHAPTER 42

Monsignor Charles Gilmartin: Sacred Heart Pastor

By Raphael H. Middeke

TIME WAITED FOR Monsignor Charles Gilmartin on several occasions during his long and memorable life. At the end it seemed as if eternity waited.

When he celebrated his golden jubilee as a priest in 1947 the homilist, Bishop James Griffin of Springfield, ended his jubilee sermon with the words: "May God be with you always, and, as the shadows lengthen across your inspiring life, may the Beloved Master of the Apostles prepare your heavenly homecoming . . ."

Eternity waited another twenty-one years. The monsignor died at the age of ninety-five, seventy-one years after he was ordained a priest.

Ordained in 1897, Father Charles Gilmartin was assistant at St. Patrick parish, East St. Louis during a particulary stormy time for Irish Catholics in East St. Louis. In 1902 he walked from the downtown St. Patrick Church north to the outskirts of the city to open Sacred Heart parish in an old store on Seventh Street north of St. Clair Avenue. Before a year ended a school had been built and the upper floor was serving as a temporary church.

Time waited for the completion of the church for seventeen years. A cornerstone for the new church was laid in 1908. The building, remembered in later years as a landmark overlooking the expressways leading to the Poplar Street Bridge, was not completed until 1925 because of a shortage of materials during World War I.

Even the highway system waited. When the interstates were planned, Sacred Heart Church was no longer at the center of a thriving parish. But the highway planners, originally interested in purchasing and razing the church, "engineered around" the building out of deference to the founding and aging pastor.

Monsignor Charles Gilmartin

For fifty-eight years Msgr. Gilmartin, until his retirement in 1960, was the pastor of Sacred Heart. He was at the center of its energetic birth and the strength of its middle age. But he also, unique perhaps to one pastor's history, saw the shadows of its age lengthen with his own. In 1967 the Irish Sacred Heart and Polish St. Adalbert joined into one parish, lending it a few last years of life. In 1979, when the engineered highway ramps presented safety problems, the church was sold to the highway department and razed.

Time waited for his death to close the church he had founded.

Charles Gilmartin was born in Marble Hill, Pa., September 5, 1873, the oldest of twelve children. At the age of four his family moved to Trenton, Ill. In 1888 he enrolled in Quincy College, Quincy Illinois, to begin his preparation for the priesthood. Six years later he was appointed to complete his theological studies at the University of Innsbruck in Austria. He was ordained on September 8, 1897, by Bishop John Janssen in St. Peter Cathedral, Belleville.

For two years he was an assistant at St. Boniface, Germantown, before going to the city he learned to call home, first as an assistant at the downtown St. Patrick's and then as the founding and only pastor of Sacred Heart parish for its first fifty-eight years.

His brother, Lawrence, followed him into the priesthood. Eight years younger than Charles, he went to the same seminaries. After resigning from the pastorate of St. Patrick parish, Cario, in 1947 for reasons of health, he died in July 1948. He was buried from Sacred Heart Church and laid to rest in the family plot of Mt. Carmel Cemetery. It would be twenty years before he would be followed by his older brother.

A theme which was developed during Monsignor Gilmartin's jubilee and other celebration sermons was charity. "His heart is so big that God had to give him a big body to hold it," Bishop Griffin said in his golden jubilee sermon. A newspaper open letter at the same time by the president of the Belleville Diocesan Council of Catholic Women was titled: "A Tribute to a Heart of Gold."

He was a very hospitable man. A friend said, "If you needed a buck, he'd give it to you." His rectory was often an open house. His sensitivity was especially evident at the bedsides of the sick. "He had a terrific bedside manner," one of his former associates said. "I always envied that."

Especially in the younger days of the parish he walked up and down the streets of his parish around the growing railroad and stockyard industries on East St. Louis' north side.

"He had a sympathetic heart, which is so great an asset to being an effective priest," the editorial writer of *The Messenger* said at the time of his death. "Much of his work was of the heart-to-heart, person-to-person sort of ministry so much in favor today."

The homilist at his diamond jubilee in 1957 noted his charity and stressed his obedience to his bishop as one of his "outstanding priestly traits." The last sentence of *The Messenger* editorial at the time of his death, reflecting a changing political climate in the church, said: "He worked through the system for the individual person. We are trying desperately to recapture that spirit of the priesthood today."

If time waited on a number of occasions for the beloved Irish pastor, the church did not wait to begin its day of renewal. Vatican II was announced by Pope John XXIII a year before he retired at the age of eighty-six.

If charity was the quality extolled in jubilee sermons, it was at particular times a gem in the rough. The volatile monsignor sometimes demanded an unusual patience and understanding — perhaps especially on the part of his assistants.

But his "Irish" temper was matched by a will and a determination best exemplified by a story he himself told often. In the late 1920s or early 1930s he gave up drinking for Lent. Knowing that alcohol had too often become a companion, he said: "If I can give up drinking for Lent, surely I can give it up for the rest of my life." And he did.

"Severe exhortation and zealous instruction were the method in the pastor's ministrations to the spiritual needs of his people," the parish's golden jubilee history said. But "severity was tempered with loving understanding and followed by encouragement," it continued.

Obviously a competent and talented priest, Msgr. Gilmartin was called upon many times to hold down diocesan offices and jobs. At different times he was Officialis of the Matrimonial Court, president of the Diocesan Catholic Charities, president of the East St. Louis Catholic school board, spiritual moderator of the Diocesan Council of Catholic Women and spiritual director of the East St. Louis Holy Name Society.

In 1921 he was named a monsignor and in 1948 he was named protonotary apostolic, the highest rank of monsignor. He was the first priest in the Diocese of Belleville to receive the honor. The only other priest in the Diocese of Belleville to be named a protonotary apostolic has been Msgr. Leonard Bauer, who succeeded Msgr. Gilmartin as vicar general of the diocese in 1959 and who is now the pastor of St. Pancratius Church, Fayetteville.

In 1939 Msgr. Gilmartin was named the vicar general of the diocese by Bishop Henry Althoff, who not only counted on him as a co-worker in the diocese, but as a friend. When Bishop Althoff died in 1946, just several months before the vicar general's golden jubilee, his co-worker and friend was named the administrator of the diocese, until the installation of Bishop Albert Zuroweste the following year.

The energetic Irish pastor was an activist and an innovator. He started the Catholic Boy Scout program in the diocese and Catholic grade school sports program. As the dean of the East St. Louis Deanery for many years, he introduced many deanery-wide lay programs and activities.

In 1902 when he opened Sacred Heart, the mode of transportation for a city pastor was walking. The monsignor changed that. He was the first pastor to use a horse and buggy for parish visitations in East St. Louis and later he amazed pedestrians by being the first pastor in East St. Louis to use an automobile to get around his parish.

When he retired in 1960, he took up residence at the Regina Cleri home for clergy in St. Louis. His last few years were spent at St. Elizabeth's Home in Belleville, then part of St. Elizabeth Hospital, the hospital in which he died on September 29, 1968. After the funeral at the parish which was in many ways his whole life, he was buried in the Mt. Carmel family plot.

Monsignor Gilmartin was an imposing man and an imposing presence in the Diocese of Belleville for many years. He was a unique man with a unique personality. But in the history of the Diocese of Belleville he will always be first remembered as the pastor of Sacred Heart parish — the parish he founded and molded. The monsignor and the parish were young together, lived a life together and grew old together.

CHAPTER 43

Father Joseph Pico: A Priest From a Persecuted Church

By Stanley J. Konieczny

THE BELLEVILLE DIOCESE has stood as a welcome, safe haven for all sorts of refugees. During Bismarck's Kulturkampf thousands of Catholics resettled in southern Illinois and made valuable contributions. This tradition continued through the years as various forms of violence and hatred have displaced people from their homes. In the aftermath of the bloody persecution of the Mexican church, the Belleville diocese gained a refugee priest, Father Joseph Pico, who made an impact by his leadership and example.

Joseph Pico was born July 29, 1884, at Alicante, Spain, where his parents, Mariano and Eladia Pico, were farmers. During his seminary days at Valencia young Pico heard an appeal for priests to serve in Mexico. The seminarian volunteered and Father Pico was ordained on Sept. 21, 1912, at Jalapa, Veracruz, Mexico, by Bishop Joachim Pagaza. "Father Pico had great compassion for the missions," explained his grandnephew, Joe Verdu, Jr.

According to Verdu, Father Pico was assigned to pastoral ministry after ordination and was later asked by the bishop of Veracruz to teach Latin at the seminary in Jalapa. During this time, he authored a number of theological works in the Spanish language. What promised to be quiet days of academic work, proved to be one of the greatest trials in Father Pico's life.

At this time Mexico was seething with civil unrest. Waves of anticlerical sentiments made life and ministry difficult for the Church. Father Pico's situation was further complicated by letters from home which reported difficult situations and requested the young priest's assistance.

One evening, as Father Pico walked in the seminary courtyard, praying his breviary, he was confronted by a breathless youth who warned him that the *federales,* or government soldiers, were planning to raid the school and arrest the priests. Father Pico reported to the rector who discounted the news as a mere rumor. The superior did offer Father Pico the option of fleeing if he wanted.

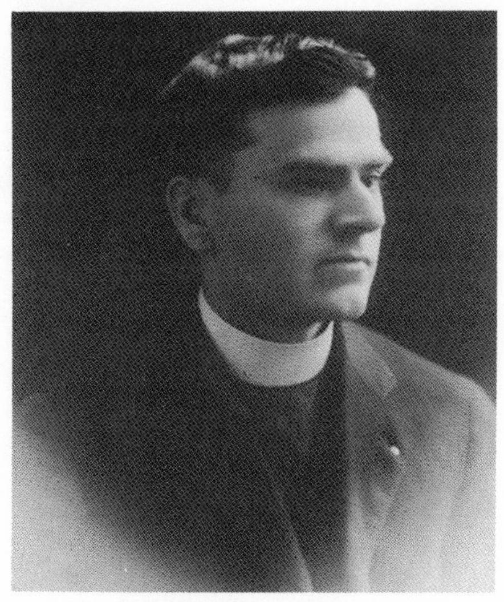

Father Joseph Pico

Verdu recalled that his great-uncle faced a difficult choice. He did not want to leave the seminary although he recognized the danger better than the rector. Yet, he had just written to his mother and committed himself to bringing his two nephews, Joseph and Angelo, to Mexico. At that time, an influenza epidemic struck the section of Spain where the Pico family lived and there was great concern that the young boys would not survive. "He was torn between the promise to his mother to come back and his desire to stay at the seminary," Verdu explained. Father Pico finally decided that he had to remain faithful to his family commitment.

"He got on a horse that night and left Veracruz. He rode by night until he crossed the Rio Grande at El Paso," recounted Verdu. Dusty and grimy from his secret crossing of Mexico, the refugee priest stopped at the first church that he saw. There, he was welcomed warmly and later was told of news reports about brutal attacks on the seminary at Jalapa.

Father Pico's trek continued as he journeyed back to Spain, where he joined his mother and two nephews. The entire family then emigrated to New York City. Father Pico ministered in a parish there while he sent letters to dioceses throughout the United States, seeking a permanent position. Archbishop John Glennon invited Father Pico to serve in St. Louis where he was appointed "pastor for Spanish people" in September 1915.

Bishop Henry Althoff of neighboring Belleville had been especially concerned about outreach to Mexican Catholics settling in the vicinity of East St. Louis. He welcomed Father Joseph Pico into the Belleville diocese in October 1920. Father Pico began his years of service to the church in southern Illinois as assistant to Father Leo Irose at St. Lawrence Parish, Sandoval. Subsequent assignments brought him closer to his ultimate mission. First, he assisted at Sacred Heart parish and then at St. Mary parish, both in East St. Louis.

Father Pico was assigned the task of organizing a new parish for the Catholics living on the outskirts of East St. Louis in an industrial community called Fairmont City. He began his new ministry by making several visits to Fairmont City. "He made a survey of the town, but he didn't dress like a priest," said Bill Longust, a member of Fairmont City's Holy Rosary parish. Longust, who was nine years old when the Fairmont City church was founded, shared his recollections of Father Pico and those of his mother, Emma, who is one of the parish's older members.

Although he started out incognito at Fairmont City, Father Pico soon attained a high profile in the community. When he came to take up residence in the town, twenty-two people welcomed him at Allen Park, which was the terminus of the streetcar line from St. Louis. Holy Rosary parish was ready to begin. Mrs. Louise Allen had donated land for the church and Bauer Brothers Construction Company had built a six-room house, which served as the fledgling community's rectory and chapel. It could accommodate approximately thirty people.

"The parish was international in character from the very beginning since it served peoples from many foreign countries," Father Pico would recall in later years. "But like the apostles on Pentecost, the pastor found that all the people — Mexican, Polish, Croatian, Spanish, Hungarian, English, Irish, and German — understood the language of faith." Father Pico celebrated the first Mass for Holy Rosary parish on his namesday, the Feast of St. Joseph, March 19, 1922. To better accommodate his congregation, Father Pico preached and made announcements in both English and Spanish.

"We had one hard time," recalled Mrs. Helen Daschke, a veteran Holy Rosary parishioner. "This was really one hard parish to start. It was a rough road, but we would work hard for Father Pico." Under their pastor's direction, Holy Rosary parishioners constructed a two-story Spanish-style brick structure, which became the parish church and school. Much of the work was done by workers from the American Zinc Company with cooperation of their manager, a Mr. Kennard.

One of the chief laborers on the job was Father Joseph Pico. "Father Pico was right in the middle of any project undertaken over here," said Bill Longust, one of the parishioners. He recalled how Father Pico started to build a concrete fence around the parish property. The priest would work all day on the outside project and then after dark he would go over to the unfinished basement of the parish building, mix more concrete by hand and pour it for the floor of this parish center. "He was a man who liked to build things. He was an awfully hard-working little priest," Mrs. Daschke added.

Father Joseph Pico realized that a Christian community was built on more than concrete foundations. In January 1924 a parish school was opened under the direction of the pastor. Various laywomen taught at the school including Otilla Claus, Marguerite Woodward, Mary Thomas, Catherine Davinroy, Helen Spitzer, Catherine Bauer, and Catherine Wieseman. This school provided an outlet for one of Father Pico's greatest interests, music. "Father Pico was very wrapped up in music, so he organized a band at Holy Rosary and taught us how to play," recalled Longust. The Fairmont City pastor served as conductor of his budding musicians whenever the group performed for parish or community functions.

He organized the St. Vincent de Paul Society in 1925 and two years later he formed the parish's Ladies' Sodality. As a member of the Third Order of St. Francis, Father Pico also promoted this calling to a deeper spiritual life and in 1927 he reported receiving ten more members into this spiritual association at Fairmont City.

Despite poor health, Father Pico never stopped working for Holy Rosary parish. On Christmas 1927 the parishioners first viewed the two new side altars which Father Pico had built by himself. "He made it happen. He put his whole life into this parish," commented Bill Longust. "It is hard for me to believe all that he accomplished in eight years."

In March 1930 Bishop Althoff transferred Father Pico from Fairmont City to St. Leo Parish, Modoc. During his pastorate, the newly-established mission of Reily Lake was attached to Modoc and during these years of the great depression, Father Pico would ride on horseback during his pastoral visits to this neighboring community. He was later assigned as assistant at St. Mary parish, Centralia and helped with its missions of St. Theresa of Avila, Salem, and St. Philomena, Kinmundy. His final pastorate was St. Catherine parish, Grand Chain, which also served the former St. Benedict mission, Sandusky. During this time, he would minister to approximately fifty Mexican railroad section hands temporarily living in Mermet.

In a certain sense, Father Pico's missionary vision found fulfillment in southern Illinois. Father Pico seemed to always be facing special challenges. Despite financial difficulties, he managed to establish a parish out of an international "melting pot" community. His later pastorates posed similar challenges, as small rural communities suffered during the great depression and then again as young men left to fight in World War II. If there is such a thing as a "comfortable" pastorate, it always seemed to elude Father Pico.

During his years at Grand Chain his health finally broke. He was diagnosed as suffering from terminal cancer. Bishop Althoff granted his request that he could serve as chaplain of St. Mary Hospital, Cairo, during his final illness. Father Joseph Pico died June 7, 1947. After a funeral Mass at Holy Rosary Church, he was buried near the altar at

Mount Carmel Cemetery, Belleville. An eight-foot statue of Our Lady of Fatima stands at the door of Holy Rosary Church as a memorial to Father Pico. It was a gift of his two nephews.

Forty years after his death Father Pico's people still remember him and readily recall anecdotes about the founder of Holy Rosary parish. Many of these stories involve his height. He stood about five feet tall, or maybe even less, and he had to use a small riser in order to reach the altar to celebrate Mass. When altar boys experienced a spurt of growth and began to tower over their pastor, they were removed from the servers' schedule. One parishioner candidly noted that when Father Pico was part of a crowd it was a considerable challenge to find him because he was so small.

Father Joseph Pico may have been short of stature, but his perseverance earned him a giant's place in the history and the hearts of the local church.

CHAPTER 44

Monsignor Robert DeGasperi: The Unique Italian

By Raphael H. Middeke

IN 1957, AT THE TWENTY-FIFTH anniversary celebration of his pastorate of St. Mary parish, Herrin, Monsignor Robert DeGasperi said: ''I have found I have had to help materially as well as spiritually because of our economic condition. I have had to help people get jobs in the mines and the factories. A man has to go after things to help all people.''

The editorial writer of *The Messenger* at the time of his death in 1966 noted that Monsignor DeGasperi probably ''anticipated the Vatican Council's concern for the dignity of the whole man by perhaps half a century.'' A ''sacristy priest'' he was not.

The Messenger editorial characterized the longtime Herrin pastor as ''the unique Italian priest of our diocese — the individualist,'' and as a ''true Father.''

Conversations with former acquaintances and parishioners recall ''the unique Italian priest'' to be sure, but also the ''true priest'' who met his people where he found them and walked and worked with them ''as best he could.''

Doing ''the best you can'' was probably Msgr. DeGasperi's favorite phrase. It was his phrase for encouragement in the confessional, often his final blessing at funerals, and the words which explained his fundamental acceptance of people in their present circumstances. More than anything else Monsignor DeGasperi was there where the people were with their present needs.

''He had a unique ability to accept people where they were,'' said Father Gerald Miriani, pastor of St. Mary, Centralia, and a Herrin native. ''Of course he asked the same for himself.''

Robert DeGasperi was born in Trent, Italy, on October 11, 1893,

Monsignor Robert DeGasperi

and was ordained to the priesthood on May 12, 1918, by Bishop Frank Egger in Brixen, Austria, where he had completed his theological studies.

The young priest served as an assistant in parishes in Italy for five years before coming to the United States, mainly to visit his father who had come to America to find work some years before. He found him in Centralia, Illinois.

After a short stay at Sacred Heart parish in East St. Louis the immigrant priest went to Murphysboro as an assistant. In 1927 he became the first resident pastor of the Ava, Willisville, and Raddle parishes. As the pastor of St. Francis parish, Carbondale, and St. Joseph parish, Equality, he also served the missions of New Burnside, Stonefort, Vienna, and Metropolis.

In 1930 Father DeGasperi was loaned to the St. Louis archdiocese to help meet the needs of the growing number of Italian immigrants in that city.

One of those immigrants was Lena Ghiringhelli who had come to St. Louis from Italy as a young bride. When her husband became sick shortly afterward and died of cancer Father DeGasperi served as a translator and supporter.

Later in 1930 the pastor of the Herrin parish, Father Ermingildo Senese, retired due to injuries suffered in a car accident, and Father DeGasperi was called back to the Belleville diocese to become the pastor of the largely Italian parish. Lena, who found herself stranded in St. Louis without a job, became his housekeeper "until I could learn the language and get a job," she said. She served St. Mary's as the parish housekeeper and cafeteria worker for the next fifty-one years.

Father DeGasperi inherited a heavily indebted and dispirited parish. It was the time of the great depression. The needs were great. John Branca, a St. Mary parishioner who was thirteen at the time, described those early years in these words: "He was everything. He was at the relief offices and the coal mines, equally concerned about the temporal and spiritual needs of the people. He was a priest and a social worker at the same time."

And he was a beggar. The burly, rough-edged priest became a familiar figure in downtown Herrin selling raffle tickets and begging for money when needed. Even though the parish was faced with a large debt he started plans almost immediately for a new school.

The parish of over 500 families included a large number of inactive Catholics, especially the men. Luring them back into the Church became a lifetime mission. Sometimes that took years. But in the meantime he developed friendships and ate at their tables — patiently waiting. But he also had a final ace in the hole which he voiced frequently: "I will get you when you die," he sometimes told hesitant penitents.

The flamboyant Italian priest, who loved ceremony, became the focus of a down-to-earth ministry which rubbed off on many of his associates. "I would have been a much less pastoral priest if the monsignor hadn't been my first pastor," one former associate said. "He didn't portray an aura of intense sanctity of the quality of Italian holy cards," Father Miriani said, "but he loved the priesthood, loved people, and gave generously. If people sometimes became momentarily very angry at him, they later continued to think of him fondly and with respect and esteem."

"He was truly happy with his life," said Bill Barras, a St. Mary parishioner and friend.

"Jobs" are perhaps the symbol of his down-to-earth ministry. When he helped someone, religion and moral background made no difference. "He put a lot of people to work," Lena said, "no matter whether they were Catholic or Protestant. We were here during the depression."

Long before civil rights became a national campaign he appealed for jobs for blacks at out-of-town company headquarters. Barras remembered taking him to a local company and when told the man he was trying to get a job for would be considered at the next opening he said: "This is a big company. There must be work for him to do right now." The man was called that day and came to work the next morning. "Of course, if the monsignor got you a job and you stayed home from work, you could be sure of a visit," Barras added.

The story of Msgr. DeGasperi, the cousin of a former president of Italy, would not be complete without comment on his political friends and involvements. A good friend of former Secretary of State Paul Powell, it was not unusual for the governor and other state officials to come to dinner at the Herrin rectory. For the monsignor, between the lines that separated church and state in his beloved new country was a huge area of gray where politicians and priests met for many reasons.

The new school was built in 1940. An addition was completed after the war. One of the first buildings to be dedicated in the diocese after the war was the new gymnasium and parish center, a huge structure which seats 1,200 people. The dedication ceremony was as much a civic celebration as a parish one, as celebrations at St. Mary's were wont to be. It was hoped that the gym would become the cornerstone of a southern Illinois Catholic high school, but those dreams were never realized.

An example of his educational foresight and interest can be found in a small 1953 news item which noted that the parish donated a classroom to make it possible for a special education program to continue in the town.

Youth were always a concern of the pastor who was sometimes called a patriarchal figure in southern Illinois. He was instrumental in procuring the leases which made the building of Camp Ondessonk possible — an instance in which his political friendships probably didn't hurt him.

The monsignor was a tease — of parishioners and bishops alike. But his humor had an edge of seriousness — usually to teach some lesson or other. His distinctive laugh is well remembered and his humor was classic. He was a brilliant and cultured man but he played the role of "dumb peasant" to great advantage.

When people talk about Monsignor DeGasperi today they are sure to say he was years ahead of his time — liturgically, theologically, and perhaps pastorally. A St. Mary parishioner said, "When you went to confession to him you never felt put down, you always wanted to do better and you were never afraid to go back." Beneath it all was a humility probably best demonstrated in his retirement days when he continued to be a pastoral priest but refused to become involved in the decision-making processes of the parish. A former associate who went to him for advice after his retirement was told: "That is in your hands now."

He is remembered as a great hospital priest, a listener, and a man who treasured freedom — his and others. He was certainly a unique man and priest who exercised his ministry "as best he could." Thousands of friends and acquaintances in southern Illinois to this day know that his "as best he could" was not a halfway effort but one which made sure the people were staying with him.

It is difficult to think of any other man who could have left the church of Herrin and the surrounding area stronger and prouder of its heritage and growth.

CHAPTER 45

Father Paul Drone, OMI: "Blood of Martyrs"

By Stanley J. Konieczny

THE BEST WAY TO DESCRIBE Oblate Father Paul Drone would be to call him an extraordinary, regular guy. The term sounds contradictory, but it captures the spirit which characterized this Belleville native who gave his life for the Church in the Philippines. Paul Drone was indeed a regular guy who loved baseball and a good joke, and who had a special knack for building and repairing. On the other hand, he also possessed a special zeal for pursuing his calling as an Oblate of Mary Immaculate. In fulfilling his call to minister, Father Paul Drone eventually paid the extraordinary price of martyrdom.

Born May 13, 1913, Paul Drone was one of eight children of the late Edward and Rose Drone. Sister Mary Urban Drone, one of Father Paul's four sisters, recalled that their parents were very spiritual and that they encouraged their children to participate regularly in weekday and Sunday Mass at the family parish, St. Mary's, Belleville. Together the Drones would follow the old tradition of visiting churches throughout the city on All Souls Day. Such practices influenced the vocation choices of Father Paul and Sister Mary Urban, who has served the Church as a School Sister of Notre Dame for over fifty years.

"I remember he was always very good to me," Sister Mary Urban recalled during an interview. "I thought he was somebody special because he was a man who loved God as much as he loved sports!"

"His favorite game is baseball," read a biographical sketch on Paul Drone published in 1933. The commencement edition of *The Dawn,* the campus newspaper of the former St. Henry Preparatory Seminary,

Belleville, added, "As a matter of fact, it was as a baseball player on St. Mary's Grade School team that he made his first visit to the college grounds . . . In the orchestra, he played cornet. As a utility man, he has no equal. . . ."

Father Paul Drone, OMI

Former prep classmates offer this remembrance of Father Drone: "Paul was a great baseball player and had a great sense of humor," said Father Stephen Wessel, OMI, who was a fellow graduate in the St. Henry's class of '33 and who made his novitate with Paul Drone. "He was a very special character," said Father Edwin Guild, OMI, who was another associate of the young Oblate missioner. "He was very energetic and most generous with his time." Msgr. Leonard Bauer, pastor of St. Pancratius parish, Fayetteville, played baseball with Paul Drone. "He was very vivacious; the kind of guy you liked to be around," reminisced the monsignor. He noted that at the seminary Paul Drone was nicknamed "Reg" because he would often use the word "regular" to describe just about anything. A fellow student Elmer Holtgrave, who would one day be called "monsignor" himself, also started calling him "Wreckless Reg." Monsignor Bauer thought that the schoolboy name was carried over in "Wreckless Reg's" ultimate vocation as a missionary. "He had a spirit of recklessness; the enthusiasm to do things," Monsignor Bauer said.

On August 14, 1933, Paul Drone recieved the habit of the Oblates of Mary Immaculate. He spent the next few years in Texas, where he made his noviate and then did his philosophy and theology studies in preperation for the priesthood. Father Paul Drone was ordained at the Cathedral of St. Peter, Belleville, on June 3, 1939, by Bishop Henry Althoff. The following morning he celebrated his first Mass at St. Mary Church, Belleville.

After another year of studies Father Paul Drone returned to southern Illinois for the summer. For a few months he ministered at St. Joseph parish, Freeburg, prior to receiving his first "obedience," or assignment, as an Oblate priest. He was informed of his assignment to the newly-formed Oblate missions in Cotabato, Philippine Islands.

A departure ceremony was held at Father Paul's home church on September 15, 1940. Bishop Althoff presided and the parish pastor,

Father Joseph Orlet, was the homilist. Father Paul and Oblate Brother Michael Braun, the first Central Province Oblates to be sent to foreign missions, left Belleville on September 25. Father Drone's sister, Mrs. Mary Rose Voellinger of Belleville, was one of the members of the Drone family who accompanied the priest to Union Station in St. Louis for the first leg of his 12,000-mile journey to the missions. "When we left him at the train station, when we bid him farewell, we never dreamt that we'd never see him again," she said. "I will always remember him as being a happy, joking person; always full of wit."

Once the missioners set sail from San Francisco on October 5, 1940, aboard the *S.S. City of Norfolk,* Father Drone kept in touch with his family and friends by letter as much as his busy schedule in the missions would allow. "He never complained about all the hardships he endured," observed Mrs. Voellinger who shared some of the letters that her missioner-brother sent to Belleville.

"All the people in my mission live along the coast where the great Pacific Ocean begins. There are about 10,000 people in the territory which extends about 190 miles along the coast. The territory is divided into six separate districts called barrios. My visitation to these missions is made by boat; sometimes by oxcart; sometimes I walk," wrote Father Drone in a general Christmas greeting which was published in the *The Messenger* in 1940.

Father Drone spent his early days in the Philippines studying the Visayan language, one of fifteen dialects used in this region. Weekends were spent visiting mission outposts. He would baptize thirty-five to fifty babies on a visit and then write home, urging his folks to tease his pastor that the missionary had more baptisms in one day than Father Orlet would have in a year. Father Drone quickly noted that this stemmed from the isolation of the communities and the scarcity of priests to serve these remote missions.

On January 3, 1941, he wrote, "The people on the whole are very good and try to do everything for you. They are very glad when the priest comes to visit them especially to say Mass for sometimes they have not seen a priest for several years. The priests here cannot take care of all the work; the field is too vast. That is the reason that we have to travel so much in order to visit the people at least once in awhile in order to administer the sacraments."

The young priest worked at building mission churches in these jungle communities and the people back in Belleville were very supportive of the efforts. St. Mary's parish held many benefit card parties for their native-son missioner. One letter would hint of a need for vestments, altar boy surplices, and other religious goods and the next would be prefaced with a warm "thank-you" to the Drone family,

Father Orlet, and the people of St. Mary's for their help. One missionary's diary recorded the fact that Father Paul and Brother Michael worked together to build a church and convent at Glan, where they were also involved in religious education and youth ministry.

Throughout this time, Japanese expansionism threatened the Philippines and the entire Pacific. On December 7, 1941, the Japanese attacked the naval base at Pearl Harbor, Hawaii, and in the ensuing war all communication with Father Paul and his fellow missioners was cut off. On December 10 the Japanese landed on Luzon, Philippines, and the struggle for control of these islands began. December 1941 marked the beginning of long years of uncertainty regarding the Belleville missionary's fate.

In 1943 it was reported that Father Paul and Brother Michael were among fourteen Oblates of Mary Immaculate who had been taken prisoners of war by the Japanese. Later, Father Drone was listed among the prisoners liberated from the infamous Santo Tomas prison camp. Such reports were indicative of the breakdown in communications during the war.

Early in the war seven Oblates had gone to the mountains near Glan as hostilities broke out in the vicinity. Eventually, two left for Koronadal, where they hoped to obtain supplies and news of the Japanese invasion. Two went to Glan for medical attention. Three remained in the mountains: Father Drone, Brother Michael, and Father Edward McMahon. They made contact with three stranded American soldiers and their two Filipino companions, who were determined to reach Australia. The missionaries decided to accompany them to assist the troops as translators and to minister to military personnel in Australia. The group left on a well-stocked, seaworthy craft, but they did not know that the Japanese already controlled the Pacific as far south as New Guinea.

The band was captured on Morotai, an island in the Celebes Sea. They were beheaded and buried in a common grave. Prior to their execution, the missionaries smuggled a slip of paper listing their names to a Catholic Filipino guard. This bit of paper was instrumental in confirming their deaths. Natives led liberation forces later to the mass grave, where they found three Oblate mission crosses buried with the victims.

"Father Drone went to the Philippines for the cause of spreading the Gospel for Christ and in doing this, he was killed. Yes, I would consider him a martyr," stated Father Edwin Guild, who was provincial of the Oblate Central Province when the bodies of the missionaries and soldiers were discovered. The survivors of the military personnel requested that the remains be transferred from a U.S. military cemetery in Manila to the United States. Father Guild presided over the graveside ceremony of reinterment. Father Drone and his companions now lie in a common grave at Jefferson Barracks National Cemetery, St. Louis County, section eighty-two, grave 219.

St. Mary Church, Belleville, was closely tied to the life of Father Paul Drone. He attended Mass there as a youth; celebrated the Eucharist there for the first time as a priest; departed from there as an enthusiastic missioner. It was only fitting that a Requiem Mass was offered at St. Mary Church for Father Paul Drone on the ninth anniversary of his death, July 2, 1951. A chalice was presented to Father Joseph Orlet in memory of the martyred priest. Father Gerard Mongeay, Oblate superior in the Philippines, eulogized Father Drone: "He had left home to give his life to Christ. He had gone to a foreign people to bring them the faith of Christ! For two years, he worked among his adopted people. Then God asked him for the supreme sacrifice of his life."

Quoting St. Ignatius of Antioch, Father Mongeau noted, "The blood of martyrs is the seed of Christians." The Oblate superior then pointed to the fruits of the labors of the three Oblates who had died in the new mission of the Philippines in 1942. Father Mongeau announced that three Filipino Oblates would begin seminary studies in Texas in the fall of 1951.

CHAPTER 46

Kate Boismenue: First BDCCW President

By Rita Renner

ON FEBRUARY 2, 1939, Bishop Henry Althoff conferred the *Pro Ecclesia et Pontifice* medal on Kathryn Frances Boismenue, making her the first woman in the Diocese of Belleville to be awarded this papal cross which was instituted by Pope Leo XIII in 1888. That historic ceremony at Sacred Heart church, East St. Louis, recognized the extraordinary service of an extrordinary woman.

In his sermon Bishop Althoff said, "Mrs. Boismenue has used her influence, power of personality, and the resources at her command to promote the interests of religion, particularly through the activities of the National Catholic Women's Council, through religious vacation schools, and through other important works. . . . She has always been an outstanding member of the Queen's Daughters and has for twenty-five years as its president very efficiently directed the destinies of this society, which enjoys pontifical approbation, and has a noteworthy record of long years of spiritual and corporal works of mercy."

Born in Gallion, Ohio, Kathryn Healy was brought to East St. Louis by her parents, Mr. and Mrs. Michael Healy, who were natives of Ireland. Their home was located in St. Joseph parish and became the headquarters for hundreds of Irish immigrants every year. An acquaintance described them as an "ultra respectable Irish family." Kate, as she was known to her friends, attended East St. Louis schools, including the Howe Institute. She eventually became a schoolteacher and worked in city schools.

Miss Healy married Louis Boismenue, a descendant of the French pioneer Nicholas Jarrot. The couple made their home in St. Patrick parish, where they raised their six children: Adele Flannery died at age twenty-two during childbirth; Marie, who became one of the first pro-

Kate Boismenue

fessional social workers in the area; Marguerite, their youngest daughter, who was deaf and remained at home keeping house and arranging flowers; Louis, Jr., who died in his teens; and Jarrot, who worked in East St. Louis until his death at age seventy-five.

Friends recalled that "one liked to pass the Boismenue home on the way home from Christmas Mass just to glimpse six happy children."

Louis Boismenue was active in civic affairs and naturally his wife became involved in these activities as well. She was a charter member of the East St. Louis Women's Club and was a member of St. Mary's Hospital Auxiliary as well as her parish sodality. This experience would prove invaluable as Kate and her friends undertook a major outreach project.

On May 27, 1896, a disastrous tornado, followed by destructive fires, devastated East St. Louis. Only a short time before, encouraged by the pastor, Rev. P. J. O'Halloran, a group of women began meeting in St. Patrick's parish rooms to sew for the poor. This group of women helped the men of the city to provide food, clothing, and shelter for the tornado victims.

Their work was so outstanding that it was decided they should form a permanent group, known as Queen's Daughters. In a short time their band grew from ten to 300 members. They participated in religious services and functions at the St. Louis Queen's Home for Self-Supporting Girls and Women at 3730 Lindell Blvd. However, their activities were mainly geared toward community and parish Catholic institutions. Their motto was "Love Thy Neighbor" and their aim was to care for the poor, underprivileged, and afflicted. Long before sewing was taught in schools the Queen's Daughters taught it at St. Patrick's, then located at 6th and Illinois Avenue.

Yet another disaster, the high water of 1903 enabled the Queen's Daughters to live their motto of charity. Many East St. Louis residents were forced out of their homes by the flood, which reached to Broadway and in some places beyond. Days and nights were spent trying to keep the water from entering the city and meals had to be cooked for the men on duty. Queen's Daughters helped with this work. They kept the coffeepots on all night long at City Hall to refresh all able-bodied men who were "out on the sandbags" protecting the levee. Clothing and other necessities were collected and the Daughters gave valuable aid.

Financial support was raised in various ways to carry on their program of charity. One of the most noted was the annual charity ball, which rivaled the Elks' Ball and was to East St. Louis what the Veiled Prophet Ball was to St. Louis. The grand march, supper, and ball were memorable events. Progressive euchre tournaments were also great social functions. Euchre games gave way to 500 and ultimately to bridge, which continued until the organization was disbanded.

In 1911 and 1912 Kate Boismenue served as president of the Queen's Daughters. In 1918 she was re-elected president and continued in this post until 1940. She directed activities during World War I and in the days of the influenza epidemic which struck many after the Armistice.

During the trying days of the Great Depression, the Queen's Daughters faced the difficult task of helping men and women who had always been helpers themselves. Demands became so heavy that working with tax-supported institutions became advisable. These were the days when Mrs. Boismenue and the volunteers reported daily to the relief offices to assist as they could.

A partial list of the services rendered during her tenure as president includes: 4397 Christmas baskets delivered;twenty-one persons buried by members and six graves donated; twelve children placed in Catholic schools; 172 ambulance calls furnished gratis; employment found for 282 persons; eighty-one children placed in Glen Addie; First Communion outfits furnished for 278 children; assistance in seven conversions; two marriages validated; two families rehabilitated; scholarships and monetary assistance provided; repair of the altar at the County Farm. (It was there that members brought ice cream and cake treats each March 17.) A total of 9976 families representing 63,223 persons received assistance.

In 1920 the National Council of Catholic Women was established as a federation of Catholic women's organizations who affiliated in response to a request by the United States bishops. The Queen's Daughters became affiliated and the East St. Louis Catholic Women's League, joined by the NCCW, visited the diocese to establish the Belleville Diocesan Council. It became the thirty-sixth diocesan council to join the federation.

Women of the diocese gathered for an organizational meeting on December 3, 1926, at the cathedral, where Bishop Althoff outlined his hopes for such a diocesan council.

He stated: "The Council of Catholic Women was already organized in several parishes of our diocese. At that time Mrs. Boismenue was appointed diocesan director. She has shown profound interest in this work and has on a number of occasions been in Washington attending to its work. It is my firm conviction that Mrs. Boismenue is best fitted to take hold of this work and to carry it on until the occasion of the first diocesan convention." Mrs. Anita Hennessy was selected as secretary.

Kate Frances Boismenue issued the invitation to the opening convention on February 9, 1927, at 9 A.M. in the cathedral. Following an opening Mass, delegates from affiliated organizations voted on a slate of officers, prepared by the nominating committee. They went on to elect Kate as their first president. After short talks by Father Cyril Haffner and Father Henry Funcke, it was agreed to sponsor Rural vacation schools and help Father Albert Zuroweste in his Juvenile Court work.

Mrs. Boismenue served as diocesan president for two years. She remained active until her death in 1949 and quite frequently served as chairman of the Resolutions Committee at conventions. These resolutions were the basis of BDCCW programming for the following years.

On Tuesday, June 21, 1949, Kathryn Healy Boismenue died in her home at the age of eighty-four. Bishop Albert Zuroweste presided at the solemn Requiem High Mass in Sacred Heart Church. Bishop Zuroweste had served as spiritual moderator for the Queen's Daughters during her presidencey. She was interred with family members on the Boismenue plot at Mt. Carmel Cemetery in Belleville.

CHAPTER 47

Mother Veronica Schmitt: A Pioneer Ursuline

By Sister Magdalene Schammel, OSU

OVER FIFTY YEARS AGO, the Ursulines of Belleville first arrived in southern Illinois. According to a news article in *The Messenger,* Father H. J. Freese, pastor of Holy Rosary Church in Fairmont City, noted "Wednesday, Aug. 27, has been written with golden letters into the history of Holy Rosary congregation, Fairmont City, for on this day three Ursuline sisters arrived to take charge of Holy Rosary parochial school."

The Ursulines of Belleville have been active in the diocese since that date. In 1946 they established their regional motherhouse in Belleville, and it became the motherhouse of the Belleville Ursulines when they became an autonomous congregation in 1983.

The person most responsible for bringing the Ursulines to the diocese was Mother Veronica Schmitt, the superior of what was then called the American region of the Ursulines of Mt. Calvary, Ahrweiler, West Germany. In 1910, when she was thirty-years old, Mother Veronica came to the United States. For the next fifty years, she gave all her strength in service to the Church through her own work as a teacher and especially through her efforts, as a superior, to guide the Ursulines of the American region.

Mother Veronica earned her teaching diploma in 1901 and taught in the public schools of Germany for three years before she entered the novitiate at Ahrweiler. From childhood on she led a very prayerful life and had thought of joining a contemplative order, but her desire to combine prayer with teaching brought her to the Ursulines. After her profession of vows in 1906 she continued her teaching career in schools staffed by the Ursulines. Upon coming to the United States Mother Veronica helped staff a rural parochial school in St. Anthony, North

Dakota, one of the first schools opened by the Ursulines in that year.

Mother Veronica Schmitt

Life in a small prairie town was vastly different from that in Germany in a large, well-organized convent. But the people were generous and responsive, and the sisters became their refuge in all problems and troubles. Mother Veronica was happy in her service to God's people and her strong will carried her through all hardships.

Mother Veronica's long tenure as a community leader began when she was appointed as superior for the sisters teaching in Onamia, Minnesota. After two years she became superior at the regional motherhouse in Kenmare, North Dakota. In 1930, when a revised constitution was approved by Rome, she was appointed vicaress of the American region.

Financial worries beset the small American region from the beginning. Crop failures year after year, combined with the Great Depression of the 1930s, resulted in such difficult conditions that St. Agnes School in Kenmare was closed for a year in 1934.

For some years the superiors in Germany as well as those in the United States had expressed the wish that the regional motherhouse could be established in a location closer to a large city where opportunities for education and other advantages would be more probable than in rural North Dakota. In February 1929 Mother Veronica petitioned Bishop Henry Althoff for a school in the Diocese of Belleville. He suggested Holy Rosary School in Fairmont City. In the summer of 1929 Mother Veronica and her counselor, Sister M. Therese Kerle, visited Fairmont City. The superiors in Germany were favorably impressed with the accounts given to them of this new mission. According to Father Freese's account, a new convent was completed for the sisters and dedicated a week before their arrival. Three sisters made up the community in Holy Rosary Convent — Sister Emily Krastel, Sister Mary Barbara Jacoby, (later known as Sister Estelle, who became vicaress following Mother Veronica) and Sister Edwarda Calkum.

The chronicles of Holy Rosary Convent tell of the following conditions in Fairmont City at the time the Ursulines began teaching there:

"The people are, with few exceptions, factory workers who are occupied in the three Fairmont City factories or in East St. Louis. Twelve different nationalities are represented here: Polish, Mexicans, Germans, Austrians, Romanians, Croatians, Lithuanians, and others. . . . Very many do not know English, therefore studies are very difficult for the children. . . . education of children had been miserably neglected all these years. . . . It is a consolation that Father Freese cooperates with and supports the sisters in their efforts." Sister Estelle told of how enthusiastically Father Freese would show off his school to visiting friends. Sister Estelle was teaching fifty children in grades one and two at the time.

In December 1930 Bishop Althoff wrote to Mother Veronica, "At the occasion of Confirmation in Holy Rosary Parish I had the opportunity of seeing your sisters. I am happy indeed that they took charge of the school. Their work is surely very pleasing to our Lord because it is for children whose parents are to a great extent poor and are of many different nationalities."

From 1938 to 1941 the Ursulines staffed St. Catherine school, Grand Chain, in southern Illinois. Due to the small enrollment and the need for teachers elsewhere, this school was closed. The same year, the sisters began teaching in St. Regis school, East St. Louis, and in St. James school, Millstadt.

With the outbreak of war in Europe in 1939, communications between the motherhouse and the American region became difficult. When the United States entered the war all correspondence with Mt. Calvary ceased. The mother general had given Mother Veronica extended authority months before the war began; therefore, she could make decisions which otherwise would have had to be confirmed by the superiors in Germany. Rome extended her term of office as superior in Kenmare, and later the papal legate in the United States extended her term as vicaress.

When the bishop of Bismarck, North Dakota, wished to change the status of the Ursulines in his diocese from that of a papal congregation to a diocesan congregation, Mother Veronica was firm in her decision not to do so. Since the thought of moving the regional motherhouse to another location was not new, Mother Veronica accepted Bishop Althoff's invitation to situate the motherhouse in the Belleville diocese. In 1942 Mother Veronica left Kenmare and took up residence in Holy Rosary Convent in Fairmont City.

As early as 1938 Mother Veronica had announced the possibility of having sisters staff Holy Childhood School, Mascoutah. This became a reality in 1943, while Father Ferdinand Weyrich was pastor. About twenty acres of land near Mascoutah were purchased and plans were made to build the motherhouse there. In 1944 Mother Veronica with two sisters moved to Mascoutah and took up residence in what was known as the "old convent."

Mother Veronica accompanied three sisters to Mounds, in southern Illinois, also in 1943. Father John Fournie, pastor of St. Mary's Church in Mound City and of St. Raphael Church in Mounds, wanted to open a school in Mounds. The furnishings of the school and the sisters' residence, all in one building, were very poor. Yet Father Fournie's contagious enthusiasm and the friendly, generous support of parishioners soon made the school not only a place of learning, but a gathering place for many activities. Father Fournie left to become an army chaplain. Father F. X. Heiligenstein became pastor, and with comparable enthusiasm he supported the small school. Taking this school was another example of Mother Veronica's philosophy that one could overcome difficulties and hardships of a material kind — it was the people that mattered.

Bishop Althoff asked the Ursulines to consider purchasing the Paccini residence in Belleville. Mother Veronica realized the advantages of moving to Belleville, so the residence was bought and in 1946 the motherhouse of the Ursulines of Belleville was established and named Holy Spirit Convent. Later, other houses in the vicinity were purchased.

In 1947 Mother Veronica managed to attend the general chapter meeting in Germany, although she almost missed going. The passports did not arrive until Congressman Melvin Price came to the rescue and had them flown from Washington to East St. Louis. The return trip was difficult, too, as she had to make the voyage on a freighter.

Mother Veronica brought with her the news that her many years as superior of the American region were at an end, and Sister Estelle Jacoby would replace her as vicaress. She was not released completely of the responsibilities of superiorship, as she was appointed first councilor and superior of the community at the motherhouse.

From 1948 to 1954 Mother Veronica was superior of the community that staffed St. Henry's school, East St. Louis. With only a few sisters to care for, her motherly traits were even more obvious than ever before. After two terms as superior at St. Henry's, Mother Veronica became superior in Mascoutah.

Her health, which had been a cause of concern more than once during her years as superior, failed visibly, and after having spent some time in St. Mary Hospital, East St. Louis, she was taken to Holy Spirit Convent. In the last years of her life she was able to give more and more time to one of her favorite apostolates — correspondence. When someone said to her that she should not be so solicitous about answering letters, she said, "But that is all I can do for souls who need encouragement and consolation; they want some visible help besides my prayers."

October 12, 1959, will be forever a memorable day in the annals of the American region. It was on this day that beloved Mother Veronica, the first regional vicaress of the Usulines of Mt. Calvary in the United States, breathed her last.

CHAPTER 48

Father Peter Harrington: Building a Black Catholic Community

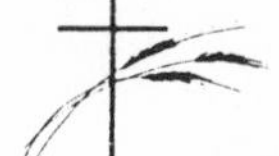

By Bishop William M. Cosgrove

SHORTLY AFTER MY INSTALLATION as bishop of Belleville in 1976, I became acquainted with four converts of Father Peter Harrington: Miss Imogene Wilson, Miss Inez Wilson, Senator Kenneth Hall, and Judge Billy Jones. Inez was one of the first four children baptized by Father Harrington when he began his ministry in East St. Louis in 1921. Through these four people I was able to see how deeply Father Harrington was loved by members of the black community of East St. Louis, especially the members of the former St. Augustine Mission. The devotion of Father Harrington's former parishioners, after these many years was impressive.

Peter Harrington was born on February 8, 1889, in County Cork, Ireland. He received his primary education in the Irish national school system. He later entered Wilton College of the African Mission Society at Cork where he completed his scholastic studies before he entered the seminary in Lyons, France. There he studied philosophy and theology. He made his vows in the Society of African Missions at Black Rock, County Cork, on June 11, 1910, and was ordained a priest of the society on July 14, 1912.

His first assignment was to a school in Cairo, Egypt, and in 1913 he arrived in Liberia, West Africa, to organize a parish at Grand Cess, where he remained for four years. In 1917 he returned to Ireland and became a chaplain to a Scottish regiment which served in the Near East, Greece, and Bulgaria during World War I. At the end of the war he became a professor of ecclesiastical history at Black Rock College.

He came to the United States in 1920 to work among the blacks of this country. Initially, he contacted Archbishop John Glennon in St.

Louis to see if he needed any assistance in the apostolate to the blacks. Archbishop Glennon told him that the Jesuit fathers were serving this need, but suggested that he contact Bishop Henry Althoff in Belleville. He was well received by Bishop Althoff, who set aside $5000 to assist Father Harrington in establishing a mission to the blacks in East St. Louis. Father Harrington began the Mission of St. Augustine at 1400 Broadway, in a building formerly owned by the Obert Brewing Company. The school was founded in June 1921, the first Mass was celebrated on the first Sunday of October 1921, and the mission was officially opened and blessed on Thanksgiving Day 1921 by Bishop Althoff.

Father Peter Harrington

Following the growth of St. Augustine over the next twenty-five years, it is easy to see how devoted Father Harrington was to the people he had come to serve, how much he truly loved them, rejoiced with them, suffered with them, and how much they loved him in return.

Pastors make an annual report to the bishop, which includes noteworthy parish events and also any public occurrences which might have an effect on the life of the parish. This usually consists of a one-page summary. Without going into great detail, Father Harrington reveals much about himself, as well as about his parish, in these annual reports.

When he established St. Augustine's Mission in 1921, there were two Catholic families and perhaps a dozen individuals. He immediately began to work with the youths, and a parochial grade school opened with the arrival of the Sisters of the Blessed Sacrament. Education of the young became the chief priority of Father Harrington and the mission.

In the early years of St. Augustine School a grade was added each year. In 1925 the sixth grade opened. The Blessed Sacrament sisters remained at St. Augustine's until 1937. Then Father Harrington invited the Dominican sisters from Springfield. Although they had no previous experience in the black community they accepted the challenge.

Almost every year, Father Harrington begins his report by stating that not much unusual took place and that there was the normal growth of the community. In 1925 he noted that the Sunday School was the largest in East St. Louis and that it was the envy of a variety of groups as well as the object of their verbal attacks.

Father Harrington's sorrow can be sensed when he mentions the death of Thomas Hall, one of the leading young men of the parish in 1930, but also his joy in seeing more than one hundred Holy Name and St. Vincent de Paul men from throughout the city march through the muddy streets to the Hall home to recite the rosary. His sorrow was also expressed when he concludes the 1930 report by stating "that extreme poverty, amounting to almost destitution in some cases, became noticeable towards the end of the year." In response to this, the sisters began to serve a hot meal every day for one penny.

On more than one occasion he refers to the annual picnic which was important for the financial support of the mission. The white parishes, priests, and people were very supportive of this picnic and in spite of the depression it was still a successful affair. In later years there was some question whether this support was occasioned by the desire to keep the black Catholics in their own school so that the other Catholic schools would not have the responsibility to integrate. In conversations held with some of Father Harrington's friends it was mentioned that there was a definite change in the attitude and support of St. Augustine's school after a black girl was admitted to St. Teresa High School.

A national organization of the Catholic Church, called the Commission for Catholic Missions among the Colored People and the Indians, each year responds to the needs of both black and Indian missions. This commission is still in existence and for the last few years has given assistance to the Diocese of Belleville. In Father Harrington's time annual requests were made to the commission. In 1934 he wrote to them describing the Mission of St. Augustine, "There seems to be a strong undercurrent movement among Negroes toward the Catholic Church. The dark side of the picture would be too long to paint. We have kept our schools open, thank God, but what a struggle! With more than a third of the Negro population on direct relief. Formerly, we could count on help from local parishes, but now most parishes can only make ends meet. I hope the board will try to increase its allowance to us this year — not that we would want to diminish the help given to other poor Colored Missions, but simply because we need all the help we can get."

This request to the commission shows how unselfish Father Harrington was and how conscious he was of those who were in need. He wanted the best for his people but he did not wish to ignore the needs of others. Judge Billy Jones and Sen. Kenneth Hall emphasized how charitable and prudent Father Harrington was. He built strong bridges between the black and the white community and the valuable support that came to St. Augustine's from the white parishes was to a great extent due to Father Harrington's ability to bring out the best in people.

In 1939 he joyfully wrote that while the parish had increased its roll by converts, now it was beginning to increase by births. During that year, four children were born into Catholics families, all former students of St. Augustine School. Msgr. Christopher Goelz, in his 1939 history compiled for the golden anniversary of the diocese, states that the mission numbered over four hundred people, the majority of them young and ninety-five percent of them converts.

World War II helped alleviate the financial stress but it also changed other things. The rotating six-day shifts made it difficult to continue the convert work. There was also an undercurrent of race tension which he mentions "but much less, thank God, than in many similar mixed-industrial communities." The greatest single focal point of race disturbance was in the crowded buses and other transportation facilities.

In 1947 the annual report is signed by Father William Dunne, the new pastor of St. Augustine. Father Harrington's term as pastor had come to a conclusion, not by his choice but because his brother religious chose to elect him as the second provincial in the American province. Apparently, Father Harrington would much rather have remained as pastor of the people whom he loved so much. He moved the offices of the society to East St. Louis but had little time to move about in the pastoral manner with which he was so gifted.

His pastorate at East St. Louis was characterized by his continuing concern for the rights and advancement of his parishioners. In one of his letters in 1948, when the possibility of a Catholic high school for Negroes was being discussed, he wrote, "Bishop Althoff had once been hopeful that eventually, Catholic Central would be opened to the Negro, but at best that would only be half of the solution: it would not take care of the girls, and it may be like poking a hornet's nest to open up St. Teresa. I have always felt that clamorous, forcible entry anywhere would only be a Pyrrhic victory, and whilst deeply wounding feelings would not help the colored so much. In fact, I was hoping that St. Augustine's was becoming so respectable that, to express it like colored folk, 'you all' may some day invite us in!"

Another instance came up in 1949 when an attempt was made to integrate the East St. Louis schools. He states in a letter: "In any ensuing discussion, one pertinent fact will be used in argument: viz. the segregation practice prevailing in our Catholic School system in East St. Louis, which is now, I think, the only large city in Illinois where it continues to prevail."

On this occasion, he also wrote a letter to the editor of *The Journal* criticizing an editorial in response to an attempt by the Negroes in East St. Louis to push for school integration. In this letter he also expressed his unhappiness that no response to a strike by the students of East Side Junior High, in opposition to integration, was made by the school, *The Journal,* or the white parents involved.

Father Harrington was re-elected provincial in 1952 but in 1954 he became ill and underwent surgery at St. Vincent Hospital in New York City, at which time a lung was removed. He returned to the mission at Tenafly, New Jersey, to recuperate. He returned to the hospital in May 1955 and his health continued to improve.

Father Peter Harrington died on December 2, 1956. As the African Mission Society reported, "He died in harness — his Mass said, his Breviary open at vespers of the day."

He was buried in the local Catholic cemetery, far from the people who loved him so dearly. They wanted him to be brought back to East St. Louis for burial, but the African Mission Society wanted him to be with them. Yet Father Harrington was not buried without someone representing St. Augustine Mission being with him.

Three men were especially close to Father Harrington, almost like sons. Two of his "sons," Judge Jones and Senator Hall, accompanied by Father Taylor, flew to New Jersey and were present for the funeral. Kenny Hall had spent most of his young years around St. Augustine's rectory. He says that Norval Hickman was Father Harrington's favorite, that he was next in line, closely followed by Billy Jones. There were many more who considered themselves special favorites of Father Harrington, because he was the type of person to whom every one was important.

At the time, John Kirkpatrick, editor of *The Crusader,* an East St. Louis black newspaper, wrote, "Years ago as a small lad, my path crossed that of Father Harrington. Though a Protestant, I found the playground and other facilities at the small Catholic parish that he founded, fostered, and fathered at 14th and Broadway, a haven for recreation and counsel.

"He was a white man, but his eyes were dim to the color of the skin. His faith was Catholicism, but he sought to help all to whom he could lend a helping hand, regardless of their religious belief."

Kirkpatrick concluded, "There would be no unrest and suffering throughout the world today if there were more men like Father Harrington. Racial discrimination, hatred and bigotry would disappear if all hearts carried the love, tenderness and compassion that he possessed.

CHAPTER 49

Monsignor Fred Witte: Ruma Chaplain

By Raphael H. Middeke

We all believe and know that in Msgr. Witte we have a most positive individual, a Sir Galahad as a fighter, an architect and a builder, a trailblazer in the wilderness, a scholar and a linguist, an educator in the ranks of the pedagogs, a promoter of every good cause, an ascetic without pedantry, a man wholly unselfish who asks no pay for anything and gives away what little he has to dispose of, a friend who puts himself and all he has at your disposition — a man who bears his many physical disabilities without a murmur.

THOSE WERE THE WORDS, admittedly biased, of Msgr. Fred Witte's lifelong friend, Father Francis J. Tecklenburg — fondly known as Teck by the whole diocese — in 1941, when the sisters' "chaplain" was made a monsignor in the convent chapel at the Ruma motherhouse.

In 1941 Monsigor Witte had been the chaplain of the Adorers' religious congregation for twenty-one years. He would stay in that capacity until his death at the age of eighty in 1961.

The chaplaincy became his life's work, and his influence in the growth and character of the Ruma community is part of the congregation's history. "His activity and the congregation's growth have been inextricably intertwined," Sister Mary Catherine Girrens, then the provincial superior, said during his fiftieth priesthood anniversary in the same Ruma convent chapel in 1959. And indeed they had.

From the very first days of his assignment in 1919 the talented and determined priest interpreted the role of chaplain to include significant responsibility in many areas of the congregation's development. His dedication to the Ruma community is remembered with love, for its generosity and its foresight. But no one denies that the good monsignor often expected to call the shots and that he did so forcefully. His influence, at least in the beginning, was "directional," Sister Mary Catherine said.

Monsignor Fred Witte

He was a man of "unusually strong willpower," Father Teck said in that 1941 sermon — a willpower which sometimes clashed with Teck's own free spirit. They were friends — but their very different temperaments didn't permit them to be always friendly.

While it is difficult to limit Monsignor Witte's influence as the Ruma chaplain to specifics, a few are memorable, if not historic.They include:

• His direction and supervision in the constuction of the new Ruma motherhouse in the 1920s, built on a dream, a talent, a determination.
• His role in the educational development and programs of the sisters, the most unique — though not necessarily the most important — of which was the successful effort to convince St. Louis University to become coeducational so the sisters could recieve their degrees there.
• His role in making the Adorers' "American" constitution canonically acceptable in Rome — an effort which almost turned into a nightmare when he refused to give up his chaplaincy at the insistence of the apostolic delegate — before the process reached a happy conclusion.

If these were memorable roles there were certainly others, including his interest in good and Eucharistic-centered liturgy. At his golden jubilee, Sister Mary Catherine said: "From his teaching, I think it has been his insistence on the liturgy as the official worship, that has left the deepest influence on the spiritual life of the sisters." Sister Olivia Forster, Althoff teacher and counselor, says: "He gave us a thorough understanding and love of the Mass which sticks with me today." Father Leo Reinhardt, his associate from 1955 to 1961, remembers being informed in 1958 that arrangements had been made for him to go to the Cincinnati liturgical convention. He looked forward to the liturgical renewal and celebrated with joy at the end of his life the revised Holy Saturday liturgy.

Fred Witte was born on May 18, 1880, in the small town of Foerde, in Westphalia, Germany, the tenth child in a bakery shop family. His father died when he was seven, which later twice threatened his dream of studying for the priesthood — first, when for financial reasons it was necessary to pursue the family's confectioner trade and later when his seminary training was interrupted during his mother's illness so he could take "care of the shop" for several years.

His recurring bouts with pneumonia and tuberculosis on two occasions interrupted his seminary training and in 1903 seemingly terminated it.

But his dream didn't die. In 1906 the young Witte came to America to pursue the goals he could not achieve in Europe.

He had written to the bishop of Little Rock, Arkansas, but had not received any assurances when he arrived in New York. He went instead to St. Louis, only to be informed that the archdiocese was not accepting additional German priesthood students.

He was sent on the road to try Belleville. The first priest he met in Belleville at the cathedral rectory door was the young German priest, Father Francis Tecklenburg, the same Teck who put into print the glowing account of achievements and character thirty-five years later.

Completing his theological studies at St. Francis Seminary in Milwaukee, he was ordained on June 20, 1909. He celebrated his first Mass at St. George parish in New Baden, his adopted parish family, since he had spent his summers with the New Baden pastor, Father Gerard Toennies.

His first assignment was as the assistant to Father Kaspar Schauerte in Murphysboro, with responsibilities for the missions of Raddle, Ava, Grand Tower, Bush, and Carterville. Father Schauerte remained his spiritual advisor for many years.

In a biographical sketch written by Sister Angelita Myerscough at the time of the monsignor's golden jubilee, it is noted that the very first priestly service was to give communion at 5:45 A.M. to the sisters who taught in St. Andrew's School. The superior at St. Andrew's (as she had been for thirty-one years) was Sister Veronica. She became the congregation's provincial superior in 1922, with perhaps a little "direction" from Father Witte. As Sister Angelita says, "in that capacity, [she shared] most fully Father Witte's efforts for the congregation's welfare."

Before those efforts were mutually pursued, Father Witte was the pastor of St. Paul parish in Johnston City and the West Frankfurt mission.

In October 1919 he was named the pastor of St. Patrick parish,

Ruma — a parish already a hundred years old.

Sister Angelita, who grew up in the Ruma parish, recalled his intense interest in the missions, which rubbed off on the parish; his encouragement of devotion to the Sacred Heart; and his religious instructions. Father Reinhardt recalled that he didn't believe in catechism answers. He would advise: "Be sure they can give the answers in their own words." The only name day, Christmas, or jubilee gifts he would accept from the children were gifts for the missions.

But his major energies were directed to the Ruma convent. The convent building itself was a problem. A new motherhouse was needed. Father Witte became the contractor and supervisor of the half-million dollar project. Originally land was purchased on West Main Street in Belleville for the motherhouse, but after it was learned that the new highway would pass through Ruma, facilitating the hauling of materials, it became more desireable to retain the present site.

Construction of the new motherhouse was an all-absorbing task. Even before it began, Father Witte was informed that he had tuberculosis and had from six months to a year to live. Doctors' suggestions to take it easy were ignored and somehow he fought off the illness.

In August 1925 the new motherhouse was dedicated and in June of the following year the chapel, originally postponed for financial reasons, was dedicated. Hindsight cannot appreciate the monumental undertaking of the project in the given circumstances.

In later years Father Witte supervised the construction of other ASC buildings programs, including St. Ann's Home in Chester, and expansions of St. Teresa Academy in East St. Louis and St. Vincent Hospital in Taylorville.

Monsignor Witte served on the diocesan building commission for many years, was a member of the diocesan commission of sacred music, and was appointed to the diocesan school board in 1920.

It is probably in the field of education that the monsignor made his greatest contribution. The education scene was changing and his foresight here was probably the most significant. Because of a lack of opportunities and because of the demand for expansion, the community's own educational progress had suffered. In 1919 no sister had a college degree and only six were state certified. In 1941, as Father Teck told it in his sermon, thirty sisters had college degrees, and 160 were state certified.

Some of this change would have taken place without the direct and forceful chaplain, but much would not have. The establishment of a four-year accredited high school in Ruma became a priority and it was accomplished by 1926.

But the St. Louis University coed story, replete with desk poundings and loud arguments, will always be part of his lore. Originally ten religious from four congregations, including three Adorers, broke the all-male tradition, but only in the school of education. One of them was Sister Etheldreda Heard, who recalls that first year in much the same way that Jackie Robinson recalled his breaking of the color line with the Brooklyn Dodgers. In 1936 Sister Etheldreda became the first woman to receive a doctorate from the university.

Monsignor Witte's loyal friendship to Ruma and the sisters was never doubted, and it was never forgotten by pastors who criticized the congregation's decision to slow the expansion program and place greater emphasis on the educational training of the sisters. That decision, fully supported (to say it weakly) by the monsignor, resulted in some refusals of requests to staff parish schools.

Sister Olivia came to Ruma as a high school freshman because she wanted to be a teacher. Becoming a religious was the result of Father Witte's "encouragement." She treasures to this day his genuine guidance. "He could take you apart," she said, "but he never left you without a good sense of personal worth."

She also found some irony in being sent to the room of the immigrant independent priest, because of her own independence. "He always assured me that independence was not sinful," she said.

Sister Edwiga Degenhardt was his housekeeper for thirty-six years. She called him a "kind and a good man," a stickler for punctuality. And yes, he was independent, and yes, he lost his temper. He also drove a mean car.

"I heard his booming voice for a month after he died," Father Reinhardt said. Someone described him as the "most typical Teuton" he knew. He had a strong, sometimes fierce temper, but "he did not hold a grudge," and he "was not quick in judgment."

Another fault: "He preached too long."

His best qualities? "Magnanimity, forgiveness, compassion, understanding, and a genuine honesty," several sisters said.

He endured stoically, by temperament. In 1927 he suffered a back injury, resulting from a flywheel accident at the convent's diesel plant. It plagued him the rest of his life. But beyond enduring, he prevailed by faith.

The Ruma chaplain died in 1961, a few months shy of his eighty-first birthday — fifty-two years after his ordination, which several seminaries insisted he was too sick to pursue. He was buried, appropriately, in the Ruma cemetery.

CHAPTER 50

Monsignor John J. Fallon: Educational Pioneer

By Linda Lehr

WHEN MSGR. JOHN J. FALLON was appointed the first Belleville diocesan superintendent of schools in 1925 he undoubtedly possessed the aspect of a pioneer embarking upon untrod territory to mark a trail for posterity. Along that trail he established landmarks in education which distinguished him as a prominent educator, not only in the Belleville diocese, but also nationally.

Although he was born in St. Louis (on May 11, 1897), Father Fallon considered himself an East St. Louisan. His family moved to East St. Louis when he was three years old. As a youngster, he attended Sacred Heart school in East St. Louis. After graduating in June 1912 he spent the next two years working for the Louisville and Nashville Railroad, during which time he discerned his call to a vocation.

Taking the first step to prepare for his priestly ministry, the young man entered St. Francis College in Quincy, Illinois, in 1914. There he became a close friend of another student from the Belleville diocese, Albert R. Zuroweste. "Monsignor Fallon had a pleasant relationship with his fellow students and he was very popular among the student body," Bishop Zuroweste recalled.

June 1918 marked young Fallon's graduation from St. Francis College. The following September he enrolled at Kenrick Seminary in St. Louis to complete philosophy and theology studies. On June 8, 1924, he was ordained at St. Peter cathedral, Belleville, by Bishop Henry Althoff. One week later, on June 25, he celebrated his first Mass at Sacred Heart church, East St. Louis.

The newly-ordained priest's first assignment came on July 2, when he was appointed assistant pastor to the Father James Gillen at St. Joseph Church, Cairo. Father Fallon's parish work was short-lived, however. He served Cairo's Catholic community only until October

Monsignor John J. Fallon

1924, when at Bishop Althoff's request he enrolled at Catholic University of America in Washington, D.C. Although Father Fallon loved working with people in a parish, he obediently honored the prelate's request.

Sending Father Fallon to Catholic University of America for specialized courses in educational work was an important decision in Bishop Althoff's plan to improve the schools of the diocese. The bishop believed that the diocesan schools needed authoritative direction so that they could be molded into an efficient and united system. With this in mind, Bishop Althoff aspired to appoint a superintendent to address the task — and the young Father Fallon was given the assignment. "Bishop Althoff chose a person for a job because of the individual's ability. The bishop knew that establishing an organized system of education in the diocese would not be easy, but he believed that Father Fallon was the right man for the job," Bishop Zuroweste said.

Father Fallon received a master's degree in education from Catholic University in June 1925. Shortly after returning to the diocese he was appointed diocesan superintendent of schools and chaplain of Notre Dame Academy, Belleville — a turning point in the history of Catholic education in the diocese.

Prior to Father Fallon's appointment as superintendent a diocesan school board, comprised of pastors appointed by the bishop, dealt with educational matters. The board was ineffective, however, because it had no authority to implement a specific program of education. Commonly, board members felt that their parish school was adequate so they did not advocate sweeping changes in education. Although diocesan schools had satisfactorily increased in number since the diocese's formation, the schools differed widely in plan, scope, and method. For example, a given course of study was not taught at the same grade level in the schools and textbooks varied from one school to another — practices which were detrimental to coordinating a uniform system of education.

With a monumental task before him, Father Fallon's first step was to conduct a survey of the schools of the diocese, focusing on teaching methods, textbooks, teachers' qualifications, and study plans. After a detailed analysis of the schools, Father Fallon devised a diocesan program of education for all of the elementary schools. The program's objective was to establish an organized and efficient system in which a given subject would be taught in all schools at the same time. Textbooks, courses of study, and examinations would be standardized. Such a program would make it possible for a student to transfer from Cairo to East St. Louis in mid-term without loss of standing. Under Father Fallon's direction, teachers' committees prepared the educational program for implementation in the schools. After much diligent work the program was introduced into diocesan elementary schools in the fall of 1929.

Like all pioneers, Father Fallon encountered obstacles and opposition. A number of pastors were not accustomed to someone "from the outside" directing the educational program of their individual parish schools. Consequently, they did not readily accept the superintendent's plan, But he had set an ideal for the schools and he was determined to transform that ideal into reality. To accomplish his goal he made long, tiring trips throughout the diocese to meet personally with pastors, sisters, and teachers. He observed students as they performed their academic work. "Monsignor Fallon traveled from one part of the diocese to another in a Star automobile," recounted Bishop Zuroweste. "It took some time to win over the priests and convince them of the value of an organized, diocesan-wide educational system, but Monsignor Fallon's great sense of humor carried him through many difficult situations," Bishop Zuroweste added.

To complement his educational plan, Father Fallon initiated the annual Teachers' Institute, at which the best ideas on educational work and method were presented and discussed. All teachers in diocesan schools were required to attend the annual meeting featuring noted speakers and educational authorities.

During Father Fallon's administration Catholic schools reached their highest point of efficiency since the diocese was formed. Furthermore, the educational system that he arranged was recognized by educational leaders as among the best in the United States. In fact, the course of studies devised by him was utilized in many parochial schools throughout the country.

As recognition for his educational accomplishments, Father Fallon was selected secretary of the National Catholic Educational Society. The educator also served as vice-president of the elementary school division of this organization. In addition, his educational program was highly regarded by the United States Department of Education.

While carrying out his work as diocesan superintendent of schools Father Fallon also served as chaplain of Notre Dame Academy, where he resided and taught religion. "Monsignor Fallon was a great leader. He was very imaginative and creative. He was willing to be innovative and willing to risk,'' Sister Noreen Slattery, SSND, former Notre Dame Academy principal, said. ''There was something inspiring about his presence, and there was a universality about his service. He did not serve just some of the students — he offered both spiritual and academic direction to everyone. Monsignor Fallon offered a motto for the Notre Dame students: 'Dare To Be Different.' When circumstances in society were not in line with Christian ideals, he encouraged them to be counter-cultural,'' she added.

Father Fallon's associates recall that he could disagree rather strongly with people at times and he had strong convictions. Yet associates are quick to point out that he was a loving, kind person who was willing to offer himself in service.

In the summer of 1934 Father Fallon was named a monsignor, elevated to the rank of papal chamberlain by Pope Pius XI. He was one of the youngest priests in the diocese to be raised to the rank of monsignor. He received the honor shortly after returning from Europe, where he had accompanied Bishop Althoff on an *ad limina* visit with the pope. In 1941 Monsignor Fallon was named domestic prelate, a higher rank of monsignor, with the title of Right Rev. Monsignor.

Among his numerous accomplishments, Monsignor Fallon initiated religious vacation schools, which provided religious education for several weeks during the summer for children who did not have an opportunity to attend a Catholic school. The educator was instrumental in developing not only the parochial school system of the diocese, but also in the establishment of Le Clerc College, Belleville, the only Catholic college for women in southern Illinois. Monsignor Fallon was president of Le Clerc from its founding in 1938 until his death on November 9, 1945.

Without a doubt, the present education system in the Belleville diocese has its foundation in the work of Msgr. John J. Fallon — an educational pioneer who marked the trail for others to follow.

CHAPTER 51

Father Peter Minwegen: Pioneer Oblate

By Stanley J. Konieczny

IT WOULD BE DIFFICULT to gauge the impact that the Missionary Oblates of Mary Immaculate have had on Catholics in southern Illinois. People from the Belleville diocese have been touched both directly and indirectly by the ministry of these brothers and priests. Whether it has been through contact with a retreat master, a visit to the National Shrine of Our Lady of the Snows, or the education of the local pastor, it is quite likely that each individual's spiritual life has been influenced by these men known as the Oblates.

The Oblates of Mary Immaculate can trace their presence in southern Illinois back to the establishment of St. Henry parish and the former St. Henry Preparatory Seminary, both in Belleville. The opening of these institutions almost parallels the creation of the central province, which coordinates the ministry of Oblate brothers and priests in nine midwestern states as well as in missions in the Philippines, Greenland, Japan, Brazil, Denmark, Sweden, and the Canadian Arctic.

Father Peter Minwegen, OMI, is a man whose life and service to the Church is closely tied to these origins of the Central Province and the Oblates in the Belleville diocese.

Peter Minwegen was born on June 27, 1881, in Kempenich, Germany, the eldest son of the late Stefan and Anna Minwegen. Growing up in Germany's Rhineland-Palatinate region, young Minwegen was profoundly influenced by two experiences. He was so impressed by a missionary's sermon that he decided to enter a gymnasium (secondary school) in Holland, where he could study to become a missionary priest.

Secondly, the aftermath of a typhoid epidemic left young Minwegen

Father Peter Minwegen

with a lifelong interest in science, nature, and health issues. He made a hobby of hydrotherapy and was a student of "Dr. Kneipp's water cure." His nephew, Father Elmar Mauer, OMI, of the Oblate Youth Ministry in Belleville, recalled that as early as 1951 Father Peter Minwegen was arguing that smoking would affect the child in the mother's womb.

He made his first profession of vows as an Oblate of Mary Immaculate on August 15, 1902. After completing his studies in philosophy and theology, Peter Minwegen was ordained on May 9, 1907, by Bishop Joseph Damianus Schmitt of Fulda, Germany. Father Minwegen's first mission was to minister to the German immigrants who had settled in Alberta, Canada. One source estimated that at the turn of the century the fertile prairies of this Canadian province attracted as many as 70,000 immigrants a year. During this time Father Minwegen did journey south into the United States, where he conducted a mission at Gretna, Montana.

His mission activities were interrupted at the outbreak of World War I. Due to the hostilities in Europe, British commonwealth countries grew inhospitable to German immigrants. Oblates of German heritage had been expelled from Ceylon and others were detained in Australian concentration camps. Thirteen Oblates left Canada and had assumed ministries in the United States by 1917. This core group would later form the nucleus of the present Central United States Province of the Oblates of Mary Immaculate.

Bishop James Schwebach welcomed Father Minwegen into the Diocese of La Crosse, Wisconsin. The Oblate headed efforts to organize Holy Cross parish, Cornell, and Sacred Heart parish, Jim Falls. In March 1919 Father Minwegen joined fourteen other Oblates for a meeting at St. Casimir Church, St. Paul, Minnesota. The result of this conference was a letter which was sent to the Oblate general administration requesting the formation of a new province for the priests working in Minnesota and Wisconsin.

Four years later Oblate assistant-general Father Max Kassiepe endorsed the recommendation for the creation of such a vice-province, which would be separate from the Canadian province. He advised that the priests obtain a mission house which would serve as their headquarters. Father Joseph Pothmann traveled south to a river city known as Cairo, Illinois, where he wanted to look at some property. En route to Cairo, he visited a priest-friend in St. Louis who recommended that Father Pothmann meet with the Bishop of Belleville, Henry Althoff.

Bishop Althoff agreed to sell the Oblates Priester's Park on the west end of Belleville with the stipulation that the religious would establish a school and a parish on the property in addition to their mission house. The deal was closed in 1924, the same year that the arch-general of the Oblates of Mary Immaculate officially created the vice-province of St. Henry of Belleville, with Father Joseph Pothmann as first provincial.

The Oblates' new Midwestern headquarters, Priester's Park, had once been a farm which had been converted into a recreation area. At one time it boasted a well-stocked lake for fishing, a hotel, roller coaster, and even a racetrack for horses.

According to a history of St. Henry Preparatory Seminary furnished by Oblate archivist Father Ronald Harrer, these pioneer Oblates immediately set to work to establish themselves in Priester's Park.

The Oblates took up residence in a frame house on the grounds while a brick building near the road became the provincial house. The bathhouse was converted into a chapel and Priester's Hotel was renovated into St. Henry College under the direction of Father Aloys Rosenthal, OMI. Ground was broken for a new addition to the hotel building and on October 4, 1926, the first thirteen students at St. Henry's were welcomed by Father Peter Minwegen, the institution's first superior and president.

The pastor of St. Pancratius parish, Fayetteville, Msgr. Leonard Bauer, was among the first students greeted by Father Minwegen. "He was a kind man, but stern. He wanted order," Monsignor Bauer said, recalling St. Henry's first president.

Despite his emphasis on discipline, Father Minwegen remained open to appeals from his students for free days when classes would be suspended.

Father Minwegen instituted festive processions for seminarians and their guests on the Sunday after the feast of Corpus Christi. Although classes usually were out of session students on campus, according to Monsignor Bauer. "Those processions made an impression on me and on the other guys, I'm sure. We stuck around for Sunday after Corpus Christi even if it was in late June," the monsignor said.

When the school year opened in 1927, St. Henry Prep hosted a festival which was highlighted by the dedication of the school's new addition. Enrollment grew from thirteen to twenty-seven by the second year that the school was in existence and larger quarters were necessary. Bishop Althoff solemnly dedicated the new wing. St. Henry's choir, under the direction of Father Minwegen, sang for the solemn liturgy. The next fall, Father Minwegen found himself back in parish ministry at White Bear Lake, Minnesota. He next joined the Oblate Mission band and for eighteen years he preached missions, retreats, triduums, novenas, and days of recollection across the country. Another veteran priest of the Belleville diocese, Father William Brandmeyer, pastor of St. Liborius parish, St. Libory, recalled his encounter with Peter Minwegen, the itinerant preacher.

In 1937, as a newly-ordained priest, Father Brandmeyer assisted Father Gerard Toennies, the terminally ill pastor of St. Michael parish, Paderborn. As his "legacy" to his parishioners, Father Toennies brought in Father Minwegen to preach one of his "fire and brimstone" missions in the German language. "You knew that you had been baptized after one of his missions," Father Brandmeyer recalled with a chuckle.

During the 1930s Father Minwegen returned to St. Henry's to preach at least one retreat for the young men at the school which he once headed. A report in *The Dawn,* the students' monthly publication, shed some light on the style of Father Minwegen. "His eloquence, striking thought, and telling anecdotes helped to enkindle in the hearts of the students a great love and enthusiasm for the important message that he conveyed to them."

Enthusiasm was a hallmark of this veteran preacher. "Uncle Peter was full of enthusiasm and would leave no stone unturned to spread the kingdom. He preached Christ and the Church in and out of season," said Father Mauer. He continued to spread the Good News to the many people who visited the Shrine of Our Lady of Sorrows in Starkenburg, Missouri, where he was stationed after serving on the mission circuit. Starkenburg was a popular pilgrimage destination with southern Illinois Catholics during the 1950s and 1960s and Father Minwegen could continue to touch the lives of the people who shared his pioneer venture in the Midwest.

He later served as the pastor of St. Joseph Church, Orient, South Dakota, until his "retirement" in 1972. He then moved to Chippewa Falls, Wisconsin, where he continued to lead a very active life. In Wisconsin, Father Minwegen celebrated his seventieth anniversary of ordination on May 3, 1977. The then-apostolic delegate, Archbishop Jean Jadot, sent him the following jubilee message: "Your years of service to the Lord and to his people have been marked with extraordinary generosity. The various roles you have undertaken — missionary to Canada, pastor, seminary rector, preacher of retreats and missions —

reflect a heart full of dedication and zeal. Your brothers of Mary Immaculate are especially grateful for your help in establishing the Central Province of the Oblates.''

A few days after this celebration, Father Minwegen fell and after hospitalization in Wisconsin, he was transferred to the Tekakwitha Nursing Home in Sisseton, North Dakota. He died on August 12, 1977, the oldest Oblate of Mary Immaculate in the United States. Father Minwegen was buried in the Oblate Seminary on the grounds of the former St. Henry Seminary, Belleville.

CHAPTER 52

Felician Presence in Southern Illinois

By Gayle Loar

"Don't worry about yourself nor what will happen to you; submit yourself to God's will without reservation and you will merit His blessing. At every moment of your life, in every circumstance, in every sacrifice, repeat these words: 'God wants it so; God permitted it.' Let this be your motto, your solace, your joy, your support in everything that God permits."

THESE WORDS OF MOTHER MARY ANGELA TRUSZKOWSKA, foundress of the Felician sisters, epitomize the foundation of this religious community.

Throughout her life Mother Angela's response to God was a simple *yes*. Without placing a single limitation on their responses, Felicians have been distinguished in their flexibility to adapt to the needs and wishes of the church, in their willingness to meet the needs of the time and in their understanding of universal service to all.

Life was difficult for the newly-founded Felician sisters in Russian-occupied Warsaw in 1855. Sharing the plight of their fellow countrymen, the sisters worked among the Ruthenian Catholics helping them both educationally and spiritually. By 1863 Poland was besieged by civil rebellion. Felician sisters nursed both their wounded countrymen and enemy troops with equal zeal.

Once the rebellion was quelled, reprisals were felt throughout the land. On December 17, 1864, the Czar demanded that the sisters disband and return to their families. Although they were scattered, the Felicians maintained contact and less than a year later Mother Angela received permission from Emperor Franz Josef to establish a motherhouse in Cracow.

Just nineteen years after their founding, the Felician sisters were

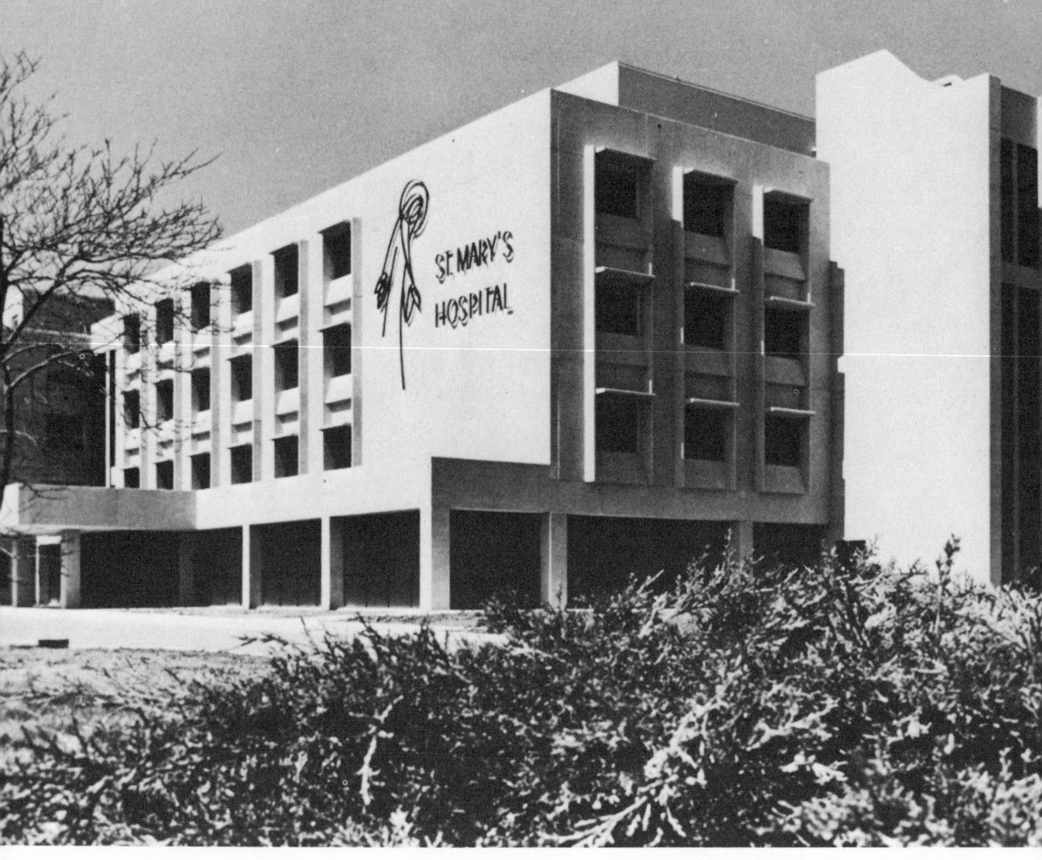

St. Mary Hospital, Centralia

called to serve in America. In 1874 Father Joseph Dabrowski, pastor of the oldest Polish parish in Wisconsin, requested the help of the Felicians. He staunchly believed that the future welfare of his people was dependent upon their being educated and trained by a religious community of their own nationality.

Despite the hardships, the community of sisters in America began to grow. Within nine years, their number increased from five to 200. They opened new houses in several Wisconsin parishes and began teaching in Illinois, Michigan, and Indiana. Although teaching was their major apostolate, they also founded orphanages, homes for the elderly, and, eventually, hospitals.

At about the same time that this Felician outreach was beginning in Poland the southern Illinois town of Centralia came into being. The child of the Industrial Revolution, Centralia was built to serve the railroad. Expansion was phenomenal; between 1853 and 1856 Centralia's construction included 274 houses, eleven stores, four factories, two churches, three hotels, a school, and a flour mill.

Just four days after the Felicians left Cracow for America Centralia's Civil War cannon signaled good news: a seven-foot vein of coal, ''black diamonds,'' was found. Coal was king in Centralia from 1874 to 1938. Then oil was discovered in 1938 and workers from Oklahoma, Texas, and Ohio flocked to Centralia's oil fields, which by 1940 were the largest daily producers in the United States, outranking even the oil fields of East Texas.

In 1939 Bishop Henry Althoff invited the Felician sisters to assume management of Centralia's St. Mary Hospital. Prior to 1939 the Poor Handmaids of Jesus Christ staffed St. Mary Hospital and taught in the parish school. As the needs of the community increased and the number of sisters decreased, the Poor Handmaids were forced to withdraw from St. Mary Hospital.

Formidable challenges faced Sister Mary Celestine, the first Felician administrator of St. Mary's, and her staff of seventeen sisters. When these Felicians arrived in Centralia from Chicago, little did they dream that in the next forty-five years, St. Mary Hospital would triple in size and achieve recognition as a fine regional health care facility.

Sister Paschalisa came to St. Mary's fresh out of school. She was missioned to reorganize the surgery department and set up policies and procedures for administering anesthesia.

''The needs were very great,'' Sister Paschalisa recalled. ''We had great difficulty getting qualified anesthesiologists at that time. Often a physician would arrange to have a fellow physician ''drop ether'' on the patient while he performed the surgery. I'll never forget the excitement and relief I felt when the anesthesia procedures were finished and our first anesthetic machine arrived,'' she said.

In her early days at St. Mary's, Sister Paschalisa witnessed the progress made during Sister Liliose's administration. ''A remarkable woman, Sister Liliose could see the direction which the hospital was taking,'' Sister Paschalisa recounted. ''Wanting so much for the hospital, she didn't wait around for things to happen. Sister Liliose made things happen,'' she recalled.

''It wasn't easy,''recalled Sister Paschalisa ''We worked morning, noon, and night. During the forties and fifties, coal mining and oil field accidents kept us busy. The oil field never slept. Flares burned constantly and midnight was as bright as day. Accidents occurred around the clock and so we worked.''

Through the cooperation of such benefactors as Hugh Murray and John E. Murphy, Sister Liliose was able to negotiate the Felician sisters' purchase of St. Mary Hospital from the Belleville diocese in 1947.

The hospital purchase was just the beginning. With the building bulging at its seams, Sister Liliose and her sisters purchased twenty acres of ground where they hoped to build a new, modern facility. Sister Liliose was also busy organizing the medical staff and working to get full joint commission recognition or accreditation.

When Sister Paschalisa became the hospital's administrator in 1951 she recognized the need to realize the dreams and plans of Sister Liliose. "I knew it was time to use the ground we had bought. It was time to build a new hospital," she recalled. Groundbreaking for the new hospital, four years in the planning, took place on November 21, 1955. "The community was ever so supportive. With friends like Hugh Murray, we just had to succeed," she said.

On March 10, 1958, Sister Paschalisa welcomed the first patient to the new 117-bed hospital. "I'll never forget it. Shortly after moving into the new hospital, I received a telephone call from a rather irate man who demanded to know what I was going to do with all those beds. I never wondered; the beds were always full."

Within ten years, hospital president Sister Miranda experienced new overcrowding problems. Under the leadership of Ben Ober and the late H. H. Pennock, Sr., the community again responded to St. Mary's needs and a forty-bed northeast wing was completed in March 1969.

The new wing brought more than an increase in the number of beds. This addition provided additional space for the laboratory, X-ray, and nuclear medicine. It also made possible a pulmonary function department and a cobalt unit. The focal point of the new addition was the rotational cobalt-sixty teletherapy unit. A first for southern Illinois, St. Mary's became the only hospital outside St. Louis and Springfield to provide this service. The business and admitting offices also found growing room in the addition.

Further expansion in 1972-73 brought St. Mary Hospital to 220-bed capacity. "Going forward, adapting to change was a must," Sister Paschalisa noted. She cited the hospital's school of X-ray technology and its affiliation with Kaskaskia College. Participants can earn an Associate of Science degree through this collaborative effort. Later drives brought space-age monitors and up-to-date medical technology to St. Mary's.

In January 1982 the southwest wing opened and included an emergency-outpatient facility, cardio-pulmonary area, medical records office, and physical therapy department. By 1983 the 246-bed facility consisted of thirty departments.

Sister Clarette assumed the presidency of St. Mary's in 1984. St. Mary's now has gained regional health care status. It has become the only hospital in southern Illinois to have an eye bank, which is sanctioned by the Lions Clubs of Illinois. This eye care facility features laser technology.

The hospital's new cancer treatment center was dedicated in May 1986. St. Mary's became the only hospital in southern Illinois, outside of Springfield and the Metro-east, to offer this capability. New programs in physical therapy and speech pathology have been launched.

This story of growth is not just the story of a building, but rather the story of the Felician sisters' growing commitment to the health care needs of the people of southern Illinois. Each new addition, whether a new wing, a new technology, or a new service, is a response — a response to a human need, a plea for healing.

Centralia and the whole of southern Illinois suffers from a depressed economy and has but faint memories of the boomtown days of the past. In their ministry of caring for the sick and injured, the Felician sisters are faced with the challenges of cost-containment, caring for the poor, the high cost of medical technology, complex issues of medical ethics, and maintaining "high touch" in a time of "high tech."

Amidst these challenges, the foremost consideration remains the same today as it was in the times of Mother Angela: how can the sisters serve God's people? The sisters' ministry is a healing ministry — one that gently touches the whole person.

Working diligently through the years, Felician sisters have devoted themselves to serving God by serving his people. As Mother Angela reached down and lifted in her arms a crying child in Cracow, so today the Felician sisters at St. Mary Hospital, Centralia, reach out with that same gentle care to the sick and injured who come to them.

CHAPTER 53

Monsignor M. J. Gruenewald: Versatile Chancellor

By Harold D. Olree

AN ACCOUNT OF THE DEATH of Msgr. M. J. Gruenewald in 1946 at age fifty-one noted the "versatile capacities" of the longtime chancellor of the Diocese of Belleville.

Until two years before his death, Monsignor Gruenewald, chancellor for fourteen years, had been secretary to Bishop Henry Althoff and chaplain at St. Elizabeth Hospital, Belleville, for more than twenty years. He headed the diocesan mission society for several years and was the first diocesan director of the Society for the Propagation of the Faith.

The account of his death in the October 25, 1946, issue of *The Messenger* said: "As chancellor of the Belleville diocese, Monsignor Gruenewald was in contact with numerous civic, religious, and industrial activities. Through these sources he became widely known throughout the area and respected for his versatile capacities."

At the cathedral Monsignor Gruenewald was a popular confessor.

Accounts of those who knew him indicate that Monsignor Gruenewald took his priesthood and his Church's teaching seriously. Despite his "no nonsense" attitude he is described as "a wonderful and kind priest" by his sister-in-law, Mrs. Ralph Gruenewald, who resides in Belleville.

Marcellus Joseph Gruenewald was born September 14, 1895, in Belleville, one of three children of Joseph Anton and Elizabeth Rudolph Gruenewald.

Young Gruenewald attended St. Peter Cathedral parish grade school and the two-year commercial high school, which was the predecessor of Cathedral High School. He pursued his college and philosophy studies at St. Francis Solanus College, Quincy, and completed his theology at Kenrick Seminary, St. Louis. Gruenewald was

Monsignor M. J. Gruenewald

ordained December 21, 1918, at the Cathedral of St. Peter by Bishop Henry Althoff.

For the first seven months after his ordination Father Gruenewald served as an assistant at St. Mary parish, Mt. Carmel. He then was assigned by Bishop Althoff to be his secretary while assisting at the cathedral. In 1922 he went to Aviston as an assistant and remained for two years. He was named pastor of Our Lady of Lourdes parish, Sparta, and of St. Anthony, Coulterville, July 2, 1924.

Within six months, Bishop Althoff again called Father Gruenewald to Belleville to be his secretary and also assigned him as chaplain of St. Elizabeth Hospital, as well as of Scott Air Force Base.

In 1919 Bishop Althoff had established the diocesan mission society "for the benefit of needy parishes and also for the general good of the diocese, if sufficient funds be on hand." In times of emergency, the bishop provided additional funds. Father Gruenewald was named director of this program shortly after his return to Belleville.

Bishop Althoff reorganized the work of the Society for the Propagation of the Faith in the diocese in 1927 and Father Gruenewald was named its first director.

Father Gruenewald was named chancellor of the diocese August 20, 1930, succeeding Monsignor Joseph Schlarman, who had been named the bishop of Peoria.

During the 1930s Father Gruenewald served as director or moderator of a number of other diocesan organizations. Some of these were health-related because of his interest and dedication to his position as hospital chaplain. These included the Catholic Physicians and Dentists Guild and the Diocesan Council of Catholic Nurses. He was the diocesan representative to the Catholic Hospital Conference. Other positions that he held were secretary of the Marriage Tribunal, moderator of the Association of the Holy Family and vice-chairman of the Friends of the Catholic University of America in the diocese.

In the fall of 1931 Mission Sunday afternoon, October 18, Father

Gruenewald launched the first "Mission Rally" in the diocese on the grounds of St. Henry Preparatory Seminary in Belleville.

Father Gruenewald was succeeded as director of the Society for the Propagation of the Faith and chaplain at Scott Field by Father F. A. Kaiser in April 1934, because of "the manifold duties and the ever-increasing work of the chancellor," according to Father Kaiser. When Father Kaiser assumed the society directorship, he wrote: "In the Diocese of Belleville, this Society is well established, and has made considerable and astounding progress under the zealous and able leadership of Father M. J. Gruenewald. . . . With all energy and devotion he has endeavored during the many years of his directorship to acquaint the people of our diocese with the lofty ideas and the eminent duties of the Catholic Church towards the vast mission field."

On July 26, 1934, Father Gruenewald was honored with the title of papal chamberlain by Pope Pius XI and he was invested with the purple robes of a monsignor September 23, in ceremonies at the St. Elizabeth Hospital chapel.

Monsignor Gruenewald became well known throughout Illinois during 1934, when he led the statewide organization of "The Good Friday Movement." That called for the merchants and businessmen of Illinois to close on Good Friday between noon and 3 P.M. in memory of Christ's crucifixion and death. He obtained the assistance of various Catholic organizations and numerous parish societies in distributing business closing signs.

The movement received strong support and cooperation from non-Catholics. In many towns and cities mayors issued proclamations closing government offices and urging suspension of commercial business activity during the Good Friday hours.

Monsignor Gruenewald also received acclaim in the diocese from fellow priests and others for his knowledge and helpfulness in the chancery office. Msgr. Christopher Goelz, author of *Fifty Golden Years,* published in 1939 to celebrate the golden jubilee of the diocese (1888-1938), said: "The writer owes a special debt of gratitude to the Chancellor of our Diocese, the Very Reverend Monsignor M. J. Gruenewald, whose valuable collaboration cannot be praised too highly. The preparation of many pages in this book was made easy by his tireless efforts in gathering data from the archives of the chancery office and from other sources."

Robert Welzbacher, former managing editor of *The Messenger*, writing on the early days of the diocesan newspaper noted: "Official news of the Belleville Diocese originated at the chancery office of Bishop Henry Althoff where Msgr. M. J. Gruenewald served as press officer."

The diocesan chancellor was given the title of domestic prelate May 15, 1941, and invested September 7, 1941. In his letter of recommendation to Pope Pius XII, Bishop Althoff wrote: "All these years he has given very faithful and efficient service, not to mention his zealous work as chaplain at the hospital and as director of the Holy Family Association."

When Monsignor Gruenewald celebrated his silver anniversary as a priest in December 1943 the homilist was Msgr. Charles Gilmartin, vicar general of the diocese. Monsignor Gilmartin praised Monsignor Gruenewald's "untiring efforts" in promoting organizations and in diocesan leadership roles. He said that the jubilarian had "fulfilled every demand made of him in the exercise of his priestly functions."

Monsignor Gilmartin said that the length of service of Monsignor Gruenewald in the various positions "was testimony to his dedication" and that the honors that had come to him "showed the high esteem in which he was held by the bishop, the clergy, and the holy father."

The vicar general added, "As chaplain of the hospital, Monsignor Gruenewald had a wonderful opportunity to be the priest at all times, and to meet every class of individual in time of distress, in time of sickness, and in time of death. No doubt many souls are in heaven today because of the ministrations of the jubilarian.

Apparently, Monsignor Gruenewald began to tire of his many diocesan responsibilities. Some who knew him said that he longed to be pastor of a parish. He resided at St. Elizabeth and it was said that he had made the hospital a virtual "parish" with appropriate organizations, including CCD classes. Finally, on July 13, 1944, he was assigned as pastor of Ss. Peter and Paul parish, Waterloo.

The next year he started a two-year parish high school with the assistance of Father Leonard Goewert, who was also stationed at Waterloo, and the Adorers of the Blood of Christ sisters. It was expanded to three years in 1946 and to four in 1947. Ss. Peter and Paul High School was the predecessor of Gibault, which opened in 1967.

Monsignor Gruenewald's health began to fail in 1945 and he spent much of the next year under medical care at St. Elizabeth Hospital, returning to his parish on weekends. One evening while hearing confessions at the Waterloo church, he suffered a cerebral hemorrhage. He died the next day, October 20, 1946.

CHAPTER 54

Edwin Irwin: Inspirational Physician

By Stanley J. Konieczny

HORATIO ALGER CAPTURED the imagination of millions of young Americans with his popular pulp novels, the first of which appeared in the 1860s. These success-through-perseverance stories continued to influence youths through the turn of the century. Certainly portions of the Belleville diocesan history have been written by women and men who seemed to have stepped out of a Horatio Alger book. The life of Dr. Edwin Irwin — physician, civic leader, and philanthropist — reflects the Alger ideal of rising to success. But this particular American dream was tempered by a generous Christian charity and concern for the less fortunate.

Edwin M. Irwin was born April 14, 1869, at Leasburg, Missouri, the son of farmers, the late John and Bridget Duhigg Irwin. He was educated in Missouri public schools and after serving a brief stint as a teacher he enrolled in the University of Missouri at Columbia. Irwin later transferred to the Missouri Medical College in St. Louis, where he graduated in 1892.

The new doctor crossed the Mississippi River and set up his practice in New Athens, Illinois, where he met and eventually married the former Emelia Flach in 1896. The couple later moved to Belleville and settled down in cathedral parish. The young family included one daughter, Agnes.

Belleville offered many opportunities for service to the newcomer. In addition to becoming involved in the cathedral Holy Name Society, the Knights of Columbus, and the Catholic Knights of Illinois, Dr. Irwin met a number of professional challenges in the city. In 1904 he became one of the organizers of the Belleville Medical Society.

During these years, he also nurtured a longtime interest in politics and the physician assumed various political offices related to the medical field. While serving on the St. Clair County Republican Central Committee, Dr. Irwin was county coroner. When the United States entered World War I, Dr. Irwin was named medical examiner for the local draft board.

Dr. Edwin Irwin

This experience lends an insight into the kind of man Edwin M. Irwin was. The February 3, 1933, edition of *The Messenger* noted, "Adjutant General Frank Dickson, commenting on the Belleville draft board, pointed out that it was unique in one respect — that every one of the members refused to accept the four dollars per diem, which would have approximated $500 by the time their period of service was over. Dr. Irwin and his colleagues, Cyrus Thompson and J. Nick Perrin, felt that it would be a blemish on their characters to send men to the uncertainty of war for one dollar a day and accept four dollars a day for doing it."

After the "war-to-end-all-wars" was over, Dr. Irwin served southern Illinois as state medical health inspector during the influenza epidemic of 1918. Throughout this time, his prominence in the community grew. In addition to his medical practice and political activities, Dr. Irwin was president of the Belleville Bank and Trust Company. It became inevitable that the doctor would gain considerable public attention and as his reputation grew, his opportunities for political advancement also increased.

In 1924 Dr. Irwin was elected to his first of three terms as a member of the U.S. House of Representatives in Washington. According to reports of the day in the Belleville *Daily Advocate,* he represented the largest constituency in the state outside of Cook County.

In the House, the representative from Belleville served on committees involved with claims, World War veterans, territories, public buildings and grounds. After his draft board experience, Dr. Irwin often showed a special affinity to veterans and their dependents. The *Daily Advocate* reviewed his record in Congress prior to his final bid for re-election and Representative Irwin proved his loyalty to veterans by his actions on the House floor.

"Dr. Irwin has been the sponsor of war veterans' legislation and during the last year (1929), succeeded in having a bill passed providing for the payment of $50 a month to veterans affected with arrested tuberculosis," the daily paper reported. The article also noted that Dr. Irwin fought to "obtain and retain" federal funds for the operation and development of Scott Air Field near Belleville.

Returning home from Capitol Hill, the retired legislator resumed his medical practice. Part of his responsibilities included serving as chief medical officer at the former St. John's Orphanage at Glen Addie.

The children at St. John's won a special place in Dr. Irwin's heart. He not only mended broken bones and wrote prescriptions at St. John's, but also dispensed a great deal of love. This love took the form of an annual Easter egg hunt, which Dr. and Mrs. Irwin hosted every year. The physician and his friends would pool their resources for memorable Christmas parties, complete with gifts of toys and clothing. It was reported that for a number of years Dr. Irwin personally paid for the clothing gifts at these parties. St. John's was home to over 200 children then.

On Thanksgiving Day 1932 Dr. Irwin came down with influenza. No sooner had he recovered when the virus broke out at St. John's Orphanage. Since his associates had contracted the flu and he was chief medical officer at the orphanage, Dr. Irwin assumed responsibility for caring for the sick children virtually by himself. The strain of the situation compounded his already poor health and weakened resistance. He died of pneumonia on Jan. 30, 1933, at St. Elizabeth Hospital, Belleville. Dr. Irwin was sixty-three years old.

That Friday's edition of *The Messenger* eulogized Dr. Irwin as "a martyr to his duty as a physician." The obituary went on to note, "A practical but unassuming Christian, Dr. Irwin's charities were numerous but without display." Expressions of sympathy came from across the nation. Bishop Henry Althoff received condolences from the headquarters of National Catholic Charities as well as from the director of the National Council of Catholic Men.

Judge Carroll Hayes, president of the Catholic Club of the City of New York, stated, "His [Irwin's] was a lifetime well spent in devotion to the Church, her charities and broad fields of human endeavor as physician and member of Congress. New York joins with Belleville in mourning his loss. Dr. Irwin's life is truly an inspiration for those of us remaining."

Bishop Althoff celebrated the doctor's funeral Mass at the Cathedral of St. Peter and Father Joseph M. Mueller preached the homily. "He was a Good Samaritan," Father Mueller said, noting that among his other lesser-known acts of charity, Dr. Irwin would pay for books and clothing for poorer children in local parish schools.

Following the Mass, Dr. Irwin was buried at Green Mount Catholic cemetery, where an estimated 3,000 people gathered in this final tribute.

CHAPTER 55

Brother Henry Heidemann: One of a Kind

By Stanley J. Konieczny

HE WAS EVERYONE'S GRUMPY UNCLE, who seemed to try so hard to hide a heart of gold beneath a gruff exterior. He never constructed a building or founded an institution; he was too busy molding boys into young men. He was a Marianist, an artist, an educator. He was Brother Henry Heidemann, SM, and as one of his former students noted, "There will only be one Brother Henry!"

Henry Heidemann was born March 9, 1905, in Breese, a son of the late Joseph and Philomena Hustedde Heidemann. After attending St. Dominic grade school, Breese, he began his high school studies at Villa St. Joseph, Ferguson, Missouri, and then entered the Society of Mary novitiate at Kirkwood, Missouri.

"Henry's older brother, Francis, entered the Society of Mary at an early age. So it was quite natural that Henry, who admired his older brother, followed God's call into the Society of Mary and gave his all to God and Mary in the area of Catholic education,"explained Brother John Maier, SM, who was in the novitiate with Brother Henry. Brother John added, "Henry was always doing things for people; using the talents God gave him to make others happy. Henry was ready and eager to please people and at the same time raise their minds and hearts to God."

After profession of first vows as a Marianist on August 15, 1922, Brother Henry entered the University of Dayton in Dayton, Ohio, where he earned his Bachelor of Science degree in business. He was now prepared to embark on his half-century ministry in education. "In the classroom as a teacher and on the playing field as a coach, Brother Henry gave himself without stinting to serve God and Mary in all the youths entrusted to his care," Brother John concluded.

Early assignments took Brother Henry to St. Louis, Chicago, and Dubuque, where he served both as teacher and coach. Shortly after profession of final vows in 1928, he returned to his native southern Illinois to teach at Catherdral High School in Belleville. After one year in Belleville, he was again transferred to Chicago and from 1934 to 1936 he served as a teacher and secretary to the provincial superior at Maryhurst in Kirkwood, Missouri. Finally, in 1937 Brother Henry came to the old Central Catholic High School in East St. Louis, a community which would be his home for most of the next forty years.

Brother Henry Heidmann

In 1940 Brother Henry was sent to Belleville, where he coached varsity basketball and baseball and served as athletic director for Cathedral High School. At the end of the school year, though, Brother Henry was back in East St. Louis. "My first experience with Brother Henry was while playing in the grade school basketball league at the old Knights of Columbus Hall in East St. Louis. He could really put on a show for us kids with his underhanded hoop shot from about twenty feet," recalled John O'Brien, principal of Althoff Catholic High School, Belleville.

"He was an important part of our lives in growing up, maturing and in setting the right example for us," O'Brien added. Brother Henry was athletic director at Central when John O'Brien was a member of the school's state championship baseball team. The student-athletes kept in close contact with Brother Henry after graduation. O'Brien had an opportunity to nurture that relationship with his boyhood mentor when in 1953 he returned as teacher and a coach at his alma mater, which had moved and was now known as Assumption High School.

As members of the athletic staff, O'Brien and Brother Henry spent many bus rides sitting and talking en route to countless sporting events. They worked together on the Assumption staff for twenty years. "Brother Henry, in my opinion, was a religious in every sense of the word," O'Brien stated. "He loved people, but he especially loved kids. Brother Henry loved tobe around youth. He was gruff," admitted O'Brien, "but that was just a cover-up for his deeper qualities. He knew he was a soft touch."

During his years at Assumption he taught at different times religion, English, history, math, general business, Latin, and commercial subjects. Brother Henry also took on various extracurricular jobs. He moderated the Mothers and Friends club, the Yearbook club, and the cheerleaders. He also served a number of years as athletic director and coached basketball and baseball. "Assumption was a place that Brother Henry cared deeply about in his own way. Even when his work load had been reduced, Brother Henry still wanted to be a part of the scene," recalled Mary Ann Beondech, academic counselor at Assumption.

"He couldn't do enough for anybody. That is one example that anyone can follow," added John O'Brien. Brother Henry Heidemann became well known throughout the East St. Louis area for his artistic abilities. His styrofoam decorations graced many a banquet table at different holiday celebrations and organization dinners. He spent hours publicizing Catholic events by painting posters and he achieved quite a reputation for his talent in calligraphy. His ability to produce Old English style print by hand graced thousands of honor roll certificates and name tags.

"He was always willing to help," observed Mary Huskey, who worked with Brother Henry during her seventeen years in Assumption High School's cafeteria. Sometimes Brother Henry would go straight from the classroom to KP duty, according to Mrs. Huskey. "He was always in the cafeteria at noontime and if we got behind with our dishes and trays, he'd get back there, take off his coat, and get right into it," she said. Mrs. Huskey remembered Brother Henry's spirit of hospitality and service extending from the cafeteria to ensuring the refreshments were prepared for various evening meetings, to manning his popcorn wagon, which was a popular concession at Assumption athletic events and area parish picnics.

All these forms of service often made Brother Henry a behind-the-scenes man. Yet his worth was recognized in 1959. The St. Philip Holy Name Society presented Brother Henry Heidemann with its annual "Apostolate Award," citing his work on behalf of Assumption High School, churches of the deanery, the Knights of Columbus and the Catholic Youth Organization.

The ultimate honor came in 1970, when Assumption's new sports facility was dedicated the Heidemann Athletic Field. Tim Krum, Jerry Murphy, and Spike Briggs spearheaded the two-year drive to build the field, according to Richard "Foz" Ryan, formerly of the Assumption High School staff. Over two hundred volunteers and area labor unions donated their services working on the bleachers, playing field, and concession stand. "Brother Henry was very proud of it, but he just couldn't see why they were doing it for him," Mrs. Huskey said.

It would seem that full-time teaching and full-time extracurricular activities would have created some sort of a "Hurricane Heidemann." Despite all of his activity he never lost sight of his spiritual roots. Brother Charles Schmitt, a longtime member of the Assumption Marianist community, remembered Brother Henry for his devotion to the Rosary and for always being punctual for community prayer and liturgy. In this sense Brother Henry lived the charism of his religious community. "He was a man of prayer; he was very outgoing to the needs of others. Brother Henry would always inconvenience himself to meet the needs of others," Brother Charles said.

This held true to Brother Henry's last day. Mary Ann Beondech remembered, "My last recollection of Brother Henry was on the Saturday when I administered a placement test to eighth graders. We provided coffee and donuts for the proctors and I arrived early that morning to set up. To my surprise, Brother Henry came and insisted on helping. As he wheeled a cart down the corridor, I noticed that he seemed weak and was trembling. Henry saw no reason to return to the residence to rest, though. He took pride in being of some assistance. It was what he wanted to do. I didn't know it would be the last time Brother Henry could do something for Assumption; the last time he could be on the scene." Brother Henry died the following day.

Father Quentin Hakenwerth, SM, then provincial of the Society of Mary, concelebrated a funeral liturgy for Brother Henry January 11, 1978, at St. Martin of Tours Church, Washington Park. Interment followed the next day at the Maryhurst cemetery in Kirkwood, Missouri. Father Hakenwerth, who currently serves at the Marianist general motherhouse in Rome reflected, "The greatest service that a religious can do for any of us is to put us in touch with God." He continued, "The more simple a person can be, the easier it is for his presence to put us in touch with the God he knows. Brother Henry's charm, as contradictory as it appeared to be, lay in the fact that he was uncomplicated. He was simple. He was dedicated to God in his heart and dedicated to people in everything that he did. He didn't talk about God very much, but he expressed the reality of the God he served in everything he did. Personally, I think people liked Brother Henry's service to them because underlying it was always another presence, sensed vividly but not articulated: the presence of God and our Blessed Mother."

CHAPTER 56

Monsignor Cyril Haffner: Du Quoin Pastor

By Raphael H. Middeke

PASTOR OF SACRED HEART and citizen of Du Quoin. That is an apt description of Msgr. Cyril N. Haffner — known as "Tubby" to the clergy and as Father Haffner to everyone else — who was the pastor of the southern Illinois parish from April 1922 until his death in May 1966.

Father Haffner came to the coal mining and farming community fifteen years after his ordination, which took place August 10, 1907. He had been the pastor of St. Joseph parish, Lebanon, for eight years and the first resident pastor of St. Leo parish, Modoc, for four years. He had built a rectory at St. Leo's while serving the parish as a mission from St. Joseph parish, Prairie du Rocher, where he was an assistant the first three years of his priesthood.

Cyril Haffner, born July 12, 1884, was one of eleven children of Nicholas Haffner and Gertrude Ley Haffner. He attended cathedral grade school in Belleville before enrolling in St. Francis College, Quincy. In 1904 he was sent by Bishop John Janssen to complete his studies for the priesthood to Innsbruck College in Austria. When ordained he was only twenty-three.

Father Henry Reis, the retired pastor of Elizabethtown, is Monsignor Haffner's nephew. Father Reis' brother, Raymond H. Haffner, is a Jesuit priest.

Easygoing, congenial, pleasant. Those are words which are repeated by those who knew Monsignor Haffner well.

Fathers Vito Lopardo and Joseph Trapp — who both served their first years in the priesthood as his assistants — used the word "lucky" for being able to spend those years with "that type of person." "That type" was the congenial, pleasant man, but most of all it was a pastor who respected them, who treated them fairly and generously. He was a gentleman, one of his close associates said.

His interests were not well hidden. One of them was the church. The church, as a building and as a place of prayer, was important in his life. "He took care of the old church. He was constantly fixing it up," said James Genesio, who grew up in the parish. "The church always had to be in perfect shape," Father Lopardo said. He was interested in beautifying God's house," said Msgr. Angelo Lombardo, who visited him often and who was himself the pastor of Sacred Heart from 1974 to 1985.

Monsignor Cyril Haffner

The church — the building and the place of prayer — was one of two great loves in his life, Genesio said.

The other was the Owls, the championship independent basketball team he was sponsored and supported, and the parish gym he planned to build for many years of his Sacred Heart pastorate. The Owls and the gym were symbolic of his interest in youth and children.

The phrase "way ahead of his time" was used by several priests to describe his youth programs and concerns. The *Du Quoin Evening Call,* on the twenty-fifth anniversary of his Du Quoin pastorate, called him an important factor in Du Quoin activities — "church, civic and athletic."

"He was good to young people," said Father Clem Dirler, the first priesthood vocation from the parish. "He supported me in every possible way," Father Dirler said.

People who remember him do not talk long before they talk about his Owls and his interest in sports. And the Owls broke the "ecumenical line" long before Monsignor Haffner had any real ecumenical interests. In fact, among interests and priorities, ecumenism placed low on the totem pole — as would be expected before Vatican II.

During his long pastorate he was a regular visitor in the school. And the kids loved him — probably for the very same congeniality and respect his associates experienced.

"The grade school kids loved to have Father Haffner come," one former parishioner recalled. "He would both ask a question and answer it.'' Another, referring to his easygoing manner, said: ''From the time of my first confession to the time I was twenty-five he always gave me three Hail Marys for my penance.''

He was also recalled as ''way ahead of his time'' liturgically and sacramentally. He looked forward to changes in the liturgy. ''He was always open to trying something different and to suggestions for better liturgies,'' Father Lopardo said.

Sacramentally, long before the council, he sometimes told people not to go to confession so often and he was not a great admirer of novenas.

An anecdotal listing of important dates in the history of the parish noted the ''traditional midnight Mass [of 1964] as the first in which Monsignor Haffner faced the congregation.''

He could be witty and amusing and he could poke fun. Father Trapp, in the early 1960s before it was the general custom, always came out in front of church after Mass. ''Monsignor called me his ''Protestant assistant,'' he said, ''but he never criticized me or asked me to stop.''

Though known as a witty man, he could be grumpy at times and tended to confine himself to his rectory and his church. He did not particularly encourage people to come to the rectory. He did not generally socialize with people of the parish. But ''he was dedicated to the sick,'' as Monsignor Lombardo put it.

Though greatly respected, he was not a civic-minded person in the sense that he belonged to organizations or was active in the community — except, of course, for his Owls and sports interests.

He never drove a car or took a vacation. Sacred Heart parish was his home and his life. In that well-defined world he could be as literal as telling his sister, Sister Henrica, SSND, when she gave him fifty dimes on the occasion of his golden jubilee: ''Ah, keep those.'' Monsignor Haffner was not a ''headquarters'' man. While he served as dean of the South Deanery under Bishop Henry Althoff, his easygoing approach to the job probably cost him an early monsignorship. And though he was made a monsignor by Bishop Albert Zuroweste in 1949 and named as one of the diocesan consultors in 1951, he was an ''outside-of-Belleville'' pastor. He seldom wore his monsignor robes and often complained about how much they cost.

Rose Zwilling, his devoted and faithful housekeeper for many years, was remembered commenting on his perspective in assessing snow flurries and blizzards. If there was an Owls game out of town and there was a near blizzard, he would say: ''It's just a couple of flurries.'' But if there was a meeting in Belleville scheduled and there were a few flurries he would say: ''We can't drive like this. There's a blizzard out there.''

Monsignor Haffner was often referred to as a gracious host — limited mostly to brother priests and servers. He was one of several priests in the area, Father Dirler said, who fostered a hospitality which was very supporting. For years he played a weekly bridge game with three brother priests who met at his rectory. He built a cabin or clubhouse behind the cemetery where he hosted guests and held servers' picnics.

Developing the cemetery was one of his longtime projects and an interest which probably ranked only slightly behind the church and the Owls.

He may have been a benign pastor, but he was in charge of the parish. He wasn't much into consultation. He made his own plans — somewhat haphazardly — and sometimes started them before he told the parishioners what they were paying for. A parishioner recalled the announcement of a plan to add a couple of classrooms and a parish meeting hall and the need for a building fund drive. When he went over after Mass to see just where the new addition would fit on to the existing school, he found the foundation already poured. But that did not diminish his respect or fondness for the priest or the pastor.

He was a pastor of his day, and a man of his day. If he was not greatly interested in ecumenism, neither was he a forerunner in the civil rights movement and was probably, perhaps even in his day, a bit chauvinistic.

A characteristic which must have created some ambivalence was the fact that his services never started on time. They always started early.

Undoubtedly, gifts and church attendance, in some circumstances, are a symbol of respect. In 1947, on the occasion of his twenty-fifth anniversary as the pastor of Sacred Heart, "1,100 Catholic parishioners and Protestant friends of Father Haffner filled the church," The *Du Quoin Evening Call* said. His parishioners gave him "a new automobile, a fine watch, and a $1,300 burse." Ten years later, when he celebrated his golden jubilee as a priest, he received $2,100, the community paper noted.

The silver anniversary guests in 1947 heard about the plans to build the parish gym and hall, which would not be dedicated until 1961, five years before the aging pastor's death. After his death it was aptly rededicated as Haffner Hall.

Monsignor Haffner wanted to spend more years as the pastor of Sacred Heart than the first resident pastor, Father Charles Klocke, who was the pastor from 1868 to 1911, a span of forty-three years. When Monsignor Haffner was buried from the church he loved, in the cemetery to which he gave a new image, he had been pastor of Sacred Heart for forty-four years.

"All my memories are pleasant memories," one close associate recalled. Certainly that was not a universal experience. But in the overall picture of the life of the longtime Du Quoin pastor and citizen, the tones of the congenial and pleasant priest are highlighted — who despite his easygoing and witty manner took his church and his parish very seriously.

CHAPTER 57

Sister Pacifica and the Little People

By Stanley J. Konieczny

"I love my Jesus best of all and to Him I will go;
For though I may be very small, yet Jesus loves me so."

THE WORDS OF THIS LITTLE PRAYER sound very simple and childlike, but they capture the spirit and drive of a remarkable woman who touched the lives of thousands of boys and girls in Belleville for over fifty years. Sister M. Pacifica Funke, SSND, taught this prayer every January to the kindergarten pupils at St. Peter cathedral grade school, Belleville. The little verse *is* Sister Pacifica, who spent her life out of love for Jesus and little children.

This special friend and guardian of Belleville youngsters entered the world on March 17, 1889, at St. Louis, Missouri, one of five children of Mr. and Mrs. Bernard John Funke. Almost prophetically, the baby girl was baptized two days later on March 19, the feast of St. Joseph, the protector of the Child Jesus. Mr. and Mrs. Funke named their daughter, Josephine.

At the age of fourteen, Josephine Funke encountered Christ in the Holy Eucharist for the first time. Four years later, she turned her life over completely to him as a School Sister of Notre Dame. Josephine became known as Sister M. Pacifica on August 22, 1907.

"I think she was well named," remarked one of Sister Pacifica's better known students, Bishop Stanley Schlarman of Dodge City, Kansas. Bishop Schlarman, a native of cathedral parish, observed that the sister's religious name is rooted in the Latin word *pax,* or peace. "She truly was the peaceful one," Bishop Schlarman said.

After professing her first vows in 1910 Sister Pacifica began her

Sister Pacifica

lengthy teaching career in the parochial schools of Cape Girardeau, Missouri, and Fort Madison, Iowa. She arrived home, at St. Peter Cathedral grade school, on August 28, 1913. Sister Pacifica spent her first ten years at the cathedral teaching the primary grades. She probably never dreamt of the impact that she would have on thousands of youngsters when in 1923, Sister Pacifica opened the door of cathedral's first kindergarten.

The early days of the cathedral kindergarten were marked by tight budgeting, but Sister Pacifica managed. She spent countless hours salvaging materials which could be used in classroom projects. According to Alice Frierdich, who assisted Sister Pacifica in the classroom for ten and one-half years, cathedral's dean of southern Illinois kindergartens would speak of processing wallpaper paste so that it could be used by her students. "Sister cut down expenses remarkably," Mrs. Frierdich said.

Operating on a shoestring, Sister Pacifica tackled a most challenging ministry. She took on a full-time job guiding awkward little hands as they tried to print ABC's; coaching timid mini-orators; coping with pint-sized dynamos who brimmed with an abundance of energy; forming young Catholics.

Yet all this did not seem to be enough for Sister Pacifica. "She worried about everybody but herself," Mrs. Frierdich commented, adding, "In everything that she did you could see that she was working for God." Sister Pacifica managed to work for God as a babysitter, who made herself available to working parents, free of charge, early in the morning before the classroom doors officially opened.

Sister Pacifica even found time to do some janitorial and maintenance work. Occasionally an associate would find her on her hands and knees, scrubbing her children's lavatories. In response to her friends' protests and offers to help, she would reply, "All for Jesus!"

Sister Pacifica acted out of love: love of God and love of children. That very element of love kept Sister Pacifica from becoming a marshmallow saint. The concept of "tough love," which is often promoted in the 1980s, had been part of Sister Pacifica's game plan all along.

Discipline became a hallmark of Sister Pacifica's kindergarten classes. Parents felt secure in turning their little ones over to the kind nun with the unforgettable smile, because this educator had earned a reputation of love and discipline. Weekly reports and updates were anticipated by the parents, who read in them the teacher's concern. Classroom difficulties were handled in parent-teacher conferences which often uncovered youngsters' latent vision or hearing problems.

In this atmosphere of concern and discipline, children grew in a loving, yet realistic perspective of the world. They learned to treat one another in a Christian manner. They learned that sometimes they would win and sometimes they would lose. Most important of all, they learned that they were someone special, because of this woman religious who could see some unique goodness in each of them.

Sister Pacifica devoted forty-seven years of her life to the role of kindergarten education. Sometimes twice a day, for a morning class and then an afternoon class, she would retrace old, familiar paths which led her wide-eyed five-year-olds to new and exciting wonders. She never intimated that the routine ever became dull or boring. Those two adjectives were never a part of her vocabulary.

This veteran of the classroom never stopped seeing miracles, especially those in the guise of tear-streaked, smudged cheeks. "One year Sister Pacifica had around 140 students and to her each was an individual. She made you see the good in each one of them," recalled Mrs. Frierdich. Sister Pacifica taught three generations in some families, yet she would be able to remember the first names of the grandparents and the students alike.

Through these years, Sister Pacifica logged a tremendous amount of homework time. Class preparation for her many learning projects and art sessions must have been staggering. She never seemed to have had much of a vacation. As soon as she ushered her class out the door for their first summer break, she began collecting greeting cards and snipping pictures for future holiday artwork and crafts.

During the school year, every minute was accounted for in the class schedule. Special projects were given ample advance time so that they could be completed in spite of the inevitable bouts with childhood illnesses. Also, students were not rushed nor were they encouraged to finish anything just for the sake of completing a piece of work. That was another way in which Sister Pacifica promoted the dignity of her little people.

Sister Pacifica's years, reputation, and mutual respect between teacher and students joined forces to create a legend of sorts, which deserves recognition. In 1960, on her golden jubilee as a School Sister of Notre Dame, cathedral parish held a Sister Pacifica Appreciation

Day.

The Belleville Junior Woman's Club voted Sister Pacifica their 1966 Senior Citizen of the Year. In 1970 the Belleville Exchange Club presented her with their Golden Deeds award.

To mark her sixtieth anniversary as a teacher, Sister Pacifica was honored at a 1970 testimonial dinner, hosted by the Cathedral Mothers' Club. Proceeds from the dinner were used to establish the Sister Pacifica scholarship fund. This was just the first of many fund-raisers that the cathedral parish family held to help create this fund.

Sister Pacifica voluntarily retired from the classroom in June 1971. As she left for the sisters' retirement home, Villa Gesu in north St. Louis, the weekly bulletin at the cathedral noted, "To chronicle the charitable works that she has performed during this time is an impossibility. She would be the very last to cooperate in such a venture. To list the number of families with whom sister has come in contact during this time would be equally impossible. We can only say thanks a million . . . for the many favors done for us."

Within a year, Sister Pacifica was dead at age eighty-two. She died April 17, 1972, at Villa Gesu. She was brought back to the Cathedral of St. Peter, where her wake was held. Bishop Albert Zuroweste and former students concelebrated a memorial liturgy for her. She was buried in the School Sisters of Notre Dame cemetery.

The story does not end with her death, because friends and admirers have worked to keep the spirit of Sister Pacifica and her ministry alive. A memorial booklet was published containing twelve prayers that Sister Pacifica had taught her youngsters. In 1977 a special tribute to the veteran kindergarten teacher began to take shape. Members of the cathedral parish began work on a Sister Pacifica quilt.

Gerry Frierdich designed the colorful blocks of the quilt, each depicting one of Sister Pacifica's whimsical art projects or lessons. The cathedral eighth grade class of '77, the last pupils that Sister Pacifica taught, stitched the blocks which were then sewn together by members of the Mothers' Club. Cathedral quilters completed the job. Sodality members furnished raffle tickets and the Holy Name Society advertised the drawing. Sister Pacifica's tribute was raffled to benefit the scholarship in her name.

This tribute reflected some of the many warm memories of Sister Pacifica that thousands of people treasure today. Perhaps Bishop Schlarman captured some of these feelings when he said, "I remember Sister Pacifica as a saint of a woman whose holiness showed in her deep love for children, infinite patience yet real discipline, deeply caring, with the great peace of God showing through her soul."

CHAPTER 58

Father Joseph Fontana: Missionary

By Stanley J. Konieczny

A DREAM WAS PLANTED in a young boy from Pinckneyville. After years of studying and hard work, that dream found its fulfillment in outreach and hardships in exotic lands such as China, the Philippines, and New Guinea. That dream was the cornerstone of the life and ministry of Father Joseph Fontana, SVD.

Joseph Fontana was born in 1907, a son of Mr. and Mrs. Anthony Fontana, who emigrated to the United States from Italy. As a student at St. Bruno grade school, Pinckneyville, Joseph would dream of being a missionary in the exotic Orient and on occasion he would share this dream with his classmates and teachers.

After graduating from St. Bruno's he entered the seminary of the Divine Word Missionaries at Techny, Illinois. Even an offer to play baseball with the St. Louis Cardinals did not deter him from his boyhood dream. On May 12, 1935, he became the first graduate of St. Bruno school to be ordained a priest. Father Fontana returned to Pinckneyville to celebrate his first Mass.

The old dream became a reality when the newly-ordained priest was missioned to northern China in 1935. Living in the Honan province, Father Fontana helped minister to the 3,200 Catholics who lived in the vicinity of the Catholic mission at Fengui and its stations in outlying areas.

His duties at Fengui included working with the catechumens who lived at the mission. He both taught them and made sure that there was enough food on hand to meet the needs of these future Catholics. Part of Father Fontana's mission work in China was supported by the Immaculata Mission Club, which was formed by an acquaintance in Queens, New York. Father Fontana also traveled by bicycle into the areas surrounding Fengui, where he would celebrate the sacraments for congregations meeting in all sorts of makeshift chapels.

Father Joseph Fontana

In China Father Fontana was dubbed Fan Chuh Hou, which means "he that belongs to the peaceful tribe." Such a nickname must reflect how Father Fontana's ministry sharply contrasted with the political and social climate of the times.

By 1939 Japanese forces had invaded most of eastern China and Father Fontana continued his ministry in an occupied land. When the United States declared war on Japan after the December 7, 1941, bombing of Pearl Harbor, Father Fontana and other American missionaries were confined in Japanese concentration camps at Shantung, Peking, and the Philippines.

Looking back on his imprisonment, Father Fontana recalled the monotony of the daily schedules and menus. In one of his newsletters from the missions he noted that he had eaten spaghetti every evening for two years while in the concentration camp.

Japanese prison camps did bring a happy reunion for Father Fontana. Msgr. Meinrad Dunn, a native of Pinckneyville and pastor of St. Joseph parish, Prairie du Rocher, told this story about Father Fontana's prison reunion.

"The late Sister Mary Regis, an Adorer of the Blood of Christ, had taught Father Fontana at St. Bruno school and had heard him talking about going to China someday. At a later date Sister Mary Regis was also sent to China with a group of Adorers from Ruma. In due time all the missionaries in China were put into prison by the Japanese," Monsignor Dunn related.

"There were many priests and sisters in this one particular prison. A friend of Sister Mary Regis, not knowing whom she was talking to, asked a man if he knew of a priest by the name of Father Fontana. He replied yes, but did not tell her that he was Father Fontana.

"The sister asked him to wait while she went to get Sister Mary Regis so she could inquire about her former student. In a short time, the sisters returned and the first words out of Sister Mary Regis' mouth, were, 'Well, Father Joseph!' The teacher and student were reunited as prisoners of war, far from Pinckneyville."

Monsignor Dunn also talked with Sister Mary Anthony Mathews, ASC, and Sister Maureen Shay, ASC, who were interned along with Father Fontana. They recalled the special liturgy that he celebrated on July 1, the feast of the Precious Blood, for them and Sisters Mary Collette Woltering, Mary Louise Utar, and Angela Frisch.

The signing of the peace treaty between the United States and Japan brought Father Fontana both his liberty and new challenges. Although he had lost sixty pounds in the concentration camp and the regimen took a severe toll on his health, Father Fontana could afford only a brief rest after his liberation. He was now responsible for the resettlement of thousands of refugees, mostly White Russians, in China. Working with the government of the Philippines, the U.S. Navy, and eventually the United Nations, he helped these people escape the Chinese Red Army. For allowing these "enemies of the state" escape, Father Fontana earned a spot on the Communist Chinese "hit list" and his bishop ordered the missionary from southern Illinois to leave China.

After a home visit in Pinckneyville, Father Fontana returned to the East as a United Nations representative. His efforts resettled the White Russians from refugee camps on the island of Samar to Australia and France. One account noted that Father Fontana's service to the displaced White Russians stood as an outreach to a desperate people for whom no one else cared.

Father Fontana returned to the States, where he served as chaplain in veterans' hospitals in Iowa and Michigan until the Divine Word Missionaries found another position for him in the missions. He was assigned to the Owen Stanley Mountain region of New Guinea. Father Fontana would preach the Good News to various tribes, including headhunters, which had very limited contact with Westerners.

The dense, rat-infested jungles of New Guinea defied any comparison to southern Illinois. Again, diet and lifestyle posed special challenges to Father Fontana, but the greatest test of this missionary was the isolation imposed on him at his new home. At first he served along with another priest at Koge, but his companion frequently ministered to the outlying stations and Father Fontana was left to cope with his loneliness.

Without any warning, Father Fontana was reassigned to a mission outpost deeper in the jungles of New Guinea. A plane took him to a primitive airstrip and he was left to spend the next several weeks to try to reclaim from the encroaching jungle the rickety shed which served as both his residence and his chapel. By day Father Fontana battled the bulrushes and weeds; by night, he fought the loneliness and the rats which continually scurried around the shed where he tried to sleep.

In his newsletter entitled, *Under the Southern Cross,* Father Fontana shared his experiences with his supporters. He wrote, "Have you ever found yourself deposited on some strange land and left there all alone to figure out things for yourself? It is quite a sensation, but not a very pleasant one, believe me."

Reflecting on his New Guinea experience, he also observed, "As I have often mentioned in my newsletter and in personal letters to my friends, one of the hardest things in a missionary's life is the lonesomeness, especially for a newcomer like myself. Being accustomed to living in the midst of things back in the States, then all of a sudden being completely cut off from even one's companions, is very hard. . . .

"I was trying my best to keep busy so that the lonesomeness would not drive me insane. I even took up carpentry work and other odd jobs which can always be found around a large mountain station. But the nights became long and I often felt homesick. Even the mountains seem to fence me in, so that I often felt like talking to them just to hear some sort of voice."

With endurance and help from his neighbors, headhunters from the Kanakas tribe, three acres of jungle were reclaimed for St. Mary mission in Goroka. A more suitable residence was built with timber hauled twenty-three miles. Next a convent was built to house Australian Sisters of Mercy. A school for natives opened and a boarding school for European residents' children was planned. Father Fontana then opened a mission station three miles on the other side of the mountain. He traveled this on foot every day to provide Mass for his people.

Emergency surgery forced Father Fontana to leave his mission at Goroka. He was making preparations to return to his apostolate among the Kanakas when it was determined that he would have to undergo radiation treatments for cancer. Encouraging reports accompanied the progress of his treatments, but Father Fontana died suddenly of a heart attack on June 24, 1958. Joseph Fontana, the man from Pinckneyville who realized his boyhood dream of being a missionary, was laid to rest at the Divine Word Missionaries' cemetery at Techny.

CHAPTER 59

John Taylor: Oblate Missionary Bishop

By Harold D. Olree

HE DESCRIBED HIS APPOINTMENT as the first American Catholic bishop in Europe as an example of the "divine sense of humor." After all, he was going into a country where Lutheranism is the official state religion and the majority of the Catholics are immigrants from about two dozen countries.

In 1962 Father John E. Taylor, OMI, a native of East St. Louis, was consecrated the first Catholic bishop in Sweden in more than four hundred years. This Oblate of Mary Immaculate was consecrated to serve in a country which had not had a Catholic bishop since the Reformation in the early 1500s.

But Bishop Taylor was used to being a missionary. When the Oblate's central U.S. province first opened its mission in Scandinavia four years earlier, Bishop Taylor volunteered to head it. He was superior of the mission in Denmark when Pope John XXIII appointed him to the Diocese of Stockholm, which includes all of Sweden plus Denmark, Greenland, Iceland, and some North Atlantic islands.

Bishop Taylor said he was surprised at his appointment but those who knew him were not. His knowledge of several languages would help in ministering to his immigrant Catholic flock in Sweden. At the time only about 8,000 of the 28,000 Catholics were Swedish. Most of the priests were also non-Swedish.

Two men who were close to him in his early years as a priest said that Bishop Taylor had a number of outstanding qualities to qualify him for his missionary-bishop position.

Father Edwin Guild, OMI, of the Shrine of Our Lady of the Snows in Belleville and a previous provincial, said of Bishop Taylor, "He was a brilliant man. He had many great qualities and was very well read and educated."

Bishop Taylor's seminary classmate, Father Stephen Wessel, OMI, who resides at St. Henry Seminary, Belleville, said, "I was not surprised at his being named a bishop." Both Father Guild and Father Wessel agreed that Bishop Taylor possessed two outstanding qualities for his position. He was "a very fine teacher and a good preacher," they said.

Bishop John Taylor

The future bishop was born John Edward Taylor on November 15, 1914, in East St. Louis. His parents were Daniel E. and Mary E. Pohl Taylor of St. Elizabeth parish. His brother, Robert, lives in Pittsburgh, Pennsylvania, and his sister, Marjorie Watts, resides in Toronto, Ontario, Canada.

He entered the Oblates of Mary Immaculate in 1933 after attending St. Henry Seminary. The commencement issue of *The Dawn,* the seminary newspaper, reported on some of the future bishop's leadership abilities:

"At the departure of [Father] Eugene Tremblay last June, the baton was handed over to 'Johnny,' who as director of the orchestra made good use of it." The St. Henry newspaper continued, "His enthusiasm caused a good number of students to take up music. As associate editor of *The Dawn* and story writer he rendered valuable service. On the ball diamond we frequently saw him in the capacity of umpire, and in the swimming pool we often witnessed his skill as the best swimmer and diver of the college. He's a staunch believer in early rising, provided it be not too early. At the recent evening frolic he displayed great ability as master of ceremonies," the article concluded.

He went from St. Henry to the Angelicum and Gregorian Universities in Rome. Bishop Taylor and his Belleville classmate, Father Wessel, were ordained in Rome on May 25, 1940, about a month and a half earlier than planned because of Italy's impending entrance into World War II.

Upon his return the new Father Taylor celebrated a first Mass at his home church, St. Elizabeth, East St. Louis. He then completed his priesthood education at the University of Ottawa, Canada, and at the University of Notre Dame.

He taught for six years at St. Henry Seminary before being named superior of the Oblates' Our Lady of the Ozarks College, Carthage, Missouri. When the order opened Our Lady of the Snows Scholasticate, a major seminary at Pass Christian, Mississippi, in 1953, Father Taylor was appointed as the first rector and superior by Father Guild.

Subsequently, the future bishop volunteered to head the Scandinavian mission in Denmark in 1958. Four years later came his appointment as bishop of Stockholm.

Bishop Taylor was consecrated September 21, 1962, in the Stockholm City Hall, since there was no Catholic church large enough. The event set the ecumenical tone of Bishop Taylor's ministry. He told the Swedish press that he was not out "to convert Lutherans to Catholicism. It is first a question of conscience," he said. "You must do what your conscience tells you to do."

The new bishop also impressed the many foreign ambassadors attending the consecration by greeting them in their own languages, Father Wessel reported.

Later, showing the sense of humor for which he was also noted, Bishop Taylor quipped, "I got more photo coverage than Liz," referring to the famous motion picture star with the same surname.

In 1968, six years after Bishop Taylor went to Stockholm, there were only twenty-three Catholic parishes compared with 1,138 state churches in the country of eight million people. But in that year, Catholics, Lutherans, and other Protestants in Sweden participated in a Lenten procession for the first time in more than four hundred years.

On a return visit to the United States in 1974 Bishop Taylor said he saw a new surge of Christianity in socialist Sweden as the nation's "restless" youth seek more in life than the material comforts of the welfare state. Bishop Taylor was home to attend the Congress of the Oblates' central U.S. province.

In the early 1970s the number of Catholics in Sweden had more than doubled, largely through increased immigration. At the time of his tenth anniversary as bishop there in 1972, Bishop Taylor wrote in one of what became known as his "circular letters" to the States:

"In these years, a number of foundations have been made, new forces have come with the arrival of priests and sisters from many lands. The large number of immigrants are being taken care of, perhaps not as satisfactorily as one would want. But with some twenty-five different nationalities in a minority group in a large country, it will take time to build a strong, homogeneous church."

Bishop Taylor traveled around Europe attending priesthood ordinations and encouraging priests to come to Sweden. He sought to alleviate the shortage of Catholic churches by obtaining an agreement from the state to use the Lutheran churches. Celebration of Mass was forbidden in the state churches, however. He also supported the building of an ecumenical center in Gothenburg, Sweden's second largest city — where Catholics were able to hold study weeks, seminars, and institutes.

Part of Bishop Taylor's missionary ministry were the Catholics among the American military population in Europe. It was while administering Confirmation at U.S. military bases in the spring of 1976 that Bishop Taylor began to suffer head pains. The diagnosis was a brain tumor. He underwent surgery and seemed to improve, but he resigned as bishop effective June 3. He died September 9, 1976 at age sixty-one at the Bridgittine Sisters' retirement home in Djursholm, Sweden, about two and one-half miles from Stockholm. Bishop Taylor was buried in Stockholm.

A comment by the chancellor of the Diocese of Stockholm, after Bishop Taylor's death, indicated that he had made great strides in strengthening the Catholic Church and its acceptance in Sweden. The chancellor wrote, "The Catholics of Sweden as well as his many friends have lost a Bishop who radiated kindness and concern for all."

CHAPTER 60

Archbishop Adolph Noser: Paving the Way

By Stanley J. Konieczny

ARCHBISHOP ADOLPH NOSER, SVD, once wrote, "With God, nothing happens by accident." This Belleville native reflected his philosophy throughout his life, which was spent in the service of the Church. It was no accident that this man who once struggled with his religious vocation later lived out his days ministering in such exotic places as Ghana and New Guinea. It was no accident that this man who had seemed destined to train missioners would one day become an outstanding missionary bishop himself. It was no accident that this leader of vision, Adolph Noser, would establish mission churches and schools which would pave the way for indigenous religious and clergy to spread the Good News in their homelands.

The future missionary was born on July 4, 1900, the first of nine children of Adolph and Katherine Hasenstab Noser, who were members of St. Mary parish, Belleville. One of Archbishop Noser's sisters, Benedictine Sister M. Tharsilla Noser, recalled growing up in Belleville at the turn of the century. "All through the years there were closely knit ties in the family. We prayed together, worked together, and sat down to meals together, each of us taking turns to say grace before and after the meal," she reminisced. "Most of our evenings were spent at home together, studying around the dining room table with just one coal oil lamp for light, then playing games or singing. Dad played both mandolin and guitar; two of the girls played the piano, one brother played the violin and Mom and the rest of us sang."

"Home life was very simple, but it was happy with the love of Mom and Dad and their beautiful example of cooperation through joys and sorrows," she continued. "They taught us fidelity to the little things in life: to sharing, to being helpful to one another and to giving to those families who were more in need than we were, even if it might be just a pan of hot biscuits or cornbread that Mom had gotten up early to bake.'' In such a family atmosphere the seeds of four religious vocations were planted: Archbishop Noser, Sister Tharsilla, Sister Paschatia, O.S.B., and the late Sister Aileen, a School Sister of Notre Dame.

Archbishop Adolph Noser

The young Adolph Noser completed his early studies in Belleville and enrolled first at St. Francis Seminary, Quincy, and later Kenrick Seminary, St. Louis, under the sponsorship of the Belleville diocese. ''He advanced rapidly in his studies in philosophy and theology,'' recalled Sister Tharsilla, but he began to doubt his vocation and left the seminary. Adolph Noser then enlisted in the army for six months, worked as a railway mail clerk, and tried electrical engineering. He was employed at Bakers Stove Foundry, but he could not find the fulfillment which he sought.

Early in 1920 Noser accompanied his sister Irene to Clyde, Missouri, where she became Sister Tharsilla of the Benedictine Sisters of Perpetual Adoration. During his time at Clyde, he spent much time in adoration of the Blessed Sacrament and upon his departure for Belleville, Adolph Noser had decided to enter the Society of the Divine Word and received the missionary habit as a novice at Techny, Illinois, in 1921.

Father Adolph Noser, SVD, was ordained in 1925 at his order's motherhouse in the Netherlands and completed his doctoral studies in Rome in 1927. With such academic credentials, the most logical assignments for young Father Noser would involve education and religious formation. So for the next twelve years, he served at various Divine Word seminaries. In 1932 he published his book of meditations, entitled *Living with God in My Heart.* Revised and reprinted in 1980 by the Daughters of St. Paul, the little booklet has sold 141,000 copies in fifteen printings.

In 1939 the Society of the Divine Word assigned Father Noser and six companions to open their community's first mission in the Gold Coast, the west African country now known as Ghana. At the time only three priests were laboring in a 7,000-square-mile territory where over 12,000 Catholics lived. With America's entrance into World War II, the missionary from Belleville was named vicar delegate of all United States Army chapels in Africa. In 1944 he was appointed prefect apostolic of this mission territory.

After the war Adolph Noser returned home and was consecrated a bishop on August 22, 1947, at Techny, Illinois, becoming the first American of his order to be made a bishop. Cardinal Samuel Stritch, archbishop of Chicago, presided at the ceremony and another native of southern Illinois, Peoria's Bishop Joseph Schlarman, preached the sermon. After visiting relatives and making a speaking tour of the Belleville diocese, Bishop Noser returned to the Gold Coast, where he was named the first bishop of Accra in 1950. His original Sacred Heart Cathedral was a humble chapel which had been built by U.S. servicemen stationed in Africa during the war.

Within six years Bishop Noser is said to have recommended that a native priest be placed in charge of the see of Accra. During his years in the Gold Coast the Catholic population tripled. Friends in America helped Bishop Noser build numerous churches and mission schools and outposts. The bishop's farewell celebrations were marked by the blessing of the cornerstone for Accra's new Cathedral of the Holy Spirit and by a personal tribute from the Gold Coast's Prime Minister Kwame Nkrumah.

Pope Pius XII extended a new challenge to Bishop Noser by naming him the vicar apostolic of eastern New Guinea in the South Pacific. He was elevated to archbishop of Madang in 1966 and consecrated that see's new Cathedral of the Holy Spirit the following year. A *Messenger* article marking Archbishop Noser's silver episcopal anniversary noted, "He is known as an able administrator with a deep understanding of the cultural fabric of the New Guinea nation. . . . Archbishop Noser is optimistic that local government and independence will succeed. . . . He expects the nation will prosper and education and religion will be fostered as communications and ways of life are improved."

During his twenty-two years in New Guinea, Archbishop Noser was instrumental in rebuilding the war-ravished island. Archbishop Noser proved himself to be a man of vision, energy, and most of all prayer during these years of growth. One of the archbishop's most ambitious undertakings speaks volumes about the kind of man that he was.

"Soon after reaching New Guinea, Bishop Adolph desired to found a community of perpetual adoration in his diocese because he felt that unless there was a powerhouse of prayer to support his missionaries in their active labors, the latter would have little success," explained Sister Tharsilla. No order was willing to send a community to Madang, so Archbishop Noser sought prayer partners in seven foreign communities which pledged one of their days of perpetual adoration each week to support of the mission of Magang.

By 1954 prayer and perseverance won out and Archbishop Adolph Noser realized his dream as he received the first candidates into the sisterhood of St. Therese, which he established at Alexishafen, New Guinea. The community of native religious was founded to serve as nurses and teachers in diocesan institutions.

In 1976 Archbishop Noser retired as head of the Church at Madang, but remained active until he died at his home on April 15, 1981. He was buried with simplicity and love on the island where he had served for so many years. Thousands passed his bier which was made of rough sawhorses, and the humble archbishop from Belleville was driven to his final resting place in a small truck-turned-hearse, decorated with garlands and wreaths of flowers.

CHAPTER 61

Professor Bernard L. Miller: Dedicated Genius

By Rev. Theodore C. Siekmann

BERNARD L. MILLER, usually referred to as Professor Miller, or more familiarly by his students as Prof Miller, was born in Pittsburgh, Pennsylvania, in 1893.

Endowed with obvious musical talents, he received early musical instruction in violin, piano, and organ. He earned a bachelor's degree from Pio Nono Normal, Milwaukee, and a master's degree from Marquette University, Milwaukee. He also attended the Wisconsin Conservatory of Music and De Paul University, Chicago.

Professor Miller was hired by Bishop Henry Althoff to be organist and choir director of St. Peter Cathedral in Belleville. Although he taught other subjects at Cathedral High School and at St. Henry Seminary, music was his life. Music was where he made his greatest contribution.

He was a kind of universal genius. If a teacher was needed on short notice, he could fill in for almost any subject. He taught Latin and Greek at St. Henry Seminary for thirty-six years. At times he also taught geometry.

Music was, however, his consuming passion.

Beside his work as an organist at the cathedral, he developed a musical program for the cathedral choir that was superb in the quality of the music chosen and in his personal direction of the choir.

The professor was also active in other musical endeavors. He gave organ recitals over area radio stations. He was band director for Cathedral High School. He was director of the Belleville Liederkranz Society, Belleville Philharmonic, and Cathedral Players Guild. He also led the glee club at Notre Dame Academy and Le Clerc College.

In addition to these musical activities, he taught at Cathedral High

School for fifteen years and at St. Henry Seminary for thirty-six years.

But his greatest achievement was his untiring service as cathedral organist and choir director for forty-five years. This included the routine organ playing on weekdays, working with the children, and behind-the-scenes work.

Professor Bernard L. Miller

Someone once tried to estimate the number of times he climbed the stairs to the cathedral organ loft. Daily at least once and often many times a day, into the night, — it would seem about 50,000 to 60,000 times, probably more.

It would be difficult to count how many times he dutifully entered the classroom day after day for so many years.

In his musical chores at the cathedral, he did not work alone. Bishop Althoff and he collaborated in producing one of the best liturgies in the nation at that time.

As so often with a genius, not everyone understood his or Bishop Althoff's true value. Still, everyone had to be impressed with the splendid liturgy in the Belleville cathedral. Bishop Althoff was always very conscientious in following the legislation and counsels of the Church.

Professor Miller, with his musical training and background, and with his own great loyalty to the Church, was able and eager to provide the appropriate music. Professor Miller also had a beautiful singing voice which was a great asset in his work. His own solo voice could fill the cathedral like a choir.

It was in a way an age of liturgical decadence. Not every church at the time was heeding the call of Pius X to restore all things in Christ and bring about a liturgical revival.

But the Belleville cathedral had a liturgy correct, majestic, and moving, for that time.

True, those were the days of triumphalism and regalism, and the liturgy could be expected on great occasions to be a magnificent drama. In Belleville it was. Probably few today would want to return to that regal type of liturgy; yet in its day it was a grand and moving event.

Professor Miller was at his best in recessionals. After a splendid pontifical High Mass with all the elaborate vestments and trappings and regal ceremonies, with the abundant bows and kisses, the church ablaze with candles and redolent with the scent of flowers and clouds of incense rising to heaven, the recessional began.

Bishop Althoff, led by servers and clad in ermine *cappa magna*, was about to exit in a colorful and dignified recessional.

Professor Miller was at the mighty organ. As the bishop left the sanctuary, Professor Miller would literally pull out all the stops. The organ thundered in an unbelievable shout of praise: glory to God in the highest! Heaven and earth were as one.

There was not a dry eye in the cathedral. Elderly men and women could be seen with tears of joy streaming down their furrowed cheeks.

Professor Miller was at the organ, dancing on the pedals, his thin hands sweeping with frenzied fervor over the keys, his eyes afire, his whole body leaping with emotion — as the mighty organ shook the church to its foundations.

The younger generation will never know the glory and the triumph that was once the Belleville cathedral.

Professor Miller and Bishop Althoff were the kind of team found only once in a century.

They were both very small and very thin men. They were both unassuming in appearance. They both, by their low-key appearance, belied the truly great men they were. Each was a person of great talent and great dedication.

Honor would come to Professor Miller. He was named a Knight of St. Gregory by Pope Pius XII in 1942.

In 1954, after he had been organist and choir director at the cathedral for thirty-eight years and after many other accomplishments in music, Professor Miller was honored as the Musician of the Year at the Southern Illinois Music Festival at Southern Illinois University at Carbondale.

After forty-five years of dedicated work at the cathedral and after his many years of teaching, Professor Miller began to fail in health. He retired in 1961 and died in 1964 at the age of seventy-one. He is buried in Green Mount cemetery at Belleville.

He was survived by his wife, the former Lydia Karr, a daughter, Julia, and three sons, Thomas B., Robert L., and Father William Miller, SJ.

On July 7, 1974, a patriotic concert dedicated to Professor Miller was held in the cathedral. His widow and family were honored guests.

Professor Miller was a loyal and dedicated man. He served well his God, his Church, his bishop, and all the people.

CHAPTER 62

Father John Henken: Young People's Priest

By Raphael H. Middeke

HUMBLE, GENEROUS, LOVED by kids and young people. That is how Father John Henken is most often remembered in words written about him and in words spoken of him by friends and acquaintances. He ministered for fifty-six years in the Diocese of Belleville, from 1895 to 1952.

"He was very modest, very charitable. He had nothing," Mrs. Millie Brennfleck, his niece and housekeeper for fifteen years, said. "He didn't have an enemy," added Mrs. Brennfleck, who now lives in Belleville.

"He made holiness attractive," Father William Brandmeyer, pastor of St. Liborius parish, St. Libory, said. Father Brandmeyer was a boy when Father Henken was the pastor of St. Damian's in Damiansville in the 1920s and 1930s.

"He taught me more about what it meant to be a priest than any priest I know," Father Francis "X" Heiligenstein once said. As a young priest, Father Heiligenstein, who died during the summer of 1983, was his associate for less than a year. (The lessons seemingly were well learned. When someone tried to explain recently what kind of a priest Father Henken was, he described him as "a Father X type.")

"All he wanted to be was a country parish priest," said Deacon Allen Agers of St. Mary parish, Mt. Carmel. When as a teenager Agers needed a place to live and study, he was directed by another priest to Father Henken, then the pastor of St. Damian's. He lived with him for several years, then followed him to St. Libory. Agers was one of a number of young men for whom Father Henken was a private high school tutor prior to their entering St. Henry Seminary. The

Father John Henken

group included Fathers Ed Arenten, Brandmeyer, and the former Aloysius Olliges, and Alphonse Schomaker — all Damiansville natives. "He worked and loved a lot," Agers said.

John Henken was born in Clinton County September 4, 1870. Before entering St. Joseph's College, Teutopolis, Illinois, he had taken private Latin lessons from Father Joseph Spaeth, the first pastor of the Bartelso parish, whom Father Henken remembered years later as "the forceful instructor."

He was ordained on June 16, 1895, and celebrated his first Mass in St. Mary Church, Carlyle. After two years as an associate and administrator in several parishes, he was appointed the first resident pastor of St. Joseph parish, Elizabethtown, and the Delwood mission. He left Elizabethtown six years later.

At the time, he was suffering from walking typhoid, which plagued him for the next three years.

After pastorates in Sandoval with missions in Kinmundy, Patoka, and Olney from 1903 to 1913, Father Henken was given a leave of absence from the diocese and taught for eighteen months at the St. Benedict Seminary in Louisiana.

With probably an overdose of humility, Father Henken attributed his leave of absence to "severe mental strain." It is no secret that the happy-go-lucky, popular priest, whose rectory was an open house for priests and parishioners alike, developed a style and a ministry not particularly appreciated by Bishop Henry Althoff, the serious, retiring and restrained bishop of Belleville from 1914 to 1946. Father Henken's free-spirited personality led in coming years to a strained relationship with his bishop and may have been a factor in the circumstances surrounding his leave of absence. At any rate, when Father Henken returned to the diocese, he served as an associate at St. Elizabeth parish, East St. Louis, for several years because, as he says in an autobiographical sketch published in the St. Liborius parish 1938 centennial book, "there was no parish open."

Humility was probably also the motivation behind omitting any mention of his literary accomplishments from his sketch. For some years he was a contributing editor of *The Messenger* when it was still owned the Buechler Printing Company of Belleville. He also collaborated with the Buechler company in founding and editing *The Schoolmate,* and *The Catholic Girl,* the first a national magazine for Catholic elementary school children and the second a national publication for teens.

The magazines were pioneers in their fields and were highly successful. *The Schoolmate* reached a circulation of almost 100,000; *The Catholic Girl* almost 15,000.

In 1916 Father Henken was named the pastor of New Burnside and the missions of Stonefort, Vienna, and Metropolis. Three years later, parishes in Harrisburg, Dorrisville, Ledford, and Delwood were added to his pastoral care. This ministry in eight parishes, scattered over the five southeastern Illinois counties of Massac, Johnson, Pope, Saline, and Williamson, made him what could well be described as the last of the circuit-rider priests of the diocese. Those years, he later said, were difficult ones. When he left the mission fields of the diocese and was named the pastor of St. Damian's parish, Damiansville, he was fifty-three years old.

Every biographer, editorial writer, and eulogizer emphasizes that he was perhaps best known as a special friend of young people. "He had a way of communicating with children," Father Brandmeyer said. "We loved his catechism classes. He made everyone feel important."

Kids didn't mind the movies he brought to town on Sunday evenings, during a day when some church authorities thought of films as an instrument of the devil. Some Damiansville oldtimers remember Christmas vespers as the time when the kids who sang in the choir were invited to the rectory afterwards for cookies and ice cream.

He is remembered especially as the priest who gave support, counsel, time, and if necessary, room and board to seminarians. It is probably no accident that four young men from St. Damian's began their seminary studies during his pastorate.

He made it "easy to be attracted to the priesthood," Father Brandmeyer said.

"He loved kids very much," was how Mrs. Brennfleck and Agers described his relationship with children.

"He loved snowstorms, too," Mrs. Brennfleck said, with a note of disapproval in her voice — a fact remembered when a blizzard kept many of his friends from his funeral, including his requested homilist.

He was a generous man, in whatever he could give. His rectory was open to anyone at any time. "Anyone could stay with us," Mrs. Brennfleck said, "and many did."

His down-home style of ministry included calling unannounced at a farmer's home after the harvest days and inviting a couple of neighbors in for a beer and a game of cards.

While happy-go-lucky and easygoing in personality, he was intensely serious about his spirituality and his ministry. "When someone came to call and he wasn't around, the most likely place to find him was in church praying," Mrs. Brennfleck said.

Though it is thirty-three years since he was buried in his family's cemetery lot next to his parents in Carlyle, he is remembered lovingly.

Father John Henken was humble, generous, loved by kids and adults of all ages. At the time of his death twenty-three Catholic communities in the diocese had been graced with his presence in a ministry that is spoken of with gratitude and good feeling to this day.

CHAPTER 63

Father Alphonse Simon: Headed Retreat Movement

By Rev. Ronald Harrer, OMI

FATHER ALPHONSE SIMON came to the Belleville diocese on April 23, 1933, as superior and rector of St. Henry's prepatory seminary. The seminary newspaper, *The Dawn,* recorded his installation in the June 1933 edition: "On Sunday evening, April 23, Rev. Alphonse Simon, OMI, was inaugurated as the new superior of St. Henry's College. The appointment had been made during the prolonged Easter holidays, and came as a surprise to the students. Very Rev. Aloysius Rosenthal, OMI, provincial, formally introduced the superior to the students and addressed them briefly, expressing his joy at having such a capable man at the head of the institution and asking loyalty and filial devotion on the part of the seminarians."

After he had finished speaking, Father Simon rose to address the assembly. He was by no means a stranger to the students. They remembered his name and reputation as a missionary in the North, and three members of the present faculty, Fathers Goetz, Ehmann, and Janssen, had been his fellow students. He had made a brief visit to the seminary earlier in the year.

Alphonse Simon was born in Russia, August 17, 1896, the son of German parents, George and Anna Jaschinski Simon. He was one of fourteen children in a family of five boys and nine girls. The Simons emigrated to Canada when Alphonse was a few years old. There he attended grade school in Saskatchewan. After a classical course at St. John's Juniorate, Edmonton, Alberta, he entered the Oblate novitiate, where he professed his first vows on August 15, 1917.

He continued his philosophy and theology studies at the Oblate major seminary in Edmonton, professing perpetual vows as an Oblate in 1920. Father Alphonse Simon was ordained a priest by Edmonton's Archbishop Henry J. O'Leary on February 2, 1923. The newly-

Father Alphonse Simon

ordained priest continued his education, doing postgraduate work at Columbia University, New York. Only one year after his ordination he was placed in charge of the Oblate juniorate at Edmonton. Later he was appointed rector of St. Paul College, Winnipeg, from 1926 to 1931.

In 1931 Father Simon came to the United States and quickly became a success as a mission band preacher at White Bear Lake, Minnesota. His activities as a preacher brought him southward into the state of Illinois. He preached two retreats at the Precious Blood convent at Ruma and later Forty Hours devotion at Du Quoin. It was on this trip that he visited St. Henry's.

Father Simon's inaugural address to the student body of St. Henry's as newly installed superior and rector was both short and eloquent. In it he expressed his pleasure at being once more among seminarians. He mentioned his former experiences as rector of schools in Canada and assured his attentive listeners that he understood seminarians. The most important point in his speech was the proposal of an honor system for the students. Carefully pointing out the difference between servile and honorary obedience, he stated that he intended to make use of the latter only. This generous offer was enthusiastically received by all the students.

The seminary chronicle describes Father Simon as a man of great intellectual achievement, extensive experience, and much personal charm. "We are proud, then, to have such a man at the head of our growing institution, and we are confident that under his guidance we will grow to a bigger and better St. Henry's."

Father Alphonse Simon collaborated with the diocesan superintendent of schools, Msgr. John Fallon, in successfully obtaining accreditation of the high school department of St. Henry's Seminary by the University of Illinois in June 1935.

During his term as superior at St. Henry's, Father Simon started the building program and established a number of diocesan scholarships. Work on the new gymnasium began in March 1941 under the direction of Father Simon. The rooms of the former red school building near Main Street, which had served for many years as the parish school and later as science laboratories and recreation rooms, were converted into a study hall, dormitories, and recreation rooms for the students of the college department. The building was renamed St. Mary's Hall. The new gymnasium was dedicated on November 16, 1941.

Father Simon also reorganized the St. John Chrysostom Better Speaking Club at St. Henry's in an effort to promote and develop preaching skills among the students.

The Belleville diocese was represented by Father Alphonse Simon at the fifth National Laymen's Retreat Conference held at Washington, D.C., from December 28 to 30, 1934. The meeting was a response to the rallying call of Pope Pius XI, who had characterized the lay retreat movement as "the great means to perpetuate and increase the fruits of faith, and the most powerful support against growing evils."

The inaugural retreats of the Laymen's Retreat League of the Belleville diocese were conducted at St. Henry's Seminary in August of 1936. Father Simon, as rector of the seminary and principal host, congratulated the retreatants in the closing address and expressed his hope that the fruits of the retreat would be multiple and enduring. He is credited with being the prime mover and shaker in the organization and formation of the Laymen's Retreat League in the Belleville area.

Responding to a new call to service within his community, Father Alphonse Simon became the fourth provincial of the Oblate Central U.S. Province in 1940. Under Father Simon's leadership as provincial from 1940 to 1949 the province grew and expanded in numbers, institutions, and apostolic works. In 1944 the minor seminary known as Our Lady of the Ozarks College in Carthage, Missouri, was acquired and opened. The Immaculate Heart of Mary novitiate house at Godfrey, Illinois, was also established during this period, in 1947.

After serving three consecutive terms as provincial, Father Simon was named first ordinary consultor and admonitor to his successor to the office of provincial by the Oblate superior general.

Father Simon is credited with founding and establishing the retreat ministry as an important apostolic work of the OMI Central U.S. Province: building and organizing the first King's House of Retreats in Belleville, Illinois, in 1951; and serving as director of the second King's House of Retreats in Buffalo, Minnesota, for sixteen years, from 1953 to 1969.

A true son of Charles Eugene DeMazenod, the Oblate founder, Father Simon was adept at recounting the beginnings of the Oblate congregation to students and retreatants alike. His depiction of Oblate origins included a description of the conditions prevailing in France at the beginning of the nineteenth century, when the Congregation of

Oblate Missionaries was born. He was fond of portraying the life of the Oblate founder, dwelling especially on his years in exile, his studies for the priesthood, the brilliant career that could easily have been his, but which he sacrificed in order to become a missionary of the poor. He delighted in recalling that in 1826, ten years after the founding, the little community had its rules and constitutions approved by the Holy See. He took inspiration from the growth and expansion of the Oblate congregation from twenty-two members in 1826 to 6,281 in 1950. Father Simon set these inspirational recollections on Oblate origins down in writing in 1948 when he authored an essay on Bishop Eugene DeMazenod, entitled "A Champion of Forgotten Men."

Father Simon retired from active priestly ministry on January 24, 1969, at age seventy-three. He took up residence thereafter in the former convent on the retreat house grounds in Buffalo, Minnesota. Failing health necessitated his admission into nursing care facilities in 1975. He received nursing care at St. Mary's Home and at the Little Sister of the Poor nursing home in St.Paul, Minnesota. On February 22, 1978, he was moved to the Tekakwitha Nursing Home in Sisseton, South Dakota.

He died of a stroke at age eighty-six at the Tekakwitha home on November 11, 1982. At his death, Father Simon had completed sixty-five years as an Oblate religious and fifty-nine years as a priest.

Funeral rites were held for Father Alphonse Simon on Saturday, November 13, 1982, in Belleville, Illinois, at the chapel of St. Henry's Seminary, where he had served as rector and superior for six years.

CHAPTER 64

Father Elmer Schuhmacher: Good Samaritan

By Raphael H. Middeke

THE EDITORIAL IN *THE MESSENGER* summed up the life of Father Elmer Schuhmacher in the words of St. Paul to the Colossians. They were part of the first reading of the Sunday between his death and his burial.

You are the people of God; he loved you and chose you for his own. So then, you must clothe yourselves with compassion, kindness, humility, gentleness, and patience. Be tolerant with one another and forgive one another whenever any of you has a complaint against someone else. You must forgive one another just as the Lord has forgiven you. And to all these qualities add love, which binds all things together in perfect unity.

The memories of Father Schuhmacher, who died in 1949 at age forty-six, could aptly be called the stories of the Good Samaritan. He had been the pastor of St. Elizabeth Church, Ava, and the missions of Willisville and Raddle for eighteen years. The memories are of a kind, charitable, unpretentious, and humble priest who often went the extra and unexpected mile. And those memories, almost forty years after his death, are very much alive.

One of the better remembered stories is of his influence on two girls, Emma and Betty. When he first met them, their grandparents, with whom they lived, had tried unsuccessfully to have them baptized. They were not practicing Catholics and the children had received no religious instructions. Father Schuhmacher met them in a Murphysboro blacksmith shop when they were thirteen and fifteen years old.

Since he was just beginning to prepare a confirmation class for the three parishes he pastored, he decided to include the girls. It was early May 1940. They lived in the country between Ava and Murphysboro.

He drove out to pick them up for class and after class brought them back home. On Saturday evening, June 22, 1940, they were baptized and made their first confession. The following morning they made their first Holy Communion and that afternoon they were confirmed at the Raddle mission. They continued their religious instruction at the regular Sunday classes.

Father Elmer Schuhmacher

That could have been the end of the story, but Father Schuhmacher thought the girls needed a high school education. He asked them to work at the rectory before and after school and during the summer months while they continued to live with their grandparents, who had since moved to Ava.

For seven and nine years, respectively, the two girls worked at the rectory, and many times during the cold winter months they were the only congregation in the unheated church. Their grandparents during this time returned to the practice of their faith.

One of the girls fondly recalled those days in a conversation recently and the gratitude they have always felt for this man who changed their lives, whose family became their family and who was "like a father and brother to us."

Elmer Schuhmacher was born in Hecker, Illinois, on September 19, 1902, the fourth of the nine children of John Schuhmacher and Mary Ellen Harbaugh Schuhmacher. After graduation from St. Augustine School he enrolled in St. Meinrad Seminary in Indiana. Bishop Henry Althoff sent him to Innsbruck, Austria, for the completion of his priesthood studies. He was ordained by Bishop Althoff in his parish church in Red Bud where his parents had moved from Hecker in 1916. The rest of his class had been ordained in Innsbruck, but he wanted his parents and his family to be present for his ordination, according to Sister Bernice, PHJC, one of three Schuhmacher sisters who joined the Poor Handmaids of Jesus Christ religious congregation. Sisters Bernice and Mary Ellen live in the order's retirement home in Donaldson, Indiana, and Sister Bernette lives at the Donaldson motherhouse. Their sole surviving brother, Clarence, still lives in Red Bud.

The newly-ordained priest served as an assistant at St. Dominic, Breese, and at the Herrin and Murphysboro parishes before he was named the pastor of St. Elizabeth, Ava, and the missions of St. Ann, Raddle, and St. Joseph, Willisville, on May 13, 1931.

It was the depth of the depression and the communities were struggling. Father Schuhmacher shared their poverty willingly. "He was satisfied with little as far as material things were concerned," said Father Francis Tecklenburg, his good friend, who preached both his first Mass and funeral sermons. "And this spirit of poverty endeared him to his flock."

Though poverty was part of the depression aftermath for many years, efforts were made to improve the church properties — sometimes depression-style. "The basement of St. Elizabeth's church and the basement on the west side of the rectory were dug by a man who needed to eat and was willing to work for meals," said a history of the parishes by Marie Palmer and Father Leo Hayes, the present pastor.

"My own favorable impressions were of his forgetfulness of self and his living poverty in his own life. He never worried about amassing wealth and had very few possessions other than his car, which he needed to get around and do the good he did," said Father Clem Dirler, who was the Murphysboro assistant several years before Father Schuhmacher's death.

Father Dirler and Msgr. Meinrad Dunn, who preceded Father Dirler as the assistant in Murphysboro, admit their respect and admiration for the country pastor who influenced and inspired them during the first years of their priesthood.

Their stories of the "very common, ordinary fellow, who was a princely gentleman," as Monsignor Dunn put it, include, too, the "going beyond the call of duty," that was so much a part of his ordinary ministry up and down the roads that led between and beyond his parish missions and the surrounding towns of Gorham, Grand Tower, Percy, and Steeleville.

Monsignor Dunn recalled the story of a man in one of his convert classes. He was driving during a rainstorm one night when he had a flat tire and no spare. It was during the war and tires were precious and rationed. For several hours no one stopped, but then a man knocked on his window and asked if he needed help. The man took his own spare tire and replaced the flat.

"What about your tire?" the grateful man asked. "Drop it off at the Ava filling station," the Good Samaritan said, "and tell them it belongs to Schuhmacher."

It was only when he dropped it off that he found out the Good

Samaritan was the pastor of the Catholic church in town. The man couldn't forget the selfless deed and it was one of several experiences which eventually led him to the Catholic Church.

Father Dirler recalled the afternoon when Father Schuhmacher "invited me to go along to help get a poor old man ready for his entrance into the hospital. Elmer helped personally to get him ready and when the ambulance arrived, helped get the sick man into it, did what he could for his aged wife who knew it was the last time that her sick husband would be with her in their home. The old couple lived out in the country some miles off of Route 3."

Father Schuhmacher's car — his one possession — was very much a part of his ministry. A hospital visit almost always included picking up a relative or friend. "He was always driving people around," Monsignor Dunn said, "to the hospital, to the doctor, and other places." Mrs. Helen Williams, who grew up in his parish, recalled: "He was most generous in using his car to transport others — especially teenagers to ball games."

Mrs. Williams recalled, as did almost everyone, his friendships with non-Catholics. He was "ecumenical before its time," his sisters said. The histories of the southern Illinois parishes note with care that parishioners and non-Catholics alike mourned his untimely and unexpected death. He was a good friend of the Methodist minister in town — too good, in fact, to suit the Methodist bishop of the day.

A non-Catholic friend later wrote an article about him and his parish because "he was the kindest man I ever knew."

He was a jovial man, Monsignor Dunn recalled, "always friendly. He had an easy way about him." People talked about his charity and kindness, but he was not without expectations. Sister Bernice recalled one of his often-voiced phrases: "God takes care of his little children if they let him."

The pastor was indeed a pastor — a man who "enjoyed visiting all of his parishioners, eating with them, and playing pinochle," said Mrs. Evelyn Sabella, who recalled him as "a great family friend and spiritual advisor."

"He was a man of ability but he did not seek advancement," *The Messenger* editorial writer said. "He pleaded with his bishop on various occasions to remain in his first and only pastorate with the people he loved."

And the people loved him in return. "The love of the people for this man of God was quite evident during the time his body lay in state. There were tears that flowed from eyes full of love. Men of the soil, farmers, his parishioners were not ashamed to cry because they knew they had lost a friend, a man whom they dearly loved."

Though he had been in the hospital for a month, his death was sudden and unexpected — a shock to his family, his friends and parishioners. He had suffered a heart attack at the last Christmas Mass of 1948, entered St. Joseph's Hospital, Murphysboro, on January 2, and died February 3, probably from a cerebral hemorrhage. Father Raymond Harbaugh, pastor of the cathedral and Father Schuhmacher's uncle, celebrated the funeral Mass on February 7. Over a hundred priests from the diocese attended. He was buried in his hometown parish cemetery in Red Bud.

Twenty-five years later, after memorial Masses in the three parishes he served, a wreath was placed on his grave — a sign that the Good Samaritan still lived in the minds and hearts of many of his former parishioners.

CHAPTER 65

Monsignor John Fournie: "A Good Sport"

By Stanley J. Konieczny

IF TEN PEOPLE WERE ASKED what does a good pastor do, there probably would be ten different job descriptions. A good pastor is a teacher, counselor, preacher, liturgist. People whose lives have been touched by the ministry of Msgr. John T. Fournie would probably add the role of coach to their criteria of a good pastor.

In his forty-three year ministry Monsignor Fournie earned an outstanding reputation for his outreach through athletic programs. A wide variety of sports programs, organized and directed by the monsignor, helped youths and adults alike feel at home in the church.

John Fournie entered the world on September 12, 1911. He was one of the ten children born to Arthur J. and Ivo Sunkel Fournie. The monsignor's mother took leadership roles in the Council of Catholic Women at the local, diocesan, and national levels.

Sister Mary John Fournie, MSSA, his only surviving sister, remembered growing up at the family home near Belleville. "Jack was just likable and lovable," Sister Mary John said. "He was a tennis nut. We had a tennis court next to our home and he'd have a couple of tournaments every summer before he left for Rome."

St. Luke parish played an important role in the formation of this southern Illinois pastor. "I think Father Vincent Hartung and Msgr. Rudolph Jantzen, both of whom served at St. Luke's, had influences on Jack's vocation. Father Hartung was the one who told him to go to Rome if he ever had the chance to study there. And Jack really did love Rome!" Sister Mary John recalled.

For over forty-two years, Sister Mary John has been a member of the Missionary Servants of St. Anthony in San Antonio, Texas. She had served as her priest-brother's housekeeper before entering religious life.

After completing St. Luke elementary school, John Fournie studied first at St. Meinrad Seminary and then St. Mary of the Lake Seminary, Mundelein. He was later assigned to Propaganda Fide College and the Gregorian University in Rome. A fellow student of Monsignor Fournie in Rome was Msgr. James Burke, pastor emeritus of St. Mary parish, Mt. Vernon.

Monsignor John Fournie

"He was a great athlete," Monsignor Burke said of his former classmate. "I attended the tennis tournaments that he played at Munich." Monsignor Burke added, "He was quite a versatile person, who made friends easily. He had the ability to bring people together."

Cardinal Francis Marchetti ordained Father John Fournie on December 8, 1935, at the North American College in Rome. The Belleville native celebrated his first Mass at the Vatican.

Returning home, he served as an associate in St. Andrew, Murphysboro, and Sacred Heart, East St. Louis. In 1940 Father Fournie was named director of the Catholic Youth Council with headquarters in the former Catholic Community House. He also became involved as a Boy Scout chaplain, a ministry that he carried out at the diocesan, regional, and national levels. He received his first pastorate, St. Mary parish, Mound City, within two years.

Father Fournie was already beginning his outreach through sports.

"The monsignor would say that he established seven tennis clubs during his lifetime; one at each parish he served," said his neice, Rita Renner.

With the outbreak of World War II, the pastor of Mound City requested permission to enter military service. Bishop Henry Althoff allowed Father Fournie to join the U.S. Army Chaplains Corps in 1944. After completing the chaplaincy program at Harvard University Father Fournie was first assigned to Camp Pickett, Virginia. He later served with the Sixty-third Infantry Division in France and Germany.

Entering the service with the rank of first lieutenant, he attained the rank of major in two and one-half years. His military decorations included the Bronze Star with Oak Leaf Cluster, Presidential Unit Citation, and the French Fouragere. At the end of the war, Major Fournie worked with American Graves Registration Command and the Vatican Relief Commission in Germany.

Father Fournie returned home and served briefly as associate pastor of St. Elizabeth, East St. Louis. He was named pastor of St. Polycarp parish, Carmi, in March 1947.

During his pastorate at Carmi, Father Fournie was named diocesan director of the Blessed Virgin Sodality and on June 15, 1950, he became moderator of the Belleville Diocesan Council of Catholic Women. He held this post for the next twenty-seven years. This appointment enabled Father Fournie to share in a special way the lifelong commitment of his mother and grandmother to the BDCCW.

Father Fournie began his twenty-five year pastorate at St. Philip Church, East St. Louis, on March 15, 1951. One of the new pastor's first tasks was to organize the St. Philip tennis club. One of the most noted alumni of the club is tennis great Jimmy Connors. "The monsignor taught Jimmy Connors his backhand. He worked a whole summer on that," Mrs. Renner said. "He was a big Jimmy Connors fan," she added.

The St. Philip athletic association came into being following the formation of the tennis club. At its peak membership the club had nearly 800 people enrolled in softball, baseball, basketball, and volleyball leagues, which were sponsored by Father Fournie's parish athletic association. To fund this program he began an annual patrons' dinner. Proceeds were used to purchase equipment and uniforms for the young athletes in his charge.

From 1953 until 1975 a variety of sports greats were featured speakers at the patrons' dinner. Ed Macauley of the St. Louis Hawks; Red Schoendienst, Joe Hague, and Al Hrabosky of the St. Louis baseball Cardinals; Larry Stallings of the football Cardinals; and golf champ Bob Goalby were among those recruited to help the St. Philip athletic association. Local coaches, sports media personalities, and even the Bush Stadium scoreboard engineer spoke during twenty-three years of patrons' dinners.

Such fund-raising activity was vital to support the "legendary sports program at St. Philip parish," which involved hundreds of people. In her 1982 history of the East St. Louis parish Sister Barbara Brumleve, SSND, noted, "The sports program grew until the parish had eighty-three teams, all in official uniforms, competing regularly in basketball, volleyball, baseball, and softball. There was also competition in football, track, swimming, tennis, and golf. Seven ball diamonds and two tennis courts became part of the parish complex."

"Father Fournie was very serious about being a priest, but he also loved sports, talking to people, and planning activities,'' commented Father Joseph C. Hays, pastor of St. Polycarp parish, Carmi. Father Hays spent the first six years of his priesthood as an associate pastor at St. Philip's with Father Fournie.

''I think determination, unlimited work, and a lot of enthusiasm describe Monsignor Fournie. He never saw difficulties; they were not there. He had boundless ideas,'' Father Hayes said. Many of these ideas were developed late at night. Father Hays noted that the former pastor of St. Philip's loved to stay up all night at his typewriter, planning new projects and activities.

''Monsignor Fournie did his best thinking at ungodly hours of the morning,'' echoed Father Robert Vonnahmen, pastor of St. Joseph parish, Elizabethtown. He served with Father Fournie for over eight years. ''Monsignor Fournie was a very dynamic, enthusiastic man, who was never satisfied with the status quo. He was always trying to improve things even when he already had outstanding programs,'' Father Vonnahmen said. He cited both Monsignor Fournie's athletic programs as well as his popular liturgies.

Father Vonnahmen continued, ''Monsignor Fournie's athletic program was unequaled in the diocese in regard to numbers of teams.'' Every child played; every child had a uniform; every child was recognized. ''That was the key to his success, he made people feel important,'' he recalled.

''Monsignor Fournie was a backer of anything good for youth. He wanted anything he touched to be first class and worthwhile,'' Father Vonnahmen commented. This type of attitude nurtured the beginnings of the Belleville diocesan Camp Ondessonk. In the summer of 1957 Father Fournie inaugurated Camp St. Philip. The program was supervised by the pastor and directed by his associate, Father Vonnahmen. In these early years, camp facilities in Grafton and Waterloo were rented.

The two priests had hoped that this parish project could grow into a camp for the entire diocese. Other priests of the diocese, including Msgr. Robert DeGasperi, Father Stephen Kraus, Father Charles Hellrung, and Father Urban Kuhl, expressed similar aspirations. Bishop Albert Zuroweste endorsed the plans, naming Father Vonnahmen director and Father Fournie executive director of the new diocesan Camp Ondessonk at Ozark, Illinois.

Father Fournie's expertise lay more in athletics than in camping, but he was an enthusiastic supporter of Camp Ondessonk and visited the facility every summer. ''He gave me a lot of freedom to do innovative things and he backed me,'' Father Vonnahmen said.

Pope John XXIII recognized the ministry of St. Philip's pastor when on July 21, 1959, Father Fournie was named a private chamberlain with the title, "monsignor." Pope Paul VI named Monsignor Fournie a papal chamberlain in 1963.

"In 1960, largely through the leadership of Monsignor Fournie, the parish began an outreach to handicapped children," wrote Sister Barbara Brumleve. "The monsignor had been going to several homes to give religious instructions to handicapped children. When a layman, Bud Vahlkamp, offered his services in the parish, Monsignor Fournie asked him to take over the instructions. Soon Vahlkamp was teaching every evening and on Saturdays and Sundays."

This catechetical program evolved into the St. Philip special education program. Sister Dolorine Daugherty, SSND, opened the parish's first full-time, special education class on September 12, 1961, with eleven students meeting in one classroom. The East St. Louis deanery Holy Name Conference assumed major financial responsibility for the program. Today, seventy children attend special education classes in five classrooms at St. Philip's.

Monsignor Fournie led his parishioners in extraordinary projects as well as the usual transitions which all communities experienced during the 1960s. St. Philip church was destroyed by fire on December 24, 1965. Yet, through hard work and generosity, a new church was built. It was dedicated on April 24, 1966, as the parish marked its 125th anniversary. In 1976 Monsignor Fournie requested a smaller parish and was named pastor of Our Lady of Good Counsel, Renault.

He suffered a massive stroke at the rectory on December 2, 1978, and died four days later at St. Elizabeth Hospital, Belleville. He was buried at the parish cemetery in Renault. The true memorial to Msgr. John Fournie, though, lives on in athletic prowess and young dreams realized; in people whom Monsignor Fournie made feel important.

CHAPTER 66

Bishop Anthony Deksnys: Settling the Displaced

By Stanley J. Konieczny

HAVE YOU EVER FELT like you were all alone in the world without anyone to whom you could turn? Have you ever had to exist from day to day without really knowing what is going to become of you? Those feelings must have been familiar to Bishop Anthony Deksnys, who as a young priest was locked out of his war-torn, native Lithuania. He came to southern Illinois as an exile, but he distinguished himself in the history of the Belleville diocese by his selfless love and concern for the displaced persons who followed.

Anthony Deksnys was born on May 9, 1906, at Buteniskis, Lithuania. His parents, Stanislovas and Vinceslava Kiliute Deksnys, farmed to support their family, which included four sons and three daughters. Stanislovas Deksnys lived in his homeland to the age of seventy-eight, when in June 1941 the first Soviet occupation of Lithuania forced the deportation of the widowed farmer. He died in a Siberian camp the following year.

Mrs. Maria Mogenis, a resident of Belleville and adopted sister of Bishop Deksnys, shared some of her memories of home life in Lithuania. "Bishop Deksnys was a happy youth growing up," Mrs. Mogenis recalled. "His decision to become a priest probably was influenced by his two uncles, Father Anthony Deksnys and Father Joseph Deksnys; an aunt, who was a nun; and some other relatives who were priests," she said.

"He was a leader in youth organizations and a good student, who always brought home a group of friends when visiting home from the seminary," Mrs. Mogenis added.

After completing elementary school at Onuskis, Anthony Deksnys completed his secondary and college studies at Rokiskis, all in Lithuania. He prepared for the priesthood at the Metropolitan

Bishop Anthony Deksnys

Seminary in Kaunas, Lithuania, and the Theological and Philosophical Faculty at Vytautas, known as the Great University, which was also located in Kaunas. Father Anthony Deksnys was ordained on May 30, 1931, in the Basilica of the Apostles Peter and Paul in Kaunas.

He was first assigned to Christ the King Cathedral, Panevezys, and later to St. John the Baptist Church, Birzai. Throughout this time he continued to work with Catholic youth. In 1936 Father Deksnys began his graduate studies at the University of Fribourg in Switzerland. He earned his doctorate in 1940. Unfortunately, the young priest was unable to return to his homeland. During the latter part of his years in Switzerland Lithuania became a pawn in a power struggle between the Nazis and the Soviets. Neither the Germans nor the Russians permitted the return of Lithuanian nationals, who suddenly found themselves to be refugees and displaced persons.

In 1941 the Marian fathers invited Father Deksnys to the United States. He ministered first in Mt. Carmel, Pennsylvania, and later in Chicago, before the late Bishop Henry Althoff extended his invitation to Father Deksnys. Bishop Althoff assigned him in January 1943 to East St. Louis' Immaculate Conception church, where Lithuanian families worshipped. In his new parish, the exiled priest worked under the direction of the late Msgr. Charles Gilmartin, pastor of the nearby Sacred Heart church.

Within ten months of his arrival, Father Deksnys faced a considerable challenge. Fire destroyed the Immaculate Conception church. A temporary structure served the parish for the next twelve years until 1955. In that year Father Deksnys spearheaded the drive to build the present Immaculate Conception Church on 15th Street and Baugh Avenue. The new structure transplanted a bit of Father Deksnys' and the parishioners' native Lithuania in southern Illinois.

Architect Jonas Mulokas designed the sleek brick structure in what has been dubbed modern, modified Lithuanian architecture. The church is rich in symbolism and artwork from the various stained glass windows, depicting the spiritual heritage of Lithuania, to the delicate woodwork and metalwork of the church's various altars, which were also designed by Mulokas in the old-country style.

Perhaps the future bishop made his greatest contribution to the Church in southern Illinois by his work in resettling displaced persons in the aftermath of World War II. At the time of the East St. Louis pastor's silver jubilee, it was estimated that Father Deksnys had resettled at least two hundred displaced persons, most of whom came from Lithuania. He helped these people as they made new homes, both in the Belleville diocese and throughout the Midwest.

The four members of the Antanas Stancius family were the first in the long line of Lithuanian refugees whom Father Anthony Deksnys assisted. "We did not know Bishop Deksnys when we came here, but he was so kind, it was like coming here and finding a brother," Mrs. Ellena Stancius recalled.

Antanas and Ellena Stancius and their daughters, Nika and Maria, had lived in Gudziunai, Lithuania, and spent four years in a displaced persons camp prior to their arrival in the United States in 1948. They were sponsored by Mrs. Stancius' uncle, John Kranauskas, a resident of East St. Louis, who along with his pastor, Father Deksnys, waded through the bureaucratic red tape of immigration laws.

"Father Deksnys helped many other families who did not have relatives in the United States," added Nika Stancius. She noted that the pastor of Immaculate Conception would process documents, furnish housing, and even guaranteed employment for newcomers. He worked as hard for strangers as some people worked for their own displaced relatives. Miss Stancius added, "He was the one who organized the Immaculate Conception parish community to sponsor other Lithuanians because without a sponsor you could not enter the United States."

The Stancius family, along with many other families who have called Immaculate Conception parish their spiritual home, treasure special memories of Bishop Anthony Deksnys. They remember that although the parish was composed of mainly working class people, the pastor could ask for anything and the people would provide it without being pressured. Father Deksnys showed his special love for the youths in his parish by encouraging them to better themselves, to enroll in college, and to apply for scholarships. Antanas Stancius recalls his former pastor's eloquent sermons and the great dignity which he brought to the celebration of the Eucharist.

While working in refugee resettlement, Father Deksnys was a close associate of the late Msgr. Elmer Holtgrave, the former diocesan resettlement chairman. Father Deksnys' apostolate to the displaced was officially recognized by the Church in 1963, when Pope Paul VI named the East St. Louis priest a domestic prelate. Bishop Vincent Brizgys, a Lithuanian living in exile in Chicago, requested the honor for Monsignor Deksnys with the endorsement of Belleville's Bishop Albert Zuroweste.

In 1966 Monsignor Deksnys assumed leadership of the diocesan displaced persons program. Two years later he became officially incardinated into the Belleville diocese. The local Lithuanian-American community and the entire Belleville diocese consider April 16, 1969, a red letter day. On that date, Archbishop Luigi Raimondi, apostolic delegate to the United States, announced the appointment of Msgr. Anthony Deksnys as titular Bishop of Lavellum with the responsibility of caring for the thousands of the Lithuanians living in western Europe.

His episcopal consecration took place in the Cathedral of St. Peter, Belleville, on June 15, 1969. Reflecting on his new ministry after his consecration, Bishop Deksnys told the congregation at the cathedral, "I am grateful to Pope Paul who gave me this cross, this charge, to take care of those Lithuanians who need consolation. His Holiness knew of the great needs of our people living outside of their homeland. They sought a bishop so that they might have this added consolation and care. This cross will be heavy at times. And that is why I ask my brother priests here, and those who could attend, to pray for me."

In a page one editorial in *The Messenger,* Father Theodore Siekmann commented on the appointment of Bishop Deksnys. "His mission will be much like that of the original apostles themselves, and not unlike the ministry of St. Patrick, St. Boniface, Ss. Cyril and Methodius, and other missionary bishops who were sent to peoples rather than to places," he wrote.

The new bishop's episcopal coat of arms revealed much about the man and his spirituality. His deep devotion to the Blessed Mother is evident by the icon of the Mother of Mercy, the central figure of the crest. He selected the motto, "Charity never fails," to reflect his long-term work with the displaced and the refugees. He incorporated into the shield the fleur-de-lis, in honor of Louis IX, his confirmation patron and the patron of the city where he ministered for twenty-six years: East St. Louis.

Bishop Deksnys left his home once again and set up his headquarters at Bad Woerishofen, West Germany, fifty miles from Munich. The community was started when bishops and priests from Communist bloc countries resettled at Bad Woerishofen. The bishop divided his time between his office in West Germany and one in Rome. He logged many miles making pastoral visits to Lithuanian communities throughout his territory.

Recently Bishop Deksnys retired and still resides in Europe. On one of his regular visits back to southern Illinois he celebrated his golden anniversary as a priest during a Mass at Immaculate Conception Church, East St. Louis. In his homily the bishop said, ''What brings happiness to the priest? To be with the people, the people who are close to Christ! I always feel at home with you, because you are the people of God.''

CHAPTER 67

Sister Rita Kampwerth, ASC: Determined Minister

By Raphael H. Middeke

"SHE TAUGHT US ALL a whole lot about living and dying."

That is how the Rev. Roger Knox, pastoral counselor and administrator of the Catherine Kasper Center in East St. Louis, summed up the gift of Sister Rita Kampwerth, ASC. Rev. Knox, a Methodist minister, was a co-minister with Sister Rita in East St. Louis during the turbulent years of the late 1960s and 1970s.

"She was a special, special person," Dr. Polly Teagle, her physician, added, echoing the words of Joseph Hubbard, Catholic Urban Programs director. "She had a special touch to do special things," he said.

Eight years after her death at the age of forty-one on June 6, 1977, the sharers of her faith and hope talked about Sister Rita as a unique Christian who changed their lives in her living and dying. She succumbed to a lingering, rare, and painful cancer — a death which was as much a part of her life as her controversial ministry in East St. Louis for the preceding ten years.

"She made a significant difference in my own life," said Sister Janet Smith, ASC, director of programs for the terminally ill in East St. Louis. Sister Janet shared Sister Rita's sickroom at Clementine Residence in Red Bud during her dying months. It was in that room that Sister Janet grew into her own personal conviction of the necessity of hospice — "that it is all right to live with someone who is dying."

But more than anything, that year of living with dying was a year of experiencing the meaning of the word "unselfish," Sister Janet said. "She taught me to be aware of other people." Discussion with visitors was never about her illness but about their concerns. During those many nights of often silent vigil Sister Janet learned to love this woman who ''slowly let go'' of the people and loves of her life with a simple and uncomplaining resignation.

''To me she was a very unselfish and dedicated person,'' said Sister Georgia, ASC, one of her five sisters. Sister Georgia, the director of nurses at St. Clement Hospital in Red Bud, also shared her ASC religious community. She took turns with Sister Janet keeping vigil at Sister Rita's bedside during her last months of dying. ''Rita was always helping out,'' she said.

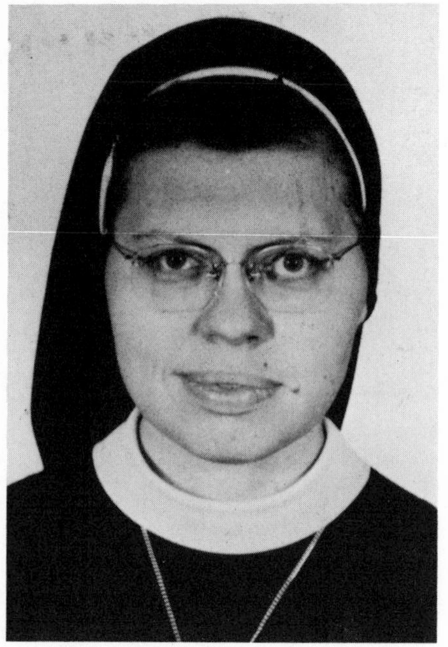

Sister Rita Kampwerth

Rita Kampwerth was born on a farm near St. Rose, Illinois, on October 26, 1935, the fourth in a family of six sisters and one brother. During her early years she became ''daddy's helper,'' and developed a relationship with her father which grew in closeness during her life. During her illness, her father, George, himself in failing health, spent many days — and sometimes weeks — at Clementine Residence, especially when Sister Georgia was out of town.

It was on trips to the stockyards in East St. Louis that Sister Rita first thought of an apostolate in that city. She later attended St. Teresa Academy as a boarding student, finishing her high school in 1956 at the Precious Blood Institute in Ruma after joining the ASC community.

The next eleven years were spent in different kinds of domestic service — sewing, cooking, supervising maintenance, and doing laundry in a seminary, a retirement home, and in a home for working girls.

''Fun loving, energetic, in touch with people,'' were phrases used to describe her during those years.

In 1966 her dream of working in East St. Louis was realized. For four years she supervised Neighborhood Youth Corps students at the academy, along with school maintenance and household work.

It was a time of growing racial unrest in East St. Louis — a tense situation in which Sister Rita became more and more involved.

In 1969 she was a charter member of the United Front — an umbrella group for organizations concerned about racial and civil justice in the city.

The Front and involvement in its tensions and conflicts became an increasing part of Sister Rita's life — at least visibly. But her involvement was never just for the cause. It was for the people of a city. For them, she marched, demonstrated, argued, and fought. Determined — bull-headed, some said — she stayed the course. Her real life, however, was with the forgotten poor, many times in the middle of the night. She was a social presence in the city of East St. Louis — but more than anything she was an uncompromising spiritual presence.

With dogged determination Sister Rita received her B.A. in social welfare work from SIU, Edwardsville, just two years before her death, to aid her in her work with the poor.

Many people "never realized what a loving person she was, what a deeply spiritual person she was," until she became sick, Sister Georgia said. Or how she spent weekends helping a sister clean and cook after a nephew's birth.

She was a bridgebuilder in a day when bridges were being torn down — in dimensions that only hindsight has been able to appreciate.

If she changed the life of Sister Janet, she also changed the life of Frank Smith, present East St. Louis city clerk, and in the late 1960s leader of the "militants" at the United Front. At the time of her death Frank Smith credited her with his gradual turning to politics. He also recalled the night Sister Rita sat on his porch all night after he had been shot at during the city's politically volatile days. Her relationship with the militants was not an easy one, but there is little doubt that the spirituality of Sister Rita had the greater influence — though not without suffering and even abuse.

"She got to the hardcore folks no one else was able to touch," Hubbard said, partly because "she stayed with it regardless of obstacles," as Rev. Knox put it.

Other observations by Rev. Knox on her ministry included:

"Amidst her own suffering, her concern for others was always evident."

"She made ecumenical ministry part of her life. Her first question was never: 'What church do you belong to?' but 'What are your needs and how can I meet them?' She led the way for ecumenical ministry to those in need. We are carrying on the work she began," Rev. Knox said. He shares major responsibility for the Catherine Kasper Center with Sister Frances Gallinatti, PHJC, a religious doctor.

Dr. Polly Teagle talked about a patient who shared a hospital room with Sister Rita, who to this day talks about the impact of Sister Rita's loving attitude. "Rita was tough and sweet all in one — warm and earthy and gracious."

Dr. Ernie Teagle said of her: "Some things I have never done since and some things I have always done since because of Rita." Dr. Ernie always stops at her grave when he passes through Ruma. "In some sense she justified the rest of us,'' he said. ''In supporting her, I was able to do things I couldn't do alone. She was totally committed, tough as nails. Her death was beautiful,'' he added.

''Her dedication and her fire were rare,'' said Mike Lucey, an East St. Louis priest at the time.

The person who probably shared her personal life more than anyone else was Sister Pauline Grady, ASC, who lived with her in East St. Louis. She said, ''The impact of Sister Rita's wide-ranging work could be felt only by daily, hourly association.'' At the time of her death, she said: ''A strong current in the depths of her being was directing her 'north wind' personality to growing self-forgetfulness and daily more demanding sensitivity to the suffering of individual people.'' For her the cause was never a theoretical one, but the happiness and well-being of real individual persons. We saw her days and nights filled with errands of mercy — like a phone call at two in the morning which took her out to stay with an elderly lady who was afraid; long hours of listening to the sorrows of the forgotten poor; help to welfare mothers to make use of their funds to buy more for their children; wiping the tears of a mother whose son had just gone to jail.''

She was ''a woman of love, courage, determination, and the core of her strength was gentleness,'' said Virginia Dowling, another charter member of the United Front.

Before she died, the city of East St. Louis presented her with a citation which ended with the words: ''We, the entire citizenry of the City of East St. Louis, extend to Sister Rita Kampwerth, ASC, our deepest and profound gratitude for the extraordinary and commendable service she has rendered to the people of our community.'' An East St. Louis memorial service ''grew out of the need of the community to celebrate her life among us,'' Rev. Knox said.

If she was controversial in the community of East St. Louis, she was also controversial in her own religious community. ''She was ten years ahead of her time in doing the things many religious are doing today,'' Sister Georgia said. ''She was a very silent person in the community largely because she was considered to be a rebel,'' Sister Janet noted.

Dr. Ernie Teagle, a Methodist, in his own blunt manner of assessment, said, ''I always got the impression she was one sister the order thought didn't turn out right. But when she got sick they cared for her in a way I have never seen anyone cared for and over the months she was seen in a totally different light.''

Two saints especially influenced her life. As a young girl she often talked about following in the footsteps of St. John Bosco, the nineteenth century unorthodox minister of youth, Sister Georgia remembers. Later she talked about the influence of St. Gaspar, a fighter for bandits and the other dispossessed and disenfranchised people of nineteenth century rural Italy.

Father John Kavanaugh, SJ, Saint Louis University professor, lecturer, and columnist, and Sister Rita's spiritual director, wrote of her before her death: "Through her patient fidelity, through her utter trust, and abandonment to the Father, Sister Rita has brought me Christ in ways no priest has yet done."

If it was in her dying that Sister Rita's living was measured and understood, her motivation remained rooted in the singlemindedness, simplicity, and determination of a rural religious family — and in a spirituality energized by the idols of saints and the love of a human father.

It was that tradition which made her a minister rather than a politician in East St. Louis — and which changed the lives of ministers, religious, and militants alike.

If unselfishness was finally her distinction, if her life was a unique gift, it was born of that tradition.

The lessons of that tradition are important, if the unselfishness of a Sister Rita is to grace our communities in the future.

CHAPTER 68

Imogene Wilson: Lesson in Understanding

By Stanley J. Konieczny

WHEN FIRST MEETING IMOGENE WILSON, she usually divulges a little secret. "I live with a Jewish lady and her son." The retired East St. Louis educator will allow some puzzlement over this clue, before she reveals with a sly smile that her special "roommates" are the Blessed Virgin Mary and her son, Jesus. "Imogene has her alarm system, but her real security is the Jewish mother and her son. She lives in their presence," observed Father Roland Mayer, SM, of the Marianist House of Intercession in East St. Louis. The presence of the Lord has been reflected through the many and varied apostolates of Imogene Wilson in the Church of southern Illinois.

Imogene Wilson was born the only child of Samuel and Adelia Wilson in Canton, Missouri. Imogene's father died while she was still an infant. Her mother and maternal grandmother, Harriet Crupper, decided to move twenty-five miles north, to Keokuk, Iowa, because of that community's excellent reputation in the area of education. Although blacks were a very small minority in Iowa, Miss Wilson remembered very little racial discrimination during her childhood. The schools of Keokuk were not segregated. "Only when you finished, there wasn't anything to do professionally," she added. Imogene Wilson decided upon a career in education during these formative years in Keokuk. The "marvelous teachers" who introduced her to the wonders of verse, prose, and history, greatly influenced her choice. "They took a great interest in me," Miss Wilson recalled. Graduating from high school, young Imogene pursued a bachelor of arts degree in history from the State University of Iowa at Iowa City. While in high school Imogene had converted from the Baptist to the Episcopal church. At the university it seemed natural for her to join the Morrison

Club of Trinity Episcopal Church. Many members of Morrison Club entered the home missions, so Imogene Wilson contacted the American Institute for Negroes. She was assigned as an English teacher to St. Augustine High School, Raleigh, North Carolina. She accompanied boarding students from St. Augustine's on shopping trips into Raleigh. These were the days when access to shops and facilities was dictated by signs restricting areas to "whites" or "colored." On one such excursion, Miss Wilson was shopping for a new dress. She began to enter an exclusive shop for whites. Her students warned her not to enter, but she went into the store anyway. "They gave me every courtesy," Miss Wilson said. After teaching for a year at State College in Dover, Delaware, the young teacher began to feel the great distance between the East Coast and her family in the Midwest. Through an agency she located a teaching position in southern Illinois. "Illinois was where I really ran into prejudice," Miss Wilson stated. Although hired to teach at Murphysboro Township High School, Imogene Wilson never conducted a single class in that building. The school board rented three classrooms in the community's grade school for black children. Miss Wilson taught in one of these classrooms.

Imogene Wilson

"I destroyed my job in Murphysboro," Miss Wilson explained in a 1983 *Messenger* Black Heritage Month feature. The segregated high school classes caused a controversy in the community. "I was asked by the black students' parents to speak at the courthouse during a public meeting on how those black children were not getting what they needed." The Ku Klux Klan marched outside the courthouse during the meetings.

When asked if she recalled being frightened, Miss Wilson replied, "No, I didn't have enough sense! My maternal great-grandfather in Missouri defied his master in slavery and I was not going to be afraid in freedom."

Friends of Miss Wilson advised her of a teaching position which had opened in East St. Louis. She applied for the job and began her forty-year tenure with the East St. Louis public school system. "When you say *the* teacher in East St. Louis, I've always heard the name Imogene

Wilson,'' commented Brother Larry McBride, SM, of the Vincent Gray Alternative High School. Imogene Wilson serves on the board of directors for the East St. Louis school which offers dropouts a second chance at a high school diploma.

Brother McBride used an interesting analogy to describe Imogene Wilson's impact on education in East St. Louis. He noted that what Joe Hubbard is to social service in East St. Louis, Imogene Wilson is to the public schools. When the institution is mentioned, one automatically thinks of the representative individual.

Looking back over her career in education, Imogene Wilson reflected, ''I always loved working with youngsters, helping them and seeing them grow. There is such a fascination.'' She includes a former U.N. ambassador, concert pianist, doctors, lawyers, and contractors among her former students.

''She probably taught everybody in East St. Louis,'' observed Jo Vallo, another friend of Imogene Wilson. The retired educator cannot travel around the Metro East area nor out of town without one of her former students stopping her to chat for a few minutes.

While teaching at East St. Louis' Lincoln High School, two factors influenced Miss Wilson to convert to Catholicism: the subject matter and the students. In order to better understand the medieval world, she began to study that society's primary institution — the Catholic Church. Miss Wilson established a rapport with Father Peter Harrington, SMA, pastor of St. Augustine mission, East St. Louis' black parish, to further her understanding. She also read extensively about Catholicism in order to respond to her students' misconceptions about the Church.

Father Harrington obviously knew the subject matter quite well. Not only did he clarify Imogene's conceptions of history, he ushered her into the Catholic faith. ''I guess I always wanted to be a Catholic. I passed the Catholic church going to grade school every day and there was just something about it that compelled me,'' Miss Wilson said.

While the seeds of her faith may have been sown long ago in Keokuk, Miss Wilson made her commitment to Catholicism at the old St. Augustine Mission. After all these years, the man who received her into the church, Father Harrington, remains heroic in stature in the eyes of at least one of his converts, Imogene Wilson.

Through service to the community, Miss Wilson has witnessed to her faith. She has been active in the Belleville Diocesan Council of Catholic Women. She has served as a member of the diocesan school board and chairman of the board of Catholic Social Service.

''Imogene was a faithful board member of our agency,'' remarked Deacon Michael Dalton, director of Catholic Social Service. ''At the very beginning of my tenure with the diocesan agency, she served as board chairman. She was an excellent board chairman who always did her homework and knew what was going on. She represented us well at public functions."

Membership on various boards, including St. Mary Hospital, East St. Louis, helped Imogene to exercise her leadership and Christian charity on a large scale, but she has also made time throughout her life to demonstrate her love in simpler, more personal ways. "If you are among Imogene's friends, for your birthday or Christmas you are apt to receive one of her famous pound cakes and a sonnet," commented Carol Scoggins.

Mrs. Scoggins observed that Imogene Wilson can count kindness, gentleness, and interest in people on her list of spiritual gifts. She added that Miss Wilson could never be called a "moral coward." This statement is evident by Imogene wilson's longtime crusade for racial justice and understanding.

After a 1968 confrontation with black radicals who interrupted her class, Miss Wilson "retired" and started to lecture throughout southern Illinois on race relations. "There is always a need for interracial dialogue," she explained.

She has tried to spread peace and understanding by speaking in area high schools and witnessing before both Catholic and Protestant congregations. Mrs. Vallo noted, "Imogene has made racial understanding her life's work. She has worked in both the black and white communities. I think she is color-blind."

Imogene Wilson shares her time with both of her loves; her love for justice and her deep love for her Catholic Church. Imogene's home parish, St. John Francis Regis, is the focal point of much of this talented woman's interest. "Whatever comes up in the parish, Imogene is there," Father Jerry Wirth, pastor, stated. "I think St. Regis parish reverences her as a lady who has contributed much to the church and the community."

Father Wirth sees Imogene as an important link with the parish's black roots. Yet she is not a relic; she looks to the future with a keen awareness of the past. At the recommendation of this senior parishioner, St. Regis parish will soon be holding a town hall-type assembly as a followup to the formation of parish council. She can look forward while still delving into the parish's past.

St. Regis' former pastor, Father Walter Barr, recalls the special friendship he developed with Imogene during his six years at the East St. Louis parish. "She always gave me the proper perspective. I credit her for the finest years of my priesthood, putting into perspective being the white pastor of a black parish," Father Barr said. The current pastor of St. Andrew parish, Christopher, added, "Imogene introduced me to some of the best-educated people I ever met. We talked a great deal about history and current events.''

Father Barr recounted, ''She would often say that she was amazed that a bunch of country boys from southern Illinois would come and serve the black Catholics of East St. Louis.'' He recalled Miss Wilson's unwavering love for the East St. Louis church and the priests who served there. As an example, Father Barr noted that every Memorial Day, Imogene and a friend still take flowers to the grave of Father Claude Taylor, SMA, who served St. Augustine parish many years ago.

Catholicism permeates Imogene Wilson's life. ''She is a deeply spiritual person, who is constantly praying,'' Mrs. Vallo offered. The rosary plays an important role in Miss Wilson's daily spirituality. She also was deeply touched by walking in the footsteps of Christ during a Holy Land pilgrimage, which she took while part of Father Roger Karban's Bible study groups.

Academics have provided the bedrock for Imogene Wilson's entire adult life and this vital dimension is permeated with the Catholic spirit. Miss Wilson made two attempts at earning her master's degree. Each time illness interrupted her studies. She finally was able to earn her M.A. in history from Saint Louis University. Imogene focused much of her research on the Catholic experience in the United States.

One would expect a lifelong educator to be an avid reader, and Imogene Wilson is no exception. Yet for her the stacks of books and unread magazines that fill her spacious East St. Louis home are more than just a collection of reading material. Imogene calls this the St. Martin de Porres library, which she hopes will eventually help others. Imogene's constant companions, the Jewish lady and her son, shouldn't mind sharing their residence with such a library.

CHAPTER 69

Roslyn Waite: "Angel of Cairo"

By Raphael H. Middeke

IN HIS LAST CHRISTMAS CARD TO HER, about six months before he died, her friend and former pastor, Father "X" Heiligenstein, wrote these words to Roslyn Waite: "I cannot thank you enough for your beautiful example of caring and sharing."

The words reflect the thoughts of thousands, perhaps, who have felt over a half-century the practical love of the "Angel of Cairo" — the description of her offered by Bishop Stan Schlarman when he was the pastor of St. Patrick parish, Cairo.

"Momma" Waite, as she was affectionately known for many of those years, developed two great loves in her life — people and her Church. Those were the loves which earned her the nomination and award in 1986 of the Spirtus Franciscanus (Spirit of St. Francis) Award from the College of St. Francis in Joliet. (The award is given annually to a lay person in the state of Illinois whose life best exemplifies the spirit and Christian love of St. Francis of Assisi. It was established in 1981 on St. Francis' 800th anniversary. The first recipient was Joseph Hubbard, director of Catholic Urban Programs in East St. Louis.)

Asked to comment on the award in May 1986, she said, "Whatever you put in the paper will suit me just fine." Later she said: "The trip to Joliet was wonderful. Cabrini (her daughter) kept on me to go. I didn't know they were going to do all that."

Today, after several bouts with cancer, heart disease, and diabetes, the door to Roslyn's apartment and heart remains open. People come to fill out "circuit breaker" forms, to get advice or to just talk. The thanksgiving for her "beautiful example of caring and sharing" will go on for many years.

Her philosophy of Christian living has been unorthodox, tough, and irreverent at times. Even an admirer has said: "I don't know why she put up with them." The "them" were those no one else would put up with — including the transients and the winos — who always found a place to stay at the Roslyn Hotel — the downtown Cairo business establishment which over a period of thirty-seven years increasingly served as the mission through which she ministered to thousands in the area. "I let everybody stay there and eat there," she said.

Roslyn Waite

Roslyn Schueing was born August 4, 1912, in the southern Illinois town of Mounds, the oldest child of Charles and Edna Travers Schueing. Her father was born in Chicago and came into the area as a railroad worker. Her mother was the daughter of one of the pioneer Catholic families in the Mounds area. It was in her grandparents' home that Mass was celebrated before St. Raphael church was built. A brother, Charles, was born in 1914.

Death in her family was almost a constant companion in Roslyn's early childhood. Her father died when she was three; her mother when she was six. Both died of tuberculosis. Two years later her brother died of diphtheria.

Roslyn was raised by her maternal grandparents, Cassie and John Travers, Sr. — where she grew up in a Catholic religious environment.

She graduated from Mounds Township High School just in time to walk into the depression. Early work included a ten-cent-an-hour drugstore job and several years as a waitress in a local restaurant.

On April 29, 1936, Roslyn married Walter W. Waite, some years her senior. Waite was a well-known county politician. He was a county clerk for thirty-two years. The couple continued to live in Mounds for the next twenty-five years.

Following the Travers tradition she was an active parishioner of St. Raphael's. For twenty-three years she was the parish organist. She took a great interest in the building and operation of the school and in assisting the Ursuline sisters who staffed the school. "Monsignor Fournie was really great for starting a lot of things and then dropping them in our laps," she said several years ago when she was interviewed by *The Messenger* for a "Faith Alive" feature. "He got the school built in Mounds and made the debt. Then Father X (Francis Heiligenstein) came; he was not one to beg for money. But we got it paid off.'' She once won a Cadillac-or-$4,000-cash raffle for the school, but gave the money back so the school could be expanded.

After her marriage she became involved in a ''hodgepodge'' of business enterprises and jobs. ''I had a little bit of everything going for me,'' she said.

The ''little bit of everything'' included a beauty shop, a car dealership, a furniture store, real estate, and earlier, a terminal barge line.

For many years she was also a deputy county sheriff of Alexander and Pulaski counties and served as a court reporter. Even today a telephone call picks up the background of the police radio.

In 1947 the Waites purchased a downtown Cairo hotel, which Roslyn managed and operated for the next thirty-seven years. The Cairo landmark — controversial in its later years — was sold in 1984, when it once again became more of a business instead of ''Momma'' Waite's place. The year 1947 was also the year the Waites' only child, Cabrini, was born.

The history of the Roslyn Hotel is as colorful as its operator — the woman who ''never turned anyone away from its door.'' As the once-prosperous river town of Cairo of 20,000 inhabitants aged into a severely depressed town of 6,000, the clientele of the hotel also changed — but the spirit didn't.

A section of the hotel has always been a home for elderly residents, but the hotel served many other purposes.

At one time it became a refuge for unwed mothers in the area. Roslyn is quick to give credit to ''Dr. Ent, who suggested fixing up a section for young girls who needed a new lease on life — he thought the hotel could serve a purpose beyond being a place in which to die with dignity.'' The doctor gave all his services to the girls free and covered hospital expenses (except for the one baby Roslyn delivered herself). A Mrs. Bidson provided the necessary clothes and a Jewish jewelry store owner purchased the necessary groceries. (He also played Santa Claus at Christmastime and helped pay for the Christmas and Thanksgiving dinners served at her hotel for anyone who needed a feast day meal. (Until a soup kitchen was started in Cairo, a meal was always available at the Roslyn Hotel.)

Some of the babies stayed at the hotel and at one time twenty-seven kids from broken homes were housed in one section. ''I still hear from some of the girls,'' Roslyn says.

At times there is a sadness in her voice as she recalls the stories of her residents who came to die as much as to live. For some years she was the conservator for what she calls the Veterans Administration boys. ''Thirty-three are buried at the National Cemetery in Mounds City,'' she says with an exact and telling memory.

The author of *The Messenger's* "Faith Alive" feature said: "Sometimes people have said that Roslyn Waite has loved too much — and too uncritically — but Roslyn says it isn't up to her to decide who should be helped and not helped. 'You always help a person when they're down,' she says.' " In the same feature she commented: "You can't be a Christian and not take care of the poor. You just can't hate and be a Catholic."

The pastor of St. Patrick at the time, Father Dean Braun, called her — as did a number of other acquaintances — " 'The Dorothy Day of Cairo.' The poor she has worked with are the poorest of the poor." he said.

Father Jerome Fortenberry, CM, her present pastor, says: "She still has the same spirit of compassion, the same concern for the welfare of others."

Roslyn's definition of charity is both modern and biblical. "I have always believed charity comes from within. Yes, you need money and you need programs, but you need to give yourself first."

Roslyn didn't overlook the need for government programs. She accepted leadership roles in federal and state housing programs, but the charity which grew out of her faith was more important.

In 1984 Father Braun said: "She is a fierce lover of the church and of the Eucharist." Although "irreverently holy," as someone called her, she is a traditional Catholic. When I asked her if she knew one of the priests involved in the river town's racial violence of the late 1960s, she said: "Yes, I went to confession to him several times." She was always involved in the organizational church. She rode the "BDCCW circuit" for many years. She was a charter member of the Newman Auxiliary and is still the South Deanery representative of the auxiliary. She was also with the first group of cooks who went to Camp Ondessonk to set up the kitchen.

At the same time, in her own way, she had broken the "color line" in the racially conscious and often racially tense southern Illinois counties long before it was profitable or even acceptable. She did it very simply: by refusing to notice color and by recognizing racism for what it was and is — a denial of God's love.

In 1961 when Msgr. John Fournie, as moderator of the Belleville Diocesan Council of Catholic Women, gave her a lay apostolate award, the award specifically noted — besides her youth work, other charitable and organizational work, her personal holiness — her work for integration.

The Waites moved from Mounds into the hotel in that same year, when Walter Waite's health was failing. He died in 1969.

Cabrini, who grew up in the hotel after the age of thirteen, was probably the cause of raising a mother's "protective temper" — which didn't necessarily need the excuse of protection — when a hotel guest's language or demeanor crossed her line of acceptance in the presence of an impressionable teenager.

Probably the most telling gift of the five decades of a faithful Christian charity has been her lack of discrimination. "She makes everyone feel important," Cabrini said. "It never made any difference whether she was talking to a wino or the pope."

A longtime friend and neighbor, Canon Ellsworth Stone, the Episcopalian pastor of the Church of the Redeemer in Cairo said: "She has ministered to thousands and to my knowledge has never turned anyone away. All the government money and programs have not been able to do what she has done."

Her half-century of charity in an often troublesome and trying environment is a monument to a steadfastness of faith. If she has not escaped her own trials — bouts with cancer, heart disease, and diabetes and, at one time, a nervous breakdown — she has known, too, the gifts of faith and celebration. She calls them the "holy-roller feeling" and "getting drunk on religion."

CHAPTER 70

Albert R. Zuroweste: Belleville's Third Bishop

By Msgr. Angelo Lombardo and
Father Clyde Grogan

On three different occasions in 1986 Bishop Albert R. Zuroweste responded to questions and talked about his life and priesthood with Msgr. Angelo Lombardo and Father Clyde Grogan. The Okawville and Carbondale pastors used the answers and the reminiscences from those visits to compose the following profile of Bishop Zuroweste, who retired as the Diocese of Belleville's third bishop in 1976 and who celebrated the sixtieth anniversary of his ordination as a priest in 1984.

OF THE MORE THAN 120,000 Catholics who make up the Diocese of Belleville, how many have been touched by Bishop Albert R. Zuroweste in some way? Many — if not most of us. To say that Bishop Zuroweste left his imprint on the diocese is to state the obvious.

Albert Rudolph Zuroweste was born April 26, 1901, the son of Henry and Elizabeth Holten Zuroweste, at 1306 Gaty Avenue in East St. Louis. Dad wanted the newborn to be named Henry. Mom said the child would be named Albert. Rudolph was his grandfather's name.

Albert grew up at 1747 College Avenue in East St. Louis with his parents and three sisters. The future bishop was baptized at St. Henry church because his parish church of St. Joseph would not be opened until the following year. Albert attended St. Joseph school and learned firsthand and up close how to build a church — truly an experience that prepared him to be the builder he was to become as a bishop many years later.

When Albert was a seventh and eighth grade student at St. Joseph's, Father Thomas J. Bannan, the founding pastor, directed the building of the new church. He trained seven men of the parish to mix concrete for the church. Each day after his religion class for the seventh and eighth graders, he rewarded the five boys who knew their religion lessons with the privilege of helping the men sift sand for the concrete. Bishop Zuroweste said: "I never saw fractions."

The Zuroweste family lived ten blocks from the parish. Albert would get up at 5:30 A.M. to serve the 6:30 Mass. He remembers those ten blocks vividly.

In the eighth grade Albert began to give serious thought to becoming a priest. Father William Trombley, the assistant at St. Joseph's in 1914 and later the founding pastor of Holy Angels in East St. Louis, began giving Albert Latin lessons. But Elizabeth Zuroweste, the bishop said, was the greatest influence and encouragement in Albert's pursuit of the priesthood.

Bishop Albert Zuroweste

After graduation in 1914 Albert Zuroweste enrolled in St. Francis College, Quincy, Ill., which was both a high school and seminary. His studies there were abbreviated because of World War I and the shortage of food.

In 1917 the sixteen-year-old Albert decided to ask Bishop Henry Althoff if he could study to be a priest for the Belleville diocese. Albert took the streetcar from East St. Louis to Third Street in Belleville. Walking toward the chancery office, he encountered Bishop Althoff, who was on his way to the dentist. "I was scared as I asked Bishop Althoff on the street if I could study for the priesthood." And the bishop responded: "Your dad is a Protestant." Bishop Althoff then told young Albert to write to Kenrick Seminary in St. Louis for acceptance. (Henry Zuroweste, Albert's father, joined the Catholic Church in 1934, ten years after Albert was ordained. Bishop Althoff's father had also been a convert.)

Albert Zuroweste attended Kenrick Seminary from 1918 to 1924. He recalled how a student from Omaha, Nebraska, and he were often confused by a certain professor. So the two students would answer in class for each other. Even after ordination the professor never knew who was who.

During summer vacations the future bishop worked in East St. Louis, first at the Illinois Coke and Refinery on Twenty-sixth Street and then as a file clerk for the Missouri Pacific Railroad. When asked about his grades in the seminary Bishop Zuroweste winked and said; "Let's not get into that."

Father Albert Zuroweste was ordained by Bishop Althoff on June 8, 1924. The first assignment for the twenty-three-year-old priest was as assistant to "Father" James Downey. Reminiscing about his time at St. Joseph's from 1924 to 1931, Bishop Zuroweste radiated in talking about his love for preaching and his love for young people.

In 1931 Father Zuroweste was placed in charge of St. John's Orphanage in Shiloh. That year was also the last time he played golf, he said. Although as a youth and young priest he was not very athletic, he enjoyed horseback riding at St. John's. The bishop referred to the four years he worked with the young people and the sisters at the orphanage as the happiest days of his priesthood.

One day in 1934 Father Zuroweste had reason to be in Bishop Althoff's office on orphanage business. Bishop Althoff was in "low spirits" regarding *The Messenger,* then privately owned. Father Zuroweste tried to encourage the bishop and told him to "appoint a young priest" as the new editor. The next morning Father Zuroweste was appointed editor of *The Messenger.*

Another day in 1935 Father Zuroweste had occasion to again be in Bishop Althoff's office concerning orphanage business. That day the bishop "was in low spirits concerning Central Catholic High School" in East St. Louis. He had just returned from a meeting of the East St. Louis pastors. The pastors wanted to close the high school. Bishop Althoff said: "I'll appoint you as administrator." Zuroweste said: "No" and encouraged the bishop to please think it over. The next day at 8:00 A.M. the letter of appointment was hand-delivered appointing Father Zuroweste administrator of Central Catholic High School.

In 1940 Father Zuroweste was asked to return to his home parish of St. Joseph as pastor. And so, until 1947, when he was appointed Belleville's third bishop, Father Zuroweste was pastor of St. Joseph's, editor of *The Messenger,* administrator of Central Catholic High School, and after 1945 the founding director of the diocesan Catholic Charities.

"Bishop, did you have any inklings after Bishop Althoff's death who might become bishop?" his interviewers asked. He had had several. One day Father Zuroweste was at the cathedral in procession with his brother priests, coming up the center aisle and "all of a sudden it hit me that someday I would occupy the bishop's chair."

He went on, "And soon after that experience, I was praying my office and came across the words *Refugium Meum Es Tu* (You Are My Refuge), and I thought 'What a beautiful motto for a bishop.'

"Then there was the evening after Bishop Althoff's funeral. I had just picked up a new 1947 Studebaker and my two assistants, Father

Ed Lugge and C. J. Cunningham, said: 'Let's go for a ride in the new car and visit Monsignor Quack in St. Rose.' We were all sitting around in Monsignor Quack's living room listening to the St. Rose pastor give his unique view of the diocese. Then one of the young priests asked him: 'Who will be the next bishop of Belleville?' Monsignor Quack responded: 'The next bishop of Belleville is sitting in this room,' and he pointed to me."

From 1947 until 1976, Bishop Zuroweste served as Bishop of Belleville. Bishop Zuroweste led the southern Illinois diocese through the post-World War II years, the fruitful and expansive 1950s and 1960s leading up to the opening of Vatican Council II, and the Vietnam era.

The bishop, as he looks back over those years, sees his major accomplishments in the field of education, through the building of our four high schools — Mater Dei, Breese; Assumption, East St. Louis; Althoff, Belleville; and Gibault, Waterloo. He also thinks of the establishment of the Newman Center at Southern Illinois University in Carbondale as a great accomplishment.

His first major building program, reflecting his continued love for the orphanage, was the rebuilding and expansion of the orphanage complex. Responding to Pope John XXIII's call in the early 1960s for more responsibility toward impoverished missions in Latin America, Bishop Zuroweste committed both diocesan personnel and financial support to Belleville's Guatemalan mission — resulting in one of the most extensive support programs in the diocese's history.

The bishop said the great joy of his years as a bishop was the ordaining of young men to serve as priests in our diocese. "It was frightening to assign a priest, hoping and praying he would be successful." Dealing with his priests was also a cause of great pain when so many priests left the ministry during the 1960s and 1970s.

It wasn't easy for Bishop Zuroweste to talk about those years of the late 1960s and early 1970s. America was torn up with the war and the civil rights struggle. The Belleville diocese, especially in Cairo and East St. Louis, experienced great racial difficulties.

Today, as an eighty-five year old retiree, Bishop Zuroweste has much time to pray and think about death. Bishop Zuroweste offers Mass each day at 7:30 A.M. and prays in the chapel from 3:00 to 4:00 P.M. The retired bishop, extremely active for so many years and involved in numerous diocesan, national, and international initiatives, finds it difficult to be so slowed down with infirmities and largely confined to his wheelchair. "This is the hardest time of my life, being so dependent with so little to do. I spend a lot of time thinking and praying about death."

"At this point in our interview," Msgr. Lombardo and Father Grogan wrote, "Sister Virgilia, ASC, came in to say goodbye to Bishop Zuroweste." She was leaving after ten years as the bishop's housekeeper. Bishop Zuroweste thanked her and gave her his blessing. Sister Virgilia responded: "Thank you for the good example you gave to me."

When asked what he was grateful for, the bishop responded: "I am thankful to God for the sixty-two years of being a priest and the many opportunities I had to serve God's people."

Editors' note: Bishop Zuroweste died of pneumonia in Belleville on March 28, 1987. He was eighty-five years old.

CHAPTER 71

Father Edwin Guild: Founder of the Shrine

By Linda Lehr

TRANSFORMING DREAMS INTO REALITY is not easy. Inherently, the process involves perseverance, hard work, faith, and an unyielding determination to succeed. Epitomizing these qualities, Father Edwin J. Guild, OMI, has seen a number of his personal dreams come to fruition during his lifetime. Yet, two of his dreams-turned-reality are fundamental to the rest — becoming a priest and founding the National Shrine of Our Lady of the Snows.

The oldest of William and Elizabeth Guild's five children, Edwin Guild was born on February 8, 1906, in the southern Illinois town of Wetaug. His parents derived their livelihood from a truck farm; thus Guild was introduced to farm work at an early age. In those days, farmland was prepared for planting by a team of horses pulling a one-bottom plow, yet the bulk of the work was done by hand. Consequently, the young Guild spent endless hours hoeing his father's crops in a constant battle with the weeds.

When the time came to attend school, the boy did not care much for the idea. "Our school was a one-teacher, one-room setup with eighty to ninety students of varying grades and abilities. Very few country children attended high school in those days. They just continued to attend the country grade school until the age of sixteen to eighteen, thus causing overcrowding," recalls Father Guild. Under these conditions, education was neither thorough nor inviting. In fact, Father Guild considers his early schooling poor, which later presented an obstacle to him in his studies for the priesthood.

In addition to inadequate schooling, the young Guild also encountered anti-Catholic sentiment in Wetaug as he suffered ridicule from both peers and adults. The Guild family patriarch was a Protes-

Father Edwin Guild

tant of Scotch-Irish descent who became angry when young Edwin did not fight to defend his beliefs. The Guild family matriarch was a Catholic who instilled a strong faith in her children, which sparked a determination to resist such anti-Catholic prejudice without a physical fight. Occasionally, however, a fight was unavoidable.

Needless to say, the religious atmosphere around Wetaug was poor. The town was a Catholic mission where Sunday Mass occurred five or six times per year. Father Guild's early religious training consisted of catechism lessons taught by his mother.

"My first association with a Catholic community and the Church came when I visited my grandparents in New-Alsace, Indiana" relates Father Guild. "At the age of nine I visited my grandparents for Christmas and ended up staying with them to attend the local parochial school during the spring semester. I enjoyed the school, the religious atmosphere of the parish, and the Catholic community. During my stay in New-Alsace, I made my first Holy Communion, learned to serve Mass and pray the rosary," he recollects.

Disappointment struck the young Guild when a letter from his father called for his immediate return home. The elder Guild needed help on the farm. Although the boy tolerated the unfavorable educational and religious conditions in Wetaug, the future held change. Several years later, the Guild family moved to a larger and better farm in Tamms, Illinois, located about twenty miles north of Cairo.

For Guild, moving to Tamms was like moving into a new world. The town had a community high school which enabled him to receive a high school education and diploma. Furthermore, Tamms offered a favorable environment for Catholics, and he did not experience prejudice because of his faith. Mass was held once a month in the Sandusky mission church, just a few miles from Tamms. Since one of the men was already an official server for Mass, the elder Guild organized a choir for the church. On the remaining Sundays the Guild patriarch drove the family to Mass in Cairo.

Growing up, Guild learned a great deal from his father which would aid him in his future life. The elder Guild was a hard worker and a good manager who was well ahead of his time in knowledge of various aspects of farming. "My father was a hard taskmaster, and he taught me to follow in his footsteps," Father Guild says. "Once he set his goals for achievement, nothing could daunt him. I similarly developed his drive," he adds.

Although the young Guild did not possess the same affinity for farming as did his father, he did follow in his father's footsteps by being ahead of his time in planning the Shrine of Our Lady of the Snows. In addition, Father Guild learned the names of all the trees and wildflowers which grew in abundance on the Tamms farm that stretched into the beautiful foothills of the southern Illinois Ozarks. Father Guild later employed this knowledge to aid in beautifying the Shrine's landscape.

Thoughts of becoming a priest had been in Father Guild's mind since his childhood exposure to the Church in New-Alsace. He made his final decision while working in his father's strawberry patch one summer. After teaching in a local school for the first year following his high school graduation, Father Guild thought he might enjoy a teaching career, but he felt a calling to the priesthood. "I loved the Church, and the ministry appealed to me in a simple, childlike fashion. I knew there was a great chasm between me and my desire to be a priest. I didn't know how I could cross the chasm or lessen it, nor did I realize the cost of my decision in terms of perseverance or fortitude required. If I had known any of these things, I might have been more frightened, and not have dared take the challenge," Father Guild explains.

The young man from southern Illinois accepted the challenge and began studying for his chosen vocation. Since the study and mastery of Latin was essential to the priesthood, Father Guild began his studies at St. Henry Seminary, Belleville, in the fall of 1927, studying only Latin. Being the oldest member of his class, Father Guild was dubbed "pop" — a name he still retains.

As his studies at St. Henry Seminary drew to a close, Father Guild decided to join the Oblates of Mary Immaculate. He persevered in his studies through the Oblate novitiate and scholasticate, taking first and final vows, and receiving minor and major orders. On June 11, 1938, at the age of thirty-three, Father Guild was ordained by Bishop Henry Althoff at St. Peter cathedral, Belleville. "I consider becoming a priest a miracle in my life," reflects Father Guild. "I was not well-suited to the priesthood. I was born into a mixed marriage, grew up amidst Catholic prejudice, and had inadequate schooling and religious training in my early years," he adds. He celebrated his first Mass at St.

Mary Church, Belleville.

Father Guild's first assignment was at St. Henry Seminary, to assist the Oblate superior in a fund-raising campaign to build a gymnasium for the seminary. Next, he was assigned assistant pastor at St. Mary church, Belleville. Following his service at St. Mary, Father Guild was appointed treasurer of St. Henry Seminary.

A short time later, Father Guild was asked by the Oblate Provincial to become the director of the Missionary Association of Mary Immaculate. The association was founded so that lay people could share in the tasks of the Oblates through prayer, good works, and financial contributions. During this time, the Oblate also taught religion and was spiritual director to students at St. Henry Seminary.

In 1942, Father Guild met Father Paul Schulte, OMI, who introduced him to the devotion to Our Lady of the Snows. Father Schulte believed that it would be good for the Oblates to promote devotion to Our Lady of the Snows in the United States for two reasons. First, devotion to Our Lady of the Snows was the Church's oldest devotion to Mary. Secondly, devotion to Our Lady of the Snows honored the many Oblate missionaries who have given their lives in the remote lands of snow and ice in northern Canada by ministering to the Eskimo and Indian people. Hence devotion to Our Lady of the Snows began, and continuing novenas commenced in her honor.

The continuing novena to Our Lady of the Snows grew in popularity, and Father John Maronic, OMI, along with Father Guild, was instrumental in establishing the first outdoor novena for the public on the grounds of St. Henry Seminary. Father Guild was quite pleased with the success of the novena, when, in the spring of 1949, he was asked to assume further responsibilities in the province. He received a letter which informed him of his appointment as provincial of the Oblate central province. As the years passed, devotion to Our Lady of the Snows and participation in the annual novena in her honor grew. "Thousands attended the closing ceremony of the novena, and the candlelight procession around the lake at St. Henry Seminary was impressive and inspiring," relates Father Guild. Due to the crowds participating in the novena, a decision was made to develop a new shrine for devotion to Our Lady of the Snows. Originally, consideration was given to dividing the St. Henry Seminary campus, so that a part of it could be set aside specifically for the shrine's development. After several studies and discussions, a decision was made to leave the St. Henry property intact and find a new location for the shrine.

"There were many permissions to secure, but we worked diligently," recalls Father Guild. "After obtaining the appropriate permissions, we searched up and down the bluffs of the Mississippi for a suitable location. After much land searching and negotiations, we found a site for the shrine. We closed the purchase of the land in February 1958, and officially began construction of the new shrine in 1960,'' he adds.

All of the elements that compose today's National Shrine of Our Lady of the Snows — the beautifully landscaped grounds, the devotional areas, the ministries for people of all ages are the embodiment of dreams of a man who learned early in life that perseverance, hard work, faith, and an unyielding determination to succeed can transform dreams into reality.

CHAPTER 72

Anne and Bolen Carter: "Dorothy Day" Catholics

By Raphael H. Middeke

DURING A VISIT IN THEIR Laclede Town apartment in St. Louis, Anne and Bolen Carter had little difficulty finding a black and white photo of Dorothy Day and their two children taken in their East St. Louis home around 1950.

It was not unusual for Dorothy Day — the devout Catholic activist and founder of the Catholic Worker Movement — to stay at the Carters' home when she passed through the St. Louis area. And it was appropriate.

Through five decades of Catholic activism and involvement, Dorothy Day's philosophy of Catholic action remained a fundamental inspiration in the Carters' lives.

The reading of an early issue of the *Catholic Worker* — Dorothy Day's penny newspaper — was the impetus which sent Bolen, a young man in St. Joseph parish, East St. Louis, across the river to help organize a Catholic Worker community, which opened the first Worker house in St. Louis in 1935.

Anne Loftus, a St. Louis schoolteacher, was a volunteer in the fledgling Catholic community.The two "Worker" pioneers became more than friends. After their marriage in 1940 they moved into Holy Angels parish, East St. Louis. Bolen was a teacher at East St. Louis senior high school.

During the following decades their involvement in Catholic action, the lay apostolate, and Catholic social justice issues — the names changed but the work remained the same — varied in focus and place, but "we never let go of the Catholic Worker connection," Anne said.

The Catholic Worker connection involved much more than happy memories and occasional contacts with the old community. While the Carters never chose to follow Dorothy Day's lifestyle, her faith and spirituality was always an important influence in their lives.

Perhaps the most significant example of that influence is the importance of the liturgy in their lives and their actions. "We have always felt strongly that Catholic action needs to be supported and strengthened by our own faith and the liturgy," Bolen said. "Linking social justice and the liturgy was one of the things so important to Dorothy Day," Anne added. "She taught us to appreciate the liturgy."

Bolen and Anne Carter

That appreciation is obviously alive for the couple, now physically frail, who admit they are mostly confined to their apartment. "We don't get to daily Mass anymore," they said, "but the Sunday liturgy at the College church is our lifeline." For the Carters, social justice — from the soup lines of the Worker houses to the pickets for grapepickers' justice to witness for peace in Nicaragua — has always been rooted in the liturgy.

An old friend, Msgr. Martin Hellriegel, the St. Louis pioneer liturgist who paid the first month's rent for the first Worker house, deepened their commitment to the liturgy as the source of their social justice concerns. In 1949 Bolen was on the program of the National Liturgical Conference when it met in St. Louis.

"Our goals were small in those days," he said. "If we could get people to say out loud *Et cum spiritu tuo* (and with your spirit), when the priest said *Dominus vobiscum* (the Lord be with you), we thought we had made a significant contribution to "participation" in the liturgy.

Involvement in the church grew in the next twenty-six years, before Bolen's retirement as an employee in the East St. Louis school district. He had been a teacher, an assistant high school principal, an elementary school principal, and an assistant superintendent before retiring in 1966 at the age of sixty-one.

The list of their activities is long and varied:

- *CCD:* Anne, especially, was active for many years in the Confraternity of Christian Doctrine as an organizer and a teacher in the parent-educator section, focusing on getting groups of young parents together for discussion and support of their faith values. In 1963 Anne received the Pius X medal for her work in the diocesan CCD program.
- *Cana Conference:* The Carters worked with Jesuit Father Edward Dowling to bring the Cana Conference, a marriage program, to the area and arranged the first parish Cana Conference at Holy Angels.

They were later associated with the National Cana Conference and helped promote the program in other cities. "Cana was a great experience and changed our lives," Anne said. The Carters, who never made a Marriage Encounter weekend, think Cana was probably the Marriage Encounter of their day.

• *Retreats:* For over a quarter century, Bolen spearheaded an effort to provide a three-day retreat opportunity for Catholic high school students in public schools. It was a unique apostolate and symbolic of the Carters' "Dorothy Day heritage" to reach out to those not in the mainstream — whether of society or the church. Bolen hinted that his membership and leadership in the Knights of Columbus — he was a Faithful Navigator of the Fourth Degree Assembly — was partly influenced by their financial support of his longtime retreat work with the public school Catholic youth of the East St. Louis area.

• *CCM:* A former president of the Diocesan Council of Catholic Men, Bolen received in 1965 the national council's St. Thomas More Award for outstanding service in the lay apostolate. The bronze bust of St. Thomas More stands on a bookshelf in their living room today.

• *Racial Justice:* Bolen's interest in the issue of race led to membership in the Catholic Interracial Council, the East St. Louis Human Relations Committee, and the NAACP. Through his initiative the Cana Conference movement was interracial from its beginning, long before the civil rights movement. A tragic and serious gunshot wound in the 1970s during an attempted holdup did not dampen his concern for racial justice.

There were other involvements and activities. In the Dorothy Day photo, there is a third "family member," a guest at the time. The Carters' home was often open for a day, for a week, or for months to someone needing a place to stay.

It was not a surprise to friends and acquaintances when in 1966 the Carters "retired" to serve as Papal Volunteers in Latin America (PAVLA) in Belize. They went as teachers and stayed for five years. They became recruiters for PAVLA and Bolen later became the director of PAVLA in British Honduras.

The same energies and passion which characterized their decades of Catholic action were not absent from their missionary experiences — returning periodically to recruit and to gather needed textbooks. And the experience planted, too, the seeds for a present passion for peace and justice in another Central American country — Nicaragua. In a younger day they would have been "witnesses for peace."

The Carters spoke of the 1971 Synod of Bishops statement which said that "action on the part of justice and participation in the transformation of the world," is a "constitutive dimension" of the Gospel. "Such a terrible word, "constitutive," Anne said. "Why can't we just say what it means?" "The works of mercy are a necessary part of what the Lord wants us to do," Bolen said. He went on to ponder the meaning of "constitutive." "It must mean that when a young man is ordained or when anyone witnesses to the Gospel, they have to be involved in a concern for social justice. Otherwise, they are not preaching or witnessing to the Gospel."

The Carters returned to East St. Louis in the early 1970s before moving to the Laclede Town apartment, where they once again became a regular presence at the local Catholic Worker house. Occasionally, they still visit the house — but even more, people there who are their friends.

Time slowed their involvements — in grape boycott picketing, in links with the Worker community, the Institute for Peace and Justice, New Lifestyles, (a prostitute rehabilitation program) and other activities — but not their passion, born of faith and the liturgy. "There are no more picket lines for us," Bolen said. But there is talk of the soul about Nicaragua and nuclear arms. They prefer the Church of today to the silent Church of yesterday — but yesterday and today, they were and are Catholic to the core, Dorothy Day style.

The Carters are the parents of two children. Their son, John, is married and lives in San Francisco. Their daughter, Sister Anne, is a religious of the Sacred Heart (RSCJ). With Sister Anne, in their weakening bodies, they share a special link. Sister Anne is confined to a wheelchair because of a sclerosis disease. In a recent editorial in the *RSCJ Newsletter,* which she edits, she speaks of her own struggles to remain active and the experience of freedom of the wheelchair. "I probably now will never make it to the Nicaraguan border to witness for peace," she wrote. But the words are not words of despair — they are words of hope and faith.

And they sound strangely like the words: "No more picket lines for us," coupled with the statement, "The Sunday liturgy at the College church is our lifeline."

Those words could not be spoken today if the liturgy had not been the root and the source of decades of Catholic activism and a growing concern for social justice. The actions would have sat down with them to taunt their frail years.

They haven't. And that is the story of their faith — and the legacy of the saint in their lives, Dorothy Day.

CHAPTER 73

Robert Welzbacher: Catholic Journalist

By Stanley J. Konieczny

IN LOOKING AT THE CHURCH in the modern world, the Second Vatican Council considered various aspects of today's society. In their comments on communications, the council fathers instructed, ''It is the layman's particular obligation to animate these instruments (of the media) with a humane and Christian spirit.'' These words echo throughout the life and career of an exceptional Catholic layman, Robert Welzbacher, who served the church in southern Illinois for over forty-years with *The Messenger.*

Robert John Welzbacher was born west of New Athens on Oct. 30, 1915, a son of George and Katherine Welzbacher. As a boy, he would shadow his favorite Uncle Peter. Consequently, the young Welzbacher was dubbed ''Pete,'' a nickname which he carried throughout his life.

Belleville's former Cathedral High School offered Welzbacher opportunities to prove himself early in life. ''Bob had to make a great deal of sacrifice to attend Cathedral High,'' recalled one of his classmates, Father Ralph Arnold. ''He came from New Athens every day to attend classes. Also, this was the heart of the depression and his family was not wealthy,'' Father Arnold added.

The 1932 edition of Cathedral's yearbook, *The Cathedra,* reveals a Bob Welzbacher who seemed to be involved in just about every activity which the school offered, from basketball to the Lettermen's Club, from the Student Spiritual Council to the Catholic Students' Mission Crusade. During these days at Cathedral High School, an important seed was sown: Bob Welzbacher edited the school's first newspaper and served as Cathedral's correspondent for *The Messenger's* Catholic high school news section.

Immediately after graduating from Cathedral High School in 1933

Welzbacher became a "printer's devil" or apprentice at Buechler Printing Company. Buechler owned *The Messenger* at the time, as well as a number of other Catholic publications. "Bob was a jack-of-all-trades at Buechler's. He did everything, working in the mechanical department and the editorial department," Bishop Zuroweste recalled. The retired bishop of Belleville worked closely with Welzbacher, first as editor of *The Messenger* and later as head of the Church in southern Illinois.

Robert Welzbacher

Welzbacher became a contributor to many of Buechler's publications. He also studied journalism during night classes at Washington University and Jefferson College, both in St. Louis. "He showed sincerity in his work, a willingness to make sacrifices of his time and an ability to do a good job," Bishop Zuroweste added, as he recounted Welzbacher's early years with the Catholic press.

Bishop Zuroweste became acquainted with Welzbacher when, as a young priest, he was named *Messenger* editor in 1934. Within three years, Buechler decided to relinquish control of the weekly Catholic newspaper and the Diocese of Belleville assumed ownership. Father Zuroweste established offices for *The Messenger* in East St. Louis and hired Bob Welzbacher as his assistant.

In his new position with *The Messenger,* Welzbacher continued to wear many hats. Working with Father Zuroweste, he would cover the news of the diocese and supervise newspaper production at the printshop. He also pounded the pavement as an advertising representative in Belleville and East St. Louis.

"That was to our advantage, because he would get the pulse of the people out in the diocese and bring it into the office," explained Bishop Zuroweste. "Bob would pick up a lot of information as he was selling ads. If people liked or didn't like something in the paper, Bob would hear about it."

During these early years, Bob Welzbacher demonstrated his devotion to the church and the Catholic press. He also told the world about the first love of his life: Dolores Vierheller. Bob and Dolores exchanged their wedding vows on Valentine's Day, February 14, 1939, at St.

Luke Church, Belleville, with Father Zuroweste celebrating the wedding liturgy.

The young couple was separated for three years, 1943-1946, when Welzbacher served on the flagship of Admiral Chester Nimitz, the U.S. Navy's Commander-in-Chief during World War II. Following military service he returned to Belleville, where Bob and Dolores raised their family of five: Richard (now deceased), Robert, James, Carol, and Gary.

After the war, Bob Welzbacher continued his service to the Diocese of Belleville through *The Messenger.* The routine continued with the diocesan newspaper. For forty-three years he would meet deadlines; write obituaries and anniversary stories; edit news service copy; cover the installation of bishops; and education stories.

Few readers appreciate the amount of planning and preparation that must go into a newspaper. Few probably realize how many hours Bob Welzbacher clocked in on *The Messenger* over forty-three years. ''He certainly put in more than an honest day's work,'' observed Msgr. Charles Nebel, who had served as *The Messenger's* associate editor from 1940 to 1943.

''I can remember him sitting at the table, proofreading with his big, red crayon,'' recalled Welzbacher's daughter, Mrs. Carol Bollman. ''Every night during the work week he would work on that paper, but he would always wait until after our bedtime. He always had that kitchen table filled with *Messenger* copy,'' added his son, Jim.

In typical fashion, Bob Welzbacher did very little to ''blow his own horn.'' After a particularly difficult week in February 1965, an unsigned article in *The Messenger,* undoubtedly written by Bob, disclosed a bit of the behind-the-scenes hassles associated with producing the Catholic weekly and betrayed a bit of the newspaperman's devotion to his craft. The setting of the article was during a strike at the former *East St. Louis Journal,* where *The Messenger* was printed.

''We could easily have said 'so what' and forgotten about the publication for that week. But instead, we made innumerable phone calls, so many of which greeted us with a negative answer, until we found several real friends of the Catholic press. These friends came to our assistance and within hours put *The Messenger* on its way to the Catholic homes throughout the diocese.''

Welzbacher's companion during these journalistic escapades was the late Msgr. Edmund Lugge. ''Father Lugge was Number One with Dad. They seemed like brothers,'' noted Gary Welzbacher.

During these years, Welzbacher saw *The Messenger* staff through moves from headquarters at the Catholic Community House, Knights of Columbus, and First Federal building in East St. Louis, and the South Third and West Washington location in Belleville. Printers were changed from the *Journal* in East St. Louis to the *Progress* in O'Fallon. The N.C. News teletype was also installed. Things had changed considerably from the old days at Buechler's. In 1967 Bishop Zuroweste named him managing editor of the paper.

"I always found Bob to be extremely friendly and delightful to work with," remarked Msgr. Joseph Schwaegel, who has served as secretary to the last four bishops and has had many occasions to work with Welzbacher. "Although he always faced deadlines, he wasn't easily ruffled. Bob always took time to be pleasant. He was a good churchman and a good newspaperman."

As if he had not already done enough, Bob Welzbacher also gave countless hours to various Catholic organizations. He was involved with the Knights of Columbus, Holy Name Society, King's House, Academy of Notre Dame advisory board, and the East St. Louis health and welfare board. He spent many hours promoting the benefit picnic for the former St. John's Orphanage. In addition to coordinating the many volunteers from around the diocese, Bob would also work his shift behind the booths at Glen Addie on the big day itself.

"Bob always had time for his fellow parishioners and fellow human beings," commented Welzbacher's former pastor, Msgr. Leonard Bauer, who had served St. Henry parish, Belleville. "He was a man of self-sacrifice, who was willing to give of himself."

The spirit of self-giving was recognized by several groups who honored Welzbacher in the course of his career. The diocesan Catholic Youth Organization presented him with its "Pro Deo et Juventute" award for the special public relations work that he did on their behalf. He was also honored by the Catholic Students' Mission Crusade.

In February 1976 Bishop Zuroweste nominated Welzbacher for a papal honor and Pope Paul VI named the diocesan editor a Knight of St. Gregory the Great of the Civil Order. "I felt that Bob had made many sacrifices for the Catholic press and was deserving of this recognition from the church," Bishop Zuroweste said. "The honor conferred on him acknowledged his ability and his devotion to the Catholic press."

In spite of so many demands and commitments, Bob Welzbacher remained a devoted family man. "He was always there when I needed him," recalled his daughter, Carol. "He always seemed to find time for everybody." She related how her dad would help her with her own homework before he started in on *Messenger* "homework." She also shared a family joke that Bob had completed twelve years of Catholic education at least five times with all the hours of homework he did himself and later helped his children do.

"They gave up a lot of things, that's for sure," Jim Welzbacher said recalling the sacrifices of his parents as they raised and educated their family. Those thrifty years were marked by coupon clipping and Bob cutting his children's hair in his basement "barbershop."

"Yet, he somehow seemed to always get everything done that needed to be done," Jim added.

Greater demands for Bob's time and giving were placed upon him after Dolores was diagnosed as suffering from a debilitating neurological disease. She would eventually require constant care from Bob and he gave it without complaint. "There was a tremendous amount of love there. I guess Bishop Cosgrove said it best at dad's funeral Mass when he said that, that was dad's Gospel — being married to my mom," Gary commented.

"He believed that everyone is asked to bear a cross. His religion gave him the ability to follow through," added Jim.

Bob Welzbacher retired from *The Messenger* in 1980 to devote himself to Dolores' care. She died in 1983. Bob puttered around the last few years of his life helping those he could and pursuing his seemingly favorite hobby — conversation.

He was stricken with an aneurysm on January 18, 1986. As his condition worsened and he became delirious, he would express two concerns: he would ask about Dolores and he would worry about work left undone at *The Messenger.* Bob Welzbacher died March 10, 1986, and was buried beside Dolores at Green Mount Catholic Cemetery, Belleville.

The people who knew and loved Bob Welzbacher often refer to his saintly patience. Yet, at least one person, his son-in-law Dave Bollman, questions if Bob actually achieved paradise. "I've always said that he would never get to heaven, because he would be standing outside the gates talking with St. Peter." Bollman said.

CHAPTER 74

Father Francis X. Heiligenstein: A People's Pastor

By Raphael H. Middeke

"I HAVE OFTEN SAID that I hope God is as easy to speak to as Father X was," said Father Jerry Feldmann, in reminiscing about his friend, Father Francis X. Heiligenstein — known affectionately as Father X by priests, family, and parishioners alike. Father Jerry was X's only "assistant," for four years at St. Augustine's in Breese. At the end of those years Father X said: "These past four years have been the happiest of my life," Father Jerry recalled, with obvious appreciation and gratitude.

Father Jerry first knew Father X as his gym teacher during his high school days at St. Mary's in Carlyle. "I formed an opinion of him then and it never changed," he said. "Father X was everything I thought a priest should be. I never had trouble picturing in my mind what a good priest is like."

Thank-you's came easy for the unassuming and self-effacing pastor. In his last Christmas card to his friend and former parishioner, Mrs. Roslyn Waite, Cairo, Father X wrote: "I cannot thank you enough for your beautiful example of caring and sharing."

Father X knew during that Christmas season of 1982 that his health was failing. He made plans to become the first "retired" associate in the diocese, after officially retiring as the pastor of St. Joseph, Equality, on July 5, 1983, but he told Roslyn Waite several months earlier he didn't expect to live till his retirement. He was buried on July 4.

It was typical of the spirit and soul of Father X to say "thank you" before talking about his health, and to think of becoming the first retired associate in the diocese.

Father X was a pastor, a priests' priest, his brother priests said; a people's priest, his parishioners said. "He always wanted to be one of his people,'' said his brother, Joseph (Toby). ''He never looked beyond his parish for identity or recognition. He never thought of himself as 'monsignor material,' a priest friend said. ''He didn't want to be one of the top-weights,'' his brother added.

Father Francis X. Heiligenstein

Asked for descriptions of the man and the priest, certain words were repeated: ''compassionate, humble, unassuming, peaceful,'' — and he ''loved kids.''

''He always told us (his brothers and sisters) that his nephews and nieces taught him so much about family life, it was very easy to talk about families with his parishioners.''

''He had a tremendous affection for kids. All kids were his friends,'' said Msgr. John Fellner, his lifelong friend.

A week or two before his death, *The Messenger* received a photo of Father X, surrounded by a group of kids, from an Equality parishioner with a note saying:

The people of St. Joseph, Equality, would like to congratulate Fr. X, our pastor, on the forty-fifth anniversary of his ordination to the priesthood. (June 11, I think.) He will be leaving us soon, and he does not want any potluck or teary farewells, so we would like for you to copy this picture of him and some of ''his'' little children he loves so well, and put a special thank you and congratulations in The Messenger, *if you will. Thank you so much.*

When he was the pastor in Mound City and Mounds in the 1940s and 1950s he would load up his station wagon with toys at Christmastime and distribute them to the kids in the area — all the kids.

The Equality note also says something significant about Father X's humility. He was a simple man, who wanted for little. One of his ambitions was to fit all his possessions into the back seat of his rented Chevy. ''He came close,'' Monsignor Fellner said.

The man who ''hated building, or anything that smacked of appealing for money,'' as one friend put it, built his parishes by being one of the people. In Breese he visited the hospital every day. He also turned the rectory into a convent and moved into a little house on the corner.

If he had a great respect for priests and parishioners alike, it was returned many times. "He had a definite feeling about people," Monsignor Fellner said. "That feeling showed."

"In all my years, I never heard him say anything unkind about someone," Father John Baggio said. "If priests started talking about another priest he would try his level best to change the subject," Father Baggio added: "He was a very holy man, totally dedicated to his job in the priesthood."

If he was holy, considerate, and unassuming, he was not a bore. His sense of humor followed him into his funeral instructions and his funeral homily.

He sometimes mentioned to Father Bill Hitpas, whom he baptized in Carlyle: "If I had known how you would turn out, I would have drowned you right then and there." In his funeral notes, after asking Father Hitpas to preach his homily, he said: "Now you can drown me." (The request to preach Father X's funeral homily came as a surprise to Father Hitpas; he learned of it only after the notes were opened.)

In the notes he also left a message for his card-playing friends. "I always played cards with (Fathers) Baggio and Fellner. Tell them they were an easy mark." Msgr. Fellner, not disputing X's assessment, said: "He had more card sense than anyone I've ever known."

He had occasionally kidded Monsignor Fellner that he would hear from him after he died. Several weeks after the funeral, someone brought him an envelope addressed to him, left in one of Father X's old moral theology books. Inside was $60, with the message: "Go and have a meal with the boys," and the sure reminder that he had kept his promise to pay a visit after he died.

His final message to his brother priests, announced in Father Hitpas' homily, said simply: "Tell the brothers it's not so bad to die. Tell the brothers."

A "Lord, have mercy," and the smell of his cigar usually announced Father X's coming. "When he came to any of our homes ['our homes' were those of his seven brothers and sisters: Marie Wolf, John (deceased), Toby, Gertrude Schomaker, Magdalen Janssen, Helen Voellinger, and Bernard] — he never knocked. 'Lord, have mercy' announced him — and you could also smell his cigar coming. He came home a lot," Toby added, "and he always said it was a blessing to have been part of a large family." In September 1982 his family filled the small Equality church to celebrate his seventieth birthday.

Francis Heiligenstein was born Sept. 20, 1912, in Freeburg, the second of the eight children of Francis X. and Ida Sintzel. He attended St. Joseph grade school and the Freeburg community high school.

He was a good athlete, his brother, Toby, recalled, playing basketball, baseball, and tennis for the high school teams.

After completing a year at Saint Louis University, Heiligenstein began his seminary training at St. Meinrad, Indiana. After completion of his theology studies there he was ordained to the priesthood by Bishop Henry Althoff on June 11, 1938.

For six years he served as an assistant at St. Mary, Carlyle, and St. Liborius, St. Libory. He was named pastor of St. Mary, Mound City, with missions in Mounds and Ullin, in May 1944.

In 1958 he began a fifteen-year pastorate at St. Augustine, Breese. For a number of years he was dean of the North Central deanery, served as vicar for religious, and as a member of the priest personnel board.

Two pastorates followed his ministry in Breese — four years at St. Joseph, Ridgway, and four at St. Barbara, Okawville.

In 1981 he began his final pastorate at St. Joseph, Equality.

Father X always had time for others. He missed few gatherings of priests and parish celebrations. Having time was part of his insistence that he wasn't born to build great churches or carry out great plans. Great builders, he knew, couldn't visit the hospital every day.

"He believed strongly in prayer. I think that is why he seemed to have such good results in their being answered," Father Jerry said.

"I believe that Father X understood better than anyone else I have known, that what we believe and do depends upon the grace of God," said his brother, Bernard. "That being a priest means trying to perform as Christ would perform in a given situation. He believed that God gave you sufficient grace to do his will on earth."

"I remember Father X as an "open-door" pastor. He welcomed everyone into his home. Often when he saw people coming up the walk, he had the door open before they could ring the bell," Father Jerry remarked.

"His house was always open, never locked," Monsignor Fellner said. "You never knew who would be there."

He was, indeed, a people's pastor. "The people in Mounds and Mound City still talk about Father X," said Sister Magdalen Schammel, OSU, who taught in the Mounds parish school during the early years of Father X's pastorate.

"One prayer God did not answer for Father X," Father Jerry said. "He told me many times that he asked God to let him suffer a long time before he died to make up for his sins. 'Life' came so suddenly for Father X. Maybe he didn't have any sins."

On the morning of June 28, 1883 he was found in a coma in the Equality rectory after suffering a cerebral hemorrhage. He died on June 30, at St. Elizabeth Hospital, Belleville.

On July 4, the day before he was to begin his "retirement" as the associate at Holy Childhood, Mascoutah, Bishop William Cosgrove was the celebrant of the funeral liturgy for this "ordinary" pastor, at St. Joseph church, Freeburg.

CHAPTER 75

Joe Hubbard: Lesson in Charity

By Stanley J. Konieczny

IF CHRIST WERE AMONG THE MANY who have been asked in the course of the past few years to write a recommendation for Joe Hubbard, Jesus would probably speak of Joe in terms of seeds and harvests. These were popular images in many of Christ's parables and they capture the essence of Joe Hubbard's charitable outreach. Small seeds of kindness, sown in Joe long ago, have yielded a thousandfold through his ministry in Catholic Urban Programs and the St. Vincent de Paul Society.

A native of East St. Louis, Joseph P. Hubbard was born Jan. 8, 1943, the youngest son of Olga and the late Edward Hubbard. He was educated at Jefferson grade school, East St. Louis senior high school and Southern Illinois University. Joe's preparation for ministry to those in need came from the men of the St. Vincent de Paul Society at the former Holy Angels parish, East St. Louis.

When Joe was only sixteen his father died after a lengthy illness. These were times of considerable need for the Hubbard household. Men from the St. Vincent de Paul Society's charity left an indelible impression on the young Hubbard, who joined their ranks as a teenager.

After he left school, Joe took a job as a bookkeeper for the East Side Levee and Sanitary District. During the next eight years his Vincentian involvement grew and Joe's work with the poor competed for every free moment.

Fellow Catholics in East St. Louis recognized Joe's growing volunteer ministry and the scope of the problems which he was trying to address. They decided to set up the necessary mechanism, which would enable Joe to better fulfill his commitment to the poor.

"We saw Joe constantly reaching out to help the poor, the old, the stranded; in short, anyone in need," recalled Bolen and Anne Carter. "We realized this unusual young man, who was embracing such work as his career, needed more scope. So, we gathered together a small group of people who also saw Joe's potential and his rare qualities."

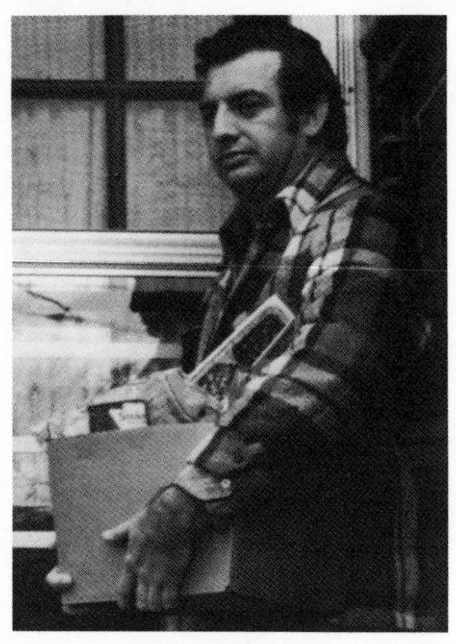
Joe Hubbard

About a dozen priests, religious, and lay people met to discuss possible ministerial opportunities for Joe. They eventually drafted a petition, which was signed by twenty people including all the priests serving in East St. Louis at the time, according to the Carters. They requested that Bishop Albert Zuroweste underwrite a small salary for Joe Hubbard so that he could formally continue his outreach under the auspices of the church.

In February 1973 Bishop Zuroweste established Catholic Urban Programs with Joe as coordinator and sole employee of the diocese's newest agency.

Bishop Zuroweste said, "For nine years previous to his appointment by me as coordinator of Catholic Urban Programs, with my approval, he worked tirelessly, without publicity or remuneration, directing the charitable programs of the St. Vincent de Paul Society, one of the oldest Catholic organizations, which serves the needy, sick, lonely, and dying."

"We often read and speak of a 'dedicated person,' " Bishop Zuroweste said. "Joe Hubbard is truly dedicated to giving service to his fellowman and does not count the cost of personal inconvenience involved in supplying this service."

Joe's new job proved to be a "promotion." As one of his previous employers noted, Joe Hubbard began to keep bankers' hours as coordinator of Catholic Urban Programs. Bishop Cosgrove, retired, once observed, "Joe is one of the few persons who can today claim to have 'bankers' hours as his work schedule. Just as one can insert his bank card for a deposit or withdrawal anytime of the day or night, seven days a week, so too, you will find Joe receiving calls for help day and night, seven days a week.

"Without exception, he responds to all, sometimes to the detriment of his own health and safety," Bishop Cosgrove added.

"There is no typical workday for Joe Hubbard," echoed Pat Albert, a public aid staff person, who chronicled a great deal of Joe's ministry while processing his nomination for the Illinois Welfare Association's Illinois Merit Award.

"Joe works all hours of the day or night — whenever and wherever he is needed. Joe is not afraid to become involved, to offer and deliver any service that might be needed. Many times in our world of red tape and regulations, Joe is seen by many as their last hope," Mrs. Albert said, adding, "This quiet, unassuming, selfless man has a strength about him that makes one start to question what we who claim to be in the human services field are really doing."

Because of Joe's unflagging commitment, there are a few less hungry people in the East St. Louis area; the future does not seem quite so threatening and uncertain for the elderly who are entrusted to Joe's care; winter will be a little less bleak for those with inadequate housing. The church of southern Illinois also benefits from this man's living lessons of the corporal works of mercy.

Listing the many facets of Joe Hubbard's work poses an awesome task. It might be easier to see how Catholic Urban Programs stacks up against the Church's call to works of charity.

• *Feed the Hungry* — Through Catholic Urban Programs, food is distributed to persons who do not qualify for government assistance or who face emergency need of food. People with good health and access to transportation often forget that just getting to the store can be difficult for the homebound. Joe Hubbard doesn't; so CUP provides transportation to and from the grocery store. Such a detail is not overlooked by Joe. Joe also helped organize the Meals on Wheels program in the Belleville area and has served as vice-president of this outreach to the sick and aged. Hubbard's Cupboard, CUP's emergency food pantry, expands from CUP headquarters at the St. Patrick parish rectory, East St. Louis, and fills the pews and aisles of the massive church. St. Patrick's becomes a sea of brown bags and cardboard boxes, filled with food and gifts for those in need.

• *Give Drink to the Thirsty* — There are many thirsts in the Diocese of Belleville: thirsts for justice, dignity, and friendship. Joe Hubbard and the staff of Catholic Urban Programs strive to relieve these thirsts. "Besides the direct services which Joe and his agency provide, Joe is very active in developing and promoting programs which will attack problems on a larger scale," explained William Kreeb of the Lessie Bates Davis Neighborhood House in East St. Louis.

"Joe sits on several boards and advisory councils and works with several community groups on such problems as welfare rights, tenant-landlord problems, and fairer utility rates,'' Kreeb noted.

• *Clothe the Naked* — Catholic Urban Programs collects clothing and furniture which is later distributed to those in need. The CUP staff frequently faces emergency needs for clothing and furniture for people who lose all of their possessions in house fires, which often plague the community.

Many people on public assistance or Social Security do not have enough money to buy needed clothing or furniture. Joe Hubbard sees to it that their needs are met. In addition to his work with the St. Vincent de Paul Society, Joe is a member of the board of the St. Francis Thrift Shop, Belleville.

• *Shelter the Homeless* — Among his many credits, Joe Hubbard can list membership on various boards that address the problem of homelessness in the Metro-East. He has served on the St. Clair County Task Force for Emergency Housing and is chairman of the Holy Angles Shelter for the Homeless. Yet, many people probably best remember Joe as the man who moved them into decent, safe shelter.

Repairs and improvements are made to the homes of the widowed and elderly, who cannot always handle the major problems of home upkeep. After outliving their relatives, the elderly find in Joe Hubbard and his associates a ''family'' who care for them with dignity and respect, insuring that they are placed in a caring environment. Transients and area homeless find a welcome haven at the Holy Angels shelter.

• *Visit the Sick* — This outreach separates Joe Hubbard and Catholic Urban Programs from other agencies. This dimension of ministry personalizes the work of CUP. Clients are not numbers; they are individuals with feelings and dignity.

Dr. Polly Teagle noted, ''Joe Hubbard loves people. What is truly remarkable about him is that he loves people that no one else seems to love: the sick, the elderly, and in particular the people who are alone and have no one else to assist them; people who are diseased and dirty and tired.''

''Joe does what others consider to be the dirty and menial work,'' commented Gerry Hasenstab of the CUP staff. ''He will clean the mess left by a sick alcoholic or will wash the floors of someone who couldn't make it to the bathroom. He will sit all night with someone who is dying alone and then turn around and put legal papers in order for a will or talk with lawyers to prevent eviction.''

He added, ''To Joe, people are people, they all deserve love, compassion and at least the basic necessities of life.''

What constitutes these basic necessities would probably be a source of debate between Joe and other social workers. Joe values letting people know they are loved; this is as important to his outreach as a box of canned goods or a used table and chairs.

Each year, Catholic Urban Programs hosts a picnic for area senior citizens. Local florists will attest that Joe orders floral remembrances for his clients, living and dead, to express his devotion and to reaffirm the importance of each person.

• *Bury the Dead* — Loneliness can greatly accentuate a sense of mortality. Joe Hubbard helps ease the pain of death for his people by handling their arrangements. People can work through CUP to plan their own funeral arrangements. Those who die alone are given a decent funeral. Often, Joe and the funeral director are the only ones in attendance for the graveside rite. Joe has been known to offer a few final words and prayers before the casket is lowered into the ground.

Joe is the closest to a survivor that some of these forgotten dead have. He serves as legal trustee or conservator for a number of elderly people.

Conducting funeral services and giving without limit have earned Joe a widespread reputation of charity, but people calling the CUP office often have a bit of an identity crisis in naming their contact. They may even ask for "Reverend Hubbard." They might not be far from the mark, because Joe has been "ordained" by his charity; ordained in the sense that his love of the poor and the elderly has left an indelible sign on his soul — a sign which witnesses to the love of Christ.

In recent years, the work of Joe Hubbard and Catholic Urban Programs has been recognized by various local, regional, and national awards. He was presented the first Spiritus Franciscanus award of the College of St. Francis, Joliet, in 1982. That same year, various local agencies hosted an appreciation dinner to honor Joe.

Joe Hubbard brought the prestigious Lumen Christi award of the Catholic Church Extension Society to the Belleville diocese in 1983. Most recently the National Catholic Development Conference gave him its 1986 Good Samaritan award.

When a person talks to Joe, his voice usually betrays fatigue. He jokes and banters until he talks about the needs of his community; then everything is serious. With characteristic good humor, he discounts his awards. That is understandable. Perhaps everything becomes less important in the face of coping daily with incredible poverty, dealing with the responsibility of being the legal guardian for total strangers, trying to combat grave poverty of spirit.

When talking with a reporter from a national magazine after winning the Lumen Christi award, Joe candidly said, "Society has a dollar or time value for everything, but you just can't put a price tag on love."

He continued, "I am convinced that God expects a lot more of you and me than of the alcoholic or the prostitute on the street corner, because we know and have experienced his love. He has given us love and grace and strength and he expects us to use those gifts to help others in need."

CHAPTER 76

William Cosgrove: Belleville's Fourth Bishop

By Raphael H. Middeke

When I am frightened by what I am to you,
Then I am consoled by what I am with you.
To you I am a bishop,
With you I am a Christian.
The first is an office;
The second a grace.
The first a danger;
The second, salvation.

THE ABOVE WORDS OF ST. AUGUSTINE were printed on the cover of the liturgy program for the installation of William Cosgrove as Belleville's fourth bishop. The words sum up both the temperament and the faith of Bishop Cosgrove. He would be the first to admit that he could have done very well without being named the auxiliary bishop of the Cleveland, Ohio, diocese in 1968, and then the bishop of the Belleville diocese in 1976.

It is not that Bishop Cosgrove wasn't interested in becoming a bishop of his own diocese; it's just that he didn't want being a bishop to change his attitudes and his priorities. He wanted to be a Christian first, then a bishop. That didn't always make the work in the office any easier.

"Bishop Cosgrove enjoyed being with people more than being a bishop for people," said Father George Mauck, pastor of the Olney and Stringtown parishes. For a period of about six months Bishop

Bishop William Cosgrove

Cosgrove lived at St. Regis rectory in East St. Louis several days a week, when Father Mauck was the pastor there.

"I saw him as someone who cared a lot about people, someone who had a genuine concern for people — especially for people and places of our diocese that were hurting," he said.

Asked in a *Messenger* interview in 1981, when he announced his unexpected retirement because of ill health, how he would like to be remembered, he said: "As someone who was comfortable among people, someone who liked to be with us and was interested in us." It is difficult not to know Bishop Cosgrove as that kind of person. He wore his joy of being with people and his interest in them on his sleeve. He said: "I felt more comfortable moving among people than doing office work."

"Why did you come here today?" he asked a packed cathedral during his installation ceremony. "Is it because I'm a bishop? Is it because of my status? Because you're my constituency? Because I represent power? Or because I'm your brother?"

He added: "We must grow in our respect for people no matter who they are, no matter how big they are, no matter how little they are."

Almost from the beginning Bishop Cosgrove wrote a weekly "Hello" column in *The Messenger,* with a kind of diary-of-the bishop's-day approach. The column put on paper names, events, and comments from the people and places who made up the Catholic family of southern Illinois and revealed a bishop who also struggled with health, weight, frustrations, anger, people, and institutions — and who had aunts and cousins, memories of home, classmates, — and who played bridge and took catnaps at the wrong times.

In one of his columns he said: "An altar boy from Elizabethtown is as important in the eyes of the Lord as Pope John Paul II." If he worried about being a bishop it was that the trappings of his office would symbolize him as someone more important than that Elizabethtown altar boy.

Whether his constituency wanted him to move among them as a Christian brother first and a bishop second, remains a question even after his retirement. His way of being a bishop received mixed reviews not only from the people, but perhaps especially from his brother priests.

There is, however, little doubt that Bishop Cosgrove pursued a vision of the church as a family and as people with consistency — perhaps, even with a bit of abandon. Asked whether some people and priests resented his priorities or his style, he said in 1981, "When I came here I decided I would be who I am."

Looking back, the bishop admitted there were frustrations, but they weren't overwhelming. "My frustrations have not been great, but sometimes when I wasn't able to facilitate movement in certain directions, I became impatient with myself." And sometimes he second-guessed that impatient, and even irritable, and blustery, Irish temperament.

Asked whether he perceived the diocese as more of a family after his five years as its bishop, he said: "I think so, though I don't know what influence I may have had on that. I think that darn column may have contributed to that. Sometimes people say that to me." It was a column revealing the soul of a bishop. And when it came to the church, Bishop Cosgrove's soul was a family soul. "Hello" kept that dream alive.

"Hello," in its casualness and its "ordinary-Joe" style was not accepted by all. Some people said it was trivial. But it was read.

Bob Welzbacher, after his retirement as the managing editor of *The Messenger,* recalled receiving a phone call from a friend the week after *The Messenger* featured a front-page photo story on his retirement. The friend said: "I just now learned that you're retiring."

"How could you miss all that publicity about it?" Welzbacher asked.

Then the sobering words: "I didn't see it there. I read about it in the bishop's column."

William Michael Cosgrove was born November 26, 1916, in Canton, Ohio, the eldest son of William and Margaret Cosgrove. His father, who was an industrial real estate salesman, died during the 1917 flu epidemic. His younger brother, Joseph, was just two weeks old. His mother lived to see her son ordained a bishop in 1968. She died in 1970.

The young Bill Cosgrove attended St. John grade school in Canton and completed one year of high school before the family moved to Cleveland. He graduated from St. Ignatius High, received his B.A. from John Carroll University, Cleveland, and completed his theological studies at St. Mary Seminary, Cleveland, in 1943. During his college years he also pursued a degree in history, completing an M.A. some years later.

William Cosgrove was ordained December 10, 1943, during World

War II. For the next ten years he was an associate pastor at St. Vincent's in Akron and St. Ignatius parish in Cleveland.

In 1953 he was named the spiritual director of the college department and professor of history at Borromeo Seminary in Cleveland, positions he held for the following thirteen years.

In 1966, the same year he was elected the first chairman of the Cleveland priests' senate, Monsignor Cosgrove (he had been named a monsignor of the first rank in 1960 and of the second rank in 1966) returned to parish ministry as the pastor of St. Henry parish in Cleveland. He was located in a biracial neighborhood, where he became actively involved in the many social concerns of the parishioners and the area. He continued as the pastor of St. Henry's after he was ordained an auxiliary bishop on September 3, 1968. In 1975 he was named the pastor of St. Paul's in Cleveland.

His work for social justice and as a leader in the Cursillo movement highlighted his years as a pastor and auxiliary bishop in Cleveland. In 1971 the city's mayor named him to the city's community relations board and in 1975 presented him with an award recognizing "his outstanding and sustaining contributions to human and community relations for thirty years."

On September 3, 1976, on the eighth anniversary of his ordination as a bishop, he was named the fourth bishop of Belleville. He was on a short fishing trip in Canada when the announcement was made. He was installed October 28, 1976.

Cleveland's auxiliary bishop came to the Belleville diocese as a bishop interested in social justice and racial concerns — an image which gave rise to both hope and fear in his new diocese. His identification with social justice was a narrow characterization, but the knowledge of his years as a pastor in a biracial neighborhood remained paramount.

Call them accomplishments, goals. efforts, beginnings — the things Bishop Cosgrove began in the diocese of Belleville were family things, justice things, people things. They were part of a vision — clumsy and clear at the same time — the way human efforts usually are.

In the five years he was Belleville's bishop he:

• Began a Christmas dinner for shut-ins and elderly, which involved as many "church family" members as guests. Dinner guests were always sure to hear a rousing rendition of the bishop's version of "McNamara's Band."

• Started a diocesan Christmas collection which was sent to dioceses in Texas, South Carolina, and Montana.

• Initiated a parish renewal program in the diocese which was used in half the diocese's parishes.

• Opened for the first time in the diocese an Office of Worship and an

Office of Peace and Justice.

- Supported and developed the church's response and ministry to minorities and the economically depressed, especially in the East St. Louis area.
- Nationally, headed the U.S. Catholic Conference effort to develop a major policy statement on energy.
- Reorganized the structure of the Office of Education
- Ordained the diocese's first class of twenty-three deacons.
- Centralized diocesan offices by opening The Catholic Center.

On May 19, 1981, Bishop Cosgrove announced that his resignation, for reasons of health, had been accepted. He remained the acting bishop until John Wurm was installed as Belleville's fifth bishop on November 4, 1981.

Bishop Cosgrove believed in dialogue, in presence at picnics and in homes, in boards, in sharing. And many people for a long time will remember that hearty and genuine laugh.

He was not comfortable with publicity and praise, and not always with his office. Perhaps, his rough-and-tumble and self-effacing Irish temperament didn't give to some the confidence and encouragement "expected" from a bishop.

If he did not always fare the best in the office of bishop, his Christian presence was a "grace," as St. Augustine said, for him, and for us.

CHAPTER 77

The Adorers' Sister Mary Catherine

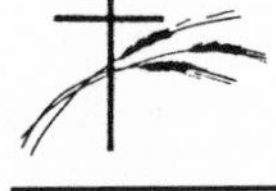

By Raphael H. Middeke

ON OCTOBER 20, 1986, Sister Mary Catherine Girrens, ASC, began a year of missionary work in Bolivia with her congregation's mission community in that South American country.

The mission journey recalls "the only doubt" the fourteen- year-old Alvina Girrens had in 1923 as she prepared to leave St. Mark, Kansas, to travel to Ruma, Illinois, to become a sister.

The Ruma sisters had been her teachers in the small Kansas town near Wichita and she "admired them." But she also thought of going to Techny, whose *Little Missionary,* published for Catholic elementary students, had stirred an interest in the missions. Ruma won out, but the interest in the missions never died.

Alvina was the youngest of the thirteen children of John Joseph Girrens and Kathryn Thimmesch — immigrants from Alsace-Lorraine and Luxembourg. Her mother supported her decision; her father was apprehensive about the distance.

She had no plans other than "just going to be a sister." Through the six-plus decades since that 1923 decision she has been a teacher, principal, directress, local provincial, and general superior of the Adorers' international congregation, traveling to many countries and many miles from that once-distant Ruma, Illinois. But her life's work and mission remained focused on "just going to be a sister."

Those years have also included an absorbing involvement in the community which has formed her and which she has helped form — an involvement which links easily the dreams of Blessed Maria De Mattias, the congregation's Italian foundress over 150 years ago, and the dreams of today's religious educators, ministers, and missionaries.

In 1927 Sister Mary Catherine began teaching at St. Teresa

Sister Mary Catherine Girrens

Academy in East St. Louis, while attending classes at Saint Louis University. From 1931 to 1934 she attended Saint Louis University full time, completing an M.A. in history.

After graduation she returned to Ruma to teach in the Ruma high school, where she remained until 1947. After 1938 she was the high school's principal and after 1945 the local Ruma superior. Her early Ruma years involved more than teaching. As directress of the junior sisters, first unofficially and then officially, she developed for herself and others a concern for spiritual development — which was to become a focus of her years as the Ruma provincial superior. (She also gained some notoriety, recalled Sister Mary Frances Newton, ASC. In a speech on the occasion of her golden jubilee in 1975, she was cited for her prowess as a softball pitcher and later as the umpire who banned sliding in softball games.)

In 1947 the thirty-nine-year-old Sister Mary Catherine returned to St. Teresa's as a history and religion teacher. Four years later she was named the school's principal. That was also the year she admitted the first black girl to the academy — an enrollment which had been encouraged by a group of students and teachers, but was challenged by a number of the students' fathers, who were told: ''Gentlemen, I had no idea I had to ask you first before I could do the will of God.''

The characteristics of the St. Teresa teacher and principal, Sister Mary Frances noted in her golden jubilee speech, included a ''presence [which] instilled wholesome fear, admiration, respect and reverence'' — and a person who was strong, patient, and a good listener. While those words might be tinged with jubilarian praise, the memory that she was ''someone who spoke from the beliefs she lived,'' recalls the lifelong ambition to be ''just a sister'' — from the rural town of St. Mark through six decades of certainty and questioning, to the mission community of Bolivia.

Sister Mary Catherine believes in the life of a religious. In 1984 in a *Messenger* interview, she said: ''It's a life I would choose again exactly as I did.'' If she talks about her life and accomplishments reluctantly, she talks about that choice — in its many dimensions — eagerly.

That choice for the new missionary is more than anything else the spirit and spirituality of Blessed Maria De Mattias — a spirit and a spirituality emphasizing a life and a ministry which makes known the redeeming love of God — especially as symbolized under the symbol of the Precious Blood of Jesus. On the eve of her mission journey to Bolivia, the veteran religious wonders whether that symbol of the redeeming Blood doesn't have special meaning in a world of violence and easy and glorified bloodshed.

In the years of reflection and re-evaluation on the writings and spirit of Blessed Maria after Vatican II, "going back to the sources was a liberating experience" personally and for the congregation, "because it was not a special ministry that formed Maria's charism, but a spirituality. The spirit of Maria's congregation is charity." That spirit supported the tremendous changes in the ministries and lifestyles of the Adorer religious.

But in 1956, when Sister Mary Catherine was elected the Ruma provincial superior, Blessed Maria was probably as much a historical saint and hero as a constant challenge to a present religious spirituality. It was a good year to be elected provincial superior. "Once again I fell heir to a good situation," Sister Mary Catherine says. The days were indeed good. The Ruma congregation had stabilized and had developed a professionalism, sometimes at the unpopular expense of withdrawing sisters from parish schools; the congregation was growing, energetic, and enthusiastic.

Classrooms were added, hospitals were enlarged and completed, a farm was bought and improved, property was purchased, and buildings were changed. But when Sister Mary Catherine recalls those years, she talks about spirituality and education and a growing sense of community. And those were indeed her interests. Theologians, liturgists, philosophers, and scripture scholars sowed the seeds of renewal at the Ruma motherhouse long before Vatican II. No one envisioned the years ahead or where the coming years of re-evaluation would lead, but in 1984 Sister Mary Catherine could say: "A tremendous growth in personal responsibility and a deepened personal prayer life are obvious good things resulting from the years of evaluation" for women religious.

In 1965, when her terms as provincial superior ended, Vatican II was ending, and the church and her congregation were changing. And the outgoing provincial, soon to be elected a general councillor and later general superior, was changing, too.

Her monthly letters to the sisters, Sister Mary Frances said, had changed, from "containing a certain amount of warnings and directives," in the early years, to encouraging concerns for civil rights, world poverty, and hunger, and choosing personally and freely witness for Christ.

In that year of 1965 she went to Rome to participate in the congregation's general chapter. She would not return (except as a visitor) to Ruma until 1983 — after eighteen years as a general councillor and general superior of the Adorer congregation.

The years after 1965 were traumatic years — but easier in Rome than they would have been in Ruma, she admits. They were the eye of the storm of the years of adaptation and re-evaluation. "We have come to a vast diversity in ministries not without a lot of perplexity and uncertainty — not without going through a good bit of the paschal mystery," she said in 1984.

The years were also confusing — perhaps even at times humbling, especially when thinking of the many sisters who left. "I think there was a great deal of suffering and questioning about how I and others contributed to the situation which led to those decisions. There was a lot of self-questioning."

Change was not, for many years, a great value. There was a good measure of rigidity in the application and interpretation of the rules. It was a day when the exercise of authority was measured by a different yardstick — as was obedience. But they were also the "good old days."

Even before the announcement of Vatican II the 1959 chapter of the Adorers began the work of updating the 1934 constitution, which was "almost all canon law with little inspiration." It would be another twenty-one years before the revised constitution would be finally approved, (though it was essentially completed in 1968.) The 1983 chapter was the first since 1959 that didn't deal with that revision.

In 1965, the year she was named a general councillor of her congregation, Sister Mary Catherine headed the international committee charged to work toward the revision of the constitution in the light of Vatican II.

In 1975 Sister Mary Catherine was elected the general superior of the international congregation of eleven provinces and missions and communities in Italy, the U.S., Poland, Yugoslavia, Brazil, Liechtenstein, Korea, India, three African countries, Bolivia, and Argentina.

In 1983, after her eight years as superior general, the Adorers' fledgling India community asked her to live with them and assist in developing their community. She stayed for three months and returned for a year later. It was there that she celebrated her diamond jubilee in 1985, and she would probably still be there if the Indian government hadn't refused to renew her visa.

Since then she has worked in the archives and has been involved in retreat work, continuing her enduring interest in spiritual development.

Perhaps, in the advent of a religious life which will never be as clearly defined as it was in the structured but sometimes also impersonal days of pre-Vatican II, one of the unique gifts of religious life is hope — in an often hopeless, fearful and worried world.

When Sister Mary Catherine left for Bolivia in October 1986 that hope was evident.

CHAPTER 78

Sister Madeline Dosmann: Morning Star of Hope

By Sister Catherine Lampe, PHJC

MORNING STAR: the star that brings in the day. Scripture writers used the image to signify *hope.* For Sister Madeline Dosmann, Daystar carried a prophetic meaning. In her encounters with the poor and needy in the Cairo district, Sister Madeline came to see the morning star as an inspiration that would lighten the way of those daily struggling with life's needs. She had a dream.

A member of the Poor Handmaids of Jesus Christ community, Sister Madeline Dosmann was born in Mishawaka, Indiana, on November 27, 1913, the oldest of seven children. Her parents were John and Edith Arnold Dosmann. At baptism she received the name Catherine Margaret.

Her father was employed by Mishawaka Rubber Industry as an office manager. Her mother was Canadian by birth. Both parents were of the staunch Catholic type for whom the Christian education of children was of prime concern. After elementary education in St. Monica's school, Mishawaka, Catherine became an aspirant in the Ancilla Domini Aspiranture school, Donaldson, Indiana.

By June 1932 she had received the name Madeline and the year saw her as a professed religious. Soon after finishing academic studies she started her first career as a teacher of elementary grades, pursuing at the same time what is frequently referred to as SS college requirements; that is, Saturday-summer courses.

Because of her Canadian lineage she became interested in the study of French; she pursued it with vim, learned it with ease and taught it with enthusiasm, even acting as a guide for students touring London, Brittany, and Paris.

After some forty years of grade and high school teaching she experienced the restlessness of "a mission fulfilled — yet so much to give." It was the lure of a lover on the hunt. Her chance acquaintance with the needy in Cairo solved the dilemma. She responded without hesitation to God's call for a second career, this time among those in grave need.

Sister Madeline Dosmann

Sister Madeline came to Cairo in September 1977. For the next four months she served as a pastoral associate to Father Stanley Schlarman, at that time the pastor of St. Patrick's parish.

As pastoral associate, she assumed a host of duties, including visiting the sick, the elderly, bringing Holy Communion to shut-ins, conducting prayer services, and providing food and clothing when such was needed and available.

Sister Madeline saw what she was doing on a weekly or monthly basis at St. Patrick's as only a fraction of an ounce on the scale of justice. The actual need of the people she envisioned would be measured in tons. Sister Madeline's dream took the form of an outreach program, which she confided to Father Schlarman, who encouraged her dream. As the next step, she secured the approval of Bishop William Cosgrove and of her own community. In both instances, approval was given along with promises of help.

With the support of Sister Joan Fisher, PHJC, Sister Madeline launched the Daystar Community Program which opened hand, heart, and doors to the needy in Alexander and Pulaski counties.

Needs of people travel along many dimensions. For a Christian the corporal and spiritual works of mercy define the way, the truth, and the life. Sister Madeline with her keen, perceptive mind and generous heart recognized in each work of mercy an invitation to minister. It was for her and her companion to discover the ways and means of doing so.

Soon after the inception of Daystar, the two sisters contacted agencies that might be of assistance. They publicized their needs in the Cairo daily paper; they took part in a radio broadcast; they appealled for food and clothing, whatever could be spared. Their efforts met tremendous response.

The day after the local newspaper had published their picture, their whereabouts and the goal of their mission, the first two clients rang the doorbell of their small Mary Katherine Casper convent, requesting food and clothing. The Daystar had risen for the needy in Cairo.

Some days later, a willing volunteer agreed to call a blind lady every day and remind her to take her medicine. That was the beginning of volunteer service. Since that day this has expanded to a modest and varied crew — some on a permanent, others on a part-time schedule.

It was a definite understanding that the Daystar Program was not to be aligned with an agency. An agreement with Bishop Cosgrove assured the sisters that the diocese would meet the administrative expenses, and an occasional booster check helped the cause along.

Advice, counsel, and help in all forms was always gratefully accepted, but the program itself remained an independent venture. Sisters and volunteer workers insisted with dogged determination to "go it on their own."

In addition to providing the tangibles, the sisters spread the spirit of goodwill and concern by their visits to the sick and shut-ins; they took meals with elderly at nursing homes and nutrition sites and sustained spiritual stamina by shared prayer and scripture discussion.

Today, Madeline's Mart, named for Sister Madeline, is the focal point of the program. The mart is one of the usual thrift shop types found in almost every city.

The first dispensary of Madeline's Mart was the basement of the sisters' convent; next it moved to a once-upon-a-time used clothing store, an unheated building with all odds against it. Bishop John Wurm, on one of his visits to the center, took note of the inconvenience and was promptly informed by Father Dean Braun that a better-equipped building was available at a reasonable price.

The bishop promised to investigate the possibility of purchasing. Before long the deal was transacted through diocesan generosity and on October 24, 1982, the purchased building became the operation center for the Daystar Program.

The Daystar Program serves more than 250 families a month with basic commodities. The food dispensaries became possible through the courtesy of a St. Louis food service program — "Operation Search." The pick-ups are always on a weekly, sometimes biweekly, schedule. Food and clothing are in the forefront of donations but almost anything and everything from "forks to furniture" is gratefully accepted.

Many meals are hosted or delivered to the needy at the holidays by Daystar. While this provision is not an integral part of the Daystar program, the hard work on the part of the staff and volunteer members, plus their close collaboration with other charitable organizations have helped to bring about this service. More than 2,100 meals have been served within the last few years.

Since January 1980 plans for an entirely new nursing home have been evolving and the structure could become a reality by 1987. This project is not to be linked with the Daystar Program currently in progress but is under the auspices of civic leadership and funding.

Once a reality, the home will be called Daystar Nursing Home because the idea for it was conceived in the minds of Sister Madeline and her companion, who spurred on its progress and were a constant inspiration to the members of the board.

The beginning of the Daystar program is to be credited to Sister Madeline Dosmann, who during those four brief months as a pastoral associate saw the possibility of a dream coming true.

Sister Madeline died from a massive heart attack on the evening of Nov. 17, 1981, just four days after she and her companion had moved into a more spacious convent. Her name will live on in the city of Cairo and its neighborhood as long as the work of Daystar lives on. For this there are the affirmative words form the Acts of the Apostles, "If this work is of God, it will perdure." To all appearances, the Daystar program is of God.

CHAPTER 79

John Wurm: Belleville's Fifth Bishop

By Father John Myler

WHERE DOES A "VOCATION" COME FROM? Perhaps the life of John Nicholas Wurm, fifth Bishop of Belleville, might show how priests are "made." The bishop's early life, his ministry in southern Illinois and his inspirational struggle with cancer, which ended with his death in 1984, can lend some insight into the roots of the call to serve the Church.

In the north St. Louis County community of Overland, Mr. and Mrs. Anthony Wurm worked hard to raise a family during the Great Depression. Anthony labored at tailor shops as a window dresser, and his wife, the former Estelle Rose Leonard, took care of the children and home.

In 1929 their seventh child was born. The oldest daughter, Mrs. Virginia Keinrath, remembers, "I can recall the night Bishop John was born. There were six of us then and being born at home, as were most of us, the older four were sent to a good neighbor's house, and the smaller ones put to bed early.

"It was the eve of Saint Nicholas' feast day. Dad strung up a rope across the kitchen wall, and hung seven socks to be filled by St. Nick. When we were brought home early in the morning, we had a new brother . . . the seventh child, and the seventh sock was also filled; more so than the other six — or so it seemed."

When Mr. and Mrs. Wurm took their newborn son to All Souls' church in Overland on December 18, he was baptized and given the name John Nicholas; John for his grandfather, and Nicholas for the saint and bishop on whose feast day he was born.

And after John Nicholas, Mr. and Mrs. Wurm took seven more children to All Souls' for baptism — a grand total of fourteen!

As John grew up the family prayed the rosary every evening after supper. The children made a little altar with two candles and a crucifix. They knelt on the floor and took turns saying the mysteries of the rosary.

Bishop John Wurm

Young John had dark eyes and dark hair, though never too much of the latter. Virginia recalls the times that, like many little tykes, John would fuss about getting his hair washed, "and Mom would say, 'It'll only take a few minutes. You only have a nickel's worth!' "

Just big enough to help with the chores, he was once told to bring in a basket of kindling for the family's old wood stoves. When little John picked up the basket the bottom fell out and someone called him "Helpless John." His brothers and sisters laughed about that the day he was consecrated a bishop.

He loved going to school, playing ball, being a scout, and occasionally pulling a prank. His sister Maureen tells the story of an April Fools' Day when Johnny called from the corner store and told the family that a helicopter was going to land on the street. "We all flew out the front door to see it and John came walking down the street, laughing, because we all fell for it. It really was a sight to see, all these Wurms out in the front yard looking for the helicopter."

The boy loved the Church, too. It seems he always wanted to be a priest. Recesses and lunch breaks were often spent helping at the parish rectory.

"And he loved to sing!" Virginia remembers. "Some Sunday mornings, when the family was getting ready for Mass, John would be singing the Mass in Latin over and over again. Jimmy, our brother, often remarked that he didn't think he needed to go to Mass . . . he'd heard it at least three times already!"

Young John graduated from the eighth grade, went to the Cathedral Latin School,and then on to Kenrick Seminary. He was ordained a priest of the Archdiocese of Saint Louis by Cardinal Joseph Ritter on April 3, 1954.

His brothers and sisters remember young Father John's visits, especially during the holidays and for big family meals. At Christmas he loved to help each family decorate their trees, and on Christmas Day he would pick up his parents and visit every brother and sister — and, by this time, nieces and nephews — with gifts for each one.

But especially, Virginia offered, "when anyone was sick or in trouble, no matter how busy or tired he was, he was always there."

Father John's father, Anthony, died two years after seeing his son ordained a priest.

Rose Wurm died in 1976 just four months after attending John's ordination as auxiliary bishop in the St. Louis Cathedral.

Bishop Wurm's brothers and sisters gathered in Belleville's Cathedral of St. Peter on Nov. 4, 1981, for his installation as the fifth bishop of the Church in southern Illinois.

In two-and-a-half years Bishop Wurm made visitations to the parishes and diocesan institutions his first priority. Bishop Wurm traveled 20,000 miles in his first eight months in the diocese, visiting the 130 parishes, sixty schools, seven hospitals, five prisons, and several nursing homes.

Bishop Wurm established St. Nicholas parish, O'Fallon, the first new parish in the diocese since 1965. The Charles and Bertha Hincke Home for retired priests was opened in 1982.

He reorganized the diocesan structure by naming seven administrative directors and restructed the diocesan vocation program. The first meeting of the Diocesan Pastoral Council was convened, the Catechist Certification program was begun. The bishop stressed improving financial support for diocesan programs, emphasized reduction of debt, and reduced both the number and scope of diocesan offices.

Strong emphasis was given to the "Come on Home to Our Family for Christmas" campaign. In 1982 the bishop sent out 1,500 letters inviting inactive Catholics to "participate again in the family life and worship of the Church." He was joined by retired Bishop Albert R. Zuroweste in taping "Come on Home" announcements, which were aired on thirty radio stations throughout southern Illinois.

A Committee of Women Religious was created with deanery representatives to better reflect the insights of these women in the diocese while the Ministry to Priests Program began in 1983. The Ursuline Sisters of Belleville was established as an autonomous congregation during Bishop Wurm's brief time in southern Illinois.

Bishop Wurm was diagnosed as suffering from cancer late in 1983. He died on April 27, 1984, after an inspirational struggle against the disease.

Where does a good vocation come from? From God of course, but very often, God sends his call through good Catholic families — in the 1930s and still in the 1980s.

CHAPTER 80

Nick Leone and Cy Vernier: Men of Charity

By Stanley J. Konieczny

FOR TWO LAYMEN OF THE BELLEVILLE DIOCESE, giving knew neither time nor season. Nick Leone and Cy Vernier, both of whom died in 1986, left the church in southern Illinois a rich legacy of giving.

A native of St. Louis, Nick Leone was born September 19, 1925, a son of Mary and the late Nick Leone. His life seemed very average. He served in the U.S. Navy and eventually settled down, marrying the former Billie Jean Wessler on January 11, 1947. The couple raised two sons and three daughters. Leone was working as a truck driver and was becoming more and more involved in lay ministry at St. Philip parish, East St. Louis.

Many people could readily identify with such an average life-style until the ordinary took an extraordinary turn. In 1973 Leone decided to work for the St. Vincent de Paul Society for one year. His "one year" of service turned to thirteen years, during which time he gave himself as full-time manager of the St. Vincent de Paul store in East St. Louis.

"Being a Vincentian is a vocation, rather than just a member of an organization," Nick Leone explained in a 1979 interview with *The Messenger.* Nick lived his vocation by ten-hour days, six days a week at the St. Vincent de Paul store. He made himself available to the poor and the lonely. His "main love" could be found in the area nursing home residents, whom he described as being "the most forgotten people in society."

"Nick just wanted to be out there and help those that he could. He just had a way with people," his wife recalled. She said that she approved of her husband's decision thirteen years ago despite the obvious sacrifices. Bringing help and hope to those in need provided great fulfillment to Nick.

Cy Vernier

Nick Leone

"Nick had that special charisma of reaching out and touching people who were suffering," commented Joe Hubbard, coordinator of Catholic Urban Programs and a fellow Vincentian. Hubbard became acquainted with Leone fifteen years ago when the two worked together on benefit picnics for the special education program at St. Philip School.

Through those years Hubbard remembers certain qualities shining through Nick Leone's outreach: his love, his care, his concern and his honesty about his feelings towards other people.

Leone's ministry ended with his battle against cancer on September 29, 1986. He was buried at the national cemetery, Jefferson Barracks, Missouri, after a funeral Mass from St. Philip church.

"You always have it in the back of your mind that more can be done," Leone commented in 1979, "and there is a depression that just comes from continually dealing with the poor. When this happens, you just sit and think. The gloom always passes, once you realize that tomorrow is another day."

In 1913 August and Sally Vernier welcomed their eighth child, Cyril August Vernier. While a student at St. Luke grade school, Belleville, the young Vernier began to develop his talents as a singer and a musician. This musical interest, which proved to be profitable to a teen growing up in the Great Depression, later provided Vernier with one of many means of serving church and society.

Cy Vernier was asked to play the organ for St. Henry parish, Belleville, in 1933, and he served that community for three years, until he became the organist for St. Teresa parish, Belleville. He did not enjoy a free Sunday for the next thirty years. Despite the fact that he had no formal training as a church organist, he served St. Mary parish in that capacity for three decades. While serving St. Teresa parish, Vernier had a profound experience that would change the course of his life.

Spring 1940 held great promise for Cy Vernier. He and Cyrilla Stark had set the date for their wedding; he was excited about his new job in a paint store in Belleville. Then one night, as Vernier was leaving his car, parked in front of St. Teresa church, he was struck by a car and critically injured. "In my prayers for recovery, I promised the Blessed Virgin I would try to do as much charity as I could in thanksgiving for my recovery," Vernier wrote in an autobiography which he prepared for his family in 1980.

Both parties in the agreement kept their promises. Cy and Cyrilla were married on August 20, 1940. They had three sons. In the meantime, when other young fathers and businessmen were intent exclusively on these concerns, Cy Vernier met his responsibilities while setting out to meet his part of this special bargain.

Vernier joined the Junior Chamber of Commerce, a group of young men who were battling the major medical problem of the day, polio. In turn he became actively involved in President Franklin Roosevelt's March of Dimes campaign for polio victims. Vernier also volunteered for the St. Elizabeth Hospital Auxiliary, which he eventually headed. As the polio threat diminished, he was able to spend more time working for the hospital, especially during expansion programs which augmented St. Elizabeth Hospital.

Children in need found a special friend in Cy Vernier. For a number of years he chaired the annual picnic to benefit St. John's Orphanage, Belleville. He was an important backer of the Mamie Stookey School for the Developmentally Disabled, Belleville, where he served on the board of directors. He also served on the board of the local Catholic credit union.

The resume of Cy Vernier's affiliations and service projects is public knowledge, but there is another side of the successful businessmen that tried to escape public notice. Vernier had a reputation for helping others without any recognition. "Cy always was ready to help the underdog; the poor person who really needed a hand," commented Art Reissen, his longtime friend and classmate from St. Luke School.

"I admired Cy's energy. He was always on the go," Reissen added. "Cy was just a promoter and a great guy."

Reissen cited Vernier's activities as a Rotarian. When the club voted to help bring crippled youngsters from Belize to the Shriner's Hospital for Children in St. Louis, Vernier came to the fore to support the project.

Cy Vernier died March 29, 1986, and was buried from St. Mary church, Belleville, where he celebrated God in song for so many years

Upon his death, Gus Lohmann told the daily *Belleville News-Democrat* "[Vernier] probably gave more things away without anybody knowing it. There was just an incredible warmth in his personality. If you needed something and you went to him, you wouldn't walk away without it."

CHAPTER 81

Rose Zwilling and Elizabeth "Hap" Meehan: Women of Faith and Service

By Raphael H. Middeke

LONG BEFORE THE PROLIFERATION of lay ministers in the post-Vatican II Church, lay individuals spent lifetimes of commitment to the Church's ministry. Two such people, totally different in personality, lifestyles, and work were Rose Zwilling and Elizabeth "Hap" Meehan. They shared only a common soul in their love for the Church, expressed in decades of dedicated service. Though no one ever talked about their vocations or called them ministers, they certainly felt called and truly were ministers and women of the Church.

Rose Zwilling spent thirty-seven years of her life as the housekeeper for Msgr. Cyril Haffner, the pastor of Sacred Heart parish in Du Quoin, from 1922 until his death in 1966. Being a housekeeper was her vocation — it was the way she served God. While the vocation of a permanent housekeeper is rare today, the gifts of Rose's life will always be treasured in the Church.

Descriptions of priests and parishioners picture her a completely dedicated woman — faithful, self-effacing, humble, never overbearing, always present. "She was a wonderful woman," said Father Henry Reis, the retired pastor of the Elizabethtown parish and Monsignor Haffner's nephew.

"No one ever complained about her, neither parishioners nor priests," stated James Genesio, who grew up in the Du Quoin parish. "She was held in very high esteem."

In the terminology of the day, one priest said, she never ran the parish, or the pastor.

Possibly the highest tribute comes from the assistants who served the parish from the beginning of the 1950s. They experienced her equanimity of service and always felt welcome. Their praise and ad-

Elizabeth "Hap" Meehan

Rose Zwilling

miration is unanimous.

She is remembered as a holy woman, but "not in the pious sense," one former assistant said. Though quiet and retiring, she had a keen interest in the church, as well as the politics of her day. She read Drew Pearson and Jack Anderson regularly, an acquaintance recalled.

Rose Zwilling was born September 25, 1890, in Stringtown, Illinois. She was the fourth of the six children of Charles and Florentine Klepfer Zwilling. She attended Cotterell public school and received her religious instruction in the Stringtown parish school — which had been opened in 1879 and was the first Catholic school in Richland County.

Little is known of her early years except that she taught in an elementary school near Stringtown for at least a year.

Records at the Ruma provincial house indicate that she attempted twice to join the Adorer community, but never made either temporary or permanent vows. She came to Ruma in March 1912 and was given the name of Sister Fortunata, but, because of illness, remained only two months.

In early 1914 Rose returned to Ruma and was given the name of Sister Antolina. There are no records of her activities or assignments, or when she left the religious community again, probably because of her health. However, friends recall her accompanying Sister Gabriel Benhoff to Lebanon in 1920. Sister Gabriel, who was blind, took over classes of an ill sister at the parish school and it is assumed Rose "served as her eyes."

She began her career and vocation as a housekeeper sometime in that same year. Father Cyril Haffner had been the pastor of the Lebanon parish since 1914. When he was transferred to Du Quoin in 1922 she moved with him.

"Her life was one of helping others," said her nephew, Herman Zwilling, a member of the Stringtown parish today. That is an apt description for the many memories of priests, relatives, and parishioners who knew her.

Her decision to return to her Stringtown home in 1935 to care for her aging parents is a striking example of the seriousness and depth of her life of service. Her mother died in 1941. When her father died in 1944 she returned to Du Quoin and continued her life as a parish housekeeper.

When Monsignor Haffner died in 1966 Rose retired to Olney. She worked for awhile for Father John Ruggles in Okawville. And during her retirement years, she spent several weeks "vacation" with him at the Bridgeport and Harrisburg parishes, recalled Father Vito Lopardo, a one-time assistant in Du Quoin. Her regular vacations during her many years in Du Quoin were taken when the monsignor was on retreat.

The "ideal" housekeeper died on June 24, 1973. She had spent the last few months of her life in a nursing home. She was buried in the parish cemetery at Stringtown beside her parents and relatives.

Elizabeth "Hap" Meehan was a woman of accomplishment, a woman of vision, and faith. Her nickname "Hap" — short for "happy" — recalled her usual disposition. Though her life was difficult and sometimes even tragic, she often said it was, all in all, "a happy experience."

There was never a doubt her happy disposition was supported by the joy of a faith which influenced much of her life. "The church has been my whole life," she once said. "My faith gave me strength to carry on when the burden became heavy."

"I am sure I am partial, but I never have met anyone with the strength and religious fervor that my mother had, and her attitude seemed to generally affect most people about her," said her son, William, a Cairo lawyer.

She earned the respect and esteem of her community; Southern Illinois University, where she was employed; and her Church. Her name is almost synonymous with the beginning and growth of the Newman Club in Carbondale, which she fostered and advised, and her push to establish the Newman Center with its own full-time chaplain. She accomplished this goal with the appointment by Bishop Zuroweste of Father Ronald Glennon as the first Newman chaplain in 1958.

Hap was born Elizabeth Griffin June 9, 1897, in Chicopee,

Massachusetts. She came to southern Illinois in 1921 with her husband, Timothy Edward, who had been hired as a state highway engineer.

The young couple first lived in Harrisburg, where Hap, a musician, directed the parish choir. When the Meehans moved to Carbondale in the late 1920s she directed the parish choir at St. Francis, and later the children's choir and the university students' choir — a ministry she performed at St. Francis for over thirty years.

Her life changed dramatically when her husband died in 1935, leaving her with little means to support herself and their three children, ages thirteen, twelve, and five. She took a job as supervisor of music in the rural school system. The Irish Catholic woman was a rare presence in the Bible-belt Carbondale area — but a presence which witnessed to a deep faith and won many hearts. "She was an exemplary woman," said Mary Garner, a family friend and 1950s Newman Club member, "who did a tremendous amount of good for the Church. Her personality and attitude did a lot in changing people's attitudes toward the Church. More than any single work she did, that was her greatest contribution."

With the encouragement and support of Father Leo Mondt, the parish pastor, Hap continued her education at the college. She received her M.A. in 1940 and was named supervisor of the university's laboratory school — considered by many in later years as one of the finest in the country. (S.I.U. at the time was a teacher's college.) As the university grew, she directed the supervision of student teachers until her retirement.

As early as the late 1930s Hap was instrumental in the formation of a Newman Club for Catholic students at the college and became the faculty advisor. In the decades that followed, accomplishment and recognition didn't dull her commitment to the Church — as choir director, CCD organizer, and teacher, but especially as Newman Club activist. Membership in the John Henry Newman honorary society meant more to her than all her academic honors combined, she said in 1953.

In 1960 in recognition of her pioneer Newman work, she was awarded the papal medal, Pro Ecclesia et Pontifice, in a cathedral ceremony.

Her life's unusual burdens did not end. Both her eldest son, John, and her daughter, Mary, died around the age of forty of lung cancer. Mary, who was divorced and never remarried, had been living with her mother for a number of years.

"Friends marvel at the accomplishments of this grandmother who goes about her business without fanfare," an early 1950s newspaper article said.

Mary Garner recalled an example of her involvement with one child in the Archway program for multiple-handicapped children. "She held this one child — blind, retarded and physically disabled — so that he would have contact with one person and know he was loved.

In 1978 the Archway program presented her with their "Grandmother Award" for devotion and love given to the children of the program.

During her retirement years she received many other honors:

• The Newman Auxiliary's "Christian Love and Service Award" in 1974;

• The "Citation Award" for her devotion to the exceptional children of southern Illinois, by the Illinois Council for Exceptional Children in 1977;

• The 1979 "Alumni Achievement Award" for distinguished service, by the Alumni Association of Southern Illinois University.

care in a nursing home. But she remained close to the Church and never lost her happy disposition. Hap Meehan died April 26, 1983.

CHAPTER 82

Sister Suzanne Schrautemyer: "A Special Time"

By Raphael H. Middeke

SISTER SUZANNE SCHRAUTEMYER, OSU, spent the several hours before midnight on the eve of her thirty-ninth birthday the way she had spent every birthday since she was a teenager — alone in her room, reflecting on her life. It was during that birthday eve reflection, on September 11, 1986, that Suzie — as she is known to her friends — decided to discontinue the chemotherapy for the cancer which was spreading in her body.

"I became intuitively aware that no form of therapy would make a difference anymore," she said in an interview in the December 12, 1986, issue of *The Messenger*. "It was time to let go. I have felt right about every surgery and every treatment in the last year and a half. I feel really right about this. I don't feel panicky or depressed, and I'm amazed at the peace I have experienced."

It was difficult to doubt that peace as Suzie sat calmly in an office chair in early December and talked about her responses to cancer, the experience of dying, and the ways of "letting go."

Letting go, she said, was "not frantic or sad. This is a very special time in my life, of entering into a new dying experience. I have died in all kinds of ways before. I have been surprised so many times in my life with new life and new growth as a result of so many 'dyings.' I can't believe that this dying will surprise me more than ever."

Letting go became "a day-by-day experience." It included a "gradual loss of taste." For a two-mile-a-day runner, it meant not only giving up running, but not walking fast, or standing for long periods of time.

But letting go especially meant giving up little by little the "enjoyment of teaching and preaching," which for seventeen years had filled most of her days.

Sister Suzanne Schrautemyer

In early September 1986, when she learned that her cancer had recurred and spread, she resigned as president of the Council of Women Religious and as a counsellor in her Ursuline community. As the cancer grew in her body she continued to work part-time as associate director of religious education in the diocesan Office of Education, realizing that she needed "to be flexible with the pain, the effects of medication, and a weakening body."

Suzanne Frances Schrautemyer was born the oldest of six children in St. Louis County, September 12, 1947. At an early age, but with much discernment — she remembers writing to over fifty religious communities — she began her affiliation with the Ursuline sisters of Belleville. In 1962 she enrolled in the Ursulines' high school, graduating in 1966. She received her B.A. from Minot State College in North Dakota in 1972. She had begun teaching theology, scripture, and social science courses at Bishop Ryan high school in Minot in 1969. In 1980 she received her M.A in religious studies from Saint Louis University in St. Louis.

Before returning to Belleville in 1980 Sister Suzanne taught in CCD programs, confirmation classes, conducted retreats, trained catechists, and taught parish adult education classes. In the Bismarck, North Dakota, diocese she had been a member and president of the sisters council and a member of the diocesan pastoral council.

In Belleville she became the novice-formation director for the Ursuline sisters and taught adult scripture and theology courses at the Ursuline convent and in parishes in the Belleville diocese.

In 1981 she joined the faculty of St. Henry Seminary as a scripture and theology teacher, continuing until the seminary closed in 1984. In the fall of 1984 she began her work in the Office of Education.

If the decision to let go was "right and peaceful," it did not preclude the fact of pain, serious physical problems, hospitalizations, and the fear of misunderstanding.

Her medication, after her September decision, was related only to pain relief. Letting go included the conscious decision of addiction to morphine, and later letting go included the awareness that medication interfered in real assessments. Her doctors, "who agreed to participate in my care," told her that this is one of the most painful ways to die, and that does scare me," she said.

Suzie feared that her decision would be seen as a desire to die. "That," she said, "isn't true. Life is more real to me now than ever and I am convinced I am faithful to the God of life."

The most painful aspect connected to this dying experience is watching the people around me wanting so much to spare me pain, wanting to lift my disease and death from me, and they can't," she said in *The Messenger* interview. "Their helplessness hurts." she said.

"I want to tell them," she said, "that it's okay. I want to invite them to come along on this journey. I want to reassure them. This is in some ways the most important time of my life and I don't want to be rescued."

Perhaps that pain was related to the uncomfortableness she expressed with people praying for a certain kind of outcome. "I think we need to pray for a disposition of heart — that peace continues and grows," she said.

"So often in our society, people know they are dying, people who love them know they are dying and no one wants to hurt anyone else by talking about it, when the healing thing to do, the loving thing to do, is to share that journey with each other."

In January 1987 Suzie began a course on Living Scripture and Being Church. She described the class, which met every other week, as a "realistic effort on my part — therapeutic for me and a need in our local church." The class had no ending date. After the second class on January 25, Suzie realized the class would probably not continue as long as she once thought.

It was Christmastime 1984 when Suzie first went to a doctor because of a lump under her right arm, which proved malignant. A partial mastectomy was followed by six weeks of radiation. During Holy Week in 1985 she discovered a new lump under her left arm. "I was really scared," she said. "So scared I didn't tell anyone for several weeks."

The diagnosis was cancer — different from the first — an unusual incidence. A bilateral mastectomy followed. At the end of June, Suzie began chemotherapy treatments in pill form, which continued, except for a short time when she lost patience with her doctor's guidance, until the birthday eve decision.

During the summer of 1986 a new lump was discovered. August tests revealed matestatic cancer to the bone in the pelvic areas and sternum. By Thanksgiving the cancer has spread to the bone marrow.A mid-January 1987 emergency room experience because of breathing difficulties revealed the spread of cancer to the rib cage.

The almost two years since Christmastime 1984 were not without anger, frustration, and depression. During the early months of chemotherapy, "I experienced a lot of anger — at God, and at myself for being angry, and also with the medical profession. I walked around with a low-grade anger for three or four months." And it was difficult to talk about the depression, she said: "I didn't want anyone to know I was really down and broken."

Suzie linked those months of anger to chemotherapy. "The surgery was behind me, but every day I was reminded that cancer was not behind me. I wanted to say it was all over, but popping pills every day told me it wasn't."

"I had to be assured that it's okay to be angry, to doubt, to be broken, and down. I don't believe my faith was insulted by my anger and doubt. I had to move through it — those real human experiences — before I could let go of it."

"In September, after my decision," Suzie said, " I told them (my Ursuline community) about my fear that they might think I was committing suicide. They took the recurrence of my cancer very hard — they experienced anger and depression also. I told them I needed them to be real. If they were angry at me for being sick again, that's okay. If they're angry at God because I might be dying, that's okay. And it's okay to show that to me. I told them I wanted them, I needed them, to be real," she said in an obviously strained voice and fighting back tears.

After *The Messenger* interview, which was reprinted in Catholic newspapers throughout the country, Suzie received about a hundred letters and fifty out-of-state phone calls. Most of the letter writers expressed gratitude for allowing them to break a silence about their own death experiences, often involving cancer, and for overcoming a fear or misunderstanding and rejection.

The letters reflected the silent response to cancer in our society, and often a misunderstanding. "It's important to realize that any kind of cancer operation causes it's own kind of depression and doubt. You don't have any control over how chemotherapy plays with your emotions — you can cry, be angry, short-tempered, and not know why. Much of that is not related to choice."

Suzie had planned to complete a second graduate degree, an M.A. in divinity, and hoped someday to teach in a major seminary. She had a pilot's license when she was sixteen and hoped someday to fly again.

Her faith changed, she admitted. "It's simpler. I used to think that some places, people, and times were more sacred than others. My experience of faith now tells me that everything, every moment, is sacred. Everything that happens is a sacrament, a moment when God becomes tangible and life is real. That's what's different."

Though Suzie pinpointed the night of September 11 as the time she knew she was dying, she began in October 1985 what she called even then a "homecoming journal." She had "journaled" — briefly described as a talking to God in a letter about the day that has passed — since 1972. "I wanted to journal seriously about the ultimate mystery in my life, whether I was dying or not. I have been very faithful — writing about what's happening in my body, my faith, my relationships. It has been a real prayer."

The thirty-ninth birthday eve decisions changed the way Sister Suzanne and many others lived some of the most important days of her life.

A second followup *Messenger* article was published in the February 6, 1987, issue — a further sharing of the experiences of a continuing journey — a sharing in which she admitted she had begun to think more about death rather than the experience of dying.

The next several months continued a roller coaster experience, with a gradual increase in morphine intake, but also occasional "good" weeks — good enough to travel several times. The Easter edition of *The Messenger* published a third sharing titled: "Celebrating Easter in the Face of Death" — Suzie's experience of Lent, Holy Week, and Easter, 1987.

After the December *Messenger* article a friend told Suzie: "Your article was an example of supreme catechesis." It is in that spirit that the interviews and this profile were pursued — encouraged by a firm but searching faith.

CHAPTER 83

James Patrick Keleher: Belleville's Sixth Bishop

By Stanley J. Konieczny
and Raphael H. Middeke

"THE DIOCESAN CENTENNIAL," Bishop James P. Keleher said in a *Messenger* interview in January 1987, "is the cornerstone of what I will hopefully accomplish in the diocese. "I see the centennial as much more than remembering the past. I also see our celebration as a time to look forward, but most especially as a time to regroup, reidentify, and reassert the fact that we are the Catholic family of southern Illinois. It seems to me that that kind of identity was present in the past and is absolutely critical if we are to accomplish anything in the future. I see that as my overriding goal for the centennial and really the overriding vision I have for the diocese," the bishop said.

Among the bishop's priorities is a continuation of the diocese's emphasis on education. "One of the characteristics of our diocese, historically, has been its dedication and commitment to education — Catholic education on the primary and secondary levels and all forms of education for youth and adults alike. There has always been an interest in education and a willingness to support it financially and develop an excellence. I admire and I hope to continue that priority of our history," Bishop Keleher said in *The Messenger* interview.

He acknowledged that "continuing that tradition is also one of our toughest goals, because of the difficulty of funding." Parishes with Catholic schools need to allot a great portion of their income to support those schools — a tough reality, but "I want to give all the encouragement I can to continuing a generous support for our Catholic elementary and high schools," the bishop emphasized. But he is also aware that we "need to continue to upgrade and assist our teachers. The effort to be fair to the great teachers in our system while helping the parishes bear their financial burdens is a very delicate balance.''

Bishop James Patrick Keleher

As the church of southern Illinois begins its second century, the dwindling number of priests and vocations will demand adjustments and changes in ministry. ''The fewer number of priests and the average age are real concerns,'' Bishop Keleher said. ''I need to be careful not to ask our priests to give what they can't. We can't put the burden of the vocation shortage on their backs.'' The bishop announced at the beginning of the diocese's centennial year that a task force would be formed to study how personnel and financial resources relate to parishes around the diocese. ''It is time for us to take a real look at what we need to do in the future — what kind of restructuring and consolidation will be appropriate.''

''Currently,'' the bishop admitted, ''the vocation picture is better than it has been in some time. I expect we will be ordaining several priests every year and that will be a great help.'' However, he doesn't think the impact of the vocation crisis has really been experienced by people. ''There are still many Masses of convenience, especially in our larger cities. But I think there is much more concern in our rural areas — in areas where the Catholic population is not very large. When the chips are down, are they the ones who will be left without the presence of a priest?'' the bishop asked.

Consistent with his vision of the church as a family, Bishop Keleher believes, however, that whatever changes are made, existing communities ''should be permitted to continue to function as parishes, even if there might not be a resident priest.''

Bishop Keleher also thinks the centennial should result in the formation, or reformation, of a diocesan pastoral council. ''I would like to see a council form itself again out of the centennial process and the planning which will take place — and perhaps out of the diocesan convocation we will have in March of 1988. Rather than resurrect a council which I had nothing to do with, just to add another structure, I would rather see a council develop out of a natural process."

In the area of ministry, after "working with my priests," Bishop Keleher called for important "collaboration with religious," and for a renewal of peace and justice concerns. He placed specific emphasis in renewing "our contact and effectiveness in our Guatemala mission."

It is obvious that the bishop views the centennial as the immediate personal and parish renewal program in the diocese. But he also thinks that gradually parish councils need to view themselves as the focus of spiritual development in the parish rather than parish administration councils.

Classifying himself as "fiscally conservative," Bishop Keleher said "we should take a good, healthy, honest look at all the programs we have and see if that is where we want to put available resources and energy. I don't think we have done that. Together with development, we need evaluation," he said.

A native of Chicago, James Patrick Keleher was born July 31, 1931, the son of Rita Cullinane Keleher and the late James P. Keleher. After attending St. Felicitas grade school and Carmel high school, the young Keleher entered the Chicago archdiocese's seminary system.

Completing his studies at St. Mary of the Lake Seminary, Mundelein, he was ordained a priest by Cardinal Samuel Stritch on April 12, 1958. Father Keleher then wrote his doctoral dissertation on St. Augustine's concept of church unity. Upon finishing his doctoral studies at St. Mary of the Lake, he was assigned as associate pastor of St. Henry parish, Rogers Park, Illinois.

Education was the hallmark of the future bishop's ministry during these years. He earned his master's degree in educational administration from Loyola University of Chicago. Father Keleher also did post-doctoral work in spirituality at the Gregorian University in Rome. He served at Niles college from 1969 to 1972. Subsequently, he was named dean of formation at St. Mary of the Lake, from 1972 to 1975. Father Keleher served as rector of Quigley Seminary, South, a post which he held from 1975 until his appointment as president-rector of St. Mary of the Lake in 1978. At Mundelein he also served as an associate professor in the department of systematic theology.

Father Keleher was named Bishop of Belleville on October 23, 1984, and celebrated his episcopal ordination at the Cathedral of St. Peter on December 11, 1985.

Dialogue has characterized Bishop Keleher's service as sixth bishop of southern Illinois. In 1985 Bishop Keleher held consulations with women religious of the diocese, as requested by Pope John Paul II. He later hosted the diocese's first convocation of men and women religious. In 1986 the bishop formed a task force for religious in southern Illinois.

Bishop Keleher convened laity forums in preparation for the 1987 world synod of bishops in Rome on the vocation and mission of the laity. During the 1986 Catholic Youth Organization diocesan convention, Bishop Keleher fielded questions from southern Illinois teens in a "Meet Your Bishop" session.

Six permanent deacons and two transitional deacons were ordained by Bishop Keleher and on June 14, 1986, he welcomed six Poor Clares to the diocese, where they established their cloistered monastery. Bishop Keleher was also responsible for the reorganization of the diocesan Camp Ondessonk and the financial council.

Addressing one of the major issues of the times, Bishop Keleher issued a special letter in 1985 encouraging participation in prayer services of thanksgiving for the harvest. The bishop regularly participated in services blessing seeds and crops as a sign of solidarity with beleaguered farmers.

"A Time of Favor," the fifteen-month celebration of the diocesan centennial, was announced by Bishop Keleher in October 1986.

BIOGRAPHIES OF THE CONTRIBUTORS

Sister Loretta Berra, ASC, a staff member of *The Messenger,* is a former teacher and principal in schools served by the Adorers of the Blood of Christ. She also served as administrator of the ASC provincial house in Ruma.

Rose Josephine Boylan's family has lived in St. Clair County since 1764. As an attorney, Miss Boylan has been active in historical preservation work since 1927 and her projects have included all three historic sites in Cahokia. Among her many awards and recognitions, she was the 1970 recipient of the President's Award of the National Trust for Historic Preservation. A longtime member of the diocesan Legion of Mary, Miss Boylan currently is a resident of the Castle Haven Nursing Center.

Sister Barbara Brumleve, SSND, formerly served in the Belleville diocese at Mater Dei High School, Breese, 1962-64, and at Althoff Catholic High School, Belleville, 1978-81. She has been involved in archival research for the eight provinces of the School Sisters of Notre Dame of North America.

Bishop William Cosgrove as ordained for the Archdiocese of Cleveland in 1943. He was both a professor of history and an inner city pastor in Cleveland. Bishop Cosgrove served as the fourth bishop of Belleville from 1976 to 1981. He is currently retired.

Sister Mary Pauline Grady, ASC, is known in the Belleville diocese for her educational and prison ministries. She has written numerous articles and books including *Alma Mater, S.T.A.; Ruma: Home and Heritage,* and *Girl in a Hurry.* Currently, Sister Pauline is engaged in prison ministry in New Mexico.

Father Clyde Grogan, ordained for the Diocese of Belleville in 1968, is the pastor of St. Francis Xavier parish, Carbondale. He has been the pastor of St. Patrick's, East St. Louis, and St. Joseph's, Equality.

Patricia Hamilton, reference-archives librarian at the Belleville Public Library, is a graduate of the former St. Teresa Academy and Saint Louis University. She authored *Belleville in 1883 and the Formation of the Public Library,* and edited the bibliography of the library's archival collection. Ms. Hamilton belongs to St. Augustine of Canterbury parish, Belleville, and is a member of the St. Clair County Genealogical Society and the Daughters of the American Revolution.

Oblate Father Ronald Harrer is the provincial archivist and records manager for the central province of the Oblates of Mary Immaculate and is based in St. Paul, Minnesota. A native Minnesotan, Father Harrer was ordained in 1970. He served in the Oblate missions in Recife, Brazil, from 1970 to 1980 and was an associate pastor in Richfield, Minnesota. He has held his current post since 1982.

A graduate of St. Mary's University of San Antonio, Texas, *Stanley J. Konieczny* is the associate editor of *The Messenger,* where he has been employed for ten years. He is active in St. Martin of Tours parish, Washington Park. He authored *The Hands and Feet of Christ,* a booklet for Eucharistic ministers, published by Alba House.

Sister Catherine Lampe, PHJC, is a native of Germantown. Her forty-year teaching career took her to a variety of schools including St. Mary, Trenton, and St. Lawrence, Sandoval, in the Belleville diocese. She is now in residence in Donaldson, Indiana, where she is considered one of the community's "free-lancers."

Mrs. Lucille Lawler is a substitute teacher, historian, and devotee of Father Elisha Durbin. She and her husband, James, of Ridgway, have six children and seventeen grandchildren.

Linda Lehr is an active member of St. James Parish, Millstadt. She is the Parish Centennial Chairperson for St. James and a member of the Centennial Heritage Festival Committee, and has been a frequent contibutor *The Messenger.*

Gayle Loar works as a marketing communications specialist for St. Mary Hospital, Centralia. She holds a master's degree in business administration.

Msgr. Angelo Lombardo, ordained for the Diocese of Belleville in 1955, is the pastor of St. Barbara parish, Okawville, and vicar general of the diocese. He has been the pastor of Sacred Heart, Du Quoin, St. Andrew, Christopher, and St. Mary, Sesser.

A member of Blessed Sacrament Parish, Belleville, *Rose Mansfield* is a member of the social studies department at Althoff Catholic High School, Belleville. She edits the annual *Journal of the St. Clair County Historical Society* and belongs to the Daughters of the American Revolution.

Raphael H. Middeke, editor of *The Messenger* since 1980, is a member of St. Damian parish, Damiansville. He is married to Bernadette Rzonca. They are the parents of two children.

Ordained in 1982, *Father John Myler* is associate pastor of St. Peter Cathedral, Belleville. He is a candidate for a doctor of philosophy degree in communications and Church history at Saint Louis University and has been involved with communications work for the diocese.

A member of *The Messenger* staff for sixteen years, *Harold D. Olree* resides in St. Louis County with his wife, Trudy. They are members of St. Joseph parish, Manchester, and are parents of three children.

Mrs. Rita Renner is a past president of the Belleville Diocesan Council of Catholic Women (1978-80) and past province director (1982-84). Mrs. Renner based her article on research, personal reminiscences of her grandmother, Mrs. Arthur Fournie, who was past president and province director of the BDCCW, and interviews with Rose Josephine Boylan, a close associate of Kate Boismenue.

A native of Caseyville, *Father Theodore Siekmann* was ordained in 1942. During his forty years in the active ministry he was pastor of St. Joseph parish, Prairie du Rocher, 1956-1964. During that time he took a leave of absence to serve as founding priest of the diocesan mission at El Progreso, Guatemala. Father Siekmann also served as editor of *The Messenger* for two years, 1968-1970. Named pastor of St. Luke's in 1968, he retired in 1982. He now lives at the Hincke Residence for Priests in Belleville.

Father Paul Stauder was ordained for the Diocese of Belleville in 1948. Currently he is chaplain at St. Clement Hospital and the Clementine Residence in Red Bud. He has produced several films on the pioneer Catholic Church in the United States.

Father John Vogelgesang, SVD, is a retired missionary who served in the Philippines and at Society of the Divine Word headquarters in Rome. Currently he is translating documents of his order from German to English at Techny, Illinois.

Robert Welzbacher, a native of New Athens, served as a printer's devil, or apprentice, at Buechler Printing Company in 1933. That began his lifelong affiliation with *The Messenger.* In his forty-three years with the diocesan weekly, Welzbacher served in various capacities. He retired as managing editor of *The Messenger* in 1980. He died March 10, 1986.

Brother Leo Willett, SM, a native of St. Joseph parish, East St. Louis, has been a Marianist since 1944 and has taught and administered Catholic high schools in Milwaukee, Fort Worth, San Antonio, Omaha, and St. Louis. He currently is stationed at Chaminade Preparatory School, St. Louis, where genealogy remains his favorite hobby.

Index

Agers, Allen 260, 262
Albert, Pat 324
Allen, Louise 178
Althoff, Henry 62, 75, 76, 78, 88, 89, 106, 112-15, 117, 119, 132, 138, 160, 165, 170, 174, 177, 179, 186, 190, 192, 195, 196, 197, 200, 211, 213, 221, 223, 224, 230, 238, 257, 258, 259, 261, 275, 280, 300
Althoff High School (Belleville) 132, 233, 302
American Zinc. Co. 178
Anna 116, 117, 118
Arentsen, Ed 261
Arnold, Ralph 312
Assumption (East St. Louis) 133, 134, 233, 234, 302
Aul, Charles 130, 131, 134
Ava 96, 110, 207, 268, 270
Aviston 112
Aydt, Henry 32, 33
Aydt, Salome 32, 34
Aydt Family 25, 31-34
Baggio, John 320
Baltes, Peter J. 35, 56-58, 65, 66, 71, 80, 83, 84, 94
Bannan, Thomas 299
Barr, Walter 292
Barras, Bill 183
Bartels, Bartholomew 100-03
Bartelso 100, 101, 102, 261
Bauer, Catherine 179
Bauer, Leonard 175, 186, 316
Bauer Bros. Construction Co. 178
Baumgart, Veronica 128, 159-63
Beckemeyer 98
Belle Prairie 125, 126
Benedict XV 138, 168
Benedictines 117
Benhoff, Gabriel 349
Benton 97
Beondech, Mary Ann 234, 235
Berger, Augustin 102
Bergmann, Frederick 109
Beuckman, Frederic 80, 81, 82, 103, 104-07, 119, 170
Bissell, William H. 44-47
Blazine, James 156
Blessed Sacrament parish (Belleville) 117, 118, 119
Boismenue, Kathryn 190-93
Boismenue, Louis 190
Bollman, Carol 315
Bollman, Dave 317
Bond, Shadrach 20-21
Branca, John 182
Brandmeyer, William 260, 261, 262
Braun, Dean 296
Braun, Michael 187, 188
Brennfleck, Millie 260, 262
Breese 34, 36
Briand, Jean Olivier 4, 5, 6
Bridgeport 351
Briggs, Spike 234
Brothers of Holy Cross 58
Brumleve, Barbara 276, 278
Bruns, John 110
Buechler, Caroline 169

Buechler, Joseph N. 169, 170, 171, 314, 316
Buechler, Louise 169, 315
Buechler, William 169
Burke, James 275
Bush 97, 207
Cahokia 4, 5, 6, 8, 9, 12, 15, 26, 28, 29, 30, 166
Cairo 41, 42, 43, 52, 53, 54, 68, 84, 117, 305, 318, 339
Calkum, Edwarda 195
Cambria 97
Camp Ondessonk 184, 227, 362
Camp St. Philip 277
Cana Conference 310
Carbondale 96
Carlyle 96, 99, 100, 263
Carmi 25, 52, 53
Carroll, John 6, 8, 11, 15, 26
Carter, Anne 309-312
Carter, Bolen 309-312
Carterville 96, 97, 207
Caseyville 117, 118
Cathedral High School 73, 131-32, 224, 257, 313
Cathedral Mothers' Club 244
Catherine Kasper Center 283-87
Catholic Boy Scouts 175
Catholic Community House 315
Catholic Center 332
Catholic Interracial Council 311
Catholic Knights of Illinois 171, 228
Catholic Physicians and Dentists Guild 225
Catholic Students' Mission Crusade 316
Catholic Urban Programs 283, 293, 323, 326, 346
Catholic Worker 309
Catholic Youth Organization (CYO) 275, 316, 234, 362
Central Catholic High School 132, 133, 233, 301
Centralia 68, 96, 182, 220, 221
Ceranski, Joseph 136, 137
Chaminade, William J. 130
Chester 160
Christopher 154
Clarette, Sister 222
Clark, George Rogers 5, 6, 7
Clause, Otilla 179
Clementine Hall (Red Bud) 66, 161
Cluse, William 75-79, 94
Cobden 116, 117, 118
Columbia 82, 89, 102, 120
Confraternity of Christian Doctrine 227, 310, 355
Connors, Jimmy 275
Coovert, William 119
Cosgrove, William 317, 321, 323, 329-332
Council of Women Religious 355
Crupper, Harriet 288
Cunningham, C. J. 302
Dahlgren 33
Dahmus, Ed 170
Dalton, Michael 290
Daschke, Helen 178
Daughters of Isabella 33
Daughterty, Dolorine 179, 278
Davinroy, Catherine 179
Day, Dorothy 309
Day, Thomas 105
Daystar Program (Cairo) 338
DeGasperi, Robert 181, 182, 183, 184, 277
Degenhardt, Edwiga 163, 209
Deksnys, Anthony 279-83
Deksnys, James 279
Deksnys, Stanislova 279
Deksnys, Vinceslava 279
Delwood 261, 262
DeMattias, Maria 64, 65
DeMazenod, Eugene 266-67
DeSoto 68
Deutreluingue, P. J. 28-29
Diocesan Council of Catholic Men 276, 311
Diocesan Council of Catholic Nurses 225
Diocesan Council of Catholic Women 274, 290, 291
Diocesan Pastoral Council 344
Dirler, Clem 237, 239, 270
Dominican Sisters 66, 200
Dorrisville 262
Dosmann, Madeline 338-41
Dowling, Virginia 286
Downey, James 77, 301
Drone, Edward 185
Drone, Mary Urban 185
Drone, Paul 185-89
Drone, Rose 185
DuBois 68, 83, 94, 95, 136
Dunn, Meinrad 246, 247, 270
Dunne, William 202

Du Quoin 67, 68, 69, 70, 236-40, 265
Du Quoin, Jean Baptiste 67
Du Quoin, Louis Jefferson 67
Durbin, Elisha 22-25, 32, 33, 48, 106
Ei, Joseph C. 132
Elizabethtown 329
Ell, Louis 118
El Progresso Mission 312, 361
Enfield (Dolan Settlement) 24, 52, 53
Engel, Peter 110
Enzelberger, John Nepomuk 31, 90
Equality 25, 49, 51, 53, 105
Evansville 76, 124
Fairfield 33
Fairmont City 114, 178, 179
Fairview Heights 119, 139
Fallon, John J. 210-35, 265
Fayetteville 102
Feldmann, Jerry 318
Felician Sisters 219-223
Fellner, John 319
Fisher, Joan 339
Flora 90
Fontana, Joseph 245-48
Fort de Chartres 1, 2, 4, 16, 166
Fort Kaskaskia 67
Fortenberry, Jerome 296
Fournie, Arthur J. 273
Fournie, Ivo Sunkel 273
Fournie, John 197, 273-278
Fournie, Mary John 273
Franciscan brothers 92-95, 101, 102
Franciscan Sisters of Our Lady of Perpetual Help 95
Franciscan Sisters of Perpetual Adoration 95
Franciscan Sisters of St. Cunegunda 137
Frank, Eugene 144-48
Freeburg 102
Freese, H. J. 194, 195, 196
French Village 13, 14, 28, 29, 90, 91
Frierdich, Alice 242, 243
Frierdich, Gerry 244
Friess, Caroline 35-39
Frisch, Angela 247
Funcke, Henry 193
Funcke, M. Pacifica 241-44
Gallinatti, Frances 285
Garner, Mary 352
Genisio, James 237, 349
Gerhardinger, Theresa 37, 38, 39
Germantown 90, 91, 100, 101, 102, 103, 115
Ghiringhelli, Lena 182
Gibault, Pierre 4-7, 26
Gibault High School (Waterloo) 7, 302
Gieryk, Theodore 59-62
Gillen, James 110, 210
Gilmartin, Charles 78, 110, 132, 172, 174, 280
Gilmartin, Lawrence 173
Girrens, Mary Catherine 205, 206, 333-337
Girrens, John J. 33
Girrens, Kathryn T. 333
Gleeson, Kitty K. 150, 152
Glen Addie (St. John's Orphanage) 73, 106, 192
Glennon, John 177, 199, 200
Glennon, Ronald 351
Goelz, Christopher 81, 110, 16-20, 171, 202, 226
Goewert, Leonard 227
Good Friday Movement 226
Goosens, Henry 82-89, 91
Grady, Pauline 286
Grand Tower 96, 207
Grant, Ulysses S. 50, 54
Gray, Vincent 134
Griffin, James 172
Grogan, Clyde 303
Gruenewald, Elizabeth R. 224
Gruenewald, Joseph 229
Gruenewald, M. J. 170, 223-26
Gruenewald, Mrs. Ralph 224
Gruninger, Charles W. 151
Guild, Edwin 249, 304-08
Guild, Elizabeth 304
Guild, William 304

Haas, Serena 162
Haffner, Cyril 236-40, 349, 351
Haffner, Gertrude L. 236
Haffner, Nicholas 236
Haffner, Raymond H. 236
Hagen, Henry 130
Hagen, Joseph 119
Hakenwerth, Quentin 235
Hall, Kenneth 199, 202, 263
Harbaugh, Raymond 272
Harkins, J. 77
Harrer, Ronald 216
Harrington, Peter 199-204, 290
Harrisburg 262, 351

Harrisonville 121
Hartung, Vincent 274
Hasenstab, Gary 324
Hayes, Leo 270
Hays, Joseph C. 277
Heard, Etheldreda 161, 209
Heck, Rita 168
Hecker 33
Heidemann, Francis 232
Heidemann, Henry 232-35
Heiligenstein, Bernard 320
Heiligenstein, Francis X. 197, 260, 293, 318-321
Heiligenstein, Ida S. 320
Heiligenstein, John 319, 320
Heiligenstein, Joseph (Toby) 320
Hellriegel, Martin 310
Hellrung, Charles 277
Henken, John 170, 260-63
Hennessy, Anita 193
Henrica, Sister 238
Herrin 97, 154, 182, 183, 184, 270
Hickman, Norval 203
Hilgenberg, Bernard 96-99
Hincke Home 343
Hitpas, William 320
Holtgrave, Elmer 186, 281
Holy Angels parish (East St. Louis) 300, 309, 322
Holy Childhood parish (Mascoutah) 196, 321
Holy Cross parish (Wendelin) 88
Holy Family parish (Cahokia) 8, 10, 11, 12-13, 16, 26, 27, 30, 112
Holy Family Association 227
Holy Name Society 171, 174, 201, 228, 244, 315
Holy Rosary parish (Fairmont City) 178, 179, 180, 194, 195, 196
Hospital Sisters of the Third Order of St. Francis 81, 95
Hubbard, Edward 321
Hubbard, Joseph 283, 290, 293, 321-26, 345
Hubbard, Olga 321
Hubbard, William 149
Hueller, Joseph 118, 290
Huskey, Mary 234, 235
Hutsch, Robert 119
Illinois Central Railroad 61, 67, 93, 96
Immaculate Conception Academy 35, 36, 38, 39
Immaculate Conception parish (Columbia) 89, 116
Immaculate Conception parish (East St. Louis) 279
Immaculate Conception parish (Kaskaskia) 16, 88
Immaculate Conception parish (Madonnaville) 89
Irose, Leo 177
Irwin, Edwin 228-31
Irwin, Emelia F. 228
Jacoby, Estelle 195-97
Janiszewski, Andrew 135-39
Janssen, John 47, 71-74, 75, 77, 81, 86, 87, 90, 94, 96, 105, 106, 109, 112, 116, 130, 136, 165, 173, 236
Janssen, Magdalen 319
Jantzen, Rudolph 271
Jarrot, Nicholas 8-11, 190, 191
John Paul II 148, 328, 360
John XXIII 153, 171, 174, 249, 276, 301
Johnston City 97
Jones, Billy 199, 202, 203
Juengling, Alma 140-43
Juncker, Henry 43, 57, 71, 76, 102, 130
Kaiser, Albert 130-33
Kaiser, F. A. 226
Kampwerth, Georgia 284, 285
Kampwerth, Rita 283-87
Kapustas, Albert 156
Kapustas, Minnie L. 156
Karban, Roger 292
Kaskaskia 4, 5, 9, 15, 16, 19, 21, 22, 26, 35, 45, 88, 89, 166
Kavanaugh, John 287
Keim, John 100, 102
Keinrath, Virginia 341, 343
Keleher, James 358-361
Kerle, M. Therese 195
Kessler, John 132, 133
King's House of Retreats 266
Kinmundy 179, 261
Kirpatrick, John 203
Kitowski, Joseph 136
Klocke, Charles 67-70, 239
Knights of Columbus 33, 55, 110, 137, 149-53, 160, 171, 228, 233, 234, 309, 311, 314, 315
Knox, Roger 283, 285, 286
Koenig, Christopher 80-82, 108, 116
Koenig, William 116
Kranauskas, John 280

Krastel, Emily 195
Kraus, Stephen 276
Kreeb, William 323
Krum, Tim 234
Kubicki, Edmund 138
Kuhl, Urban 276
Ku Klux Klan 151, 289
Laymen's Retreat League 266
La Cantine 29
Lambert, Louis A. 50, 52-55
Larmer, John 41, 42, 43
Lawler, Joseph 31
Lawler, Michael Kelly 22, 24, 42, 48-51
Le Clerc College 213, 257
Ledford 262
Le Grand, Joseph 118
Lenzini, Don 156, 157
Leo XIII 71, 190
Leone, Nick 345-48
Leve, G. 80
Liliose, Sister 221
Limacher, Paul 81
Lincoln, Abraham 10, 46, 47, 50
Linderberger, B. L. 170
Loftus, Anne 309
Lohmann, Gus 348
Loisel, Jean Francois Regis 26-30
Lombardo, Angelo 303, 236, 237
Longust, Bill 178, 179
Longust, Emma 178
Lopardo, Vito 351, 237, 238
Lucey, Mike 286
Ludwig, Evangeline 161
Lugge, Edmund 301, 314
Maier, John 232, 233
Malec, Raymond 138
Marianist House of Intercession 133, 134, 288
Marion 97, 154
Maronic, John 307
Marquette, Jacques 167
Mary Celestine, Sister 221
Mary Regis, Sister 246
Mary Stella, Mother 162
Mascoutah 196, 197
Mater Dei (Breese) 33, 99, 302
Mathews, Mary A. 247
Mauck, George 328, 329
Mauer, Elmar 215, 217
Mayer, Roland 288
McBride, Larry 290
McCabe, Patrick 40-43
McLeansboro 25, 52, 53
McMahon, Edward 188
Meehan, Elizabeth "Hap" 349, 351
Meehan, Timothy E. 352
Meehan, William 351
Meinhardt, Louis 132, 133
Menard, Pierre 19-21
The Messenger 73, 90, 101, 104, 106, 114, 119, 121, 122, 170, 262, 300, 312, 316
Metropolis 25, 182, 262
Meurin, Sebastian 4
Meyer, George 130
Meyer, Leo
Meyerpeter, Eugene 133
Mierzowski, Luke 92-95
Miller, Bernard 59, 170, 259
Miller, Julia 259
Miller, Lydia K. 259
Miller, Robert L. 259
Miller, Thomas B. 259
Miller, William 259
Millstadt 28, 29, 102
Minwegan, Peter 214-18
Miranda, Sister 222
Miriani, Gerald 181, 183
Moczydlowski, Julian 137
Mogenis, Maria 279
Morrison, August 140
Mound City 54, 117, 121, 197, 274, 295, 318
Mounds 121, 197, 294, 318
Mount Vernon 121
Mueller, Joseph M. 230
Muloka, Jonas 279
Murphy, Jerry 234
Murphy, John E. 221
Murphy, John T. 149-53
Murphy, Loretta S. 150
Murphy, Thomas 150
Murphysboro 33, 96, 109, 110, 111, 160, 207, 268, 270
Murray, Hugh 221, 222
Myer, Leo
Myerscough, Angelita 207, 208
Nashville 62, 114
National Catholic Rural Life Conference 99, 166
National Catholic Women's Council 190
Neuhaus, John 65, 66
New Athens 228
New Burnside 182
Newman Auxiliary 351, 352, 353

Newman Center (SIU) 302
Newton, Mary Frances 334, 335
Niemeyer, Arthur 142
Notre Dame Academy 39, 257
Noser, Adolph 253-56
Noser, Adolph (Sr.) 253
Noser, Ailene 254
Noser, Katherine H. 253
Noser, M. Tharsilla 253, 254
Noser, Paschatia 254
Notre Dame Academy 211, 212
Ober, Ben 222
Oblates of Mary Immaculate 160, 185, 249-52, 264-67, 306
O'Brien, John 233
Odin 68
Office of Education 332
Office of Peace and Justice 332
Office of Worship 331
O'Halloran, Patrick 77, 82, 83-86, 191
Okawville 75, 351
Olivia, Sister 209
Olivier, J. 12, 26, 28
Olney 25, 261, 351, 328
Orlet, Eileen 150
Orlet, Joseph 187
Ostlangenberg, Kaspar 45
Our Lady of Good Counsel (Renault) 3, 277
Our Lady of Lourdes (Sparta) 225
Our Lady of Perpetual Help 136
Our Lady of the Visitation (St. Philippe) 1, 3
Paderborn 102
Palmer, Marie 270
Paschalisa, Sister 221, 222
Patoka 261
Paul VI 278, 281
Pennock, H. H., Sr. 222
Pensoneau Family 12-14, 29
Pico, Joseph 176
Pieper, Francis 110
Pinckneyville 68, 245-48
Piopolis 25, 32, 33, 52, 53, 65, 125, 126
Pius XI 213, 226
Pius XII 165, 167, 227, 255, 259
Pocahontas 102
Polish Roman Catholic Union of America 60
Pond's Settlement (Waltonboro) 24, 42, 48, 53
Poor Clares 362
Poor Handmaids of Jesus Christ 81, 102, 140, 221, 269, 337
Posen 136
Pothman, Joseph 216
Prairie du Rocher 2, 3, 4, 5, 9, 15, 16, 28, 166
Precious Blood Fathers 144
Precious Blood Institute 161, 288
Precious Blood Sisters 34, 63, 66, 76, 88, 110, 125, 126, 128, 133, 159-63, 205-09, 227
Price, Melvin 197
Prudent, Eugene 155, 156
Pruess, Arthur 170
Quack, John 302
Queen's Daughters 85, 190, 191, 192, 193
Raddle 96, 182, 207, 268, 269, 270
Radom 38, 61, 62, 68, 92, 93, 94, 95, 136
Red Bud 89, 160
Reineke, Augustine 36, 102
Reinhardt, Leo 206, 208, 209
Reis, Henry 236, 349
Reissen, Art 347
Renault 3
Renault, Philippe 1-3
Renner, Rita 275
Repking, Mary Theresa 125-29
Reyling, August 32
Richard, Gabriel 15-18
Ridgway 55
Ritter, Joseph 343
Rosenthal, Aloysius 264
Rosiclare 105
Rothermich, Leo 133
Royalton 97, 154, 155
Ruggles, John 351
Ruma 66, 110, 126, 127, 128, 159-63, 265, 333, 349
Ruma College 66
Ryan, Richard 234
Sabella, Evelyn 271
Sacred Heart parish (East St. Louis) 79, 132, 172, 173, 177, 182, 190, 193, 210
Sacred Heart parish (Du Quoin) 38, 67, 68, 69, 70, 93, 94, 237-40, 349
Sacred Heart parish (Zeigler) 154, 158
St. Agnes Children's Asylum 140
St. Adalbert parish (East St. Louis) 133, 136, 137, 138
St. Albert the Great parish (Fairview Heights) 119

St. Aloysius College 85
St. Aloysius parish (Royalton) 154
St. Andrew parish (Christopher) 97, 291
St. Andrew parish (Murphysboro) 109, 110, 155, 275
St. Ann parish (Nashville) 112
St. Ann parish (Raddle) 270
St. Anne parish (Fort de Chartres) 1, 16
St. Ann's Home (Chester) 162, 208
St. Anthony parish (Beckemeyer) 96, 98
St. Anthony parish (Coulterville) 225
St. Augustine mission 199-203, 290
St. Augustine parish (Breese) 321
St. Barbara parish (Okawville) 75, 112, 321
St. Benedict mission (Sandusky) 179
St. Boniface parish (Evansville) 121, 124
St. Boniface parish (Germantown) 90, 91, 100, 102, 164
St. Bruno parish (Pinckneyville) 68, 245
St. Catherine parish (Grand Chain) 179, 196
St. Cecilia parish (Bartelso) 100-01
St. Charles Borromeo (DuBois) 39, 93
St. Clare parish (O'Fallon) 127
St. Clement Hospital (Red Bud) 127, 166, 284
St. Cyril parish (East St. Louis) 119
St. Damian parish (Damiansville) 112, 156, 260, 262
St. Dominic (Breese) 33, 34, 36, 102, 232, 270
St. Elizabeth Hospital (Belleville) 139, 140, 175, 224, 225, 226, 227, 230, 346
St. Elizabeth parish (Ava) 110, 268
St. Elizabeth parish (East St. Louis) 73, 155, 261
St. Francis parish (Carbondale) 182
St. Francis Student Aid Society 82, 118
St. George parish (New Baden) 207
St. Henry parish (Belleville) 314, 345
St. Henry parish (East St. Louis) 137, 197
St. Henry Seminary (Belleville) 170, 185, 226, 257, 258, 260, 264, 265, 267, 306, 307, 355
St. James parish (Minstadt) 196
St. John Orphanage 72, 73, 82, 106, 140-43, 171, 230, 315, 346
St. John the Baptist parish (Piopolis) 25, 31, 33, 34
St. John Nepomucene parish (Dahlgren) 33
St. Joseph parish (Cairo) 42, 210
St. Joseph parish (East St. Louis) 299 301, 309
St. Joseph parish (Elizabethtown) 261, 276
St. Joseph parish (Equality) 105, 182, 318
St. Joseph parish (Freeburg) 321
St. Jospeh parish (Lebanon) 236
St. Joseph parish (Prairie de Rocher) 236, 246
St. Joseph parish (Ridgway) 321
St. Joseph parish (Rosiclare) 105
St. Joseph parish (Willisville) 270
St. Lawrence parish (Sandoval) 155, 177
St. Leo parish (Modoc) 236
St. Liborius parish (St. Libory) 36, 260, 321
St. Libory 102
St. Louis University 161, 208-09
St. Luke parish (Belleville) 39, 72
St. Martin of Tours parish (Washington Park) 235
St. Mary Hospital (Cairo) 179
St. Mary Hospital (Centralia) 220-23St. Mary Hospital (East St. Louis) 72, 78, 80, 81, 291, 197
St. Mary parish (Belleville) 106, 107, 185, 186, 307
St. Mary parish (Carlyle) 261, 319, 321
St. Mary parish (East St. Louis) 177
St. Mary parish (Herrin) 180, 181
St. Mary parish (Mound City) 320
St. Mary parish (Mt. Carmel) 144, 225, 260
St. Mary parish (Mt. Vernon) 274
St. Mary parish (Sesser) 97
St. Mary parish (Shawneetown) 25, 105
St. Mary Magdelen parish (Todd's Mill) 61, 68, 135
St. Michael parish (Paderborn) 89
St. Michael parish (Radom) 59, 61, 62, 93, 94
St. Nicholas parish (O'Fallon) 344
St. Pancratius parish (Fayetteville) 175
St. Patrick parish (Cairo) 41, 42, 53, 83, 173, 293, 296, 339
St. Patrick parish (East St. Louis) 77-80, 82-85, 132, 172, 190
St. Patrick parish (Pond's Settlement) 24, 42, 105
St. Patrick parish (Ruma) 66, 207-08

St. Paul parish (Johnston City) 207
St. Peter Cathedral parish (Belleville) 35, 36, 45, 57, 71, 74, 96, 112, 121, 164, 165, 166, 171, 173, 186, 210, 225, 242, 257-59, 345
St. Philip parish (East St. Louis) 14, 29, 30, 90, 116, 117, 118, 119, 120
St. Philippe 1, 2, 3, 5
St. Philomena 179
St. Polycarp parish (Carmi) 276
St. Raphael parish (Mounds) 197, 294
St. Regis parish (East St. Louis) 196, 329
St. Rose parish (St. Rose) 127, 284, 302
St. Sebastian 33
St. Stephen parish (Caseyville) 117, 118, 119, 156
St. Stephen parish (Flora) 90
St. Teresa Academy (East St. Louis) 34, 66, 72, 128, 201, 202, 133, 161
St. Teresa parish (Belleville) 346
St. Teresa of Avila parish (Salem) 179
St. Thomas the Apostle parish (Millstadt) 28, 29
St. Vincent de Paul Society 165, 171, 199, 201, 322, 323, 345
St. Vincent Hospital (Belleville) 73
Ss. Peter and Paul parish (Waterloo) 40, 57, 81, 136, 227
Sandoval 68, 261
Schammel, Magdalen 321
Schauerte, Kaspar 96, 108-11, 207
Scheller 93, 95
Schlarman, Bernard J. 165
Schlarman, Joseph 73, 75, 112, 131, 164-68, 171, 225, 255
Schlarman, Philomena 165
Schlarman, Stanley 241, 244, 293, 339
Schmitt, Charles 235
Schmitt, Veronica 194-97, 207
Schnepp, Gerald 134
Schomaker, Alphonse 261
Schomaker, Gertrude 320
School Sisters of Notre Dame 35, 36, 37, 38, 39, 57, 69, 94, 131, 185, 241-44
School Sisters of St. Francis 95
Schrautemyer, Suzanne 354-58
Schueing, Charles 294
Schueing, Edna 294
Schuhmacher, Bernette 269
Schuhmacher, Bernice 269
Schuhmacher, Clarence 269
Schuhmacher, Elmer 268-72
Schuhmacher, John 269
Schuhmacher, Mary Ellen 269
Schulte, Paul 307
Schultz, Charles 130
Schwaegel, Joseph 315
Scoggins, Carol 291
Scott Air Base 165, 225, 226, 230
Seebald, Thomas 130
Seifert, Charles 97, 154-58
Senese, Ermingildo 182
Shawneetown 22, 25, 31, 32, 41, 48, 49, 50, 52, 53, 105, 106
Shay, Maureen 247
Shrine of Our Lady of the Snows 304, 306, 249
Siekmann, Theodore 119, 281
Simon, Alphonse 264-67
Sisters of the Blessed Sacrament 250
Sisters of Charity of Nazareth 23
Sisters of the Holy Cross 54
Sisters of Mercy 14
Sisters of St. Francis of the Providence of God 95
Sisters of St. Joseph 28
Slattery, Noreen 213
Smith, Frank 284
Smith, Janet 283, 284
Society of the Propagation of the Faith 224, 225, 226
Society of African Missions 199-204
Society of the Divine Word 144, 245-48, 254
Society of Jesus (Jesuits) 9, 10
Society of Mary 130-34, 232-35
Society of St. Sulpice (Sulpicians) 15, 16, 17
Southern Illinois University (Carbondale) 51
Spaeth, Joseph 100, 261
Spitzer, Helen 179
Stancius, Antanas 280
Stancius, Ellena 280
Stancius, Maria 280
Stancius, Nika 280
Stone, Ellsworth 298
Stonefort 54, 182, 262
Stringtown 328, 350
Stritch, Samuel 255
Sulkowski, Vic 155, 157, 158
Sullivan, Catherine 151
Sweeney, Charles 77
Tamaroa 68, 93

Tamms 305
Taylor, Claude 292
Taylor, Daniel E. 250
Taylor, John E. 249-52
Taylor, Mary P. 250
Taylor, Robert 250
Taylor, Zachary 45, 49
Teagle, Ernie 285
Teagle, Polly 283, 285, 325
Tecklenburg, Francis 121-124, 170, 205, 206, 207, 270
Terepka, John 61
Thebus, George 170
Third Order of St. Francis 179
Thomas, Mary 179
Todd's Mill 33, 68
Toennies, Gerard 207
Trapp, Joseph 236-37
Trappists 10, 144
Travers, Cassie 294
Travers, John, Sr. 294
Tremblay, Eugene 250
Trombley, William J. 153, 300
Truszkowska, Mary Angela 219, 222
United Front 284, 285, 286
Ursuline Sisters 194-98, 344-355
Utar, Mary Louise 247
Vallo, Jo 290
Vatican II 174, 313
Verdu, Joe, Jr. 176
Vernier, Cy 345-48
Vernier, Cyrilla S. 347
Vernier, Frances 169
Vienna 182, 262
Vincent Gray Altenative High School 133
Virgilia, Sister 303
Voellinger, Helen 187, 320
Voellinger, Mary Rose 187
Vonnahmen, Robert 276
Waite, Cabrini 293, 296-97
Waite, Roslyn 293-97, 318
Waite, Walter 294
Wansing, Marian 161
Washington Park 235
Waterloo 160
Welzbacher, Carol 314
Welzbacher, Dolores V. 313, 316
Welzbacher, Gary 314
Welzbacher, George 313
Welzbacher, James 314
Welzbacher, Katherine 313
Welzbacher, Richard 315
Welzbacher, Robert 226, 313-17, 329
Wessel, Stephen 186
West Frankfort 154, 207
Western Catholic Union 171
Wetaug 304
Weygandt, Sebastian 170
Weyrich, Ferdinand 196
Wieseman, Catherine 179
Willisville 182, 268
Wilson, Adelia 288
Wilson, Imogene 199, 288-92
Wilson, Samuel 288
Wirth, Jerry 292
Witte, Fred 159, 161, 205-09
Wolf, Marie 320
Woltering, Mary Collette 247
Woodward, Marquerite 179
Wurm, John 342-44
Wurm, Maureen 344
Zerr, Clementine 63-66
Zeigler 154, 155, 157
Zielinski, Simon 136, 137, 138, 139
Zuroweste, Albert 132, 142, 143, 153, 166, 167, 168, 171, 175, 193, 210, 211, 212, 276, 298-302, 313, 322, 344, 351
Zuroweste, Elizabeth 299
Zuroweste, Henry 299
Zwilling, Herman 351
Zwilling, Rose 238, 349, 350

MarquetteGravierAllouezSt.CosmeMarestGibaultRenaultMenardMeurinBergierLevadoixFlaget
BadenRivetOlivierLawlerDurbinCloostereRaddlMoosmullerDuffyHanaganLambertZerrKlo-
ckeBauerHilgenbergMuensterFischerHaterBergmanMahoneyHenkenDeGasperiSchauerte
ReuschEnzlbergerWiemarCluseSpaethMcCabeBloesingerRoehrigOstlangenbergBrandmeyer
SeifertBrumleveAntonSchellerGajewskiReidelbergerBerndtPanickLimasWegmanO'Halloran
BrennanHartungReinekeLohmannDemingCollinsDowneySauerGoeltzKorandoVossSpeckmanMohr
GieryMadajKowalskiPieszchalskiPriesRynakiGrajekZgoninaLabudaDudzikWollowskiTenepka
CzerniejewskiTerepkaRoesbergTecklenburgCimarolliTaggartBooshertKreinWittenbrink
WibretKillianMarhonicBurakMiddekePenjakPfisterMulliganLacroixChandlerDaussard
CoffeeMorrisonSullivanSwithLebkucherChewMcCarthyGoughBaumannSiekmannDutton
CoyneCraigCyganD'ArcyCywinskiClarkFoleyGajewskiGenettiFaheyFahrnerRaslawksiHalvachs
GroganGryzmalaKeserauskisHlavekHennessyMenestrinaMenendexMaldanadoKroupaMcDonnell
HowelMeehanManninoKlemmeDonzeSpannagelBottaniBueskingGregorichMojzisKeatingSchaefer
EckertSchottDelaneyWolfBussGreerWebbFlachMetzerGreimanTakmajianDonleyWilkinsonPruett
JonesJohnsonHarrisEdwardsCowgillBielickeCahnovskyBurkeBrelloBogachiBournDonahueDiaz
MerscherFruecheSchumacherHoltgaveMolitorStockmannStrubhartOttensmeierKolmer
SchultePeekPoettkerLampeGoestenkorsStrohmannLagerHempenLaurentDillmanLitteken
KuhlZurlioneKeimGoelzBartelsHoffmanMuellerKueterBeckerHeidemannGrimmerBretzBudde
TimmermannPhilippsGraweScmittKruseVandeLooTheisingGebkeWellinghoffGeoffrayHuene
KlinekorteGausepohlWesselmannWinkelerKolpFaukeDetermannDulleKoopmannDustFerguson
SchillerRibbingBergmannBrueggemannHuelsmannOverbeckMarkusFeldmannWempeStrootMer-
scherRobbeStueverKorandoTougawBrushShieldGaleKaercherHeiligensteinHaselhostPerjakBun-
gayMeirinkFoppeScheibelDonneNieburTaphornReinekeGuttersohnGoewertHentschelRuterman
HusteddeRascheHitpasHorstmannLoddekeKluthoNiemannJansenDennoAngulisSpainKubrick
KolesinskisDrasdofskiNowickiZajokowskiVenegoniGaravagliaMossmanEovaldiGrezlakNagy
SwinjonskiVincentiZeboskiKonkielMazaiarzSimonDeMatteiLaurensEschmanVoellingerArnold
SchmidtBaquetHechenbergerFellnerSchobertHoffO'ConnellHladyshewskyBaggioStauderFrerker
ThousvenotVosmikBlaesDiekemarFleskrenLeonardMoerchenRensingZacharskiZimmermannHogg
IslerLeChienBretschVillemainReutermannVanCanhLeVoellingerKaefholdBeckWekemanIrose
Kuh!sPeikeBeuchmannFreantPeppenhorstGerversmannFoecheHeitmannOstermannFidelerRoberg
EchelmannHilmesLandwehrRohrNordmannSimsMurphyHolthausSchoenKharkoffKampwerHusted-
deKahrhoffKampwerthHusteddeSchneiderPetersLanghauserVanDornBodenburgMahataFriederich
EllCunninghamDriscollDunnKastnerRoweEichenseerMargasonScherrerLinnemannHutschMcEvilly
StetzenKlappBussonGuerrettazGaffinettPanaraceBollheimerPoulterWaggandLevyBourqueTobin
TobinRombaughKovacHenneberryPabstPabarcusOssickSandheinrichSartorySaugetVivianoSoucy
SmithRoustioRigneySchaltenbrandSchlechtSchlueterSvobodaSwartztrauberSzewczykSzezepaniak
ThomasVosseWainwrightPetersonNeffHayesWigginsWilliamsZittelWhiteheadPetersonNeffHayes
WigginsWilliamsZittelWhiteheadYordyYsaraVanderPluymNeffAlbersBedelBresnahanDeMonge
BurnsDuffClimacoCourtneyKaminskiFitzgeraldEnskatHeckerBradyFedakCaraviaCannadyCipf
DrevickiBarroncoAmesAllenBergkoetterBozzaBommerscheimBloemerBarbieriAuthBerensGaskill
GoydaGrandcolasHassKeckHoeffkenOerterKimutisKujawskiMagillMeyerMillerMaagPiekKoch
PratleReisO'BryanRujawitzSchlarmanSchandleValloweTorresSforzaVogtWambergueYettke
WesterheideBergerBachWachtelAgneMoorekernDissettTimperReimeSaxParkerFournieObernhefe-
manDuttonHahnmannLinhoffBodewesZwieslerBeckerSporsFitzmorrisRuenseterDemickMaty-
chowickFietsamMonkenLoiselLohmanGillenJantzenSondagCoerverFenainMcCormickEschenfel
derMeisenbeckPetrovichSentinkskisMunierKenneyHorellsMuddSimpsonO'HaraDiverBurgess
TragesserKriegerCollignonScheppingQuackGleichMcMahonBrefeldBellmannKunkelKeleherDutton
MarquetteGravierAllouezSt.CosmeMarestGibaultRenaultMenardMeurinBergierLevadoixFlaget
BadenRivetOlivierLawlerDurbinCloostereRaddlMoosmullerDuffyHanaganLambertZerrKlo-
ckeBauerHilgenbergMuensterFischerHaterBergmanMahoneyHenkenDeGasperiSchauerte
ReuschEnzlbergerWiemarCluseSpaethMcCabeBloesingerRoehrigOstlangenbergBrandmeyer
SeifertBrumleveAntonSchellerGajewskiReidelbergerBerndtPanickLimasWegmanO'Halloran
BrennanHartungReinekeLohmannDemingCollinsDowneySauerGoeltzKorandoVossSpeckmanMohr
GieryMadajKowalskiPieszchalskiPriesRynakiGrajekZgoninaLabudaDudzikWollowskiTenepka
CzerniejewskiTerepkaRoesbergTecklenburgCimarolliTaggartBooshertKreinWittenbrink
WibretKillianMarhonicBurakMiddekePenjakPfisterMulliganLacroixChandlerDaussard
CoffeeMorrisonSullivanSwithLebkucherChewMcCarthyGoughBaumannSiekmannDutton
CoyneCraigCyganD'ArcyCywinskiClarkFoleyGajewskiGenettiFaheyFahrnerRaslawksiHalvachs
GroganGryzmalaKeserauskisHlavekHennessyMenestrinaMenendexMaldanadoKroupaMcDonnell
HowelMeehanManninoKlemmeDonzeSpannagelBottaniBueskingGregorichMojzisKeatingSchaefer
EckertSchottDelaneyWolfBussGreerWebbFlachMetzerGreimanTakmajianDonleyWilkinsonPruett
JonesJohnsonHarrisEdwardsCowgillBielickeCahnovskyBurkeBrelloBogachiBournDonahueDiaz
MerscherFruecheSchumacherHoltgaveMolitorStockmannStrubhartOttensmeierKolmer
SchultePeekPoettkerLampeGoestenkorsStrohmannLagerHempenLaurentDillmanLitteken
KuhlZurlioneKeimGoelzBartelsHoffmanMuellerKueterBeckerHeidemannGrimmerBretzBudde